# COMPETENT SUPERVISION
## *Making Imaginative Judgments*

RUTH R. MIDDLEMAN
GARY B. RHODES
*Raymond A. Kent School of Social Work,*
*College of Urban and Public Affairs,*
*University of Louisville*

PRENTICE-HALL, INC., Englewood Cliffs, New Jersey 07632

*Library of Congress Cataloging in Publication Data*

Middleman, Ruth R.
 Competent supervision.

 Includes index.
 1. Social work administration—United States.
I. Rhodes, Gary B.  II. Title.
HV91.M47  1984      361.3'068'3      84-14377
ISBN 0-13-154881-6

Editorial/production supervision
 and interior design: Kate Kelly
Cover design: Lundgren Graphics, Ltd.
Cover art adapted from Linda Luking.
Manufacturing buyer: John P. Hall

Prentice-Hall Series in Social Work Practice
*Neil Gilbert and Harry Specht, editors*

Printed in the United States of America.
10  9  8  7  6  5  4  3  2  1

ISBN 0-13-154881-6      01

Prentice-Hall International, Inc., *London*
Prentice-Hall of Australia Pty. Limited, *Sydney*
Editora Prentice-Hall do Brasil, Ltda., *Rio de Janeiro*
Prentice-Hall Canada Inc., *Toronto*
Prentice-Hall of India Private Limited, *New Delhi*
Prentice-Hall of Japan, Inc., *Tokyo*
Prentice-Hall of Southeast Asia Pte. Ltd, *Singapore*
Whitehall Books Limited, *Wellington, New Zealand*

*Dedicated to the potentialities we all possess.*

# CONTENTS

## PART II    APPROACHING THE WORKPLACE

Chapter Three
PICTURING SUPERVISION
*A Transition*

Chapter Four
THE PROFESSIONAL IN THE ORGANIZATION

# PART III    KEEPING UP: DOING THE WORK

# PREFACE

Supervising the work of others has enjoyed a relatively long life in the social work profession. It is as old as the early moves to systematize the helping impulse into a casework that would be fair, objective, and informed by the science of the times. Social work arose in organizations; and there was always the need for its activities to be teachable—starting with the early agents and volunteers. Various means were devised to exchange ideas and to convey the know-how to others. The detailed process record of practice, for example, dates back to the 1890s and Baltimore where Mary Richmond initiated the habit of mailed exchanges with workers too distant to see in person. They mailed her their case notes and questions about what to do next; she answered with minute instructions for accomplishing specific tasks.[1]

Much has happened since those earlier times: within the social work profession, in other professions and disciplines, and in the wider realm of our multi-cultured, close-linked Space Age World. This book aims to take account of some of these developments, and to propose a direction for supervisory practice today. It seeks to continue the aim of connecting the more abstract concepts and the values concerning the desirable ends of social work practice with the realities of present work-a-day life. No longer is it fruitful to attempt a minute step-by-step

[1] Muriel Pumphrey, "Lasting and Outmoded Concepts in the Caseworker's Heritage," *Social Casework,* vol. 54, no. 5 (May 1973), 259–267.

set of instructions to meet specific tasks. For they are too varied and changeable today. Instead, we offer various conceptual schemes about aspects of service delivery and its supervision, profiles to help you assess where you and your organization are, certain tasks and illustrations of the elements of supervision, and suggestions geared to help you reconceptualize the orientation you will take and the particulars you will pursue to elaborate your work.

Our use of the term *supervision,* rather than *management,* and the use of a language system familiar within the traditions of social work (to the extent possible) is deliberate. While management is a popular concept today, we have selected supervision as our overarching concept for the following reasons:

1. It embodies an aspect of social work's value base and tradition too precious to lose, despite the complexities of modern organizational accountability requirements.
2. We view managerial requirements as central and crucial, but not as the single construct which encompasses what supervisors need to know and be about.
3. We seek to appeal to all levels in an organization and to connect clinical with policy and planning viewpoints. Thus, there may emerge a mentality of shared responsibility and accountability for *interdependent* work, a shared professional culture.
4. And we speak also to those in private practice, to the soloists, partnerships and practitioners now at work in the corporate firms where proprietary as well as service mentalities obtain.

We realize this is an ambitious, complex goal. Any push toward synthesis *and* analysis may be but an empty hope in view of the science of our times, itself in flux. Even the juxtaposition of competence and imagination is a paradox which may both invite and turn-off some persons. For competence tilts toward the "hard" sciences, "precise" technologies while imagination may conjure up expectations of non-rational, irrational, even mystical intentions. Yet, our commitment is toward linking these two facets as equally critical for functioning in today's workplace, in fact in the world.

The purpose of this book is to enhance the competence and imagination of supervisors with regard to supervisory tasks, so that these supervisors could behave in such a way as to enhance the worker's competence and imagination in relation to practitioner tasks. This same purpose holds for supervisors as they work with their "higher-up's" since they can have an impact enhancing the competence and imagination of administrators. And such thinking and doing by supervisees may ask more of their supervisors at the same time as they are being helped to become competent/imaginative in their work with clients.

In other words, our stance is a transactional, reflexive one. We have set much of our emphasis within organizations since most social work is practiced and supervised there. We shift back and forth between organizations and persons because interdependent workings demand transactional thinking. We start in the middle so to speak and we expect reverberations flowing back and forth. Much organizational "development" has focused downward hoping to replenish worker performance only to discover the "top" wants change at the bottom while remaining as they are (a special version of victim blaming: "if only the workers were better workers"). More recently, we find moves in the direction of bottom-up decision making are in fashion; yet it remains to be seen how much managers and administrators can really adjust to what is asked of them by such an approach.

In its most general sense, the concept supervision need not describe only the supervisor/supervisee relationship. It could be thought of as designating the major thrust of social work and other provision of services, whether it aims at redirecting others' behavior, replenishing, or adding to what others are about. Appreciating the elements of responsibility and authority, of control and enhancement has broad pertinence. The subtleties involved will matter for the relationship of supervisors with workers, workers with clients, parents with children, adults with aging parents, and children with pets.

Our stance is that study and practice of the supervisory role matters to all practitioners and that it should be addressed by all students as a requirement of their professional education. From our teaching experiences, we find that involvement with and analysis of supervisory issues yields learnings whether or not the students have been supervisors in the past. We have seen how informed supervisees can make a difference from the perspective of their worker-role.

And yet we know from our surveys of curricular organization in social work education, and from how courses in this general area are described, how variously this content is placed among "concentrations": required? elective? "touched on" as a component of practice at BSW levels? sometimes left entirely to post-masters or continuing education? And we know that most teachers need more than one text to flesh out their preferred emphases, not one text; just as no one approach, or school of thought, is adequate to inform any component of social work practice. Even in the 14 "introductory" social work texts produced in the 70s, according to Ephross and Reisch's analysis of orientations, considerable obvious and subtle variability exists in ideology, assumptions about society, the nature of change, and what social work should be about.[2] Should we expect anything different at the supervisory level?

Some learners (and teachers) prefer a "nuts and bolts approach" and we have provided certain particulars. But, in the main, this is not a nuts and bolts approach. It is not a package of things one can do tomorrow. The very words "nuts and bolts" would link us with a mechanistic, technique-mentality which we believe is now too characteristic of much organizational experience in the workplace, and has led persons to feel they are only cogs in a great machine—valuable so long as they work well or do not wear out. Nor have we separated the conceptual from its application (as some might prefer), for this, too, has obscured reality in both class and field learning and thinking, and created its own conceptual, political, and status issues over the years.

---

[2] Paul H. Ephross and Michael Reisch, "The Ideology of Some Social Work Texts," *Social Service Review,* vol. 56, no. 2 (June 1982), 273-291.

Our major goal is to approach a grasp of a whole which may provide a framework from which you can think your way toward the demands your practice imposes. We think practice should be *practiced,* not merely described, talked about, or analyzed. Yet all these facets have value.

This book is organized in both lineal (straight-lined) and non-lineal (recursive, looped) fashion. Its lineality involves the flow of the organizing sections: I, *Getting Oriented*; II, *Approaching the Workplace*; III, *Keeping Up: Doing the Work*; and IV, *Developing the Position and the Organization.* This aims to sequence the chapters in relation to some considerations about the nature of supervision, moving through elements in the situation, and looking ahead. The recursive loops will become obvious as you find us spiraling back to earlier points, now with additional information. It is an attempt to show a relationship among a series of "causes" or discussions, as for example the influence of history upon supervision in social work (and other professions), the relationships between key elements of the community's mandate for service provision as this relates to the specialness of human service organizations, and the interactional elements (possibilities) which may be selected and given priority.

In Chapter 1 we look at the special type of supervision which developed in social work—one that should be educative as well as administrative, and that was carried out mainly through a one-by-one, individual, tutorial structure. In Chapter 2 we introduce the concepts *competence* and *imagination,* and relate these to our way of conceptualizing supervision. We introduce three major philosophical world views which affect what different persons believe and value. In Chapter 3 we offer a general analytic paradigm for analyzing situations, a *Foursome* mentality, which seems appropriate for perceiving and imagining patterns and multifaceted thinking rather than dichotomies. Chapter 4 focuses on the Community Mandate (the components involved in bringing people-serving services into being) with special emphasis on the domain accorded social wellbeing, i.e. the *social* services.

In Chapter 5 we introduce our conceptual scheme for understanding supervision: a process and practice comprised of nine key functions which express the organization's internal structural integration, its delivery of services system, and its linkage with the external environment. These comprise the central supervisory task, and are described and illustrated through various practice vignettes. Chapter 6 loops back to the organizational context in greater detail to examine its enormous effect upon supervisory possibilities. A framework for understanding different organizations in terms of their purposes, structures, and inherent advantages/constraints is described. In Chapter 7 we loop back to Chapter 5 (Supervisory Functions) and highlight two of these—career socializing and teaching—because it is these two which will vary according to the particular backgrounds of supervisees.

In Chapter 8 we return again to the organization as an arena filled with opportunities and obstacles related to the pursuit of quality, responsive service provision. We consider the possibilities for expanding opportunities for dealing with professional/organizational imperatives. Chapter 9 concludes by returning to the two themes which have anchored this book: competence and making imaginative judgments. With respect to the competence theme, practice principles and derivitive directives connected to the nine functional imperatives of the supervisory role/ tasks are offered. The imaginative theme is re-introduced as growing out of the competence theme, as a matter of flexible perspectives and diversity in analyses of situations.

Perhaps our most fundamental position is that learning about supervision, in professional education and workshops, should reflect the realities of the practice of today, and aim to enhance it. We have been helped in the first instance by the willingness of the National Association of Social Workers' national staff in allowing us to review preliminary printouts of their 1982 *Professional Social Workers Data Bank Questionnaire* and other demographic data. While NASW is not the only organization where social workers affiliate, it is the profession's most representative and "biggest" voice numbering about 95,000 members. We hope our efforts, which have culminated in this book, contribute to the enhancement of practioners' and organizations' responsiveness to the pressing human needs of our times.

As we think about the many persons who have contributed to the emergence of this book, we recall the inspiration provided by our own teachers who were never satisfied with a static profession. Our conceptual schemes have been refined through trial and error in many classes, institutes, and workshops over a number of years. We appreciate the helpfulness of these many practitioners, students, and colleagues who were both learners and teachers with us. More specifically, as our footnotes acknowledge, we have benefitted from the contributions of Anne Davis, Gale Goldberg, Larry Hopkins, Claude Drouet, Lon Johnston, and Darrell Payne. Beulah Rothman, Marion Wijnberg, Martha Wahl, John Longres, and Linda Stetson offered critical reactions to various parts of the manuscript. The special caring, support, and assistance of Lynn Rhodes provided a continuing impetus to believe in and work at the tasks. At the technical end, we received valuable support from Penny Marler and Chris Bader. Special thanks go to Harold Lewis who voluntarily read an elongated version of the manuscript and believed in its value. Finally, we wish to acknowledge the useful reviews of Reva Holtzman, Rose Dobrof, and Eris Ginn.

# CHAPTER ONE
# THE SPECIALNESS OF SOCIAL WORK SUPERVISION

## INTRODUCTION

Supervision in social work is special. It differs from supervision in other professions or occupations in its traditions, definitions, and literature descriptions. Social work is special because of its origins in organizations—nonprofit ones—that are distinctive in terms of agency and professional vulnerability, a scarcity heritage, and a general cultural difference from mainstream American values that appreciate the successful, achieving movers and shakers. It is special because the values of the profession lead to concerns for justice as well as efficiency, for freedom as well as security, and for equality of opportunities which, as De Tocqueville noted, may be less elevated than those of Europeans but more just and therein great and beautiful.

It is special because the purposes of social work and the service agencies are diverse. They include work with involuntary as well as help-seeking clients, with persons who "bother" the community, harm their families, abuse others, and generally disturb, and who need an outreach approach. Such complex practice requirements call on more than the development of a trusted relationship with clients. And the supervision of such services demands both a broader, diversified knowledge base and attention to sharpening the quality of treatment or therapy. In this chapter, we shall consider some aspects of social work's unique history and service conditions. We shall then examine how these produced a special social work brand of supervision.

But what is *so* special about social work supervision? We submit that the most "special" aspect of the profession's supervision is a tradition, ideology, and literature that emphasize that supervision ought to be *educative* rather than merely administrative, and that it is best carried out through a *one-by-one* individual, tutorial structure. We think this is a commitment that most human service organizations are not supporting currently. We shall explore aspects in the profession's development that have contributed to the creation (and to the undermining) of the educative and individualized components of supervision.

Ordinarily, workers in all organizations are helped to grow and develop on the job as part of their career movement—whether in social service settings or in any other field. In fact, they are *expected* to grow in experience and competence in all cases. Social work's special version of this occupational requirement was its investment in a 1- to 1½-hour individual conference held weekly with each worker—an individually tailored tutorial arrangement with the supervisor. This represented an enormous "official" resource investment of persons and money by the organization.

In most other occupations, workers do *not* get such individualized job-development attention. Once hired, they are expected to take care of developing their knowledge and skills by learning outside the workplace. Occasionally, they may be sent by the organization to special training programs. Competition for advancement based on demonstrated competence (or political intrigue and acumen) is the motivator for self-development on the job. Mainly, the organization-sponsored staff development is attended to through training programs (in-house or external) and informal collaboration and consultation among the workers. And, at a still more informal level, as Levinson describes (1978, pp. 98-101), a mentor system might operate. The mentor is more than an ordinary teacher, advisor, sponsor, or supervisor. This is a person typically several years older, with greater experience and seniority in a given field, who supports and helps the novice in pursuing a career goal—that is, who believes in this person and creates space for him (the "him" is accurate in this context).

The mentor is a mixture of parent and peer—a teacher of skills and intellectual development. The mentor is a sponsor, host, and guide into the occupational and social world, who is acquainted with its values, customs, resources, and cast of characters, and who is an examplar, a counselor, and an offerer of moral support in stress. This intense, emotional relationship ordinarily ends in bitterness when the mentor is "overthrown." This personal, unofficial relationship is *not* like educative supervision, which was openly planned and made available to all workers in the social agencies as the profession developed. We shall look at this aspect of supervision further.

## CHANGING DEFINITIONS OF SUPERVISION

Kadushin, a prominent supervision theorist, pointed to the changing definitions of *supervision* in the literature: as *educative* in the 1965 *Encyclopedia of Social Work*; as *administrative* in the 1971 *Encyclopedia* (retained in the 1977 edition);

and as *administrative, educative,* and *supportive* by his own definition (1976, p. 38). Kadushin, who sees the supervisor as an administrative officer, elaborates the administrative, educative, and supportive functions fully (pp. 39-271), along with an evaluative function that is conceptualized as a component of both administrative and educative supervision.

Miller, who contributed the recent *Encyclopedia of Social Work* discussions (1977, 1544-1550), viewed supervision as essentially "an administrative process for getting the work done and maintaining organizational accountability." Reviewing the historical development of supervision, he noted that emphasis fluctuated between the two major functions: administration and teaching.

So supervision has been viewed in diverse ways: as educational; as administrative; as administrative and educative; as administrative, educative, and supportive (the most prevalent viewpoint); and, in our view, as a role and process involving nine functions—humanizing, managing tension, catalyzing, teaching, career socializing, evaluating, administering, changing, and advocating.

Our curiosity about these fluctuating definitions and our observations of current practice led us to seek data on the proportions of education and administration in current supervisory practice. We observed an increase in complaints from workers about the lack of any educative, supervisory help on the job. Students in supervision classes had similar reports about their prior work experiences. These heightened our interest. We examined empirical studies of supervision in the 1970s and early 1980s to find out how much educative supervision was actually reported in agency-based supervision. As a simple working definition, we think "educative" supervision concerns enhancing the professional development of the practitioner, while "administrative" is related to the organization's need for efficiency and accountability.

## EDUCATIVE SUPERVISION

### Research on Educative Supervision

Considerable attention has been devoted to workplace organization, teams, and training (e.g., Barker and Briggs, 1978; Schwartz and Sample, 1971), but we have limited ourselves to research on the focus and content of the supervisory relationship. Empirical research that offers clues about this area of supervision has been limited. (See Note 1 for a summary of the work of Kadushin, 1974, 1976; and Shulman, 1982.) Our own preliminary study examined research by Johnston and Drouet (1982) on 27 supervisors employed in private social agencies and Payne's study (1982) of 29 supervisors in the public sector in Kentucky. We explored the actual versus the desired amount of time supervisors devoted to teaching, to administering, and to the other seven functional components we identified as elements of supervision. We defined *teaching* as "devising and conveying to others information that will increase their knowledge and skills" and *administering* as "related to activities of planning, decision-making, and workload management as demanded by the service-delivery situation." Our findings suggest that supervisors in private social agencies spent most of their time administering (35 percent); teaching ranked third in terms of time allocation (13 percent). In terms of desired allocation, teaching ranked in third place (21 percent); administering ranked fourth (13 percent). In the public agency, supervisors spent most of their time administering (33 percent); teaching ranked second in time spent (30 percent).[2] With regard to preferred allocation, these supervisors ranked administering first (30 percent) and teaching third (20 percent). These results suggest that supervisors are aware of the importance of teaching and of the need to give it more emphasis in comparison with administering. Moreover, although public agency supervisors, both in practice and in preference, acknowledge the importance of teaching, they give priority to administering. We believe these findings highlight the dilemma for the contemporary supervisor in maintaining time and commitment to teaching in the face of administrative duties and the demands of the other seven supervisory functions.

Social work supervision is perhaps also unique in the gap between the imagined, idealized *oughts* of supervision and the way it *is*: the discrepancy between nostalgia about "good old days," when you could count on deepening your competence during agency work under the watchful, helpful eyes of the supervisor, and the workaday world in the 1980s, when time pressures limit the opportunity for guided individual, tailor-made teaching and learning. Let us look closer at educative supervision in the social work profession.

### Emphasis on Educative Supervision

To have a hand in another's professional development, to become a supervisor, was a career goal to cap years of crafted practice expertise. It was a valued move. Educative supervision was an attractive opportunity for knowledgeable, seasoned practitioners, and an appealing learning situation for the newer workers. It demanded and drew on everything that supervisors had learned in professional education, and many of them considered it the most interesting part of the profession. In the supervisory relationship, learners discovered insights and self-awareness; their own risked attempts at helping were recorded and discussed; and then, using the new insights, they adapted their approaches and attempted them again. The social work profession developed a rich literature that documents the use of practice knowledge as a basis for developing theories and formulating key principles. This literature also records what has been learned about how supervisors should go about teaching others to acquire skilled practice.[3]

Kadushin describes educative supervision as the major intramural (i.e., within-agency) avenue for teaching the knowledge and skills needed for social work practice (even though this may be augmented or superseded eventually in one's career development by workshops, institutes, and other forms of in-service training). He describes this supervision as "providing optimum opportunities for individualizing learning needs in response to educational diagnoses of the idiosyncratic learning patterns of supervisees" (1981, p. 641). Acknowledging that supervision is sometimes defined either as administrative responsibility with educative components or as educative with administrative components, he holds that the educative function is central in any case,

> . . . as a principal avenue for the education and training of inductees to social work positions . . . in almost all social welfare agencies . . . who come to the position without any prior knowledge of social work [or] . . . with some prior education . . . at community-college level, at the bachelor-level major in social work, or at a masters' degree level. The supervisor, as educator, has responsibility for assessing what the new appointee knows and can do and then formulating an agenda of training that is appropriate. Even with the recruit who comes with full professional training, the supervisor, as educator, has the responsibility of helping the appointee translate general knowledge and skills so that they are applicable to the specific functions and tasks of the particular agency. . . . Intramural agency educational supervision provides the supplementary internship training for refinement of knowledge and skills in ongoing clinical contacts with clients (1981, pp. 640–641).

Other professions have not emphasized supervision as the main means for inducting newcomers into a professional role. Nor have they used the intimate, individual format of educative (or traditional) supervision in social work, even to "the recruit with full professional training." Toren (1972) criticized this type of social work supervision as follows: (1) What is supervised is a set of relationships and activities not directly observable. (2) Supervision is carried out through a relationship system having no *formal end point.* (3) Supervision in this relationship system covers practice judgments as well as administrative issues, sometimes going against professional ethics (pp. 75; 76). She argued against the supervision in social work of an "invisible practice"—one the supervisor never observed directly that relied on the worker's attitudinal conformity achieved through a shared value base. This attitudinal conformity, or common ideology and orientation, controlled the quality and substance of the practice. It was assured through an induction system that featured careful selection, training, and evaluation, with agency supervisors playing a critical role. In fact, selection often settled upon those applicants who appeared as if they would best fit into the agency as it existed, not those who looked like boat-rockers.

The learning process for the social work novice was one of gradual insight development, an increase of self-awareness distinguished in the professional sense as "conscious use of self." Through this conscious use of self, the novice learned new actions and behavior in the service of clients. This was the major goal of the intimate, all-purpose relationship with a more seasoned, experienced worker: the supervisor. Such learning was a slow-developing process that did not end with the masters' degree, but in fact continued throughout agency work, sometimes without diminishing emphasis. For some workers, the never-ending process of increased knowledge and skill development was a cherished component of professional work; others chafed at the restraint on their autonomy, described by Epstein (1973) as "mandatory tutorial education," and the implied dependency that the relationship nurtured. In all cases, it was an expensive, time-consuming arrangement for the agency. It worked well so long as practice orientations were relatively stable and similar, external funding and service provisions were consistent, and competing knowledge and skill-teaching modalities of other professions did not intrude. These forces, of course, did surface.[4]

### Changing Orientations

When the educative component of supervision has been considered separately from the administrative part (e.g., workload assignments, review, planning, and coordination), most discussions of the content and process of the supervisory sessions reveal shifts in approach that parallel the theoretical advances in social casework and social work. The format was dyadic on the whole until, in the 1960s, especially in the public-agency sector, team and group supervision gradually appeared. The supervisor was an "officially" designated expert and the supervisee was a seeker of knowledge and skill. As can be seen in Table 1-1, the assumed expertise of the supervisor in the early days of social work was in the activities and tasks of the job; in the 1920s to mid-1960s in self-awareness and personality dynamics; and more recently, in the performance of various roles and functions required by complex systems. In other words, these were the areas that the supervisor was supposed to know a lot about and be able to teach others.

There are many ways to instruct others. We have identified three general descriptors to characterize changing orientations of supervisors over time: from coach, to counselor, to conferee. In each of these orientations the goal for supervision is effective service to the clients. The routes toward helping the supervisee learn to offer such services differed with the times.

The *coach* is master of the specific tasks to be accomplished. Performance of these tasks is closely monitored through a master-novice relationship between supervisor and supervisee. The emphasis is on teaching via precept and example. Instruction focuses on right and wrong ways to be and do. The supervisor is concrete and directive and is respected as an authority based on knowledge and skills developed in the "school of hard knocks."

The *counselor* is master of personality dynamics, self-awareness, and the elements of a relationship that are needed for the process of giving and receiving help. Here, teaching depends on the development of a trusted relationship where feelings can be shared openly and explored in terms of origins and dynamics. In this way, insights into one's self, and consequently into others' feelings and actions, can be accepted. In the self-discovery process, the supervisor is a guide who teaches through inductive questions out of specific incidents of the learner's service to clients.

The *conferee* is master of many roles, for example, helper, enabler, planner, advocate, mediator, counselor, broker. The conferee knows when to take these different roles, what cautions and consequences are part of doing so, and what activities comprise each role. The conferee is a collaborator, a consultant, a coordinator, a delegator, a negotiator, and most of all, a master of the complexities of

**TABLE 1-1  Perspectives on Supervision**

| ROLE ANALOG | EXPERT/ MASTER OF* | ORIENTING THEORIES/ PHILOSOPHIES | VIEW OF CLIENT | ROUTE TO GOAL THROUGH | APPROACH OF LEARNING |
|---|---|---|---|---|---|
| Coach | Activities<br>Tasks | Pragmatism<br>Behaviorism<br>Empiricism | Needs to learn | Mastery of operations | Observation, approximation, feedback, correction, action |
| Counselor | Personality dynamics<br>Use of self, relationship | Dynamic psychology<br>Personality theories<br>Existentialism<br>Phenomenology | Needs to understand self; feelings, attitudes, insight | Disciplined use of self | Action/reflection<br>Conceptualization<br>Enactment |
| Conferee | Diverse roles and component behavior,<br>Coordination and distribution of tasks and resources | Role<br>Systems<br>Cybernetics<br>Exchange<br>Communication | Is a consumer<br>Needs access to resources, justice | Negotiated distribution of resources and decision making | Task analysis<br>Problem assessment |

*Note: In each of the three roles, the expertise or mastery is posed as an *assumption* of the role and orientation. We do not intend to imply that all supervisors *were* experts. Supervisors in any orientation may lack competence in knowing and executing their work.

current organizational life. The conferee concept is derived from the notion of the conference (see Middleman and Goldberg, 1974). The conferee role is *egalitarian and facilitative*. It creates structures for enhancing others' achievements. The conferee role may involve becoming coach or counselor, if this is acceptable to the supervisee (when and if the learning circumstances demand such teaching—for example, in relation to learning specific skills or to sensitivity awareness). The conferee orientation is broad and encompassing. It is a poised-for-action anticipatory stance with an instructional component. As such, it is responsive to what supervisees need to learn more about in order to deliver services of high quality. The knowledge to be taught may be related to self-awareness, sensitivity to others, understanding of the service systems, or understanding of the diversity of particular tasks that supervisee and supervisor face. Since our focus at this point is on the educative aspect of supervision (more than the administrative aspect), we need to add that "conferee" differs from "case manager." (In our view, case manager is an administrative line-role that springs more from the service system's delivery needs than from workers' learning needs. It is critical, and it is a current response to the system's needs for economy, efficiency, accountability, accessibility, coordination, balance, and continuity of services.)

Let us pause briefly in our history to explore your attitudes about supervision as you may have experienced it in the past. To do this, try to recall supervisors you have known, and think about what ideas and behaviors you preferred to see in a supervisor. No doubt you have noticed that there are certain supervisory attitudes and behaviors that you hope to cultivate in yourself. Also, there are probably others you may not wish to repeat, and these can be put aside. Remember: the cycle can stop with you! You need not repeat what you have experienced unless you actively choose to do so. Before you continue, we encourage you to complete Appendix B, Supervisor Preference Checklist, which will help you imagine what kind of supervision you value or aspire to cultivate.

## INFLUENCES MAKING FOR TRADITIONAL (EDUCATIVE) SUPERVISION

Traditional, educative supervision flourished mainly from the 1920s through the mid-1960s and was known as the "growth" model (Epstein, 1973; Wijnberg and Schwartz, 1977), as the "worker-centered" (Gitterman, 1973) or the "existential supervisee-centered" orientation (Kadushin, 1974), or the "insight-oriented" and "feelings-oriented" approaches (Cherniss and Egnatios, 1978). This orientation is described by Kadushin as follows:

> Supervision [is] concerned with the development of the supervisee's self-understanding, self-awareness, and emotional growth. The supervisee has the principal responsibility for what he wants to learn, and the focus of supervision is on the *way* the worker does his work and the nature of his relationship to the client. (1974, p. 294)

According to a second view of this type of supervision:

> Supervisors undertook to modify the attitudes of their students so that they might be able to function more effectively in their casework relationships. Professional education in social work was concerned not only with the knowledge imparted to students, but also with their personality growth. (Wijnberg and Schwartz, 1977, p. 108)

Several factors have shaped what is now known as traditional (educative) supervision. Some that seem important in our view are (1) the social agency's close linkage with professional training, (2) the dominant influence of casework, (3) the combined administrative/educative functions to be carried by the same supervisor, and (4) the adherence to supervisory rather than consultative structural arrangements. We shall review these factors before we look at supervision in the 1980s.

### The Social Agency and Professional Training

We shall see (in Chapter 6) the heavy influence that the social agency, with its traditions and conventions, has had on social work practice. The social agency also greatly influenced both the view of what the supervision of social work practice should be like and what professional training would become. Miller saw this close association between agency and the evolving professional training schools as a force that tended to obscure the more general, administrative thrust of most supervision. Speaking of the influence of the training programs that accentuated the teaching function, Miller states:

> The literature on supervision reflects this influence, explicitly or implicitly, using a conceptual model for supervision of social agency practice similar to that for graduate training for social work practice. The overlapping objectives and important similarities have, however, tended to obscure important distinctions between a model for supervision directly related to the delivery of services and maintenance of service standards and a model that must reflect the special requirements—teaching and socialization—of education for the profession. (1971/1977, p. 1545)

Miller went on to discuss the confusion that this educational emphasis imposed on the supervisory relationship. As the "quasi-therapeutic relationship" was presumably the central component of supervision that was necessary and sufficient for learning and for working, effort was required in order for "keeping means and ends in perspective and both related to work, agency function, and maintenance of standards of service" (p. 1545). By questioning the self-awareness emphasis as a possible detriment to specific service elements, Miller was really assaulting one of social work's most sacred cows.

Another unique historical feature of social work was its pattern of professional training and education. Unlike psychology and psychiatry, the class- and field-learning experiences in social work were linked in an articulated pattern in which professional learning experiences were provided *before* graduation. This pattern connected the educative and the training components more closely in social work than in the allied professions. It also brought the professional school into a determining position by which practitioners in agencies might be acceptable as fieldwork supervisors. And when agency practitioners became fieldwork supervisors for a professional school's program, they also tended to supervise the rest of the staff (who might not be in any educational program) in line with the "new psychology" learned as part of their own master's degree programs. As Miller observed, educative goals were encouraged for *all* staff, and this at times ran counter to the more ordinary administrative role of the supervisor. In other words, the educative was elevated at the expense of the administrative.

In other occupations, supervisors have acted more as foremen or administrators, and the education or training of the workers has been accomplished either outside of the job or in clearly graduated guild statuses (apprentice, journeyman). But for social work, the supervisor had to be concerned with the educative component. This happened partly because of the close linkage with the professional schools and the status this linkage imparted to certain practitioners; partly because of the lack (until the late 1960s) of other identified standards and certifications set by the profession or licensing agencies; and partly because the community sanctioned agencies, not individual practitioners, to provide social services. All these factors determined that agency supervisors would have a deep concern and stake in the quality of the work, and not merely the amount of it or the arrangements for it.

It was only natural that agency work and professional education and training were intimately connected through most of the profession's development. This situation was called "the myth of the agency as partner" by Middleman (1973): a myth that school and agency *were* partners, that formal education and agency work needed close, if not identical, theoretical orientations and objectives. The myth also accented that theory would be learned in the school and applied in the agency and that this psychology of practice would be sufficient to inform and guide all practice. Mainly, the myth allowed the professional schools to *direct* the agency supervisors (field instructors) to synchronize the fieldwork of students with the newly developed practice theories and methods. Quite naturally, out of their administrative supervisory roles in the organization, the agency supervisors also introduced these approaches to "good" practice to other staff. There was a need to spread the new gospel to all staff.

There are some subtle distinctions among the concepts *educative, education,* and *training* and what these imply about *learning* and about the profession's history. The close connection historically between the social agency and the developing professional school, which we have just described, tended to confound education and training, the general and the particular, the abstract and the concrete. We shall return to this theme—education versus training, school versus agency, class versus field teaching and learning—after we consider the differences between *educative* (adjective) and *education* (noun), and the influence of this distinction on professional *education* and its *training* agencies. Many experiences are *educative* but not necessarily *education* in its formal sense. There is learning "from the street" and learning "from the school," and either type of learning is educative. Educative, in the sense of informative or instructional, refers not only to school experiences, but also to learning derived from work or life experience. And approaches that can be thought of as education or training are both educative. All professions have some mix of education and training as required educative experiences.

All of the helping professions have independently evolved systems for induction, acculturation, knowledge and skill promotion, and monitoring, credentialing, and standard-setting. The induction and evaluation of practice involve some education and some training. *Education* ideally should produce professionals who are differentiated from their earlier selves and from all other learners, who can both do and doubt, and who enjoy complexity, ambiguity, and making independent judgments. *Training* deals with similar operations, uniform outcomes, and achieving a given level or standard of performance that has been determined in advance by others to be good, right, in the best form, or most sensitive and insightful. The training deals with the rules, policies, practices, and professional norms that have been ordered into some set of ideas and behaviors that the novice must learn in order to deliver a reliable, accountable practice in line with the goals and special functions of the profession and sponsoring agency. Training uses a teaching/learning approach that is deductive (general to specific) and didactic (telling, showing). Education needs a teaching/learning approach that, over and above the deductive, is also both inductive (specific to general) and evocative (questioning, exploring)— that is, it needs a deductive/inductive approach.

The influence of graduate education in the young profession of social work, busy with professionalizing itself, heightened the importance of educational supervision vis à vis the training component. Moreover, it emphasized the production of a professionally socialized practitioner, rather than one who might merely meet the administrative requirements of agency work. We shall return subsequently to consider "training," since this is an aspect of current supervisory practice that is "in" so far as agency interests are concerned.

### Casework and Supervision

The enormous influence of casework on all of social work and on supervision must also be considered. It was through the intellectual contributions of casework theorists that supervision theory was formulated. So, it was only logical that supervision came to be a mode of practice complementary to casework. The ideal type of supervision has been one-on-one, intimate, regular, retrospective, and introspective, much like casework. This supervision was based on the supervisee's written process records and was comparable dynamically to the contacts that the supervisee had with clients. The content and the process paralleled those of social casework and combined to form a potentially powerful learning modality for the novice, which came to be known as educational supervision.

Casework has determined the profession's major thrust theoretically, programmatically, and organizationally. The influence of casework theory and practice on the totality of social work is well documented in all accounts of the historical development of the profession. Casework has been the predominant orientation of educators and the major practice specialty throughout the profession's history. This heritage must be recognized for its contribution to the very existence of social work supervision, but it also bears responsibility for the conservative form that most social work supervision has followed as compared with developments in other professions.

Miller describes this development as follows:

> As services expanded and became bureaucratically organized and method [that is, casework] began to be conceptualized in "scientific" and "treatment" terms, a strong individualized tutorial approach emerged in supervision, corresponding to the emerging individualized case approach. (1977, p. 1545)

For all practical purposes, the supervisory approach of status in social work has always been a one-by-one, individual tutorial arrangement, just as a one-by-one mode of helping remains the favored context for delivering social work services and the predominant way in which social agencies have organized the work. We think this is mainly a function of numbers; in the final analysis people do what they are most comfortable with, what they know how to do and are trained to do, despite the task. And for social work, this task has been serving individuals, and serving them one by one. The one-on-one casework approach has been the preferred mode of work in organization as well as in private practice. According to a 1976 survey of services offered by social workers in private practice, 63 percent was individual treatment, 19 percent marital couples, 8 percent groups, and 7 percent families (Wallace, 1982). Casework's domination of the substance and form of supervision has been recognized in the literature; yet the heavy reliance on a one-on-one supervisory approach persists in social work literature as the most authentic way to supervise.

Miller (1960) criticized the emphasis on casework-type supervision as being far from ideal for group work and community organization practice. He described the frustration that group work supervisors experienced in trying to connect the agency reality with what was taught to them as good supervisory practice. He reported many group workers' discount of the usefulness of theories that make sense only to the teachers of practice and "those in highly specialized, controlled, and protected situations," (p. 69) and he questioned the utility not only of the elaborate recording and regularly scheduled conferences that this supervision required, but also of other "luxuries." Miller pointed out that the heavy emphasis on relationship and the emotional and comfort components in the learning process diminished the attention to giving active, supportive direction to actual work with groups, giving service, developing programs, and the various instructional, information- and advice-giving aspects of supervision. Epstein also described the mismatch of supervision with group work, community work, and research—approaches that

are "highly visible, subject to public appraisal" unlike the "more private and obscure" casework. She summarized the research that pointed to the advantages
of team and group modes of workplace organization over traditional supervision
(1973, p. 146). Kutzik's history further clarifies the circumstances that kept traditional supervision in place over the years (1977b).

It was inevitable that supervision of persons in organizations would have to
accommodate conceptually to, and make use of, knowledge other than that from
individual psychologies and personality theories. Concepts from systems theory,
role theory, sociology, organizational and group dynamics theories, and task- and
motivation-related knowledge have been recognized as useful for understanding
persons, work environments, and supervision. And, as we shall explore, in addition
to this elaborated, expanded knowledge base about persons, work environments,
and practice approaches, the last twenty years have seen an explosion of information about instructional technologies, theories of teaching and learning, and diverse
formats for influence approaches—most of which have been annexed from practice
in allied professions. These have influenced the way in which organizations pursue
the stimulating, controlling, and monitoring of the services offered—in short, they
have influenced the substance and form of supervisory practice.

### The Administrative-Educative Supervisor

Since it was necessary for supervisors—ordinarily administrative personnel—
also to assume educative responsibilities, social work developed a curious role that
combined administrative and educative functions in the same person. This arrangement became the arrangement of choice for social work, and the issues surrounding
it are complex.

Administrative supervision typically is linked to career advancement and
organizational performance, while educative supervision is linked to learning, to
one's sense of confidence through competence in practice. As to the debate and
arguments that have surrounded this situation, an extensive literature exists in the
journals, dating from the 1950s. Some of these have been collected as "classical
statements and critical issues" by Munson (1979b) and present the historical developments and proposals advanced by concerned theorists and practitioners in
earlier years. Here, we shall propose a few focusing questions that may orient you
to some of the concerns that have continued to haunt the profession.

Shall we assume that the supervisor who is knowledgeable in the administrative area is equally knowledgeable in the clinical realm? Or that one who is skilled
in intervention with clients is expert in work-load management, budgets, and other
administrative matters? Beyond knowledge requirements, are the values complementary? Are double reportings, with the potential for alliances or discords, more
(or less) productive for the organization, for the workers, than a combined accountability? The administrative linkage must be line-connected. So, in order to coordinate efforts and services, reporting and recording accountability must be overseen
and enforced by someone in the next higher level of the organization's hierarchy.
But must the educative function be a line one, or can it be a staff (consultative)

function? And should the educative role last forever simply because the administrative role must be ongoing? One of the authors still painfully recalls that after twenty years' post-masters practice, the agency hierarchical "supervisor" would ask any time they disagreed about a practice approach, "Why are you so reactive?" Should agency seniority and administrative position power necessarily imply superior practice judgment and competence?

Epstein (1973) summarized the historical trends and developments within this administrative/educative dilemma, a problem she called "oversupervision in social work." She described several practice and theoretical shifts. There was the tutorial arrangement, where the supervisor was mainly educator. Then there was a structural shift, where the administration and teaching functions were located in different persons, with the individual conference played down in favor of group learning through seminars, consultations, and the like (leaving the worker free to choose among available experts or use supervision sparingly). There followed a group or team emphasis, where the supervisor was leader-administrator or was not a supervisor at all in the administrative sense, and where the education was assigned to someone outside the group. Finally, there were some situations where practitioners worked autonomously or independently, perhaps employed by new agencies or special projects spun off from traditional agencies, or under the auspices of organizations directed by professionals from another field, such as education or psychiatry.

Munson proposed a dual model of supervision that aimed to distinguish client-centered questions from agency-centered issues. His arrangement would separate the clinical and administrative tasks, with a supervisor and a one-on-one structure for the administrative part and a consultant and group conferences for the clinical part. Through this arrangement, he expected that the interactions involved in clinical work would be free from administrative constraints and evaluation (1979a, p. 340).

Social work, more than other professions or occupations, developed a dual type of supervision (administrative/educative) because of its historical requirements. It was a profession, as we have said, born and bred in social agencies out of the demands of the work to be done. Professional education in social work was conceptualized by the agency-based practitioners. Instead of remaining in-house, professional training was systematized, lodged in training schools, and developed, subsequently, in universities. The heritage has been one of service first, education or training second, as derived from a service mission. Agency work and professional education and training have been intimately connected through most of the profession's development. The supervisor, as an agency employee, had administrative responsibilities and then added an educative role with staff and students. In short, social work started in agencies and moved to educational institutions to educate for this work, while many other professions (e.g., clinical psychology, psychiatry) were conceptualized in The Academy and moved from there to find a practice arena for their graduates.

It was a unique tradition among professions that the service component, the actual dealing with problems, was a central part of professional education. Since the practitioners became the theoreticians, the educative pattern always has been rooted in service provision, and field experience always has been a central part of professional education. The centrality of service to social work education and its difference from traditions in medical education have been described (Kutzik, 1973a/1973b). The social work emphasis on learning from the realities of service was a factor that seemed to justify the combination of educative and administrative supervisory functions. And since it was the agency, not the individual worker, that the community "authorized" to do social work, it made sense for the agency— through the supervisor—to assume control of the programs and practice pursued in its name.

This administrative/educative combination has consumed the intellectual energies of many. Closely related to this matter, social work developed another traditional pattern that we shall now review—that is, the emphasis on supervision to the detriment of consultation. Many of the factors already described played a role in this situation. So let us look more directly at this aspect of agency practice.

### Supervision and Consultation

Supervision and consultation are two principal ways to assure the training component of professional practice—that is, to control and standardize performance. These processes depend on some sort of in-profession, collegial collaboration that starts with the induction of the new recruits and continues throughout their professional careers.

There are, of course, many varieties of supervision and of consultation—no one formula for either. Yet some general distinctions may be clarified by using role titles for these processes: trainer, consultant, supervisor. Immediately, we can imagine the trainer dealing typically with some staff group (in-service meetings, workshops), the consultant responding to requests from either individual workers or a team or unit, and the supervisor most likely dealing with workers in one-on-one conferences. Another distinction among these three influence modes is the person(s) who determines the goals for the contact. In the training event, the trainer or faculty typically plan and set out the goals. In consultations, the consultee chooses the goals, determines what material to discuss or present, and evaluates the helpfulness of the consultation. And in the supervisory situation, the goals may be mutually determined, or they may be set by the supervisor or field-instruction curriculum, with some input from the supervisee; and evaluations presumably are mutually determined.

Beyond these target, goal-setting, and evaluation distinctions between training, supervision, and consultation, other key differences can be cited between supervision and consultation. Supervision involves a line as opposed to a staff relationship. It is not optional, and its rhythm and frequency usually are set by the supervisor. It is a superordinate/subordinate relationship, with the supervisor holding the power, no matter how collegial the relationship may seem to be.

Supervision is periodic and has a specified regularity. The supervisee not only implements the advice, directions, or suggestions proposed and planned during the sessions but also reports on the outcomes at a future meeting. Supervision is a relationship between unequals and has been most successfully used in instances where the supervisee is not similarly educated and trained as is the supervisor (for example, is a volunteer or a paraprofessional). Levy (1973) cites several power differentials that favor the supervisor. These power advantages include: assigned control over the supervisee by the agency, including accountability reporting; mediation and interpretation between the worker and the higher-ups; a role in hiring, firing, salary increases, promotion, personnel records, references, and long-range employment fortunes; greater access to agency information; and the expectation that the supervisee should reveal personal information to the supervisor.

Consultation assumes a voluntary meeting between professional peers, initiated by the consultee who seeks advice or reactions from a selected consultant, presumably because the consultant has expertise in the area of concern. The meeting may, but need not, be regularly scheduled: It can be episodic, on an as-needed basis, and the results of the consultation may or may not be accepted. There is a take-it-or-leave-it mentality, depending on the consultee's determination of the worth of the consultation. These differences between consultation and supervision are mainly structural. Kadushin, however, emphasizes a qualitative, content difference pointing to an added measure of expertise for the consultant:

> . . . some special knowledge and skill different from, or beyond that, possessed by the supervisor. . . . The consultant begins where the supervisor ends . . . [and] has either a higher level of knowledge of the same kinds of content with which the supervisor is concerned, or a specialized kind of knowledge and skill which the supervisor is not expected to have. (1977, p. 1545)

While it may be that some consultants have specialized knowledge or skills that justify their role, we tend to see the major distinctions between supervisor and consultant in structural, role-related, line-versus-staff statuses.

Both supervision and consultation are types of collaboration among helpers aimed to combine knowledge and skills so as to improve service to clients; still, as discussed above, they may have differing dynamics and assumptions. Supervision involves unequal statuses; consultation involves equal statuses. Supervision requires, at least implicitly, following the supervisor's advice, opinions, and orders; consultation is a take-it-or-leave-it event judged on the basis of its merits in the eyes of the consultee. Supervision is continuous and unending; consultation is episodic, taken as needed. Supervision is evaluated either mutually or by the supervisor; consultation is evaluated by the consultee. The supervisor has a power advantage over the supervisee; the consultant is a conferee who collaborates and forms an egalitarian relationship with the consultee. While there are shades and differences within each format, we have emphasized the extremes in this discussion, so that key differences can be appreciated.

An extensive historical review by Kutzik (1977a/1977b) has illumined the subtle differences between the events in the fields of social work and medicine (also psychiatry) that have led to alternate professional emphases. These include differences in the training of the novice professional-to-be, and in the norms affecting interaction among the accredited professionals. The development of training and applied practice norms in medicine dates from the 17th century; in social work from the end of the 19th century; and in psychology from as recently as 1963, when the Mental Health Act launched a clinical psychology and counseling that looked more to psychiatry than to social work for training norms (Hart, 1982).

According to Kutzik's analysis of the medical and social work fields, both professions used and confused the processes of supervision and consultation during their formative periods—the 17th and 18th centuries for medicine and the past eighty years for the young social work profession. In medicine, for example, the university-educated physician actually supervised the apothecaries and others in medically related occupations but usually described these meetings as consultations. In social work, at least since the 1930s, "much of what has gone on has been consultation," despite its description as supervision (Kutzik, 1977b, p. 51). Kutzik supports this conclusion by quoting Kadushin's description of "supervision," which Kutzik (p. 51) claims is "unmistakably described and even explicitly characterized as [consultative]":

> The traditional literature in social work supervision suggests an image of the supervisor which . . . is that of a person who establishes full and free reciprocal communication with the supervisee . . . resulting in optimization of supervisee autonomy and discretion; who has a problem-solving orientation toward the work of the agency, based on consensus and cooperation . . . rather than power-centered techniques; who values a consultative-leadership relationship in supervision rather than a subordinate-superordinate relationship" (Kadushin, 1976, p. 116).

Kutzik (1977b) claims that the mistake of treating supervision as consultation has been positive for the physicians' practice, while the mistake of considering a consultation arrangement to be supervision in social work has diminished the status and role of professional social workers. This supervisory tradition has impaired the social worker's ability to collaborate freely with other professionals, especially in multidisciplinary settings. It has retarded the achievement of licensure as well as of vendorship status in national health insurance plans.

Kutzik proposed a supervisory format approximating that of medical education: time-limited, postgraduate training-supervision followed by full professional status and consultative relationships. His observations, like those of numerous others in the literature of the past two decades, proposed time-limited, "close" supervision and instruction only for neophytes and inexperienced professionals, and "routine" supervision and consultation for the experienced professionals. Case conferences and staff meetings devoted to exploring program and policy issues would be viewed as consultation, and much in the educative realm would be "packaged" as in-service and training programs for groups of staff.

## SUPERVISION IN THE 1980s

Writing in the early 1970s, Epstein identified forces that would work against the total reliance on supervision to ensure and transmit the qualitative component of professional social work practice:

1. The nationwide program of the NASW to certify social workers who are qualified to practice independently may loosen the bonds of close tutorial supervision.
2. The kinds of social work being practiced and workers' educational levels are becoming increasingly diverse.
3. The traditional roles of professionally trained practitioners are shifting to ones that require higher levels of skill, as workers with undergraduate degrees receive more recognition.
4. There is increasing evidence that more professionally trained workers are going into private practice.
5. Increasing numbers of professionals are urging that the purpose of graduate training should be to prepare students for self-regulated practice (1973, p. 5).

Most of these predictions have come to pass, as we consider them from the vantage point of today and look at social work in the 1980s (with the possible exception of the recognition accorded the B.S.W. degree vis à vis other undergraduate degrees in the public sector). We shall follow these themes further and add certain others, more obvious at the present time.

### Standards, Certification, and Licensure

There is increased recognition within organizations that consultative rather than strictly supervisory arrangements, especially among seasoned professionals, should be featured in current delivery systems. This development has been hastened and made more feasible by the recognition of the profession's ACSW credential, a stable NASW membership category comprising over half of its membership. This credential signifies that these practitioners may self-monitor and self-regulate their own practice and are competent to be self-supervising in terms of the qualitative substance of the work. As of 1984, moreover, 35 states have achieved some form of legal regulation of social work practice, a development that has diminished the sole reliance on supervisors to attest to the quality of individuals' competence. Table 1-2 reveals the diversity surrounding licensure from state to state.[5] A nationally applicable licensure examination has been developed by the American Association of State Boards of Licensure and some movement toward reciprocity among states has been made. Definitions and specifications of social work performance standards for basic and specialized levels of practice with their relevant knowledge, skills, abilities, values, and tasks have been identified and published by NASW (1981). These criteria will help clarify and publicize matters related to the standard-meeting, classification, training, and interpreting aspects of professional assignments. These factors, which may be considered as an aspect of the maturation and

**TABLE 1-2  Levels of Practice Regulated—Renewal Periods***

| | Title | Initials | Education | Experience Required | Current Employment Required | Exam Required | Renewal Period |
|---|---|---|---|---|---|---|---|
| ALABAMA | Independent Practice | — | MSW | +2[17] | | YES | 2 years |
| | Certified Social Worker | LCSW | MSW | +2 yrs. | NO | YES | |
| | Graduate Social Worker | LGSW | MSW | [18] | NO | YES | |
| | Bachelor Social Worker | LBSW | BSW | | | YES | |
| ARKANSAS | Licensed Certified Social Worker | LCSW | MSW | +2 years | NO | YES | 2 years |
| | Licensed Master Social Worker | LMSW | MSW | | | YES | |
| | Licensed Social Worker | LSW | BSW | | | YES | |
| CALIFORNIA | Licensed Clinical Social Worker | LCSW | MSW | +2 years[3] | NO | YES | Annual |
| COLORADO | Licensed Social Worker II | LSWII[11] | MSW | +5 years | NO | YES | 2 years |
| | Licensed Social Worker | LSWI | MSW | +2 years | | YES | |
| | Registered Social Worker | RSW | MSW or BA | +2 years | | NO | |
| DELAWARE | Licensed Clinical Social Worker | LCSW | MSW | +2 years | NO | YES | 2 years |
| FLORIDA | Clinical Social Worker | LCSW | MSW | +3 years[24] | NO | YES[25] | 2 years |
| IDAHO | Independent Practice | — | MSW | +2 years | NO | NO | Annual |
| | Certified Social Worker | CSW | MSW | | | YES | |
| | Social Worker | SW | BSW[14] | | | YES | |
| ILLINOIS | Certified Social Worker | CSW | MSW | +2 years | NO | YES | 2 years |
| | Social Worker | SW | BA | | YES | YES | |
| KANSAS | "Specialties" | | | | | | |
| | Master Social Worker | MSW | MSW | +2 years | YES[6] | YES | 2 years |
| | Baccalaureate Social Worker | BSW | BSW | | | YES | |
| KENTUCKY | Independent Practice | CSW | MSW | +2 years | NO | YES | 3 years |
| | Certified Social Worker | SW | MSW | | | YES | |
| | Social Worker | | BSW | | | YES | |
| LOUISIANA | Board Certified Social Worker | BCSW | MSW | +2 years | NO | YES | Annual |
| MAINE | Independent Practice | | MSQ | +2 years | NO | YES[20] | 2 years |
| | Certified Social Worker | CSW | MSW | +2 years | | YES | |
| | Registered Social Worker | RSW | BSW | +2 years | | YES | |
| | Associate Social Worker | ASW | BA or | 6 years | | YES | |
| MARYLAND | Independent Practice | CSW[10] | MSW | +2 years | NO | YES | 2 years |
| | Certified Social Worker | GSW | MSW | +2 years | | YES | |
| | Graduate Social Worker | SWA | MSW | | | YES | |
| | Social Work Associate | | BSW | | | YES | |

**TABLE 1-2 (cont.)**

| | Title | Initials | Education | Experience Required | Current Employment Required | Exam Required | Renewal Period |
|---|---|---|---|---|---|---|---|
| MASSACHUSETTS | Independent Clinical Social Worker | ICSW | MSW | +3 years | | YES | |
| | Certified Social Worker | CSW | MSW | +2 years | NO | YES | |
| | Social Worker | SW | BSW or BA | | | YES | |
| | Social Work Associate | ASW | AA/BA | | | YES | |
| MICHIGAN | Certified Social Worker | CSW | MSW | +2 years | NO[6] | NO | Annual |
| | Social Worker | SW | MSW or BA | +2 years | YES[7,6,13] | NO | Annual |
| | Social Worker Technician | SWT | 2 yr. BA or | 1 year | YES[8,6] | NO | |
| MONTANA | Licensed Social Worker | LSW | MSW | +2[26] | NO | YES | 2 years |
| NEW HAMPSHIRE | Certified Clinical Social Worker | CCSW | MSW | +2[27] | NO | NO | — |
| NEW YORK | Certified Social Worker | CSW | MSW[4] | | NO | YES | 2 years |
| NORTH CAROLINA | Certified Social Worker | CSW | BSW | | NO | YES | 2 years |
| | Certified Master Social Worker | CMSW | MSW | | NO | YES | |
| | Certified Clinical Social Worker | CCSW | MSW | +2[28] | NO | YES | |
| | Certified Social Work Manager | CSWM | BSW | +2[28] | NO | YES | |
| NORTH DAKOTA | Licensed Social Worker | LSW | BSW | | NO | YES | 2 years |
| | Licensed Certified Social Worker | LCSW | MSW | | NO | YES | |
| | Independent Practice | | MSW | +3 | NO | NO | |
| OKLAHOMA | Independent Licensed Social Worker | LSW | MSW | +2 years | NO | YES | Annual |
| | Licensed Social Work Associate | LSWA | BSW | +2 years | NO | YES | |
| OREGON | Registered Clinical Social Worker | RCSW | MSW | +2 years | NO[19] | NO | Annual[19] |
| PUERTO RICO | Social Worker | | BA-MSW[1] | +2 years | NO | NO | None |
| RHODE ISLAND | Registered Social Worker | RSW | MSW | | NO | NO | Annual |
| SOUTH CAROLINA | Registered Social Worker | RSW | MSW[5] | | NO | NO | Annual |
| SOUTH DAKOTA | Independent Practice | CSW-PIP | MSW | +2 years | | YES | Annual |
| | Certified Social Worker | CSW | MSW | | NO | YES | |
| | Social Worker | SW | BSW | | | YES | |
| | Social Work Associate | SWA | AA-BA | | | YES | 2 years |
| TENNESSEE | Independent Practice | — | MSW | +5 years | NO | NO | Annual |
| | Master Social Worker | MSW | MSW | | NO | NO | Annual |

| | Private Practice | | | + Exper.²² | | | |
|---|---|---|---|---|---|---|---|
| TEXAS | Certified Social Worker | CSW | CSW | | NO | NO | Annual |
| | Social Worker | SW | MSW | | | YES | Annual |
| | Social Work Associate²³ | SWA | BSW | | | YES | Annual |
| | | | HS/BA | +SW exp. | | YES | Annual |
| UTAH | Independent Practice¹⁵ | — | MSW | +years | NO | YES | Annual |
| | Certified Social Worker | CSW | MSW | | | YES | Annual |
| | Social Service Worker | SSW | BSW | | | YES | Annual |
| | Social Service Aide | SSA | | | | | |
| VIRGIN ISLANDS | Social Work Associate | SWA | AA BA | | NO | | |
| | Social Worker | SW | BSW or BA | +2 | NO | | |
| | Certified Social Worker | CSW | MSW | | NO | NO | |
| | Certified Independent Social Worker | | | | | | |
| | Social Worker | CISW | MSW | +2 | NO | | 2 years |
| VIRGINIA | Clinical Social Worker¹⁶ | CSW | MSW | +3 years | NO | YES | 2 years |
| | Social Worker | SW | MSW | +3 years | | YES | 2 years |

*National Association of Social Workers, compiled by Myles Johnson.

¹Act provides eligibility for either of BA + 2 years post graduate study (MSW), BA + 1 year post graduate study + 2 years experience, or BA with Social Work major (BSW) + 3 years of experience. (P.R.)

²1972 amendments provide eligibility for MSW, BSW + 3 years of experience, BA + 5 years experience, and 1 year Social Work Master's study + 1 year other MA study—2 years experience. (Cal.)

³One year of experience must be in a hospital, clinic, or agency and providing psychotherapy. (Cal.)

⁴Master's or equivalent degree in Social Work. (N.Y.)

⁵Or membership in NASW on May 29, 1968. (effective date of Act). (S.C.)

⁶Legal resident or employed in the state (Mich.) (Kansas).

⁷Or has the equivalent of 4,000 hours of voluntary service. (Mich.)

⁸Or has the equivalence of 2,000 hours of voluntary service, was previously certified, or has AA in Social Work. (Mich.)

¹⁰Only Certified Social Workers may practice independently. (Md.)

¹¹Only LSW-11 with 4 years experience may practice independently, other two levels have title protection only. (Colo.)

¹³Employment not required if person has an accredited BSW or MSW, or was previously certified. (Mich.)

¹⁴BA in "related fields... approved by the board" recognized. (Idaho).

¹⁵Includes specialty license as "Clinical Social Worker." (Utah).

¹⁶Previous titles continued temporarily. (Va.)

¹⁷Experience required in 2 years full time or 3 years part time; 4 years full time or 5 years part time for specialty license. (Ala.)

¹⁸For six years from May 23, 1977, an LBSW may be granted applicant with BA and two years of full time continuous employment as a social worker. (Ala.)

¹⁹Renewal requires one to have been "actively engaged" in practice during registration period. (Ore.)

²⁰Applicant must submit evidence of qualification to practice independently. (Maine).

²¹Period for renewal to be set by Board. (Mass.)

²²Dept. to establish procedures including "the number of years of acceptable Social Work experience." (Tex.)

²³The SWA certificate was open for application for two years only ending August 1983 (Tex.)

²⁴The MSW must have "a major emphasis or specialty in direct patient or health care services," and be CSWE accredited. Doctoral degree need not be CSWE accredited. (Fla.)

²⁵Exam is to be "prepared by dept." or State professional organization." (Fla.)

²⁶MSW or "doctorate" required plus 3,000 hours in psychotherapy in past 5 yrs. Three references also required (Mont.)

²⁷"2 years or 3,000 hours of post-masters supervised. paid clinical experience." (N.H.)

²⁸The Certified Clinical S.W. requires the CMSW license; the Certified S.W. Manager requires a CSW license (N.C.)

increased complexity and specialization of the profession, are discussed in Chapter 6. For additional discussion of these factors in terms of in-profession and extra-profession influences, as well as the emergence of the many professional associations in which social workers are active, influenced by and influencing others, see Hardcastle's extensive review (1981).

At the state level, NASW and Clinical Society chapters are increasingly engaged in political activity aimed at obtaining vendorship status for social work clinicians (that is, payment for services by insurance firms that now mainly favor the powerful physician lobby). More practitioners in the mental health and health fields seek an acknowledgment and financial support of their specialty expertise.

### Changing Agency Norms

Internal agency norms are changing toward more participatory, consultative, and interdependent orientations to mutual learning. Consider, as an example, the recent journal report of one system, claimed with enthusiasm and pride as an innovative approach to supervising "flexible enough to meet today's needs but still grounded on the solid philosophy and practice experience of the past" (Dublin, 1981, p. 234). It is a family service agency, proud of its professional, quality standards where the "new" emphasis is upon supervisory groups of three to five staff members who represent a mixture of experience levels and expertise which are process-oriented and developmentally focused, comparable to a family-focused service approach. Through this type of supervisory group an arena is provided in which group process parallels family process. Workers learn from multiple sources, and more experienced workers may "rethink and re-work already integrated knowledge and have the opportunity to be exposed to new ideas and perspectives brought by newer staff members" (Dublin, p. 235).

The values and emphases reported here are *not* reminiscent of traditional educative supervision, a situation where the seasoned staff were to teach the newer staff and where the integrated knowledge that the supervisor had refined was to be discovered and followed by the supervisees. Yet this example is evolutionary within the social work profession's "way" of constructing a structure for supervision paralleling the structure of service: The format of the learning experience is easily transferrable to the format of service (supervisory dyad : casework dyad; mixed "family" learning/teaching group : family practice). Using our role analogs, we see in the *conferee* realm the normative aspects of mutuality of teaching and learning, but we think there is also a *counselor* component involved, with its emphasis on relationships and deliberate use of self.

It is interesting that this example is reported from an established family service agency—a field where traditional, educative supervision was pioneered. The family-service field has contributed much innovative practice theory and revised communication, transaction, and intervention approaches. It is a leading-edge practice arena where workers from several disciplines (social workers, psychiatrists, psychologists) have teamed up and collaborated in evolving revised approaches to treatment or therapy. In the teaching/learning realm, however, we think many of the methods of instruction are *training* ones, reminiscent of the coach phase of social work training, using advanced techniques and formats mainly imported from the related professions.

Kaslow's discussion of these trends, developed in special institutes and programs aimed to produce family specialists, is a clear analysis of "six didactic" orientations to teaching marital and family therapists, least emphasizing the "traditional model"—that is, where supervisor and supervisee meet periodically each week before the next session and discuss material identified in the written process record (1977).[6] We disagree that the traditional social work orientation was clearly didactic, a matter we shall elaborate in Chapter 7.

### The Increased Publicness and Diversity in "Knowing" the Mysteries of Practice

Here we emphasize the forces within the realm of knowledge and how knowledge is conveyed, a matter closely linked to the changing norms just reviewed. The knowledge base has become enormously complex and expansive. This development is the result of increasing diversity in many areas: the tasks facing social workers; fields and specialties; populations of interest; related knowledge from other disciplines. Reid (1981) offers an extensive map of this territory. The knowledge explosion is consistent with the diversity of the profession and the accelerating advances in theory and research. The available literature is extensive, with many journals to review, both within social work and in the many other related fields. Yet, as David Austin observes (1983), it remains a knowledge base in which the *practice* component consists mainly of principles "almost entirely (derived) from codified practice wisdom," and in which empirical investigation was perhaps mere "window dressing" related to the drive for academic recognition of the profession (pp. 372–373).

Nevertheless, opportunities for continuing education have proliferated—workshops external to agencies; entrepreneurial, roving consultant/trainers; new choices (despite financial strains) made possible by air travel; television; audiotapes; video modules; and the elaboration of various instructional techniques. All of these have made social work practice more public.

In large part, supervisory approaches have been transformed by these advances in educational theory, instructional techniques, and accessibility. Since World War II, advances in communication theory and technology have gradually swept through universities, training institutes, and continuing-education enterprises, so that today's workplace is pervaded by a new mentality of lifelong learning and do-it-yourself approaches to skills enhancement, sensitivity, and career development. Social work, like all professions and occupations, has felt this influence. These newer approaches to supervision aim at modeling behavior, exploring assumptions and values, refining observations, enhancing self-perceptions, and stimulating creativity (Kaslow, 1977). They are claimed to be holistic approaches to whole-person learning. They focus on immediacy and interactional learning (a combination of values, knowledge, feelings, and behavior) through action and observation more than reflection, discussion, and gradual insight development. In general, they aim to speed up the learning process and to extend it beyond the one-to-one format. More accurately, they are *training* approaches, not educative supervision.

It would be hard indeed for the sage supervisor of days past to compete with the vast array of learning modules, videotapes of master clinicians, and other packaged instructional devices that have been developed by instructional technology specialists and are available through scores of catalogs. The development of this commercially produced hardware and software has been supported in recent years by federal and state training grants. As a result, there has been and will continue to be a transformation in educative supervision. We do not propose that this is "better," only that it *is*. The transmission of the experience and expertise of the profession no longer depends on a verbal imparting from master practitioner to novice. This information is preserved in a rich literature of books, videotapes, audio cassettes, and other materials prepared and "immortalized" either by the masters themselves or by others who wish to preserve (or capitalize on) particular treatment approaches. Supervision and teaching need no longer be merely a word-of-mouth, master-to-novice affair. Much can be read about and viewed. The formats are as diverse as are the materials—making the one-to-one tutorial arrangements not a necessity. Class and group modes, self-instruction using books, tapes, and computers are all possibilities.

Presently, knowledge and skills are public information. They are publicized, attractively packaged, and widely accessible. There are still a few "master gurus" around, in professional schools and in training workshops, whose personal image will attract aspiring clinicians. But in the main, most supervisors and trainers need to take a more egalitarian stance, to be more aware of andragogical theory, of the psychology of adulthood, and therefore of a diverse repertoire of teaching/learning approaches—particularly those that appeal to the learner as a self-directing determiner of what needs to be learned. For example, in discussing value orientations for field instruction based in "adult learning modes," Bogo (1981) stresses maximization of collegiality, informality, mutual respect, collaboration, openness, risk-taking, accepting and valuing difference, expressing conflicting views, inquiring attitudes, curiosity, and enthusiasm. Clearly, these values also apply to supervisory practice.

It is interesting that the new modalities of instruction seem to affect social work education at beginning level and at the specialized level more than at the more traditional master's level. That is, competency-based instruction at the B.S.W. level, like the institutes, workshops, and nondegree programs in marriage and family therapy and other specialties, seems to be most geared to using such technologies as telephones, one-way screens, and video equipment. Courses at the master's level seem to remain more traditional in emphasis and format, although teaching methods here have become increasingly more diverse (e.g., logs, maps, force-field analyses, simulations), just as supervision in the field has diversified through greater attention to varieties of instructional design.

There is a logic and sequence here that makes sense. At both B.S.W. and specialty levels there is a training emphasis—an emphasis on mastery of the "is" as precisely as possible. The "is" at the B.S.W. level includes basic aspects of the values, knowledge, and skills fundamental to social work practice; and the "is" at specialty levels pertains to the elaboration of particulars within a given area of practice. In between these two training areas, at the M.S.W. level, the emphasis is on broadening and deepening a base of theories and on finding ways to evaluate and expand them. There is an emphasis on questioning and developing a guiding frame of reference that will lead to self-monitored decisions and to greater latitude for discretionary judgments. It is an emphasis on education and discovery, and education for discovery, discovering what is but also finding what might not now be known.

At each level in career preparation, more emphasis is now accorded to the training component in both class and field experience—that is, to directing learners to master the predetermined, "right," particular targeted behaviors and to perfect them. Now, educational approaches that are both didactic and experiential are better understood by more instructors, both in formal classes and in agency experiences. So far as educational sophistication is concerned, the waves of the future are swelling around us today: computer-assisted instruction; competency-based education; multimedia, modular learning; behavior modeling; self-directed and self-paced learning; contract learning. These and other modalities are geared to pitch skill development, sensitivity, awareness, and values exploration. The supervisor, in short, is surrounded by instructional strategies and technologies that boggle the mind, that make the interview/conference into only one among many possible approaches.

Finally, the accreditation of social work education exists as a component in social work's multiple educational levels and career entry points, and as a factor in social work's linkage to related professions in the accretion and dissemination of knowledge, and in the diversity and complexity of current times (Council on Social Work Education, 1982). Its policy and thrust acknowledge not only standards related to the historical continuity of social work education and its enduring philosophical base, but also an emphasis on flexibility and openness in curriculum designs. The emphasis encourages programs in tune with changing social processes. This implies a current, future-oriented perspective, and an openness to practice innovation, interdisciplinary work, emergent knowledge, the impact of changing social movements or forces, and needs of various populations requiring the profession's attention.

### Other Influences

Three other influences that have had enormous effect on *supervision,* especially on the supervisory role, are these: (They will be discussed in more detail later in this book.)

External and intraprofessional quality assurance, accountability, and control
Increased complexity and differentiation among and within service programs
Uncertainty about the resources and programs of service agencies

Regarding external influences, we think of changing public policies and the enormity of their influence on all services: health, mental health, social, educational, environmental protection, personal protection, justice. Standards, principles, guidelines, regulations, accountability systems flow downward from federal, state, municipal, and political-economic interests, and these, in combination, have imposed new controls on agency operations. In the health field we cite the impact of directives from the Joint Commission on Accreditation of Hospitals, its influence on priorities for accreditation of community health services, and its "creation" of Balanced Service Systems priorities. These priorities are now appearing as directives state by state, and they will seriously affect career directions of social work "therapists" as they become reclassified as case managers. We think of the impact of the guidelines established by the National Institute of Mental Health (1977), affecting community support programs, and of the general impact that this body has on all mental health professions that seek support in line with established priorities and with favored professions now receiving financial support. And we see the influence of the 1978 President's Commission on Mental Health, as well as other commissioned "directives" that influence how programs will construct their services. In child welfare, the influence derives from PL 96-272, the Adoption Assistance and Child Welfare Act (1980); comparable specifics could be provided in relation to all human services.

We experience these as "declassification," "reclassification," and other actions by personnel departments state by state, exerting great influence on the workplace and career opportunities of social workers at all levels. The effects of these trends include: relabeling and retrenchment of middle managers; elimination or curtailment of consultation, or of Consultation and Education; and emphasis on revenue-producing services. In general, we refer to emphases drawn from operations research and systems analysis concepts—for example, output rather than input; mandatory goals and objectives; zero-based rather than line-item budgets—and other "strategics" that are devised for accountability and control of resources and that also include "quality" as part of the mission. (Just what is meant by quality is a matter best left to the mindset of the discipline or interest group that has defined the term.)

In the health field, Coulton (1979) analyzed approaches to quality assurance in various hospitals. She describes computerized information systems revealing outcome data, peer-review mechanisms (e.g., Peer Service Review Organizations, or PSROs, comprised of professionals and developing means to monitor the quality of service), and systems geared toward guaranteeing client access to the health system. Another example of professional self-monitoring in the clinical realm, related to vendorship status for social workers, is the NASW's current activity in developing social work peer-review programs for treatment cases, both at state chapter levels and nationally (Evans, 1983). Comparable moves are underway in related mental health professions.

In terms of the increased complexity of service systems, we refer to the diversity of backgrounds and orientations among "helpers," including their different education and training, loyalties, and preferences. Other factors include the time constraints imposed by increased complexity; the many rules, procedures, requirements, reports, confronting workers and all levels of organization-based practice; and the continuous emphasis on doing more in less time, and with reduced financial resources and personnel. And we see the desire by large, complex organizations (and some in the profession) to "lose" supervision within a conceptualization of administration and management—a move that may rationalize and technicalize the work, serving organizational standardization and accountability needs more than worker individualization and learning needs.

All of these forces must be seen against the shifting, uncertain commitment to human need, a theme that will appear throughout this text, since it most seriously affects all practice.

> EXAMPLE: A recent telephone call from an M.S.W. graduated in 1969 with clinical license and extensive experience as a therapist. His current position in the community mental health center was manager of outpatient services, with 25 percent of his time spent in managerial work, 75 percent in direct clinical practice. The question: "I am asked to become a case manager. What *is* this position?" When he was asked whether the center had distributed material about what such a transfer meant, and about where the rationale came from, the response was, "They are doing it at another center and it is working well."

The implications of this example need not be detailed. As with all shifts, there are gains and losses. For the profession, we must ponder not only what we may do or not do, gain or lose (if only we could forecast futures), but also the direction in which we are heading.

## CONCLUSION

Because educative supervision has been central and "special" to social work supervision in the past, we have described it and reviewed its empirical and historical aspects. Kadushin describes it as a major component of supervision, along with administrative and supportive functions. Michael Austin retains its importance as a training role, and adds the three roles of direct service specialist, organizational specialist, and personnel specialist (1981). From our review, we think this educative function has been greatly diminished during the past twenty years, and that it is drifting toward extinction, in contrast to its prevalence in the days when social work was developing its theoretical foundations. We conclude that part of the specialness of social work supervision is a literature that continues to idealize educational, traditional supervision, and that there is a gap between this and the realities of today's service delivery world (one which features a 20 percent turnover among first-level workers yearly). But, at least since the 1950s, there has also developed a literature, mainly a series of journal articles, that has argued against and questioned the predominant beliefs about supervision.

Part of the specialness of social work supervision, as compared with that in other fields, is that it should be educative; happen regularly, periodically (not "on the fly"); and take place in a one-to-one structure. We questioned whether these conditions are being met in current practice. Three general teaching approaches were identified as guiding the orientation of supervisors: two traditional ones, coach and counselor, and the newer stance that we called conferee. These were oriented respectively toward mastery of particular activities and tasks; mastery of deliberate use of self in relationships; and mastery both of the ability to assume diverse roles in relation to the environmental demands and constraints—that is, to the impinging tasks—and of what supervisees need to know in order to carry out their tasks.

We have tried to account for some of the specialness that characterizes social work supervision. We believe this specialness is partly due to the contextual influences of the social agency, to the unique history of the social work profession, to its pattern of professional education and training, and to the early requirement for some elaborated supervisory (agency) control over practice. We have also described the heavy imprint from casework theory, which has been the dominant influence on all social work theory and practice—a conceptual and political reality that has created, for better and for worse, social work's brand of supervision. Other features, unique in social work's traditions, are the agency pattern of having one person fill both administrative and educative functions, and the reliance on supervision more than consultation.

Supervision in the 1980s has become more consultative in organizations (a development acknowledged in our conferee supervisory role analog); in some organizations the very job title has been replaced by *manager* or *director,* and this has led practitioners to define themselves this way. Yet while there has been a drift in organizations away from traditional, educative supervision, there is no drift away from the need for stimulating, career-expanding, learning experiences in the workplace at all levels of practice. In fact, the reverse is true. There is more need for discrete approaches to ongoing learning and professional development. The educative function of supervision still remains, but it is joined by eight other functions, and so it must be performed with great precision, economy, and know-how. In a sense, the supervisor must become an administrator of the learning experience— planner, coordinator, and sometimes directly the teacher.

Fortunately, even as the service systems and the practices needed by them have grown more complex and specialized, the social work profession has matured. It has profited by the knowledge and technology developed through its own efforts and efforts in other professions. In days past, it was left to the supervisor to preserve the standards and substance of the work; this responsibility is now shared with others, distributed elsewhere, and decentralized more broadly in the profession: Teaching, ensuring competent practice, and inventing approaches to assist another's learning—to *guide* practice know-how—have been extended to others beyond the supervisor.

Through extensive research and theory development in the general field of education, in recent decades, more is known now about the learning/teaching situation itself. Yet much more needs to be known in order to tailor learning situations to specific learners in line with teaching and learning theories. Nevertheless, there now exists a rich "smorgasbord" of theory and technique—much more than was available to the educative supervisors of the past, who gave their supervisees individualized tutorial instruction yet, essentially, approached them through a single, particular teaching orientation. We have given up much when we give up educative supervision. We give up a tailor-made approach for a ready-made approach. And as with store-bought clothing in comparison to designer costumes, we may sacrifice quality for economy unless we are able systematically to build a knowledge of individuality and idiosyncracy into the consultative and teaching approaches. Mass production in teaching design will *not* do!

Effective teaching involves discrete, differentiated approaches attuned to the characteristics of the individual learner (even when grouped with others); to the characteristics of the learning setting; and to the characteristics of the subject—informational domain—that is being taught. For social work, this informational domain is *social work practice:* its institutional bases, settings, populations, tasks. And the informational domain requires clear articulation not only of specific knowledge but also of the attitudes, feelings, and skills needed to be known, and how these may be taught. Since more is known now about each of these elements, the supervisor as teacher can make more differentiated, elaborated, and sophisticated use of instructional strategies and skills.

In the chapters to come we shall discuss these realms in further detail: learners' individual differences (Chapter 2); moving from supervisee to supervisor (Chapter 3); aspects of service delivery (Chapter 4); contexts of social work practice (Chapter 6); contexts of the tasks and approaches to learning or teaching them (Chapter 7); ways to increase the opportunities to do so (Chapter 8); our reconceptualization of supervision (Chapter 5); and our directives toward becoming a competent, imaginative supervisor (Chapter 9).

We know more about the informational domain itself, and more about the transmissibility of social work from person to person, than in years past. The requisite knowledge and skills have been described in an expanded literature. The NASW has formulated more specification of standards, of levels of practice, and of specialties. Clinical societies and health, pediatric, and other specialty groups have articulated specific definitions and descriptions of practice. More is known theoretically and conceptually, and more technology is available to enable the profession to license, test for competence, and monitor the quality of practice. It is easier these days to specify objectives for instruction and to devise means to evaluate and measure how well the intended knowledge or skill has been learned. As we shall see in Chapter 7, more needs to be done in the specifics of instructional design. We share Munson's view that "much of the literature [on supervision] defines the functions of supervision without developing models to organize and implement these functions" (1979a, p. 344). Yet having made great inroads toward gaining a sophistication about the learner, the learning situation, and the domain to be learned, we aim to push on, to progress further.

You may wonder just why educative supervision has remained an ideal in the literature when the reality is so at odds with this picture. We think the importance of educative supervision for social workers resides deep within the profession's value base. In the social work profession, the growth and development of individuals toward the fulfillment of their inherent potential always has been a priority commitment. This includes caring about the worker's development as a professional. The ideology runs deep, despite lack of personnel, time, and other resources. A diversified approach to supervision and to teaching and learning seems to be required to meet today's agency realities. The situation today demands eclecticism in supervisory approaches, and this demand goes beyond systematizing, rationalizing, and technicalizing the workplace. For the workplace is a people place, and people are hardly about to be rationalized.

In Chapter 2 we shall explore two overarching imperatives of the supervisory task: competence and imagination. We shall consider certain influences that have worked toward conformity in perspective, thinking, and actions. We shall also deal with other perspectives that lead toward differences in perceptions, to longing for uniqueness, and to persons' desire to make their special imprint on their work (and their total living experiences).

Before moving into Chapter 2, we suggest you turn to Appendix A. You will notice that there are suggested *For Further Thought* discussion questions, tasks, and other experiential activities which should be pursued at the end of each chapter.

## NOTES

1. Kadushin's findings (1974, 1976) have been enormously influential in bringing conceptual clarity to the various aspects of social work supervision. After studying 469 supervisors and 384 supervisees, he reported activities, attitudes, and perceptions of discrepancies between ideal and actual supervisory practice. Since context is crucial for determining supervisory practice, we view this survey as two distinct studies reported together, rather than as one study. We think Kadushin was actually looking at two different supervisory situations and thus two different "supervisions." According to Kadushin, "the promotion of the MSW social worker from practitioner to supervisor often involves a move from a private to a public agency; from a smaller to a larger agency; from a psychiatric-mental health, medical, or school social work setting to a public assistance or child welfare setting" (1974, p. 289). In the large, public agencies where Kadushin's supervisors were working, practice requirements differ in substance and process from those of the smaller, private agencies where many of his supervisees worked. Among Kadushin's findings, the following pertain to the educative-administrative situation.

It appears that supervisors in Kadushin's study wanted to teach more than supervisees wished to be taught. Twenty-six percent of the supervisors saw themselves as a teacher, but only 3 percent of the supervisees saw themselves as students. In the main, supervisees described the relationship as that of colleague-collaborator (60 percent), while only 30 percent of the supervisors described it in that way. The supervisors' valuation of their teaching role is further underscored by their reported *satisfactions* in supervising (1976, pp. 265–268). Ranked first was helping supervisees grow and develop in professional competence, mentioned by 88 percent of the supervisors surveyed; ranked third was sharing social work knowledge and skills, mentioned by 63 percent; and ranked sixth was helping supervisees grow and develop as persons, mentioned by 37 percent. In terms of *dissatisfactions,* the second-most-disliked aspect of the supervisory job (mentioned by 53 percent) was the heavy job responsibilities that took time away from work with supervisees. As to this finding, Kadushin commented that it reflected the interference of work pressures with instructional goals. Also, 26 percent of the supervisors identified the conflict between administrative, evaluative, and educative aspects of the relationship with supervisees as a source of dissatisfaction.

But let us now look at the supervisee side of the situation. In terms of *dissatisfaction* with supervision, only 21 percent of those surveyed thought there was not enough regularly scheduled, uninterrupted conference time. Additional dissatisfactions that we believe are related to the educative component of supervision were these: supervisor is not critical enough so as to know error (26 percent), does not provide much real help with problems with clients (25 percent), is capricious and arbitrary in use of authority (23 percent), is too controlling and dominant, thus restricting autonomy and initiative (20 percent). In terms of supervisee *satisfactions*, on the other hand, 40 percent thought the supervisor helped with client-related problems, 34 percent with their professional development, 27 percent with stimulation of thinking about theory and practice, 24 percent with feedback as to performance. The contradictory nature of supervisees' reactions leads us to conclude that the findings are equivocal at best.

Perhaps the most interesting difference between supervisees and supervisors is the supervisees' low level of response to any of the criteria. Their highest response in any *satisfaction* category was 44 percent, in any *dissatisfaction* category, 35 percent. Their "other" (miscellaneous) dissatisfactions totaled 22 percent. Our calculations showed that the average response rate for the supervisees was 21.3 percent in the dissatisfaction area and 24.1 percent in the satisfaction area. This contrasts with the more obvious trends for supervisors. Here the highest response rate in the supervisory satisfaction category was 88 percent; the highest response rate in the dissatisfaction category was 71 percent (and miscellaneous responses were 2 percent). It is hard to account for the supervisees' responses by demographic factors. They were drawn from the 1972 *NASW Directory of Professional Social Workers,* as were the supervisors, and they tended to differ from the supervisors only in average age (i.e., five years younger).

Shulman conducted an elaborate study of supervisory role, supervisory context, and job stress and manageability among Canadian workers in child welfare, nursing, and residential treatment (1982). His findings are based on responses from 109 supervisors. He used workers' responses (671) only if their supervisor had also responded to the survey questionnaire. In terms of educational background, the supervisors and workers ranged from community college and technical school diplomas to M.S.W. degrees. The frequency (availability) of supervision and the emphasis of supervision in the professional development of the worker (educative versus administrative emphasis) are particularly germane to our concerns here.

The average supervisor set aside an amount of time for regularly scheduled individual supervisory conferences somewhere between "a little of the time" to "sometimes." These individual conferences were, on the average, once a month; group sessions "sometimes regularly scheduled" averaged twice monthly. Workers reported that their supervisors were available when needed "a good part of the time."

Supervisors thought they were stretched too thin and spent too much time on management and coordination rather than consultation and supervision—a factor described by Shulman as central to workload stress. Typical process comments from the supervisors referred to: too wide a span of control, stress of expected versus possible level of service, press of other meetings, involvement in high-risk cases, policy and planning projects, paperwork, and other heavy demands that detracted from the opportunity for case consultation, availability to workers, and regularly scheduled conferences.

The data revealed that supervisors spent 39.4 percent of their time in supervision and consultation (and, in preference, wished to spend 45 percent of the time in such activity). In addition, Shulman found that 11.8 percent of the actual, direct time spent with supervisees was devoted to "teaching practice skills." We calculate that the time spent directly with supervisees *and* devoted to teaching practice skills approximates 5 percent or about 2 hours weekly. Considering the monthly supervision sessions (predominantly with individuals and even allowing for some group meetings twice monthly) and the "too wide span of control," we are led to wonder how diluted these two hours of teaching per week become and to question how much of an actual emphasis on teaching there is.

2. This finding is inflated beyond what might be expected, since 8 of the 29 supervisors in Payne's study were part of the Child Protective and Dependency Unit. This unit was singled out by the American Humane Association in 1981; and the Association mandated that supervisors increase the teaching component of their jobs, owing to the high incidence of crises and violence against children.

3. Classical accounts that emphasize teaching and learning and that have guided supervisors include Robinson, 1936/1949; Reynolds, 1942/1965; Towle, 1954; and Williamson, 1961.

4. For other reviews of the history of supervision in social work, see Kadushin, 1976, pp. 1–38; Kutzik, 1977b, pp. 25–60; Abels, 1977, pp. 1–59; and Munson, 1979b.

5. Not included are the recent (1984) licensure regulations achieved in Georgia, West Virginia, and Iowa.

6. In addition to the "traditional" model, Kaslow identifies these training approaches:

*Cotherapy*—the supervisor and supervisee work in tandem as a treatment team and (ideally) discuss and review the work between sessions.

*Direct supervision using delayed feedback*—the supervisor watches or listens to recordings (videotapes or audio tapes) or views the session through a one-way mirror. The supervisor observes directly while the session is going on, or shortly thereafter, and interprets dynamics soon after the session.

*Direct supervision with instant feedback*—the supervisor watches through a one-way mirror or on a video monitor and interrupts to redirect and influence the treatment during the session (through a telephone hook-up, a "bug" in the ear, or even direct entrance into the situation).

*Group supervision*—learners and supervisors meet after group observations of sessions where each student has had a turn to act as therapist, while the other students observe. Students discuss one another's work in front of the group.

*Role-playing techniques*—the supervisor and supervisee reenact key episodes of the therapy hour, with the supervisee playing the role of therapist or reversing to the role of client (with the supervisor taking the complementary role) in order to gain emotional or cognitive understanding of the situation as it was or might have been.

## REFERENCES

ABELS, PAUL A., *The New Practice of Supervision and Staff Development.* New York: Association Press, 1977.

AUSTIN, DAVID M., "The Flexner Myth and the History of Social Work," *Social Service Review,* 57, no. 3 (September 1983), 357–377.

AUSTIN, MICHAEL J., *Supervisory Management for the Human Services.* Englewood Cliffs, N.J.: Prentice-Hall, 1981.

BARKER, ROBERT L., and THOMAS L. BRIGGS, *Differential Use of Social Work Manpower.* New York: NASW, 1968.

BOGO, MARION, "An Educationally Focused Faculty/Field Liaison Program for First-Time Field Instructors," *Journal of Education for Social Work,* 17, no. 3 (Fall 1981), 59–65.

CHERNISS, GARY, and EDWARD EGNATIOS, "Clinical Supervision in Community Mental Health," *Social Work,* 23, no. 3 (May 1978), 219–223.

COULTON, CLAUDIA J., *Social Work Quality Assurance Programs: A Comparative Analysis.* Washington, D.C.: NASW, 1979.

COUNCIL ON SOCIAL WORK EDUCATION, "Curriculum Policy Statement Revision." New York: 1982.

DUBLIN, RICHARD A., "Supervision as an Orienting and Integrating Process," *Social Casework,* 63, no. 4 (Spring 1982), 233–237.

EPSTEIN, LAURA, "Is Autonomous Practice Possible?" *Social Work,* 18, no. 1 (March 1973), 5–12.

EVANS, JAMES, "Memo to NASW Chapter Executive Directors and Presidents on Peer Reviewers." Washington, D.C.: NASW, 1983.

GITTERMAN, ALEX, "Comparison of Educational Models and Their Influences on Supervision," in *Issues in Human Services,* Florence W. Kaslow and Associates. San Francisco: Jossey-Bass, 1972.

HARDCASTLE, DAVID A., "The Profession, Professional Organizations, Licensing and Private Practice," in *Handbook of the Social Services,* Neil Gilbert, and Harry Specht, eds. Englewood Cliffs, N.J.: Prentice-Hall, 1981.

HART, GORDON M., *The Process of Clinical Supervision.* Baltimore: University Park Press, 1982.

HERSEY, PAUL, and KENNETH H. BLANCHARD, "Grid Principles and Situationalism: Both! A Response to Blake and Mouton," *Group & Organization Studies,* 7, no. 2 (June 1952), 207–210.

JOHNSON, MYLES, "Levels of Practice Regulated and Renewal Periods," in *State Comparison of Laws Regulating Social Work.* Washington, D.C.: NASW, 1983.

JOHNSTON, LON, and CLAUDE DROUET, "An Analysis of Social Work Supervision in Private Social Service Agencies," unpublished essay. Louisville, Ky.: Kent School of Social Work, 1982.

KADUSHIN, ALFRED, "Professional Development: Supervision, Training, and Education," in *Handbook of the Social Services,* Neil Gilbert, and Harry Specht, eds. Englewood Cliffs, N.J.: Prentice-Hall, 1981.

————, *Consultation in Social Work.* New York: Columbia University Press, 1977.

————, *Supervision in Social Work.* New York: Columbia University Press, 1976.

————, "Supervisor-Supervisee: A Survey," *Social Work,* 19, no. 3 (May 1974), 288–297.

KASLOW, FLORENCE W., "Training of Marital and Family Therapists," in *Supervision, Consultation, and Staff Training in the Helping Professions,* Florence W. Kaslow and Associates. San Francisco: Jossey-Bass, 1977.

————, "Group Supervision," in *Issues in Human Services,* Florence W. Kaslow and Associates. San Francisco: Jossey-Bass, 1972.

KUTZIK, ALFRED J., "The Medical Field," in *Supervision, Consultation, and Staff Training in the Helping Professions,* Florence W. Kaslow and Associates. San Francisco: Jossey-Bass, 1977. (a)

————, "The Social Work Field," in *Supervision, Consultation, and Staff Training in the Helping Professions,* Florence W. Kaslow and Associates. San Francisco: Jossey-Bass, 1977. (b)

LEVINSON, DANIEL J., *The Seasons of a Man's Life.* New York: Ballantine, 1978.

LEVY, CHARLES S., "Ethics of Supervision," *Social Work,* 18, no. 2 (March 1973), 14–21.

MAIER, HENRY, "Chance Favours the Prepared Mind," *Contemporary Social Work Education,* 4, no. 1 (May 1981), 14–20.

MILLER, IRVING, "Supervision in Social Work," *Encyclopedia of Social Work* (16th ed.), 1971; rpt. New York: NASW, 1977.

————, "Distinctive Characteristics of Supervision in Group Work," *Social Work,* 5, no. 1 (January 1960), 69–76.

MIDDLEMAN, RUTH R., "The Myth of the Agency as Partner," in *The Centennial Proceedings: 1973 Social Welfare Forum.* New York: Columbia University Press and the National Conference on Social Welfare, 1973.

MIDDLEMAN, RUTH R., and GALE GOLDBERG, *Social Service Delivery: A Structural Approach to Social Work Practice.* New York: Columbia University Press, 1974.

MUNSON, CARLTON E., "Authority and Social Work Supervision: An Emerging Model," in *Social Work Supervision.* New York: The Free Press, 1979. (a)

————, ed., *Social Work Supervision.* New York: The Free Press, 1979. (b)

NASW TASK FORCE ON SECTOR FORCE CLASSIFICATION, *NASW Standards for the Classification of Social Work Practice, Policy Statement 4.* Silver Spring, Md.: NASW, 1981.

PAYNE, DARRELL, "Knowledge and Skill for Supervisory Leadership," unpublished essay. Louisville, Ky.: Kent School of Social Work, 1982.

REID, WILLIAM J., "Mapping the Knowledge Base of Social Work," *Social Work,* 26, no. 2 (March 1981), 124–132.

REYNOLDS, BERTHA C., *Learning and Teaching in the Practice of Social Work.* 1942; rpt. New York: Russell and Russell, 1965.

ROBINSON, VIRGINIA P., *Dynamics of Supervision Under Functional Controls.* Philadelphia: University of Pennsylvania Press, 1949.

————, *Supervision in Social Casework.* Chapel Hill, N.C.: University of North Carolina Press, 1936.

SCHWARTZ, EDWARD E., and WILLIAM C. SAMPLE, *The Midway Office: An Experiment in the Organization of Work Groups.* New York: NASW, 1971.

SHULMAN, LAWRENCE, *Skills of Supervision and Staff Management.* Itasca, Ill.: Peacock, 1982.

TOREN, NINA, *Social Work: The Case of a Semi-Profession.* Beverly Hills, Calif.: Sage, 1972.

TOWLE, CHARLOTTE, *The Learner in Education for the Professions as Seen in Education for Social Work.* Chicago: University of Chicago Press, 1954.

WALLACE, MARQUIS, "Private Practice: A Nationwide Survey," *Social Work,* 23, no. 3 (May 1982), 262–267.

WIJNBERG, MARION H., and MARY C. SCHWARTZ, "Models of Student Supervision: The Apprenticeship, Growth, and Role Systems Model," *Journal of Education for Social Work,* 13, no. 3 (Fall 1977), 107–113.

WILLIAMSON, MARGARET, *Supervision–New Patterns and Processes.* New York: Association Press, 1961.

# CHAPTER TWO
# ENTERING THE WORLD
# OF SUPERVISION

## INTRODUCTION

In this chapter we shall introduce you to two central concepts that the title of this book highlights: competence and imagination. The concepts are mutually reinforcing—each affecting the other—and work in tandem when the supervisor meets the demands of the work situation, when the supervisor and supervisee(s) interact so that the purpose of the organization is actualized. The competent person is one who can do what needs to be done effectively. This takes a certain degree of imagination, since the tasks of effective practice are not fixed. But we all can remember persons who may occupy roles that affect the work of others, who have been acknowledged as competent and *who see themselves* as competent, yet whose competence is rooted in a time and place that has vanished from contemporary work life.

While true competence involves imagination, some persons continue to "pass" as effective supervisors and are supported in their roles by certain accoutrements of organizational life—seniority, political behavior, the "club" network, survivor tactics. Imagination, on the other hand, *demands* competence: It is difficult to be imaginative without first mastering the basic components of the tasks involved in the work. Imaginative judgment is neither sheer wildness nor unfettered innovation. More nearly, it is the recombination of well-known elements into new patterns. These reconceptualizations "work" because they encompass the known and respond to the present and future—not because they are "different."

## COMPETENCE

Competence is a relatively young concept in the social work literature. It entered the vocabulary of social work in the 1970s and it is equally new in the literature of education, training, research, and measurement. The competence literature—stimulated by recent attention to matters of accountability, standard-setting, and development of professional credentials and licensure—relates competence to the demonstration of the knowledge, skills, and abilities that are needed for a particular performance. Before the concern with *competence,* the social work vocabulary used the terms *skill* or *skilled* to describe social work practice of high quality.[1] But unlike skill(s), competence requires some specified standard or level of task performance designated *a priori,* with certain criteria and procedures of assessment to separate competent from incompetent practice. Competence, then, is inferred from a performance (via written, oral, or interactional events) that is judged. Competence may be assumed to mean some aggregate of knowledge, judgment, experience, style, self-image, and skills that are applied when and where needed in relation to the impinging tasks.

We assume that competence is an attribute of a high-ability professional. It accounts for the personal impact. But it represents more than personal qualities, for it includes the environmental context as well. A competent supervisor has the capability of meeting the immediate tasks with knowledge and skill as well as detecting the more remote situational elements—the patterns beyond the immediate situation. As an action concept, competence concerns what one does (or did do) in relation to a changeable (often cantankerous) environment. It is not a "once-for-all" quality inside a person, but a transactional concept that links the practitioner and the service situation.

So, you may think of competence as a variable entity that changes according to where you are and what you do. For example, one of us recently spent two weeks in Germany, and it was immediately and painfully evident that the previous sense of competence in executing the ordinary activities of everyday life was soundly shattered. It takes time to regain competence when every action demands deliberate attention and new learning. Some of the same kinds of adjustments, although less total and dramatic, must be made on the job. Competence must be continuously cultivated and recultivated—for it is affected by the work setting, the age of the worker, career changes, new tasks and problems, and so forth.

We were taught when young, practice makes perfect. This may have worked for the early tasks of everyday living, for behaving in a world that seemed relatively orderly or changing only gradually. It may have worked when the values, norms, and ideas of the times were what one was supposed to learn. One cannot practice such an adage today; a revision is required. *Practice plus feedback* (knowledge of results) *makes perfect.* Practice by itself merely makes permanent.* In our view, the implications of such a revision for supervisory competence suggest the myriad,

---

*This formulation was suggested by Simon Slavin.

subtle, reciprocal interactions between supervisor and supervisee plus special sensitivity to the particular impact of contextual and situational demands which must be known and adjusted to continuously by the watchful practitioner.

When we think of competence, we must conjure up an action and a performance image. This image involves much more than what you know or think you should or would do in a given situation. It is what is expressed in the living moment, with appreciation of its consequences as well as its immediate impact.

We deal with competence issues in this book as we identify, define and describe, illustrate, and provide opportunities for experiencing the varying components of the supervisory role. In our discussion, these issues will be anchored in and related to conceptual material that illumines aspects of both organizations and the wider environmental context in which the supervisor practices. In the Appendix, we provide checklists and instruments for you to construct a profile that may offer clues to how you see yourself and how you look at organizations, both now and after you move through this book. But like all such "instructional, subjective instruments," they will offer merely clues and approximations, not "is's," and they should be regarded this way. They may help you "see" what you believe and can do *now,* and they may help you build on your knowledge, beliefs, and goals for increasing your competence.

And we shall offer conceptual schemes that clarify our view of supervisory functions, organizational imperatives, and ongoing professional development. We pose these schemes as an orienting frame of reference, applicable to current work and adaptable to emergent issues. We caution that our conceptualizations constitute merely one among many possible (always arbitrary) ways of arranging information. We shall augment this conceptual material with experiential assignments and suggestions that may offer opportunities to try out your ideas and practice refining them through actions. Through these emphases, we aim to touch you as you develop in competence. Our goals are for intellectual and experiential opportunities to examine *being, doing,* and *becoming* in terms of competence as a supervisor.

## IMAGINATION

A second goal is helping you use your imagination, so that you avoid rigidity in thinking and in action. To the extent that you reformulate what you know when you address a new situation, you must draw on your imagination. Imaginative judgment is the creative component of your work. This is the part that attracts many to social work and other occupations concerned with people. And in imagination, the artistry and style of the practitioner come to the fore. We view imagination (creativity) much as we view competence—as a transactional concept. That is, it is not fixed within the person once and for all. Rather, it may be expressed when the situation is conducive to its expression.

All of us have imagination. In the course of living and working, however, it may be nurtured or stifled—depending on the environmental context in which we express ourselves. At work, while we may have the potential for being imaginative in our practice, our imagination may or may not be encouraged, depending to a great extent on the situation of the workplace. The T.G.I.F. syndrome and the abundance of leisure time and after-hours activities, hobbies, and avenues for imaginative pursuits suggest how separated from the work itself imagination and creative expression have become for so many persons these days.

Two requirements for using your imaginative ideas are security and challenge (Pelz, 1976). While these may seem antithetical, the combined effect may stimulate the production of imaginative thinking. Our sense of personal security is related to self-confidence. Self-confidence is derived from a combination of components such as competence, intellectual independence, self-reliance, and autonomy. Our sense of challenge springs from our inherent curiosity.

The interaction of self-confidence and curiosity is expressed through the play of imagination, provided the workplace also nourishes both security and challenge. Organizations provide security in numerous ways, including: resources (money, staff, equipment, time); opportunity to control your resources and make choices about your work; reasonably attainable expectations for achievement and for task and role performances; visible recognition of achievements; and the promise of continuity of effort. Organizations provide challenge through the diversity of tasks, through the openness of opportunities for determining priorities and assignments, and through the structures (policies, procedures, regulations) that offer support and flexibility for innovation.

It is hard to be imaginative in organizations that reward only rule-following, safe behavior. It is hard to be imaginative where there is too much challenge and too little security, or too little challenge and too much security. And yet, the organization is *us*. We cannot imagine that "they" will not let us do this or that, that "the system" or "those others" are responsible for what happens and how it happens. For "the enemy" is us! A huge obstacle to imaginative thinking is the habit of viewing ourselves as somehow separate from the big picture.

In this book, we aim to challenge your imagination. Therefore, we emphasize different ways of thinking about and looking at things. We rely on your desire to deliberately cultivate other ways of "knowing," so that you can increase your repertoire of information-processing skills and your flexibility in imagining new possibilities. And to free the imagination from the ordinary ways of thinking, we shall stress diversity in perceptions.

## LOOKING AT SUPERVISION

This book is devoted to looking carefully at supervision, perhaps in unaccustomed ways. We think our perspective is fresh, unique, optimistic. Do you notice that we framed our picture of supervision in visual terms? This was deliberate—to capture your attention and fix it on certain key aspects of the supervisory scene.

We see attention as the major (but limited) human resource that one brings to any situation. It is the psychic energy that controls our consciousness. Attention limits our expectations and actions. It filters in or excludes what we may think about, feel, hope for, or experience. In other words, what we attend to—including how long and how hard we concentrate on any thing (whether "out there" or inside us)—determines what matters to us.*

We hope to sharpen the intensity and inclusiveness of your vision of supervision by focusing on certain aspects and by providing a multifaceted view of the elements of elements. (You may discover some of your blind spots, or ours.) In focusing on supervision in this way, we hope to gain an in-depth view: through the angles we offer, through our zoom in on the patterns and networks—the regularities out of which the particulars emerge; through our highlight of certain links and critical joints in its underlying structure; through our attention to the chiaroscuro of our subject, with its rich shades of light and dark; and through our magnification of supervision's electrifying potentialities.

## A New View

Ordinary dictionary definitions of supervision suggest such actions as directing, inspecting, controlling the work of others, overseeing, and observing as a spectator. We shall take a different view and consider supervision as super-vision—that is, extraordinary vision. So we must first consider vision. Vision has been defined in three ways: (1) as the act or power of seeing; (2) as a mental image or imaginative contemplation; (3) as the ability to perceive something not actually visible. Supervision, then, can refer to having the capacity to see more clearly the larger picture in the realm of work. It can refer to having unusually imaginative ideas beyond what has been considered. And it can mean even entertaining the wildly impossible or the opportunities that others do not see.**

Not only do physiological abilities to see what we look at differ from one person to another, but they also systematically decline for all of us as we age. Moreover, we use binoculars to bring near what is afar, and microscopes to examine what is miniscule. While we know when we use sunglasses to filter out glare, we are often in the dark about the rose-colored mental lenses that distort our perspective. Looking is different from *seeing*.

## Professional Looking

Common sense has it that seeing is believing. Perhaps this works for much of our daily activity. We propose a different adage: Believing is seeing. We actually "see" with our brain, not just our eyes. Furthermore, as we shall argue: *Conception befuddles perception.*

---

*We realize that modern physics and psychology (and Eastern thought) tell us there is no "out there"—that the "out there" is created by our own consciousness of "it." For now, we use a simplistic, apparent construction of reality.

**A class assignment by Larry Hopkins suggested this connection between vision and supervision.

Our brain synthesizes sensations from several sensory receptors. The ears, body muscles, skin, and eyes are all involved in the visual perception system. Moreover, we have the human distinctiveness of self-consciousness—of seeing ourselves seeing. We also have the special professional requirement of developing what has been described as *disciplined looking* (Goldberg and Middleman, 1980; Middleman, 1983). And disciplined looking is only one component among the complex array of perception and cognition issues that confront social workers. We like to see what we know already and what we expect to see—the familiar. Our professional assignment, however, demands a particular kind of "seeing," a special self-awareness as a precondition for other awareness. This specialized seeing has an extensive history and importance in social work practice, and it is usually termed "conscious use of self."

George Miller's astronomy analogy is useful as we think of the social work supervisor. Astronomers try to understand the laws of planetary motion so as to predict where the moon is going to be and then, where to aim their telescopes. But they can control only their instruments, not the moon (Elizabeth Hall, 1980). In our case, we can gain deliberate control only over our self—our instrument—by knowing where to look, how to look, what to look for, and thus what to "see." And if we are good enough lookers, we can do as the king in *The Little Prince* (St. Exupery, 1943/1971), who would command the sun to set, having determined the precise moment when the conditions were right for this event to happen; or, in some modern terms, we can "go with the flow."

The eternal challenge, of course, is to look at the world with childlike wonder, to be ready to look at the old sights in new ways, to find novelty in the commonplace, to refuse to neglect the ordinary, to see many sides and dimensions,

**FIGURE 2-1  The irregular object. Assume you must describe this figure to listeners who cannot see it except through how you talk about it. You want each of them to reproduce it on a sheet of paper. What would you tell them? (Adapted from Bateson, 1979)**

What Is This?

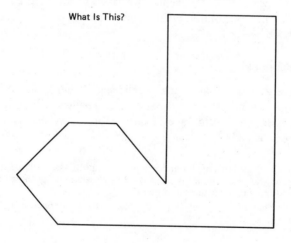

and to gaze defiantly at confusion. We hope we may help you cultivate *super*vision about supervision.

Professional looking implies not only the self-conscious awareness that it is *we* (in all our uniquenesses) who are doing the looking; but it also demands that we deliberately try to see the "other" from diverse perspectives—that is, that we analyze any situation in multifaceted ways. The irregular object pictured in Figure 2-1 illustrates what we mean.

Let us consider some implications of the fact that the "same" object can be described in many different ways. A central value of the social work profession is that all persons are different and unique, and that this difference must be respected by the practitioner. Various theories deal with individuals' growth and development and with practice interventions; the aim of these theories is to explain individuals in their similarities and variability, and then to propose ways to deal with them (the social work practice approaches). Both values and knowledge bases in social work affirm individual difference. But it is almost impossible to comprehend how very different each person is (and how unique each practitioner is).

### Individuals' Views

We have used this irregular object in classes and institutes as a looking experience for hundreds of students and supervisors, always with the same interesting result (see Figure 2-2): All versions of looking (except versions 4 and 5) have been represented in every group, no matter how small the number of members. There is simply no *one* way to "see" things, even though commonsense behaving and thinking makes us act as if there is *a* way. There are at least five different ways of describing this irregular object, none of which is "wrong." Each person responds to certain features of the stimulus (and of the environment) out of ideas in his or her own memory.

The irregular-object experiment reveals cognitive styles (for example, holistic versus analytic), as well as other previously learned concepts that affect what one knows when looking at something. For those who saw a boot or other object, the response was to the figure as a whole, as one central image. Alongside the descriptive words that are used to label this response (analogic, iconic, holistic), recent research suggests this is a right-brain-hemisphere response, one attuned to overall pattern. It would be hard to have another person actually reproduce this object from such a response. It is an intuitive reaction to subtlety and nuance. This kind of response is often a quality of supervisors—one that they may not be able to label or explain or teach to another person, but that nonetheless is a qualitative grasp of a situation. Moreover, the ability to respond this way is often thought of as "the art" of practice—an *intuitive, holistic sensitivity.*

Those who saw a hexagon and two triangles operated out of some specialized knowledge (derived from geometry and mathematics), or they would not have been able to label these shapes. They noted some regularity between the unusual object they saw and other objects "seen" in their imagination and known from past study.

FIGURE 2-2   The irregular object (possibilities)

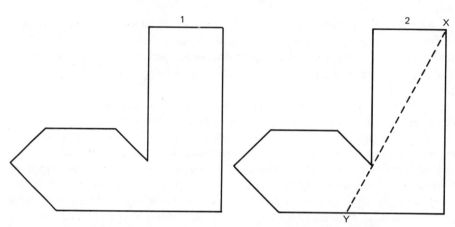

A boot; a toilet; a kind of J;
a backwards L; a silo with
a barn, etc.:
*analogic, iconic, holistic*

Three geometric figures; in fact,
if a line xy is drawn, one
sees two triangles and a hexagon:
*scientific, mathematical, linear*

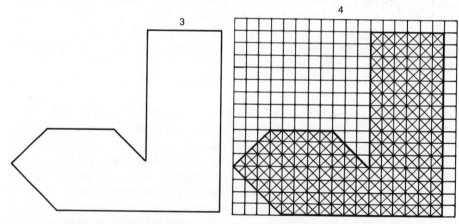

Staring at the top right, go south
with the line for two inches, then
west for two inches, etc.:
*operational, processual*

Make a grid around the object and
report yes/no for each box with
respect to whether it contains
part of the object or not: *digital, analytic*

5 Another way, it is an enclosed figure made of black lines printed
on a white page: *structural, contextual.*

Seeing such relationships—and mentally generating hypotheses to account for such associations—is the stuff of *empirical, scientific, linear inquiry.*

Persons who selected version 3 showed a value of the process in communication. They broke the matter of reproduction down into component parts (i.e., they operationalized the task) and gave step-by-step directions for another to follow. There would be many ways to operationalize this task (for just one example, telling listeners to move their pencils north, south, etc.). Mostly, persons start from some point at an angle and proceed from there, usually clockwise, with a set of sequenced "instructions"—that is, with a commitment to *process.*

The fourth method—i.e., to make a grid and have a yes/no answer for each square in terms of whether or not the object occupies it—is most exact (provided the grid is small enough to capture detail). This approach implies some knowledge of electronics or of computers or other digital, discrete ways of thinking. As the enlarged half-tone block shows, this method is used to transmit halftone newspaper illustrations and TV pictures, and it reflects a valuing of the *analytic, quantitative, digital* orientations.

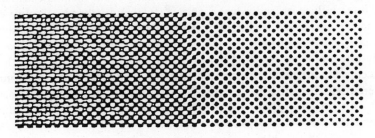

HALFTONE EXAMPLE

The fifth approach focuses mainly on the environment or context. People who answered in this way are dealing equally with the materials of the stimulus, noticing the ground more than the figure—or, perhaps, the environmental context and forces are concerns that are noticed *before* aspects of the individuals are seen (i.e., background before foreground). To extend this a bit further, such a response is sensitive to the anatomy or the *structure* of what is seen. This is just as valid a way to think about things as any of the previous ways. So far as the relation between figure and ground is concerned, this way of seeing can be called transactional, slippery, or unitary.

For supervisors, it would be important to be able to see any situation from *all* these vantage points. For imaginative supervisory practice, you need to appreciate the structure of the situation, the step-by-step processes over time, their component activities, the totality of forces involved, the discrete elements, and the associations of components; and you need to bring to bear whatever specialized knowledge (theories, research findings, practice wisdom) you already possess.

## THREE CONSTRAINTS ON HOW WE SEE THINGS

But there is another point to be made here that grows from these different ways of describing something. Any of these methods of description contributes nothing to an explanation of the object or situation; they are merely ways we find to identify the "it" in terms that we can understand in relation to what we know about things and how we habitually look at them. How we explain what we see must grow out of our limited descriptions and will always be arbitrary according to what we are able to notice. So, our explanations are arbitrary; even more so, then, are the interventions we select to use, which should be related to how we explain things to ourself and our clients. All of this is a humbling realization for practitioners. It suggests how arbitrary description, explanation, and intervention really are, how different and unique to each practitioner these activities may be, and how interventive-practice theories do not necessarily flow from descriptive, explanatory person-in-environment theories. Knowledge *about* does not tell us what to *do about* a situation.

Our way of looking at things and of thinking about them is constrained by at least three influences: individual cognitive style; cultural and collective conventions; and the norms and traditions of our profession or discipline. Cognitive styles are attitude- and value-based, learned preferences that are qualitative dimensions, and they affect *how* we perceive, remember, think, cope, and interact with others. Cultural conventions, also rooted in values, affect what has importance in our world and, therefore, what we *want* to perceive. Professional and academic norms and traditions further qualify the "right" way to think and pursue understanding (i.e., what we believe we *should* consider).

### Cognitive Style

At the individual level, cognitive styles are process dimensions. They are neither content-based, nor do they have to do with intellectual ability (IQ). They deal with *how* we process information rather than *what* we process or *how well* we do it. Major typologies of approaches to thinking processes have been proposed (see Jung, 1923; Witkin, 1974; Kolb, 1976; Hill, 1976) and have been advanced through studies of individual psychology. Messick (1976) described nineteen lines of research on cognitive style, including: convergent versus divergent, analytic versus global, impersonal versus social, risk-taking versus cautious, rigid versus flexible. In all instances, these stylistic dimensions are described as more or as less suitable to certain environmental circumstances, not as better or worse ways of thinking. Such research stands to affect many assumptions and values of traditional U.S. approaches to teaching and learning, to gender and ethnic differences, and to the stigmatization of all who may process information in other than rational, lineal, analytic ways.

## Cultural Influences

At the collective (cultural) level, anthropologists and sociologists have shown how differences in world view are constrained by a generalized consciousness that affects both how persons process information and what they value as important to think about (see, for example, Mead, 1946; Kluckhohn, 1949; Edward T. Hall, 1959/1965/1976; Berger and Luckmann, 1967). The elder Pribram (1949) described four culturally different preferences in social philosophy and valued patterns of thought. The U.S. tradition emphasizes inductive and pragmatic reasoning —a preference that differs from other traditions that may value intuitional, deductive, or dialectic ways of reasoning. Harvey (1966), using psychological tests with university students, extended his study into the realms of culture, values, belief systems, and social systems; and Maruyama's studies are increasingly focused on cross-cultural differences in values, ethics, and total outlooks on living and being in the world (1974/1980/1983).

## Professional Conventions

At the profession or discipline level, there are additional influences on how one should think—conventions of the field. There is the science versus art division, with the first camp interested in general relationships and lawfulness and the second with the particular, the unique (Snow, 1970; Hudson, 1966). Disciplines have been differentiated further along an abstract/concrete dimension and along an action/reflective dimension (applied versus pure or basic), yielding four "families" with distinctive epistemologies: the social professions, the science-based professions, the natural sciences and mathematics, and the humanities and social sciences (Wolfe and Kolb, 1979).

Within each discipline-family a particular approach to the "knowing" prevails. This can be seen by examining such aspects as valued unit for study, dominant philosophy, evaluation and reporting of knowledge, method of inquiry, and definition of "truth." For example, in terms of dominant philosophy, the social professions favor pragmatism; the science-based, empiricism; the natural sciences and mathematics, structuralism; and the humanities and social sciences, organicism (Wolfe and Kolb, 1979; see also Kuhn's classic work, 1970).

Academia and the funding agencies have traditionally placed highest value on one particular world view: on the methods of inquiry and evaluation used in the natural sciences and the science-based professions (empiricism, structuralism, positivism)—a situation in which social workers, clinicians, and social scientists have fit with difficulty. But there is increased recognition not only of the many ways—and not one "right" way—of knowing and of reporting this knowledge, but also of the diversity of human approaches to inquiry and the necessity for new paradigms to look at the human condition (Reason and Rowan, 1981). More critiques have been published on the limitations of the methodology and reasoning styles of the "hard" sciences when applied to social events.[2] These challenges are aimed at logical positivism and various elements of the classical empirical approach—linear thinking, reductionism, quantification, objectivity, and so forth. Curiously, these assumptions and concepts gasp for life or have been abandoned by the philosophers of science, physicists, and many in the social sciences more readily than by theorists in social work.

Beyond the general conventions of the social professions, social workers hold certain perspectives that stem from the traditions and norms of the profession. These include: an action orientation, action despite incomplete information or inadequate resources; a feeling or person orientation; a social conscience, a value orientation concerned with the disadvantaged, the stigmatized, the oppressed person. A female perspective is operative. Despite the preponderance of men in the top administrative roles, a female mentality prevails, owing to the number of women in the work force and their contributions as major theorists and teachers of practice.

As with any profession, there is the ideal of altruism rather than self-interest, which in social work is expressed as a service mission—a commitment to the social good and the well-being of all individuals. Other influences stem from the organization-based (rather than individual and entrepreneurial) locus of most of the work. Career incentives come more from professional service ideals than expectations of monetary advantage; in fact, the practitioner is led by tradition to expect personal sacrifice in the economic realm. Bureaucratic norms curtail independent activity in favor of organizational and collegial considerations. Working in arenas where others (other professions, politicians, citizens) may determine the thrust of the work and where the resources are uncertain, inconsistent, and usually insufficient further affect social workers' spirit of independence. For most of the professions' history, practitioners have learned to make do, to function within a milieu of scarcity and watchfulness, in a climate where their services have been regarded with suspicion if not distaste.

Social workers' political perspective has been mainly liberal, rather than conservative or radical (Longres, 1981); and their efforts have been determined and constrained largely by the dominant social interests. While by tradition some continuous perspective and energy always have been deployed to social reform, social workers have worked mainly within the overall social-economic-political system as a force that conserves the dominant ethos, preferring perspectives of information sharing, enabling, facilitating, and conciliating.

We have tried to show that your perspective as you think about supervising will inevitably be affected by three influences: (1) your individual way of processing information (cognitive style), (2) the effects of your particular culture and traditions, and (3) the general conventions of the social professions and particularly, of social work. Let us now relate this more directly to you as a supervisor. You will need to start by considering where you are now.

## TAKING STOCK OF YOURSELF

You are thinking of becoming a supervisor—tomorrow or at some more distant point in your career. Perhaps you are supervising now and wish to bring more conceptual clarity to your role. Or maybe you have no such intentions; you are moved to think about supervisory issues from your discontent with your own experiences as a supervisee and your hopes for a better work situation. All of these circumstances will benefit from examination of certain elements and issues related to supervising.

You can use the ideas you will encounter in this book whether you are a supervisor or a supervisee, since the substance of what happens between you and other(s) results from a transaction in which each person affects the other. Because of this, the particulars of supervision should be knowledge useful to every social worker, no matter which side of the desk one occupies nor where one sits in the team or group. All parties to the transaction are responsible for making supervision work.

Although becoming a supervisor requires shifting your perspective and mastering some new ways to think and act, do not assume that you are starting from scratch or know nothing of what is involved. You come with your life experience and work experience, with your conceptual schemes and theories of social work practice, your knowledge of human behavior and environments, and your familiarity with evaluation and assessment. You will build on what you know. As supervisor, you are not, presto, some new breed, but merely more of what you always were. What you will have to give up is your do-it-yourself mentality. Now you will need to work through others much more of the time and, hopefully, learn to gain your own satisfactions through others' accomplishments.

You have much to go on. You have been supervised throughout most of your life. You have known being watched, warned, and directed. You have known introductions to expectations and activities many times over in the past—by parents, bosses, other supervisors—in diverse realms and worlds. All such experiences and the recollections they evoke will help you now as you review the thoughts and feelings you have accumulated over the years. Some generate nostalgia—happy and appreciative images; others are painful—experiences you would wish to avoid. All will help you frame your way of supervising others.

As you work at constructing the kind of supervisor you aim to be, it is tempting to do what you know from your past experiences. These memories stick in your mind, surfacing when you encounter situations resembling those you have met before. We urge you to suspend all such judgments and start afresh. The complexities of organizational life leave room for diverse interactions. It will be helpful to start imagining yourself in the supervisory situation by looking at some of your current ideas about supervising. To help you get a picture of where you are now, we encourage you, before you read any further in this book, to complete Appendix C, *Current Profile*; Appendix D, *How I Look at Supervision*; and Appendix E, *Your Working Style.*

In completing Appendices C, D, and E, you will develop a baseline for thinking of yourself as a supervisor. This perspective on how you see yourself as supervisor is further influenced by cultural and discipline-based thinking preferences, which have affected beliefs about how social workers should and should not think. Mainly, we identify three world views that historically have conditioned how knowledge is approached.

## WORLD VIEWS

World views have been discussed in different disciplines under diverse labels, for example, paradigms, models, logics, structures of reasoning, epistemologies (Maruyama, 1974). They have been called patterns of thought (Pribram, 1949) and "the pattern which connects—the metapattern or pattern of patterns" (Bateson, 1979). The concepts *epistemology* and *model* have entered the social sciences and social work as popular ways to describe new systems of thinking, and as more "precise" ways of organizing views about situations and interventions. Models are especially popular, perhaps because they speak across disciplines, linking the social sciences with the "hard" sciences. A model may be a small, *tangible* replica of some planned construction (a model airplane), or a full-size simulation of a "thing" to examine its workings before it is *really* used (a mock spaceship that we see on TV). Or it may be abstract and symbolic, using words, numbers, notes, or acronyms, to express through a few symbols a message having only an arbitrary link with the world of things. In either case models are most valued to the extent they accurately represent relevant components of some larger object or situation, provide a grasp of how the components are interrelated, and are *predictive* of future workings. But models that deal with complexities that include persons and human situations have limited predictive value, yet may have great *descriptive* value.

In the helping professions, models have been used to impart order to ways of thinking and ways of doing, and their use has been mainly in the descriptive. In the person-in-environment situation, however, the interrelatedness among components cannot be clearly known. Therefore, there are hazards in using "models" and other research conventions in ordering or organizing human transactions so that they appear to be "true" as prescriptions for practice, when such models are more accurately "schools of thought." As you will see, we shall *not* talk in terms of models of supervision or propose precise interrelationships among interdependent components. There are, as yet, too little empirical and experimental studies of the components and elements that we identify as aspects of service delivery tasks, functions, and supervisory approaches. But we shall identify our preference in world view (i.e., our paradigm, our epistemology); as a meta-view or frame of reference or metaphor or belief system, this world view influences our beliefs about "being in the universe," and leads to "the models" we pose. These models are created, first, within belief systems that prescribe a permissible "reality" for each of us and, second, within the limits of what the "science" of our age allows us to entertain as ideas (and thus, as actions). Throughout this book we shall continue to discuss concepts such as practice orientations, mentality, frame of reference, and metaphors and world views. We begin by illustrating three world views with a slogan (metaphor) for each, and by describing them briefly.

1. Our world is a perpetual-motion machine, a giant clock once wound up (by God), that is running its predetermined course.
2. Our world is a game of chance, a lottery where we have increasingly fewer tickets to use.
3. Our world is a kaleidoscope, one among many, where we happen to be. It and we move and flow continuously, with certain unexpected, potentially diverse patterns and configurations. But the pattern may pop into a totally new arrangement as we notice and manipulate the it and ourselves.

### The World as a Great Machine

This is the mechanistic world view of classical physics that became a model for the "hard" sciences, the natural sciences, and the social sciences. This mechanical metaphor animated science and philosophy from the late 1600s until the middle 1800s and still influences how you should go about "knowing" in a scientific way. It derived from Newton's classical mechanics and Déscartes' philosophy of dualism, which viewed the universe as a great machine whose orderly workings could be known through logic and intellectual insight, through rational thought. There were mind *and* body, spirit *and* matter—two independent realms. Newton added experimentation and observation—the empiricism of Bacon—as the way that seemed adequate to describe all natural phenomena. Concern was with theoretical schemes and logical systems that could be verified through experimentation, with certainty and predictability, and with universal laws. It was a world that would be knowable eventually, a world whose hallmarks were causality, linearity, determinism, forces external to elements, experimentalism, objective observers, and observable facts.

### The World as Lottery with Diminishing Tickets

Newton's mechanical laws of classical physics were hoped to extend generally to all science, but history proved otherwise. There was no grand theory applicable to all science, no universal law of cause-and-effect mechanics. A radically different view, proposed in the 1870s by Ludwig Boltzmann, was of a patterned world possibly evolved from a chaotic sea of randomly moving particles *by chance*. Working in the area of thermodynamics, Boltzmann advanced the second law of thermodynamics, which became known as the entropy law, and a *statistical* mechanics in which change was seen as moving from order to disorder. This law grew to animate systems theory, information theory, cybernetics, and eventually, social work practice. In this lottery, probability world, cause is abandoned in favor of tracing probable trends. Statistical techniques separate out (to the extent possible) the chancy fluctuations from steady trends. System, the opposite of entropy, *is* order; and notions of pattern, feedback, redundancy, and multicausality replace concepts of forces, linearity, and cause and effect. A key concept, equilibrium, is useful in dealing with two types of change: (1) growth in complexity through differentiation, and (2) adjustment to external change. Equilibrium and balance are central imperatives, and negative feedback is the means by which balance is maintained. In the case of living organisms, as neurologist Walter Cannon described, this tendency to maintain a state of internal balance was called homeostasis—a state of continual fluctuations.

### The World as Kaleidoscope

This is a world where fluctuations are central and change moves from disorder to higher levels of order. Instead of the laws of cause in the machine world, or the laws of chance and entropy in the lottery world, kaleidoscope thinking[3] appreciates the patterns of instability—those recurrent random fluctuations that lead to order through selective choice—to a new order out of chaos. This world involves instabilities and fluctuations; understanding it requires looking at the whole cycle, the totality, especially the shifts among the subparts that drive systems to new levels of form and function. The very fluctuations, which were previously excluded as a margin of error, become the focus of interest. Key notions here are potential, possibility, instability, positive feedback (or feedforward), transformation, self-organization, and nonequilibrium conditions. So, uncertainty, instability, fluctuation, change, and nonequilibrium are seen as natural occurrences in this world view of open systems characterized by a high degree of exchange within and among systems and environments.

## CONCLUSION

We began this chapter by discussing competence and imagination, the two central components of the kind of supervisory performance we discuss throughout this book. Both were described as transactional entities, rather than as qualities residing within the supervisor. Further, we introduced a theme that will be emphasized throughout this book—that the organizational context and broader environmental influences affect and are affected by the supervisor. We then introduced, in the Appendix, three observational and informational questionnaires. These can be used to show how much variation there is in the ways people react to and make sense out of their world, and to help you know how you see yourself in several dimensions of the work experience. We suggested that your perspective is shaded by individual cognitive style, by culture and tradition, and by the conventions of your profession. Finally, we described three basic views of the world that have affected how philosophers, scientists, social workers—and thus supervisors—have been led to think about the world in which they live and act.

If we believe the world is mechanical and we are but cogs in a giant machine, then we live by mechanical rules. If we believe the world is one of equilibrium and exhaustion, then we live to predict and try to control process and structure in order to delay our inevitable demise. But, if we believe in a "dancing" open world (Zukav, 1980), an ever-changing and increasingly complex pattern of energy and matter, then we live to positively amplify creative forces, to experiment with change, to marvel at the power of the unseen, the unimaginable-yet-possible. For the supervisor, this would mean seeing the regularities *and* the random events, the fluctuations and uncertainties as well as the routines and controls, and appreciating the possibilities of the as-yet-unknowable new structures that may emerge from the confusion that often seems to characterize the workaday world.

Each of the three world views is applicable today in certain situations. The Newtonian view helps us develop cures for diseases, construct giant skyscrapers, and design ingenious machines and assembly lines. It is useful for explaining physical phenomena and constructing systems that work, like simple machines. The lottery view helps describe and analyze the processes of closed systems that are characterized by symmetry, bounded equilibrium, negative feedback, and entropy. It helps us understand the homeostatic processes in the human body, formulate

A view of the unseen and unimaginable. (*Photo courtesy of Edward Herser.*)

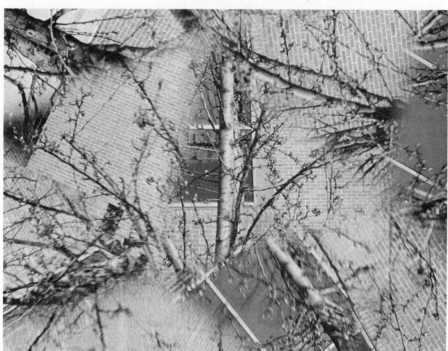

the conversion efficiency of power plants (necessary in designing such plants), construct engines and automobile tires that can withstand the heat caused by friction, and understand the equalization of temperature between hot and cold water or air in a closed receptacle.

Finally, the view of world as kaleidoscope provides us with a reality matrix emphasizing the possible, visualizing the unseen, conceiving the unimaginable. It guides us in analyzing and describing complex, interacting systems and processes, processes of amplification as well as control, where complexity probably begets complexity and flexibility probably begets flexibility. This view appreciates the influence of the disparate forces of politics, economics, and ecology on the outcome of disruptions to the equilibrium of physical, biological, or social systems.

The world as kaleidoscope involves a mindset that goes beyond the concepts of the clockwork machine, beyond duality and linearity, beyond diminishing options, to concepts and actions that reflect the possibilities of vibrant ever-changing patterns. In this world, the unimaginable becomes the possible, instabilities become opportunities for positive feedback, for *feedforward,* to drive living systems to a higher achievable level.

We aim to show how the kaleidoscope world view will affect the supervisor at work. We shall begin in Chapter 3 by looking at our picture of supervision and the pushes and pulls you are likely to encounter in moving from supervisee to supervisor.

## NOTES

1. Middleman (1977) described four basic orientations to skill that have influenced how "skill" and subsequently "skill components" have been taught in schools of social work. (1) As an entity that is informed (knowledge-based), action, intentioned, and idiosyncratic (bearing the imprint of institutional and individual styles). These elements, according to Lewis (1976) comprise the structure of professional skill: knowledge, action, values, and style, which he differentiated further in terms of degree (preprofessional, professional, and advanced professional). This approach to skill was congenial with the elaboration of various methods (casework, group work, community work) and activities (skill in interviewing, in observing, etc.).

(2) A second orientation views skills as desirable attributes of the helper, or what qualities one needs to *have* or *be.* An influential example in this tradition is contributed by Rogers comprised of genuineness or congruence, empathic understanding, and unconditional positive regard by the helping person, an orientation later extended beyond work with individuals to encounter groups (1961; 1970).

(3) A third approach to skills viewed them as actions the helping person needs to *do* to accomplish tasks which were analyzed into their component elements. A key example is Fine and Wiley's *Functional Job Analysis* (1971) which described the functional tasks of dealing with data (e.g., coordinating, comparing), people (e.g., persuading, instructing), and things (e.g., controlling, operating). Another conceptual approach to skill components in this *doing* orientation is Middleman and Goldberg's formulation beginning with the task and deriving subcomponents in the interpersonal area (e.g., dealing with feelings, managing interaction), in the technical area (e.g., data gathering, analyzing) and the development of skills labs for such instruction.

(4) Middleman also described her newly emergent conceptualization of skill components for which theoretical elaboration and instructional methods remained at a formative stage. In this approach, one begins with the situation, and skills are conceptualized as a potentiality that

awaits a context or situation in which the other(s) think or act differently because of the intentional actions of the helper, or conversely where the helping person thinks or acts differently because of the impact of the other(s) on her or him. This implies teaching for "transactionalism," for example, for flexibility, responsiveness, openness—an approach that remains a basic orientation and underlying assumption in this text. *Competence* literature added a further component to the skill or skills formulations: standards (specifying what the skill consists of and what constitutes performing it well).

2. See, for example, Scheflen (1977), Mitroff and Kilmann (1978), Haveliwala (1979), and Bateson (1979) for the social sciences; Pascale and Athos (1981) and Ouchi (1981) for organizational and managerial behavior; Middleman (1980) for group work practice; Middleman (1983) for clinical practice; Hoffman (1981) for family practice; Vigilante, Lodge, Lukton, Kaplan, and Mason (1981) for social work theory building; and Heineman (1981) for social work research. See also the interesting exposé of "The Flexner Myth," on the historical attempts of the social work profession itself to become "a profession" by pursuing "alien" traditions and professional high-status academic norms, ill-suited and diminishing to the profession as well as limited by the fashionable, yet internally questionable logic of the times (Austin, 1983).

3. To pursue these world views more fully, you would need to study writings from several disciplines, about the philosophy of science, for example, K. E. Boulding, *Ecodynamics* (Beverly Hills, Calif.: Sage, 1978); J. Bronowski, *The Common Sense of Science* (Cambridge, Mass.: Harvard University Press, 1978); F. Capra, *The Tao of Physics* (New York: Bantam, 1977); M. Gardner, *The Ambidextrous Universe* (2nd ed.) (New York: Scribners, 1979); E. Jantsch, *Design for Evolution: Self-Organization and Planning in the Life of Human Systems* (New York: George Braziller, 1975); W. Lepowski, "The Social Thermodynamics of Ilya Prigogine," *Chemical and Engineering News,* 57 (April 16, 1979), 30–33; I. Prigogine, "Order Through Fluctuation: Self-Organization and Social Systems," in E. Jantsch and C. H. Waddington, eds., *Evolution and Consciousness: Human Systems in Transitions* (Reading, Mass.: Addison-Wesley, 1976); J. Rifkin, *Entropy* (New York: Viking, 1980); and N. Weiner, *Cybernetics* (Cambridge, Mass.: M.I.T. Press, 1948).

# REFERENCES

AUSTIN, DAVID M., "The Flexner Myth and the History of Social Work," *Social Service Review,* 57, no. 3 (September 1983), 357–377.

BATESON, GREGORY, *Mind and Nature: A Necessary Unity.* New York: Elsevier-Dutton, 1979.

BERGER, PETER L., and THOMAS LUCKMANN, *The Social Construction of Reality.* Garden City, N.Y.: Anchor, 1967.

DE BONO, EDWARD, *Po: A Device for Successful Thinking.* New York: Simon & Schuster, 1972.

————, *Lateral Thinking: Creativity Step by Step.* New York: Harper & Row, 1970.

FINE, SIDNEY A., and WRETHA W. WILEY, *An Introduction to Functional Job Analysis: A Scaling of Selected Tasks from the Social Welfare Field.* Kalamazoo, Mich.: The Upjohn Institute, 1971.

GOLDBERG, GALE, and RUTH R. MIDDLEMAN, "It Might Be a Boa Constrictor Digesting an Elephant: Vision Stretching in Social Work Education," *Contemporary Social Work Education,* 3, no. 3 (December 1980), 213–225.

HALL, EDWARD T., *Beyond Culture.* New York: Doubleday, 1976.

————, *The Hidden Dimension.* New York: Doubleday, 1965.

————, *The Silent Language.* New York: Doubleday, 1959.

HALL, ELIZABETH, "Giving Away Psychology in the 80's," *Psychology Today* (January 1980), 38+.

HARVEY, O.J., *Experience, Structure, and Adaptability.* Itasca, Ill.: Peacock, 1966.

HAVELIWALA, YOOSUF, ALBERT E. SCHEFLEN, and NORMAN ASHCRAFT, *Common Sense in Therapy.* New York: Brunner/Mazel, 1979.

HEINEMAN, MARTHA B., "The Obsolete Scientific Imperative in Social Work Research," *Social Service Review,* 55, no. 3 (September 1981), 371–397.

HILL, JOSEPH E., *The Educational Sciences* (rev. ed.). Bloomfield Hills, Mich.: Oakland Community College, 1976.

HOFFMAN, LYNN, *Foundations of Family Therapy.* New York: Basic Books, 1981.

HUDSON, LIAM, *Contrary Imaginations.* New York: Schocken Books, 1966.

JUNG, CARL G., *Psychological Types.* London: Pantheon, 1923.

KLUCKHOHN, CLYDE, "The Philosophy of Navaho Indians," in *Ideological Differences and World Order,* F.S.C. Northtop, ed. New Haven: Yale University Press, 1949.

KOLB, DAVID A., *Learning Style Inventory: Technical Manual.* Boston: McBer and Company, 1976.

KUHN, THOMAS S., *The Structure of Scientific Revolutions* (enlarged ed.). Chicago: University of Chicago Press, 1970.

LEWIS, HAROLD, "The Structure of Professional Skill," in *Social Work in Practice,* Bernard Ross, and S.K. Khinduka, eds. Washington, D.C.: NASW, 1976, 3–13.

LONGRES, JOHN F., "Social Work Practice with Racial Minorities: A Study of Contemporary Norms and Their Ideological Implications," *California Sociologist,* 4, no. 1 (Winter 1981), 54–71.

MARUYAMA, MAGORAH, "Mindscapes and Science Theories," *Current Anthropology,* 21, no. 5 (October 1980), 589–608.

————, "Paradigmatology and Its Application to Cross-disciplinary, Cross-professional and Cross-cultural Communication," *Dialectica,* 28 (1974), 135–196.

————, "Cross-Cultural Perspectives on Social and Community Change," in *Handbook of Social Intervention,* Edward Seidman, ed. Beverly Hills, Calif.: Sage, 1983, 33–47.

MEAD, MARGARET, "An Application of Anthropological Techniques to Cross-national Communication," *Transactions of the New York Academy of Science,* Series 2, 9 (February 1946), 133–152.

MESSICK, SAMUEL, and ASSOCIATES, *Individuality in Learning.* San Francisco: Jossey-Bass, 1976.

MIDDLEMAN, RUTH R., "The Role of Perception and Cognition in Change," in *Handbook of Clinical Social Work,* Aaron Rosenblatt, and Diana Waldfogel, eds. San Francisco: Jossey-Bass, 1983, 229–251.

————, "The Use of Program in Group Work: Review and Update," *Social Work With Groups,* 3, no. 3 (1980), 5–14.

————, "The Skill Component in Social Work Education: Semantics, Pragmatics, and Instructional Heuristics," paper presented at the Annual Program Meeting, Council on Social Work Education, 1977.

MIDDLEMAN, RUTH R., and GALE GOLDBERG, *Social Service Delivery: A Structural Approach to Social Work Practice.* New York: Columbia University Press, 1974.

MITROFF, IAN, and RALPH KILMANN, *Methodological Approaches to Social Science.* San Francisco: Jossey-Bass, 1978.

OUCHI, WILLIAM, *Theory Z.* Reading, Mass.: Addison-Wesley, 1981.

PASCALE, RICHARD T., and ANTHONY G. ATHOS, *The Art of Japanese Management.* New York: Simon & Schuster, 1981.

PELZ, DONALD C., "Environments for Creative Performance Within Universities," in *Individuality in Learning,* Samuel Messick and Associates. San Francisco: Jossey-Bass, 1976, 229–247.

PRIBRAM, KARL, *Conflicting Patterns of Thought.* Washington, D.C.: Public Affairs Press, 1949.

REASON, PETER, and JOHN ROWAN, eds., *Human Inquiry: A Sourcebook of New Paradigm Research.* New York: John Wiley, 1981.

ROGERS, CARL, *On Encounter Groups.* New York: Harper & Row, 1970.

―――――, *On Becoming a Person.* Boston: Houghton Mifflin, 1961.

DE SAINT EXUPERY, ANTOINE, *The Little Prince.* New York: Harbrace Paperbound Library, Harcourt, Brace & World, 1943, 1971.

SCHEFLEN, ALBERT E., "Classical Biases and the Structural Approach to Research," *ETC,* 34, no. 3 (September 1977), 290–300.

SNOW, C.P., *The Two Cultures: And a Second Look.* New York: Cambridge University Press, 1970.

VIGILANTE, JOSEPH E., RICHARD LODGE, ROSEMARY LUKTON, SHARRON KAPLAN, and ROBERT MASON, "Searching for Theory: Following Hearn," paper presented at Annual Program Meeting, Council on Social Work Education, Louisville, Kentucky, 1981.

WITKIN, HERMAN A., "A Cognitive-Style Perspective on Evaluation and Guidance," *Proceedings of the 1973 Invitational Conference on Testing Problems.* Princeton, N.J.: Educational Testing Service, 1974.

WOLFE, DONALD M., and DAVID A. KOLB, "Career Development, Personal Growth, and Experiential Learning," in *Organizational Psychology* (3rd ed.), David A. Kolb, Irwin M. Rubin, and James M. McIntyre, eds. Englewood Cliffs, N.J.: Prentice-Hall, 1979, 535–563.

ZUKAV, GARY, *The Dancing Wu Li Masters.* New York: Bantam Books, 1980.

# CHAPTER THREE
# PICTURING SUPERVISION
## *A Transition*

## INTRODUCTION

In choosing a kaleidoscope view of the world, we join with others from the philosophy, science, and social science communities who view the world as open, evolving, changing, and expanding. As we described in Chapter 2, the way one looks at and thinks about self and situations affects what one does and the words one uses to talk about professional behavior. In fact, the very words one uses can advance or limit one's openness to the possible. For example, Pascale and Athos (1981) cite Japanese managers' positive views of dependency, ambiguity, and indirectness in contrast to U.S. managers' views. Similarly, Jantsch commented on differences in behavior of successful and unsuccessful managers in human service agencies; the successful ones were intuitive, capable of tuning into and moving with the stream, while the unsuccessful ones looked for a rational explanation for the movement of the stream (1975). Social work's history and literature reveal a consistent commitment to persons *and* environments, or persons *in* environments, or persons/environments, or the linkage point *between* the person and the environment. There always has been the dual concern. Of course, at certain times in the profession's short 75-year life, you could find main preoccupations with the "person" part or the "situation" part, largely influenced by the economic-political-intellectual *Zeitgeist* of the moment. But there was *never* a time when both components were not seen as our mandate, never a time when *all* energies of the profession were devoted to one part alone.

This dual commitment has been a source of social work's uniqueness among the professions. It has been a source of complexity in terms of the valued and needed knowledge, the practitioner roles, the identification and orientations, the research agendas, and the methodological conventions that make up social work. The double imperative also has been a source of within-group conflict, an asset with a drawback so far as unified voice, image, and influence are concerned. The passionate commitments to treatment versus justice, to cause versus function, to containment versus reform are well-known chapters in the profession's history. At the individual-practitioner level, each person makes some choice of special energy investment (not necessarily once and for all fixed), but not without awareness of the profession's *social* mission.

## TOWARD A DIFFERENT PICTURE AND VOCABULARY

When we consider social work practice and its supervision, we encounter a profession that is multifaceted. It is comprised of diverse fields of practice, specializations, roles, orientations, and interest groups. It is and has been constrained by the Indo-European language system and thinking style that favors dichotomy. It is no longer productive, however, to think in terms of either/or, this/that, or *any* x and y. To look and think *pattern,* on the other hand, necessitates the abandonment of all twos, all dichotomies, all dualities. At the very least we must cultivate thinking and talking in trichotomies, in threes, and even in fours or mores. As you will notice as you read, our discussion of supervision and concepts related to it will always be framed in units of threes and fours.

Let us start by applying a "fourness" mentality to imagine any situation in which you are engaged in any activity with another person. *It is never merely the two of you interacting: It is always a foursome.* The components of this foursome may be thought of as follows:

The *me*—looking with all my biases, knowledge, fears, comforts, . . .
The *it*—what I am looking at; the "it" as separate from "me" is a construct for analytic convenience only
The *context*—what surrounds "me/it": others, objects
The *history*—past, present, forecast of happenings and possibilities

This general approach can be applied to actions, to thinking, and to looking at situations, and it can serve as a general orientation to analysis. Let us apply such an analysis to supervision. We shall call this the *foursome mentality.*

## THE SUPERVISORY PICTURE

In Chapter 2 you were asked to examine yourself and, hopefully, you began to imagine what you would do as a supervisor. Now picture the situation further. Here, you are an actor in a configuration that includes supervisor, worker, client, and context. Each affects what happens. In this situation you may be the supervisor or the worker. Regardless of your particular position, you are only one actor among four actors. The configuration includes supervisor, worker, and client transactions within a specific, active context. For now, think of context as the organization and all the myriad forces that affect it. The context has as much or even *more* effect on what happens as any of the other three actors.

As you consider the four actors, assume that each is equally dominant. Now, practice imagining a change in these dimensions. Make each actor the dominant one and think about what happens to the picture of this situation: dominant supervisor . . . dominant client . . . dominant worker . . . dominant context. Obviously, accentuating any of these components will change the total balance of the situation. Let us consider an example to illustrate each dominance situation:

DOMINANT SUPERVISOR: In this example, "dominant supervisor" is represented by the director and the assistant directors. Agency C is a subunit of umbrella system U. Its staff includes a director, two assistant directors, seven counselors, and many volunteers. Each assistant director is in charge of a different service area, but the counselors and volunteers work in both areas and thus report to each assistant director. Job dissatisfaction is at a high level for all the staff members. Five of the seven counselors have been employed less than six months; all three of the supervisory staff are sending out résumés. The volunteer pool is at its historical low point. Although there are weekly staff meetings, most communication occurs as gossip. At staff meetings the director does most of the talking and does not seek input from others. Staff is informally divided into "new" and "old," with only the "old" group of four persons doing any talking. No minutes are kept of the meetings. The director is the only one who has any contact with U system. He works no scheduled hours, and much of his work is done at U in a different part of town. So, staff have little contact with him, often do not know where to reach him if problems arise, and do not know his hours or what he is doing for them.

DOMINANT CLIENT: Mrs. C, a slim woman 35 years of age, has been receiving welfare for over five years. She has three children, ages 13, 11, and 5. Two of the children were fathered by her husband, who deserted her nine years ago. The third child was fathered by her current boyfriend, who promised to marry her when he obtained a divorce from his wife. This promise was made five years ago. Mrs. C is very nervous and easily intimidated. She becomes extremely dependent on her social workers and calls them frequently for advice. Any change in staff or service systems greatly upsets her.

Six months ago, Mrs. C called her worker to say she was having a serious problem with her 11-year-old son, Robert. He was behaving badly in school, had begun to steal small things from neighborhood stores, and generally was difficult to control. She asked her worker to visit her at her home. The worker went about a week later. At that time the worker suggested that Mrs. C get in touch with the local Child Guidance Clinic, regarding the problems she was having with her son, and left the telephone number of the clinic for her.

A month later, Mrs. C called to say her son had been picked up by the police and placed in the Children's Shelter. He had run away for a few days and Mrs. C did not know where he was until the police located him. She said she had to appear in court and was frightened. The worker assured her that since this was a first offense, the case would probably be dismissed with a warning. The worker then asked if Mrs. C's son was going to the Child Guidance Clinic. Mrs. C explained that she had lost the telephone number and the worker gave it to her again.

A few days later Mrs. C called and said she was still having trouble with Robert and wanted the worker to visit her. When asked if she had contacted the Child Guidance Clinic yet, Mrs. C replied that even if she called, she would have no way of getting there for appointments, since she had no car and lived quite a distance away with no public transportation available. The worker explained that the Welfare Board could supply transportation for clinic appointments. Further, there is sometimes a waiting list at the clinic so that Mrs. C should try to get on the list immediately.

About a month later, Mrs. C called and told the worker she felt she could not handle Robert at home any longer and would like to place him either in a foster home or in a state institution. The worker visited the home and spoke with Mrs. C. At this time Mrs. C showed the worker the application she had received from the Child Guidance Clinic—almost 6 pages long and quite detailed. Mrs. C told the worker that if she did go to the clinic, they might ask her personal questions about her relationship with her boyfriend and with her son's father, and she didn't feel she could talk about those things to strangers. She wanted the worker to help her with Robert. Besides, she had found the application too hard to fill out, since the questions involved many specific details (such as ages of toilet training) and she couldn't remember these details.

About a month ago, Mrs. C's son was picked up by the police on a charge of incorrigibility placed by his mother. He is presently living at a residential treatment center for boys.

DOMINANT WORKER (The following two examples illustrate situations where the focus is on the worker):

EXAMPLE 1: I (the supervisor) had to fire a part-time group worker, John, when I was director of a community center. John worked with activity groups for elementary- and high-school-age boys. During his first six weeks of employment, John lost his temper several times. For example, he shoved and hit two boys. After the first incident, I instructed him about agency policy regarding physical management. After the second time, I gave him a stronger reprimand and planned steps to resolve the conflict. After the third time, in the face of strong community pressure and threat of legal action, I fired John. What made me so uncomfortable as I think back on this, is that I had assumed a responsibility for his behavior after the first episode. That is, I thought I could teach him to control his behavior and I believed I shared in the responsibility for the situation, because he had been inadequately trained (orientation to the position) by me, and because when he was hired, his aggressive tendencies were not assessed accurately.

EXAMPLE 2: While I was a supervisor for the Salvation Army Family Services Bureau, a problem developed with the secretary, who began to come in late in the morning. She had always been very conscientious and highly efficient in managing her work, so I overlooked the problem for several days. When

Trudy's lateness began to become more regular and began to inconvenience the office staff, I talked with her and asked if anything could be done about this. She told me she was having car trouble. Also, she was finding it difficult to get her 4-year-old daughter up and ready and to the babysitter's house by 8 o'clock. She said that she would try harder with her daughter and that by next payday she could afford to have the car fixed. Trudy was a single parent and I understood her dilemma. Also, she appeared sincere about trying harder to get going early in the morning.

After a few weeks of promptness, Trudy once again began to slip in late. The rest of the staff were becoming irritated and resentful of her, and she was creating a lot of tension for everyone.

DOMINANT CONTEXT: (In the following agency, the context is overly emphasized.) X is a child welfare agency where the supervisors all sit upstairs in private offices and caseworkers sit downstairs with partitions between them. On both sides, there is a "we-and-they" mentality. Also, conflict exists between foster care and protective services. The P.S. staff sees the foster care staff as getting more support, doing less work, and being somewhat incompetent. Twelve forms per child are required every time a child comes into foster care; some of the information is redundant. According to one of these workers, "I never take kids anymore; it is just not worth the hassle."

A recent issue, especially troublesome to the director, is that the protective service workers fail to fill out medical forms on children they have removed and placed in foster care. Twice recently, children were exposed to foods causing allergic reactions. Despite repeated conversation with the workers about the forms, the situation has not improved.

The director blames staff members for not filling out the forms and wants to force them to do this. The staff complain about the inadequate leadership of the director, the lack of support for their difficult work, and the many demeaning and demoralizing incidents they have with superiors. They claim there has not been a staff meeting in more than a year and a half, and that their input is never taken seriously, so they do not fill out the circulars that ask for input. According to the director, there are no staff meetings because they are unproductive. Also, the director feels that the staff members never contribute input to the agenda or respond to requests for information.

We have tried to provide a general framework for you to use in analyzing supervisory situations: First, we suggested that you conceptualize four components in each situation to be examined: (1) the *observer* (you), (2) the *it* (the situation you are considering), (3) the *context* (the situation's relation to wider forces), and (4) the *time dimension* (the situation's history, process). Then, we showed that the *it* component (what you are considering) can be conceptualized as four actors: (1) supervisor, (2) worker, (3) client, and (4) context. Further, we presented practice illustrations in which each of these four components was dominant in a supervisory situation.

What if an analysis of your particular situation reveals that it is out of balance? For now, we are concerned that you be able to make just such an identification. Later, in Chapter 8, we shall describe approaches to changing the situation that may help bring things back into better symmetry. We leave you with the general idea at this point of bringing about a new realignment through one of two ways: (1) reduce the salience of the dominant influence, or (2) increase the salience of any of the three subordinate components.

## MAKING THE TRANSITION TO SUPERVISOR

As a social worker, you probably have encountered clients with problems associated with transitions and crises. Many clients presented problems reflecting the stress, strain, tension, and conflict that accompany changes in role, situation, or context. Generally, you responded by working with clients to develop new ways of satisfying needs. You might have assisted clients in developing new skills or enhancing and reorganizing prior skills in order to meet new demands and expectations. Also, you might have focused on improving elements of the external environment that were troublesome (Golan, 1981). Whether you are a new supervisor or a supervisee anticipating advancement into the supervisory role, you will probably experience similar problems of transition.

Problems of transition for social workers moving from direct service to supervision have received attention in the past few years. Educators and professionals in practice have increased their study of the preparation of social workers for managerial roles (Patti and Austin, 1977; Patti, Diedreck, Olson, and Crowell, 1979a, 1979b; Holloway, 1980; Ewalt, 1980; Austin, 1981; Scurfield, 1981; Epstein, Savage-Abramowitz, and Weissman, 1982). One set of transitional issues concerns the reactions you might have in moving into the new, the unknown, and the unimagined. In a new situation and role, you often experience uncertainty about what is expected and whether you have the knowledge necessary to meet new challenges. For some of you, perceived threats to self-image or self-confidence will arise from the need to ask questions or from admitting to not knowing the particulars of the new situation and context. Typically, these concerns subside as the new gradually becomes familiar. With experience you will learn that prior knowledge and skills are useful in meeting new demands. Also, interactions with others can help you with role clarification and the development of a more realistic understanding of your new responsibilities.

Transition to the supervisory role involves a second set of critical concerns that characterize supervision in the social service organization. Various approaches have been followed in efforts to increase professional understanding of the transitional issues facing a new supervisor. Some have emphasized the role discontinuities between direct service and supervision (Patti and Austin, 1977; Patti et al., 1979b; Holloway, 1980; Austin, 1981). Others have sought to identify similarities between direct service and supervision (Epstein et al., 1982). Another focus has been on transition in a particular agency setting, such as mental health (Ewalt, 1980). Also, a few empirical studies have dealt with the transition experiences of supervisors (Patti et al., 1979a; Scurfield, 1981). Whatever the approach, there is general agreement that the most critical issues are as follows: use of authority; relationship orientation; accountability and evaluation; and agency politics and organizational dynamics. We shall explore each of these briefly.

## USE OF AUTHORITY

The use of authority is generally thought to be the most difficult aspect of transition from practitioner to supervisor. The difficulties you will face as a new supervisor are not the result of assuming authority for the first time. Instead, the difficulties are related to a broadened perspective and a change of emphasis in your use of authority. As a worker, your practice behavior was probably directed toward benefiting the clients assigned to you. In the practitioner role, you possessed authority, the authority of knowledge and skill, which you applied in the helping process. You probably used your authority within the boundaries of respect for and enhancement of maximum client autonomy. This may have been reflected in your willingness to wait for the client to believe in and accept your expertise before you exerted your own influence to produce change. Such behavior probably reflected your concern for self-determination, as well as an egalitarian approach to using your authority.

In contrast, as a supervisor, you will be expected to use authority in more directive ways. While you may seek consensus, if supervisees refuse to accept the legitimate authority inherent in the role, you will be expected to press for compliance with agency standards (e.g., x number of client contacts per week). The tension for the person in transition from practitioner to supervisor arises from uncertainty about how to deal with the differences between client-centered and agency-centered practice. The difference between supervisor and supervisee in using authority is a matter of emphasis. In the supervisory role, the expression of prior knowledge, values, and skills will involve new forms of behavior consistent with a broadened perspective. For example, you will need to shift your concern for maximum client autonomy to a more circumscribed view of worker autonomy. The more limiting view reflects the supervisor's responsibility for facilitating worker performance that is consistent with agency goals and objectives (e.g., concern for the timely submission of paperwork).

When you assume the role of supervisor, you are granted, at a minimum, organizationally legitimized authority (power to influence or direct thought, opinion, behavior). This authority establishes supervisory prerogatives related to initiating actions, making decisions, allocating resources, and setting expectations for worker performance. As a supervisor, you will be responsible for guiding the efforts of all your supervisees in behalf of their clients. Sometimes when you, as a supervisor, comply with organizational expectations, workers may think that you are infringing on their discretion and professional judgment. For example, you may have to require more attention to records in anticipation of an audit. Or you may have to assert yourself in getting supervisees to be more consistent about coming to work on time. These changes in emphasis may produce stress and tension in the new supervisor. You can help yourself through these authority-related transition problems by using your knowledge and skill to earn legitimacy from your supervisees.

This "legitimacy of authority" must be earned by the supervisor in order to successfully manage the authority issues that emerge during transition. As a new supervisor, you can seek to earn legitimation of your authority by involving supervisees in an exploration of the uses and limits of supervisory authority. For example, you can implement an approach (within the constraints of agency goals and procedures) to making decisions based on supervisees' knowledge about specific situations and supervisees' skills useful in those situations. As a supervisor you could include your supervisees in the thinking and planning for adjustments in caseload assignments. This could help you earn their legitimation of variable assignments based on differences in experience or differences in number of service-intensive, high-risk clients. Following such an approach to planning and delegating work will help you earn legitimacy by establishing a framework for equity and consistency. Consistency in the following areas will be especially important in gaining supervisees' respect for your use of authority:

1. Developing clear definitions of goals and objectives
2. Setting equitable expectations for quality and quantity of work
3. Balancing supervisees' backgrounds and needs with agency requirements
4. Balancing use of praise with use of constructive critical feedback

Another way for you to earn legitimacy of supervisory authority is by using supervisory judgment responsibly to differentiate areas of freedom of choice from areas of limited or no choice. Supervisees can be actively involved in exploring new approaches to doing the work (e.g., managing time, handling paperwork) or in developing content ideas for staff meetings or teaching events. These are areas with some freedom of choice. In contrast, as a supervisor you may be involved in confidential discussions of sensitive organizational issues (e.g., budget reductions, layoff policies and criteria). These discussions may lead to decisions that you are expected to implement. To gain legitimacy from supervisees, you will need to share the outcome of these discussions, information about how decisions were made, and implications for supervisors and supervisees. For example, suppose you are a supervisor in an agency that has experienced 15 percent reduction in state revenue allocation. Administrators and program developers have explored grant possibilities to no avail. Faced with this situation, staff reductions were discussed. There was consensus that the agency could not adequately fulfill its responsibilities to clients and the community if it reduced its work force. So, it was decided to consolidate some administrative staff functions, reassign personnel as appropriate, suspend merit increases for all personnel, and reduce cost-of-living increases from 7 percent to 5 percent. Clearly, this decision will affect you and your supervisees, and they have a right to hear this proposal directly from you.

In dealing with matters of limited or no choice, you can enhance your credibility by developing an assertive style. Using authority in these areas will involve assertive communication about your perspectives on change, both downward to staff and supervisees, *and* upward to your superiors. So, in the preceding example, you would need to share the proposed agency salary and personnel allocation policy with supervisees in an open, straightforward manner. Following this discussion, you might share supervisee concerns or objections with higher-level administrators in a similarly assertive fashion. The critical task is to be assertive rather than either nonassertive or aggressive in your relationships within the agency. As an assertive supervisor in this situation, you would express your ideas, pro and con, about aspects of the proposal and your feelings about how it will affect you and your supervisees. You might note your opposition to the freeze on merit increments because of the discounting of supervisees who have done outstanding work. Such an approach will encourage supervisees to be equally candid. The nonassertive supervisor would not share such ideas and feelings and would present the proposal in a manner designed to avoid conflict and minimize hard feelings on the part of supervisees. Supervisees are unlikely to have a clear understanding of where they stand, where their supervisor stands, and whether their ideas and feelings matter. An aggressive supervisor would present the proposal as a *fait accompli* and indicate that the supervisees had better go along or else. . . . Clearly, the assertive approach is much more likely to earn for you the legitimation of your authority by your supervisees. This approach allows you to earn this legitimacy at the same time that you fulfill your supervisory obligations as mandated by the agency.

Earning your authority and using it appropriately involves differentiating among three concepts: being an authority (having knowledge, skills, experience); being in authority (having agency legitimacy of role); and being authoritarian (using directive, controlling, punitive approaches to supervisees and the work). Being an authority requires sensitivity in sharing and applying what you have learned from integrating your knowledge, skills, and experiences. This sensitivity is critical if you are to avoid being perceived as elitist or superior and are to achieve success in creating a climate that reinforces dignity and ongoing professional development. Being in authority is an inherent part of the role of supervisor. The challenge you face is to develop a workable balance in using your authority. You will need to balance the responsibilities for agency legitimacy with the responsibilities for earning and maintaining legitimacy of your authority with supervisees. Being authoritarian is what you should work to avoid. The authoritarian approach reflects a lack of sensitivity in applying your expertise and an abuse of the inherent authority of the role.

## RELATIONSHIP ORIENTATION

Relationship issues also can be a source of stress for the supervisor in interactions with supervisees, supervisory peers, and higher-level administrators. Two primary relationship orientations are evident in social services in an agency context. One orientation, the expressive, involves openness, rapport, trust, and an intimate sense of caring in relationships. The second orientation, instrumental, involves functionally specific, task-centered relationships and concerns for productivity and accountability (Kadushin, 1976). As a direct-service worker, you had relationships with peers that probably were characterized by collegial norms; the same expressive qualities were probably emphasized in your worker-client relationships. In making the transition to supervisor, you will probably experience tension in shifting from expressive relationship orientations to more instrumental relationship orientations. In blending and balancing these two orientations, you may experience a sense of loss at no longer being part of the group and its expressive, collegial norms. Rather than withdrawing into isolation and loneliness as a supervisor, you will need to develop an alternative support system. This new system of support may include professionals in other community agencies, as well as membership in professional organizations like NASW. As a supervisor, you will be challenged to temper your expressive orientation with the instrumental orientation as you develop and maintain equity in relationships with all your supervisees.

Changes in relationship orientation may also involve tensions in working with your supervisory peers and higher-level administrators. In relating to other supervisors, your needs and expectations for collegiality may be met with reactions that reflect the instrumental, task orientation. Higher level administrators are likely to expect you to ensure staff compliance with their directives. In fact, they will reward you for demonstrating your loyalty and ability to produce good results in a manner consistent with their values. Each supervisor is expected by both superiors and supervisees to achieve the best possible outcomes for the agency and its clients within the constraints of available resources. So, if you adopt an expressive orientation (i.e., trusting and sharing) to supervisory peers, you are likely to suffer frustration and disappointment. This would be particularly true if your ideas are used by others to competitive advantage. Consider the situation where a new supervisor shared ideas on a possible approach to job sharing that might increase supervisees' opportunities to develop new knowledge and skills. A supervisory peer then developed the ideas into a proposal and submitted it to the administrator. The administrator liked the idea and authorized the supervisor to implement the proposal as a demonstration project with his supervisees. In situations like this, you may not only be frustrated, but you may also be criticized by your supervisees for not doing better in protecting their interests.

As a supervisor you will often be faced with the conflict between acting to establish your individual prominence with superiors and acting to enhance the benefits for your supervisees. One way to manage these pressures is by practicing the deliberate use of your influence in developing and maintaining relationships at all levels. This will involve mixing and matching your expressive and instrumental behavior to fit the tasks and the context. As an example, consider a situation where the administrators decide to keep the agency open two evenings a week. You can approach supervisees by encouraging them to express their feelings and reactions with you and with one another (expressive orientation). This could be followed by planning with the group an approach that satisfies expectations for expanded coverage (instrumental). Then, you can communicate to the administrators the supervisees' feelings and reactions, plus a plan of action (a mix of expressive and instrumental). This example also illustrates another aspect of dealing with relationship issues in transition. You can reduce your tension and anxiety as a supervisor by purposeful use of self in working with and through others to set priorities and guide action consistent with professional standards. This combination of approaches will enable you to demonstrate your sensitivity and responsiveness to these different relationship demands.

## ACCOUNTABILITY AND EVALUATION

Accountability and evaluation demands are familiar to all social service personnel. The transitional problem for the new supervisor is shifting to a broader concept and vision of these two demands. In terms of concern for effectiveness, this shift is reflected in the difference between a process orientation on the one hand, and a product orientation to accountability and evaluation, on the other hand. The process orientation emphasizes the subtleties of practice and usually focuses on means to achieve program goals in meeting client needs (e.g., client self-awareness, client awareness of need for intervention). A product orientation emphasizes measurable, observable outcomes and focuses on indicators of the success probability of a program for an entire agency's client population (e.g., client employment following a job-skills training program, increased family problem-solving skills following a family counseling program).

In the social services, both process and product orientations are important. Process and product outcomes are important in evaluating performance consistent with standards of professional social work practice. Product outcomes are important in satisfying client, agency, and public demands for accountability. Ordinarily, such outcomes are measured in terms of tangible, valued changes or improvements in the client, in the client's environment, or both. As a worker, you probably approached accountability and evaluation in terms of process and process outcomes (e.g., client reports feeling better; client is satisfied, at some level, with the helping relationship). Moreover, you may have emphasized matters of importance to specific clients, rather than matters of importance to all clients and all workers. As a new supervisor, it will be important for you to support the process concerns of your supervisees. In addition, in fulfilling your responsibilities of accountability and evaluation, you will need to emphasize measurable outcomes. Your task will probably be one of increasing supervisee attention to specific outcomes that can be used as evidence that the agency has attained its program goals. In practice, this may include contracting for specific number of counseling visits, stating service goals in concrete terms, and recording specific examples of changes in client behavior, feelings, attitudes, or situational circumstances.

Other transitional problems may arise from your relationship with higher-level administrators. They will probably expect you to emphasize the quantity as well as the quality of services delivered by your supervisees. The quantity/quality demand is likely to produce conflict between you and your supervisees. Social work practitioners generally focus on responding to the needs and requirements of each client as the highest priority, regardless of competing demands of other clients or program areas. As a worker, you also may have resisted the pressures of time, quantity demands, and limited agency resources while attempting to provide services for the maximum benefit of a particular client. This approach to service delivery is similar to the principle of "optimizing" in making decisions (March and Simon, 1958). As a supervisor mandated to assure quantity of services provided in a qualitative manner, you will seldom be able to consider each worker and client as the service unit of highest priority. In your middle-range position, it will be important to recognize that each program area is competing for resources that are insufficient to maximize the need satisfaction in each worker-client situation. So, you probably will find yourself expecting action that reflects the best alternatives available within the reality of scarce resources. Such an approach to service delivery is conceptualized as *satisficing* (March and Simon, 1958), and when pursued with good professional judgment, it can be consistent with ethical principles for making choices.

While you are working to satisfy the demands of accountability and evaluation, your supervisees may confront you with feelings that you have *sold out* to the administration. These feelings may be a response to your efforts at focusing their attention on accountability to the agency, its goals, and resource allocations. Most likely, these feelings will be related to performance reviews of their service delivery—a method of ensuring accountability to the agency. As a supervisor, you will need to use your influence to help supervisees recognize that both quantity and quality are necessary social service realities and that satisficing is a viable approach to balancing these concerns. In addition, it will be important for you to demonstrate sensitivity to supervisee concerns by emphasizing both effective and ineffective areas of performance. You can point out that evaluating performance through recognition of strengths and limitations is similar to the processes involved in planning. Both these processes (supervisory performance evaluations and client assessments) involve drawing on strengths in working on limitations, as well as developing mutually agreed-on action plans to foster change or improvement. Such an approach is one means of earning supervisee support and legitimation of your authority in this area. Then, evaluation can be connected to accountability in terms of individual performance (process) within the context of agency expectations. In addition, you and your supervisees will be able to relate their performance to behavioral and attitudinal changes in clients served by the program (product). This approach to accountability and evaluation approximates the demonstration of accountability that is expected by higher-level administrators and the general public.

## AGENCY POLITICS AND ORGANIZATIONAL DYNAMICS

Successfully managing the transitional issues previously identified probably will require that you, as a new supervisor, come to grips with the realities of agency politics and organizational dynamics. You may have to direct your efforts to dealing with two sources of tension that are related to these realities. One source of tension is uncertainty about how to deal with the limits on the open sharing of ideas among supervisory peers. As a worker, you probably valued sharing ideas as one approach to stimulating your own thinking and the thinking of others about practice issues. As a new supervisor, you will often face the possibility that others may take ideas you share openly and use them to their own advantage. Also, you will be expected to keep organizationally sensitive issues confidential. A second potential source of tension is the recognition that as a supervisor, you will now be accountable not only for your own performance, but for that of a whole group of supervisees as well. As a worker, you probably concentrated on your own performance and its impact on clients and assumed that others would do the same in accordance with professional standards. As a supervisor, you will likely be challenged to demonstrate your ability to produce and to motivate your supervisees to produce valued results. You will need to respond to this challenge if you are to protect benefits for your supervisees and enhance those benefits. In addition, your responses will be an important determinant of whether higher-ups recognize you as a supervisor who gets results.

In order to deal with these tensions, it will be important for you to examine the system from your superiors' perspectives. This will involve familiarizing yourself with agency operations, including: who makes what kinds of decisions; who are the informal leaders; what is the agency's philosophy about service; and what are the existing linkages to the community power structure and to client-advocacy groups. Also, you will probably benefit from spending some of your initial time on the job analyzing your role in the complex network of personal, program, and administrative relationships. This will include identifying similarities and differences in expectations for your behavior by supervisees, supervisory peers, your immediate supervisor, and top-level administrators. Further, you will want to compare and contrast your assignments and the assignments of other supervisors within your program area, as well as in other program areas in the agency. Identifying who relies on you and whom you can rely on will be important as well. Learning the system will help you establish your professional and agency identity as a supervisor.

Establishing your supervisory perspective and identity can be facilitated by accepting what you do not know or understand as a challenge, not a deficit. Accepting the challenge is the first step toward deliberately increasing your knowledge of political and organizational issues that are new to you. This will involve conscious effort to restructure your thinking from the individual case, the particular, to thinking of wholes and patterns. Thinking in this new way will help you in analyzing the networks around you in which you are a participant. Sharpening your ability to anticipate future trends will be useful when you must think about alternatives so that you are ready no matter what occurs. Anticipatory thinking will help you develop a mental set on likely variations in formal and informal system responses to agency issues. For example, which individuals, groups, departments, programs are open to and supportive of creativity and innovation? Are there persons, groups, departments, or programs that oppose any idea that might require rigid adherence to rules and regulations? How closely do others monitor your day-to-day activities and those of your supervisees? Considering the agency as an organized political system will probably lead to recognition of opportunities you might have to take advantage of degrees of freedom within the rules, regulations, and politics of the agency and community. Asserting your professional self as a supervisor will enable you to surmount the many transitional issues you face and will strengthen your chances for success in dealing with agency politics and organizational dynamics.

## CONCLUSION

As we have seen, moving from worker to supervisor will open up a totally new dimension of organizational life to you, will pose different demands and rewards, new tasks and skills. We believe the supervisor-worker relationship is where the influence of organizational authority and professional identity collide, collude, or connect. It is of great consequence that you gain the know-how and optimism to carry out an enlightened role performance, whether as supervisor or supervisee. As supervisor, there is great opportunity as a third party, standing midway between administrator and workers, to make the organization a more effective and exciting place to work. Even as a supervisee, it is possible to work strategically from the lower position in the administrator-supervisor-worker trinity. Now, whether you are a supervisor looking at the administrator-*supervisor*-worker unit or a supervisee looking at the supervisor-*supervisee*-client unit, you should enlarge this picture by adding the *context. Your unit of attention remains a foursome.* With this additional perspective, you can start thinking of new possibilities as supervisor; and as supervisee, you can learn how to survive despite the vagaries and vicissitudes of an incompetent supervisor—a critical skill in and of itself.

The literature of the profession suggests that future development rests on role definitions in the human services field, on the way organizational contexts are structured to manage the services, and on the creativity necessary to mesh one's knowledge with the imperatives of service (Hanlan, 1972; Dinerman, 1975; Washington, 1978; Skidmore, 1978; Austin, 1981). Many M.S.W.s have assumed positions as administrators, supervisors, or consultants within two years of graduation (Kadushin, 1976). We believe it is crucial to think about supervision as you consider the task of social work, to anticipate and plan ahead. Career trails are unclear these days: workers become supervisors and supervisors become workers again with alarming speed as organizations shift and change in line with the tumultuous times.

We think persons should have more control over their lives. Typically, this attitude is focused more toward homelife and leisure time than work life. And yet, work life consumes a third of our lives. We shall aim to eliminate the separation between control in homelife and control in work life from a belief that one need not submerge those well-developed habits of decision making and judgment simply because jobs include an accountability hierarchy. We shall seek ways to enhance active participation for supervisor and worker enroute toward encouraging involvement rather than apathy. This, after all, is what the workplace and staff members need.

Picturing supervision and yourself as supervisor will require you to extend your thinking in threes and fours into the broader context of social work practice. As a primarily agency-based profession, social work is and has been subject to shifting forces in the broader social, cultural, political, and economic environment. In your efforts to gain for yourself and your supervisees greater control over your practice and the workplace, you will need to develop conscious, deliberate means for influencing, as well as responding to, the ebb and flow of diverse forces internal and external to the organization. In Chapter 4 we shall further elaborate the picture of supervision, with specific reference to issues confronting supervisors and supervisees.

## REFERENCES

AUSTIN, MICHAEL J., *Supervisory Management for the Human Services*. Englewood Cliffs, N.J.: Prentice-Hall, 1981.

DINERMAN, MIRIAM, "Options in Social Work Manpower and Education," *Social Work*, 20, no. 5 (September 1975), 348–352.

EPSTEIN, IRWIN, ANDREA SAVAGE-ABRAMOVITZ, and HAROLD WEISSMAN, "Training 'Clinician Managers' in Community Mental Health Settings: A Progress Report," *Social Work Education Reporter*, 30, no. 1 (January 1982), 10–15.

EWALT, PATRICIA L., "From Clinician to Manager," *New Directions for Mental Health Services*, 8 (1980), 1–9.

GOLAN, NAOMI, "Building Competence in Transitional and Crisis Situations," in *Promoting Competence in Clients: A New/Old Approach to Social Work Practice*, Anthony N. Maluccio, ed. New York: The Free Press, 1981.

HANLAN, ARCHIE, "Changing Functions and Structures," in *Issues in Human Services*, Florence W. Kaslow and Associates. San Francisco: Jossey-Bass, 1972, 39–50.

HOLLOWAY, STEPHEN, "Up the Hierarchy: From Clinician to Administrator," *Administration in Social Work*, 4, no. 4 (Winter 1980), 1–14.

JANTSCH, ERICH, *Design for Evolution: Self-Organization and Planning in the Life of Human Systems*. New York: George Braziller, 1975.

KADUSHIN, ALFRED, *Supervision in Social Work*. New York: Columbia University Press, 1976.

MARCH, JAMES G., and HERBERT A. SIMON, *Organizations*. New York: John Wiley, 1958.

PASCALE, RICHARD T., and ANTHONY G. ATHOS, *The Art of Japanese Management*. New York: Simon & Schuster, 1981.

PATTI, RINO, ELENORE DIEDRECK, DENNIS OLSON, and JILL CROWELL, "From Direct Service to Administration: A Study of Social Workers' Transitions from Clinical to Management Roles. Part I: Analysis," *Administration in Social Work*, 3, no. 2 (Summer 1979), 131–151. (a)

————, "From Direct Service to Administration: A Study of Social Workers' Transitions from Clinical to Management Roles. Part II: Recommendations," *Administration in Social Work*, 3, no. 3 (Fall 1979), 265–275. (b)

PATTI, RINO, and MICHAEL J. AUSTIN, "Socializing the Direct Service Practitioner in the Ways of Supervisory Management," *Administration in Social Work*, 1, no. 3 (Fall 1977), 267–280.

SCURFIELD, RAYMOND M., "Clinician to Administrator: Difficult Role Transition?" *Social Work*, 26, no. 6 (November 1981), 495–501.

SKIDMORE, REX A., "Administration Content for All Social Work Graduate Students," *Administration in Social Work*, 2, no. 1 (Spring 1978), 59–73.

WASHINGTON, ROBERT O., "Social Work in the Future and Implications for Social Work Education," *California Sociologist*, 1, no. 2 (Summer 1978), 193–204.

# CHAPTER FOUR
# THE PROFESSIONAL
# IN THE ORGANIZATION

## INTRODUCTION

We believe our society has developed a set of institutionalized responses to conditions that threaten the realization of human potential for various population groups. This network of institutions is described and defined as the welfare state (Schottland, 1967; Wilensky and Lebeaux, 1965). Welfare, in this sense, is a broad term covering more than the public, stereotypic concept of welfare as income assistance. The welfare state construct is based on principles derived from a belief that society has a public responsibility to provide for the well-being of its citizens. Commitment to this belief is reflected in public education, the Social Security system, housing, medical care, environmental protection, income transfer programs (e.g., AFDC, veterans' benefits), and personal social services (e.g., mental health, day care) (Rein, 1970; Kahn, 1973). While acknowledging these welfare state commitments, it is imperative that social workers be consciously aware of persisting challenges to these commitments: fluctuating support for taxation to finance these commitments; competing vested interests seeking to establish their programs as the highest priority; reluctance to accept the redistribution and reallocation of resources to narrow the gap between the "haves" and "have-nots"; bureaucratic inertia that is criticized by both the public and consumer groups; and limited use of a future "forecasting" perspective in planning and implementing policies to ensure that programs actually achieve the expected goals (Galper, 1973; Wilensky and Lebeaux, 1965).

## COMMUNITY MANDATE

The legitimacy of the helping professions, and of the programs and services they manage and deliver, stems from a public sanction or mandate. This mandate is evident several ways: in licensure and regulation of professions; in state or local government approval of incorporation articles for private and public nonprofit organizations; and in federal, state, and local legislation that determines social policies for organizing and delivering services. These mandates reflect a set of value-based commitments to structures, programs, and services to which and for which social service organizations and human service professionals are accountable.

The community mandate is comprised of four components:

1. The competent supervisor
2. A responsive provision of service
3. A dynamic organization
4. A context

We shall describe each briefly and then return to them in depth to show that each of these four components involves a triad of concepts.

The *competent supervisor,* you, are central in fulfilling the community mandate. Competent supervisors have the opportunity to be major architects in making operational the commitments embodied in welfare state principles. They are usually the fulcrum on which demands for accountability in quality and quantity of services are balanced against competing needs and expectations of workers and clients. In this role, competent supervisors are compelled to use their "super-vision" to coordinate the work of self and others in promoting responsive provision, reinforcing the dynamic organization, and "seeing" the context for what it is—a field of forces with opportunities and constraints that can be influenced and used for positive purposes. Competent supervisors are persons who radiate and maintain a certain presence as professionals. This "presence" will be described in this chapter in terms of leadership, dignity, and wisdom.

*Responsive provision* is the basic delimiter of what we are about as professionals and what service organizations are expected to offer. Service provision is characterized by turbulence associated with the shifting waves of support, and with resistance in establishing national, regional, and local priorities for public policy. We are familiar with the battles for and against categorical and block grants, the pros and cons of public-sector versus private-sector responsibility, the obligations to national defense versus the obligations to social welfare ("guns or butter")— society's pendulum swings between entitlements to a certain quality of life, on the one hand, and social provisions as acts of charitable good will, on the other hand.

Given the inherent tension, conflict, and fluctuating priorities, responsive provision becomes a very delicate process for all involved. Responsive provision will be described in terms of resources, needs, and skills.

As one type of *dynamic organization,* social service agencies must satisfy certain functional requirements. They must provide services that are needed (goal orientation), demonstrate that these services have an impact (accountability orientation), and respond to strains in terms of what and how many services are necessary (constraint orientation). Thus, to fulfill the community mandate, to achieve goals that have a desirable impact, an organization must anticipate strains and be prepared to respond to them. We shall describe three elements that contribute to such an organization: stability, effectiveness, and adaptability.

*Context,* as we have said, surrounds every situation. Contextual factors that must be recognized by the competent, imaginative supervisor will be elaborated in greater detail in Chapter 6.

## THE COMPETENT SUPERVISOR

We start with the competent supervisor, the subject of this book, whose traits are leadership, dignity, and wisdom. To illustrate how these combine into competent and imaginative performance of supervisory work, we suggest that they determine *what* will be done and *why; how* it shall be done; and *what cautions* or *timing* will be factors. Leadership is the focus for imagining the purpose or mission of the supervisory task; in the process of supervision, leadership generates the excitement for the work and inspires others to pursue a goal, to meet the challenges and opportunities. Dignity concerns involvement with others in the sharing of supervisory purposes, and consideration for how others are treated as partners in the enterprise. Finally, wisdom has to do with the subtleties of timing and pacing, with what is deliberately not done, with what is sequenced for another day or avoided altogether. In combination, each component builds on the others into an orchestrated composition that is on target, considerate, and realistic.

It is, of course, usually better to illustrate with a positive rather than negative example to make one's point. But we shall take a risk and give an example of the utter opposite. Here is a recollection of one worker who was asked about a most memorable example of supervisory behavior:

> This was a large public facility and there were twenty of us workers. The agency was facing cutbacks and a reduction in staff had been hanging over everyone's head for months. Rumors and speculation abounded. Finally, the day came when the social workers were to hear from the department head just who was to be fired. We were gathered in a staff meeting. The department head's method? "You . . . you . . . you . . . and you. Don't show up for work after this week." To me it was obvious. This person's method was insensitive and, yes, even cruel.

Let us apply our analysis foursome to this situation:

1. *The me looking*—the worker who recalled this incident called the department head insensitive and cruel. Yes, this constitutes an obvious first impression of the event. However, perhaps the department head was overcome with other feelings: embarrassment? impotence? futility? anger at the bind? We can't be sure. Who was this person? male, female? age? and so forth. We don't know, but it is easy to be outraged in this situation.

2. *At it*—Several persons from a staff of twenty were given one week's notice, and in a curt manner. The situation was a public one. It was a one-way, directive communication. The waiting was over. Shock. Relief that it was someone else. Dismay. *Emotions*. Fear. Desperation.

3. *With its history*—This was not a surprise; it was expected for several months. It had been demoralizing and tension-producing. Yet there were hopes for avoidance and especially for self-preservation. When the news broke, it was swift and sudden.

4. *And its context*—The impetus came from outside the unit, from the economy of the state and from the national scene. It was not isolated as an event, but was tied up with the general economic system, with the political shifts at national policy level.

We can also examine this incident analytically to account for the lack of competence in the department head's action:

*Leadership*—The cutbacks were not in the staff's interest. Rather, they were in the system's interest, at least in terms of making do with the amount of resources available. Probably, they were not in the system's interest in terms of service delivery, although some systems might have more staff than necessary. More likely, the department head was merely reactive, not proactive. One cannot assume that leadership was exerted in this situation unless the department head had some say in deciding who left and who stayed.

*Dignity*—This process was an assault, a violation of the staff's dignity. Despite the painfulness of such announcements, there are more considerate ways of dealing with such a blow—for example, private conferences that include two-way communication, and a sharing with all staff of certain general information (criteria) concerning the method of making decisions on terminations. Most importantly, it would have helped to have some overt expression by the department head of personal feelings, discomfort, or whatever in this situation, and some acknowledgment of the difficulties for all involved.

*Wisdom*—Are there any wise ways to deal with firings and layoffs? We think so. These ways begin with hiring practices and are reinforced by periodic performance evaluations, by frequent communication between department head and staff as to the climate of the organization, and by development of openness and trust to the greatest possible extent (even in times of shrinking resources). In short, painful as terminations are, they may be tempered by the style and quality of the action, which include timing and setting. We turn now to think further about leadership. What exactly is it? How can we best determine its components and cultivate them?

### Leadership

The essence of leadership has been the subject of occasioned voluminous study. Understandably, many have pursued its "secrets," the knowing of which would have great practical value for executives and organizations. Diverse orientations and schools of thought can be identified. There is "the great man theory" (leaders are born, not made), which has resulted in the search for traits and attributes contributing to effective leadership (extraverted personalities, height, speaking ability, etc.). This approach began with identifying persons known to be great leaders and then studying their lives and general behavior with the hope of determining key leadership variables from their backgrounds. Despite disappointing findings in this tradition, it still lives. An example is, "The great manager is born; so much of him is instinctive" (Siu, 1982, p. 1).

Alternatively, a sociohistory approach to leadership held that "the times make the man." According to this line of thought, a great leader was that person who just happened to be in the right place at the right time. Leadership was a response to the situation, and attempts have been made periodically to explain the rise of a Lincoln, a Churchill, a Franklin D. Roosevelt, a Martin Luther King in these terms. Leadership as a response to situational variables has been one of the aspects studied by those interested in small-group behavior. In these studies, the qualities important for leadership were found to vary, depending on the task and the situation. Such small-group studies concerned who was in the central position, who controlled the communication, who embodied the group values, and so forth (Stogdill, 1974).

Probably the earliest leadership study in small groups was the pioneering action-research of Lewin, Lippitt, and White in various leader styles: democratic, autocratic, and laissez faire (1939). While these terms suggested the effects of each style on group productivity and the consequences of various leader behaviors, they did not deal with what qualities are needed to earn a position of leadership. Other important small-group studies, in the human relations tradition, were undertaken by Bales and associates and may be thought of as a functional approach to leadership (1950). Here, leadership was attributed to the person(s) who performed the requisite tasks for the group's survival. The work was done with a leaderless group, and the object was to determine who would become a leader. Findings reveal that there need not be "a" leader, merely various persons doing the tasks required by a group. In any group a balance between task behavior and maintenance behavior was needed. What was important was that both kinds of functions be performed, even though they could be performed by different persons.

*Leadership in organizations.* From these beginnings in small-group study, leadership theory and research moved to broader organizational settings. Focusing on the leader, researchers abandoned an emphasis on leader traits in favor of interest in the behaviors or actions that leaders typically used in doing their jobs. This approach yielded two behavioral clusters: consideration (e.g., being accessible, treating workers as equals, explaining one's actions) and initiating structure (e.g., scheduling the work, criticizing poor work, insisting on working at full capacity) (Stogdill and Coons, 1957). Other studies refined the general behavioral clusters and conditions for satisfaction (Halprin and Winer, 1957; House, 1971) and specified key behavioral dimensions of support, interaction facilitation, goal emphasis, and work facilitation (Bowers and Seashore, 1966). Filley described three types of leaders, and the organizations these leaders would be part of: the craft type, the promoter, and the administrative leader (1978). The first two types lead largely through their personality and the third via a set of learned skills.

These studies are instructive as we think about the leadership component of supervision, but they must be approached with caution and tentativeness on three counts: (1) semantic confusion (i.e., leadership versus managership), (2) the problem of generalizing from corporations to social agencies, and (3) the uniqueness of the social work supervisory tradition and method. We shall explain briefly each of these issues.

*Semantics*—The studies indiscriminately mix leadership and managership—a distinction we aim to make in our consideration of leadership. While most of these studies claim to deal with leadership, they actually deal with managerial behaviors. As we shall explain, we see both leadership and managership as important orientations for the social work supervisor. We shall deal with leadership in this chapter and with managerial skills as a component of "administering," one of nine functions of a supervisor (see Chapter 5).

*Organizational context*—The organizational leadership theory and research was based mainly in the corporate, for-profit sector, not in the nonprofit, public organization. We would need to question the wholesale applicability of such findings to those organizations that have typically been the home for social work and its supervision. Social work has been offered primarily under nonprofit, public auspices described as "ambiguous performance environments" (Davis, 1979) and "scarcity situations" with values and assumptions that attend such circumstances (Das, 1981).

*Social work's unique supervisory tradition*—We are cautious about generalizing from broad organizational studies to social work because of the unique, historic patterns of supervisory tradition and the method of social work supervision. We see this historical phenomenon as having no exact historical counterpart in other organizations. We see the intensive, one-to-one supervisory pattern, spawned mainly within the private-agency sector, as enormously influential in the profession's supervisory theory development and its literature. This has no close comparable role elsewhere (e.g., a middle-management person concerned equally with accountability matters and teaching/learning issues).

With these three special concerns in mind, we will consider the extensive organizational leadership research conducted since World War II. All such research can be assigned to one of two camps: (1) the *one-best-style* viewpoint, and (2) the *it-all-depends* perspective. Curiously, each approach considers two variables—the task to be accomplished (also known as output, production, etc.) and the person element (worker satisfaction, consideration). Both orientations view leadership as some mixture of these two variables and as residing neither within a person nor in a situation exclusively. But here the commonality ends: The one-best-style school of thought holds that there is a best style that can be used across diverse situations, while the situationalists see leadership as controlled by the situation, with no one style suitable for all situations.

The one-best-style approach is exemplified in the work of McGregor (1960) and Argyris (1975), who argue for Theory X or Y and Model I or II, respectively; in Likert's Systems 1 through 4 (1967); and in Blake and Mouton's 9, 9 managerial-grid (1981). The situationalist approach is represented by Fleishman (1953), Fiedler (1967), Hersey and Blanchard (1977; 1982), and Reddin (1970). These theorists propose that different forms of leadership are contingent on different situations, and they aim to fit the leadership approach to the situation. These two major divisions in the leadership literature make the situation muddy at best, but not unlike similar controversies among personality or learning theorists. According to Blake and Mouton (1981), the differences are highlighted by the treatment of the major variables—task concerns and person concerns. That is, when the variables are treated as independent of one another and additive to one another, a high degree of both components would lead to high direction and high reward for compliance—a paternalism or maternalism. When they are treated as interdependent, as in Blake and Mouton's managerial-grid approach, the high degree of each component is seen as a compound of shared responsibility between leader and others, or teamwork. Clearly, two approaches that rest on a high degree of concern for task and person, yet that lead to two different leadership outcomes—teamwork versus paternalism—seem indeed incompatible. Yet, as Hersey and Blanchard counter, Blake and Mouton are examining attitudes—feelings or predispositions toward or against doing something. This is different from actual, observed behavior. "Situational Leadership describes how people behave while the Managerial Grid appears to describe attitudes or predispositions toward production and people" (Hersey and Blanchard, 1982, p. 207). We would suggest that the approaches to managerial (leadership) style are contradictory at best.

*Leadership in social work supervision.*    Considering the differences (and confusions) in leadership theory and research, the distinctions between private and public service organizations, and the uniqueness of social work's supervisory mechanism, we feel comfortable in offering our own line of thought about the leadership component needed for competent supervision. Zalesnik (1977) described leaders and managers as distinctly different persons, a viewpoint we partially share. Still we think that knowledge of each orientation can help persons nurture the underdeveloped side of themselves. Leaders are lonely persons who are active in relation to goals. They shape ideas rather than respond to them. They change the way people think about what is desirable, possible, and necessary. Leaders work to extend choices, develop fresh approaches, open issues for new options, project ideas into images that excite others. They create excitement in the workplace and seek out risk and danger, especially where the opportunities and rewards seem high. They are concerned with ideas, but not details, and with what the events and decisions mean to others. Leaders are goal-oriented and visionary. They establish missions, tolerate ambiguity, and are concerned with the future where clarity is not possible and events are unpredictable. Leaders see problems as opportunities for turning failures into successes. They inspire others, attempt to produce change and even encourage and provoke change.

Managers emphasize rationality and control. They are problem solvers, essentially, and excel in persistence and hard work. They are tough-minded, analytic, and tolerant of diversity. Managers seek consensus, good will, and agreement. They see the job as an enabling process that involves combining persons and their ideas through the skilled management of the interaction. The manager develops strategies and makes decisions to help the process along via the skills of negotiating and bargaining, coordinating and balancing, as well as rewarding and punishing. They act to limit choices and are concerned with how things get done, with relating to people in accordance with their roles. Managers like working with people, but want to survive more than take risks (Zalesnik, 1977). They are results-oriented; they accept the missions and determine how to accomplish them. They strive for order and coherence, try to keep the everyday activities in order, hate vagueness or tentativeness, try to correct failures, depend on systems, and make these systems work. They attempt to adjust to change when change seems necessary, but they also may see change as a threat to the smooth functioning of the organization, to the well-managed routine.

The distinction between leadership and managerial styles is not trivial. These two concepts have been used interchangeably in both the general organizational literature and in social work supervision texts as well. The confusion and mixing of these entities is more than a semantic quibble. Just as painters are not necessarily artists, managers are not necessarily leaders. The literature has emphasized managerial knowledge and skills, not the fine points of leadership. The rational methods of solving problems are fairly easy to teach and describe; it is quite another matter to teach persons how to select the best goals or to find the ways around organizational obstacles, or to juggle the stresses and strains of a real-life impasse. The orderly, rational elements of organizational work—with their elements to be identified and serially attended to—can easily be taught as skills to master and techniques to be known; the innovative aspects of organizational work are more difficult to lay bare.

We see leadership as a qualitative dimension intimately related to the person of the supervisor. Perhaps in this sense, we align with those who have considered leadership a trait, gift, intuition, and so forth. It is a part of the greatness, mystery, and charisma of certain persons whose very way of being encourages others to want to follow their ideas and ways. Leadership has to do with visualizing ultimate purpose and meaning, with imagining the *what ifs,* with raising awareness of values, with questioning the mundane, and with inspiring others to do the same.

As a noteworthy example of leadership, Harry Hopkins comes to mind. Close adviser and innovator of Roosevelt's New Deal, social worker Hopkins was described as follows in a *Time* story about Roosevelt's centennial:

> . . . perhaps the most remarkable of all the New Dealers . . . a gangling and often brusque idealist . . . Born to poverty as the son of an Iowa harness-maker, Hopkins had worked one summer among the slum children of New York City's Lower East Side, and . . . spreading money among the poor became Hopkin's life passion. . . . Hopkins violated the rules that most Americans had learned in childhood: that taking charity was shameful; that unemployment was shameful; that a man who couldn't feed himself and his family was hardly a man at all. "People don't eat in the long run, Senator," he said to one legislator, "they eat every day." By nightfall of Hopkins' second day as Federal Relief Administrator, he had telegraphed seven Governors and arranged more than $5 million in emergency grants. He hired the unemployed for the winter in all kinds of part-time jobs that needed doing, such as repairing roads or teaching the illiterate. (Friedrich, 1982, pp. 24–25)

Both leadership and managership are important for the supervisor. Both need to be understood and cultivated. We shall try to identify both aspects in this book. We do admit that we hope to accent the qualities and cultivation part of leadership more than the more technical elements of managership. Conceptually, when we picture the competent supervisor, leadership is one among three crucial elements (leadership, dignity, and wisdom). On the other hand, managership (a key element in administering) is only one of nine functions discussed as crucial to the supervisory role. This says something about our value orientation.

Before we go further, we must alert you to the fact that already in Chapter 2 you were involved in matters of managerial behavior and leadership thinking. We ask that you refer back to Appendix E, *Your Working Style,* and reread the questions and profiles of the accommodator, morale builder, negotiator, task master, and collaborator. Hopefully, these now take on more meaning, for they are descriptions that apply to the managerial component of the supervisory job. Now review Appendix C, *Current Profile,* and its components. Recall that this deals with creativity and imagination, and with field-dependent or independent ways of processing information. This instrument, we suggest, has a greater connection with leadership mentality. Thinking about the two instruments further may help you gain more understanding about elements of management and leadership.

We think supervisors are both leaders and managers—both leadership and managership are possibilities that supervisors may cultivate, if they conceptualize the differences and nourish, even value, both aspects in themselves. In fact, the two elements may balance each other. Too much leadership (idealism) may be tamed by the managerial self; too much managership may be enlivened by allowing leader impulses to gain expression. We do not reserve leadership for the one or the few persons at the top of the organization. In fact, part of our aim is to decentralize some of the top-of-organization mentality down through the ranks, so that many are moved to see themselves as imaginative thinkers and actors—as leaders—in the workplace. We do not believe too many cooks spoil the broth, especially if they all notice what each one is doing. Rather, we think that many involved cooks watching the pot will result in a tastier meal—that this will yield zestful, spicy results through a variety of inputs.

We believe that leadership potential exists in every supervisor and that it only needs cultivation. We believe this leadership is important to cultivate because the workplace is a place of people. In this context, the supervisor's thinking is involved in the intuitive, the empathic, the emotion-laden and turbulent, the intense and sometimes disorderly struggles of individuals. It goes against a mentality of rationality and control. It is the part of the supervisor that others may love and hate, may wish to identify with, may feel intensely about. It is the part that is a powerful influence on the thoughts and actions of others, a power that makes workers want to follow the supervisor's lead. Such charismatic leadership does not result merely from the position-power of the role. More nearly, to use Burns's distinctions, it is a *transforming* and not a *transactional* leadership (1978, p. 4). This transforming type of leadership "looks for potential motives in followers, seeks to satisfy higher needs, and engages the full person of the follower [in] a relationship of mutual stimulation and elevation that converts followers into leaders" (p. 4). The more prevalent kind of leadership, transactional leadership, is rooted in exchanges between the supervisor and worker—for example, favorable evaluation for compliance —and not the stimulation of a new venturesome self. The leadership component of competent, imaginative supervision is this potentially transforming leadership that entices others around the person to see and use their inherent leadership qualities also.

### Dignity

Dignity, a second key element of supervisory competence, highlights social work's historic commitment to people and causes. The profession has a heavy ideological base and a tradition concerned with values—that is, with what is good and just for persons and for society. Dignity is a value; its pursuit and preservation are ethical imperatives. The dignity of the individual is expressed in the preamble to the NASW's Code of Ethics. It was acknowledged emphatically in Miller's review of social work's value dilemmas, "above all, our business is with dignity" (1968, p. 33). *Toward Human Dignity* headlined the 5th NASW Professional Symposium (Hanks, 1978). Indeed, no value is so central, so nonnegotiable for social workers as dignity. The dignity of the individual has served throughout the profession's history as a buzzword that signified what we are to be about and how we should approach clients—that is, with respect for their inherent worth despite possible differences from personal or societal norms and preferences.

Yet relatively little attention has been accorded the dignity concept when the worker, not the client, is concerned. The dignity of the individual has not been a paramount consideration with respect to social workers themselves nor to the tasks of social work. We believe it is important that the worker's inherent dignity be respected and nurtured for two reasons: (1) It is a rational and coherent approach to service delivery. It seems hardly possible that workers can convey a spirit of dignity to clients if they are at the same time experiencing personal indignity themselves. (2) It is a moral imperative. Consideration of the worker's inherent dignity will suggest a set of ethical actions that supervisors should follow.

It is all too easy to assume that the dignity of the social worker is accorded prominence. In reality, the hurly-burly of workaday organization life with tasks to accomplish, deadlines to meet, conflicts to resolve, and decisions to make, often relegates ordinary dignity to the status of a luxurious amenity that would be nice to have were there only enough time! It is this lack of dignity that Beck described as "the dehumanization of the human services (using) measures of a morally bankrupt management technology" (1978, p. 11). To experience these issues more fully, we suggest you turn to Appendix A, Chapter 4, For Further Thought and Action . . . , and look at item 7, which deals with dignity.

Indeed, the very dignity of social work as a profession is at stake today. As if the profession were responsible for social policy and program failures, for the political and economic life and strife of the times, social work's image has been scapegoated and diminished along with "the liberals" and others alarmed with the ill-fare of society. Social workers have championed the rights of the oppressed, advocated justice and equity for all, aligned themselves with unpopular causes and populations that others might prefer to ignore. They have contended with an unpopular image through most of their profession's history. This has been the case whether in interdisciplinary team meetings, or in professional and organizational infights, or at national social policy levels where programs and people-based planning are shuffled about as if they had a contagious disease.

What is dignity? It is a mindset that comes from within despite external circumstances. It is easier to feel your own innate dignity when others look upon you as one who has dignity. But you can have dignity despite others' valuation. Remember Charlie Chaplin's little tramp? He had dignity. He was the little guy: weak, nervous, poor, alone. But he managed to rise above adversity and to give his superiors their licks without denying or disguising his own frailties. The little tramp sustained a jaunty air of self-assurance despite his dilemmas—nothing destroyed his innate dignity.

There are other examples. Frankl dealt with instances of human dignity despite the horrors of concentration camp life. Such dignity involved the ability to choose a particular attitude despite a given set of circumstances, to preserve a vestige of spiritual freedom and independence of mind, and to make a decision about personal, mental, and spiritual states (1963). Perske formulated an approach to the developmentally disabled described as "the dignity of risk" (1972). By this he meant that living involves risking and acting with courage; offering only safety, shelter, and protection is an affront to one's dignity—it is an indignity. We think of the dignity of a seventy-three year old black woman confined in a state mental hospital for over fifty years. The social worker who connected with her worthiness and finally arranged for her moving out of the hospital recalls:

"She looked like a queen with her long silver hair arranged in a coronet. She fought to keep it from being cut in the institutional bowl style and managed to style it herself without tools. She made hand-stitched ruffles for her collars and cuffs from the old sheets. She dressed in the style of an elegant lady of the early 1900s, sat straight and erect, looked you in the eye, refused to conform, and radiated dignity.*

Dignity has many forms, but it has certain key aspects. It is freedom from inferiority, acceptance of self, acceptance of one's own imperfections without needing to deny them. It involves the ability to risk, choose, use personal initiative, and take a chance. At the client level, dignity has to do with a belief in self-determination, deciding and making choices in your own behalf. At the worker level, it has to do with involvement and participation in matters that affect your work life. According to Rosow,

> The majority of American workers indicate that they consider it their right to participate in decisions that affect them directly on the job. To advance human dignity at the workplace in the public sector, it is important to turn attention to the options for greater employee participation. (1979, p. 13)

It is the dignity issue that lies at the core of the popularity of Quality Circles, an approach to line-worker decision making and participatory management imported from Japan that is now sweeping through American corporate life (Middleman, 1982). Personal dignity is related intimately to the essence of all professions (for example, to freedom for professionals to follow their own discretion and judgment in practice decisions as contrasted with merely following a set of rules; and to the insistence within the profession that ethical and competence issues be monitored through peer review, for the profession's self-determination).

Supervisors who are concerned with worker dignity need to find opportunities for greater worker participation in what happens, to accept the workers' contributions and activity once they are involved, and to encourage self-directed work. To view others' achievement as evidence of your own and to become satisfied, even excited by this, you must often change your own mindset. Competent supervisors radiate dignity and accord it to those around them. They allow others the freedom to learn from their own mistakes. This takes subtle, seasoned judgment. How do you protect the organization from serious mistakes and yet allow workers the opportunity to develop out of their own trial-and-error learning? How do you protect client interest and preserve worker freedom to learn at the same time? Implied here are qualitative judgments that supervisors must make out of their own sense of respect for others and belief in their dignity and responsible judgment. It is a matter for supervisory competence and imagination, for considerate and ethical judgment.

Lewis connects dignity with ethical behavior.

---

*Personal correspondence from Caroline Mayes.

One can fail in almost any aspect of administrative judgment and yet retain self-respect. But failure to engage in ethical behavior is to yield to unprincipled practice, and unprincipled practice erodes an administrator's core of personal dignity. (Lewis, 1977, p. 121)

Dignity has to do with what is the right thing to do, whether or not this is practical or good for the organization. A dignity ideal values actions that enhance others and show consideration for them, a quality of concern for them and their very being. Dignity is enhanced by, but is not dependent on, an environment or circumstance that nourishes it; it can exist despite dehumanizing circumstances.

Honoring the injunction to respect others' dignity has special importance in social work because of the power differentials involved. Workers hold power over clients. Clients rarely have a chance to "shop" for a competitive service more to their liking. Also, supervisors hold power over workers, while administrators hold power over supervisors. All are fairly "locked into" their organization with its services, where alternatives, options, and choices are in short supply. Levy details various issues calling for ethical decision making by supervisors because of the relatively disadvantaged position of supervisees (Levy, 1973)—that is, calling for what is right to do and not necessarily what is efficient or most practical (see Note 1).

### Wisdom

Wisdom is the third important attribute of supervisory competence. It is a concept rarely encountered in the literature of the profession. We do, of course, find the notion *practice wisdom* occasionally. But when this is invoked, it is often used apologetically, perhaps proudly. It acknowledges the experience-rich persons who work skillfully despite a lack of formal professional education, or intuitive persons who operate effectively, but are unable to conceptualize or convey to others exactly what they do or why they do a particular thing. These are persons who have developed "the smarts" in their own idiosyncratic ways. Practice wisdom is a respectable kind of know-how; it is not what we have in mind by wisdom. We use wisdom in its more classic sense—a special sagelike kind of knowledge. It is akin to King Solomon's judgment that threatening to cut a baby in half would reveal the true mother, since she would give up the baby rather than allow it to be killed. We may approach the sense of this kind of wisdom through Reynold's discussion of the development of the new teacher in a chapter aptly titled "Subject Matter in its Place" (1942/1965; see Note 2).

The "wise" supervisors approach wisdom when they can put the system's work in its place and seek the point of living contact between each supervisee and the agency goals. Such supervisors know how to keep preoccupation with outcomes from getting in the way of working through others. They have outlived the stage of "supervisor knows best" and the irresistible need to control the work of the unit. While they may know well what needs to be done and how it should probably be done, their real work is scarcely begun until they discover the joy of developing others' curiosity and capacity to have impact.

We believe that wisdom entails a commitment to ongoing professional development, both personally and as a staff. This commitment can be demonstrated in word and deed. It has to do with an attitude of being a continuous learner, a student of the rich fabric that is social work. It implies openness to new ideas and learning opportunities, to your finding room for such stimuli and taking advantage of them, as well as to your encouraging others toward such pursuits. Standing for the importance of continuous refurbishing of personal knowledge and skills—for ongoing professional development—is a necessary but insufficient condition for wisdom.

Wisdom is more elusive and subtler than mere questing for knowledge. It suggests reliability, having the good track record, being someone that others can count on. It means being "well-seasoned." Wisdom is experience. It is the ability to know a variety of possible outcomes before plunging into any one action, to call on past experience and possibly to predict chances for possible ideas or actions. It has to do with an experience perspective; with a reflectiveness about the newest fads; and with a fair amount of cautiousness and respect for what has been tried in the past, plus imaginative curiosity that allows innovation as opposed to rigidity. Wisdom includes knowing and coming to terms with the profession's roots. This special knowledge includes a professional sense of meaning, as well as the ability and the courage to play the odds well.

This kind of wisdom also involves cultivating a mindset that is prepared to entertain the unknown—a new, perhaps alien idea or experience—a mentality of "planned emptiness" (Middleman, 1979), of openness in perception that entertains rather than dismisses the unfamiliar. This orientation includes an attitude of anticipation and tentativeness that features a provisional assessment of data that may be disordered and incoherent. Involved here is a pivotal readiness for this open perception, as well as the skills of planning that will allow for enjoyment in preparing for contingencies. Such pivotal anticipatory readiness suggests valuing flexibility while maintaining a generalized, poised concern for such tasks as getting information, communicating, seeking feedback about your impact, keeping options open, looking ahead, living with ambiguity, and realizing in advance that you may fail to meet your objectives in some situations, and yet not feeling personally inadequate.

Wisdom, according to Bateson (1980), involves a search for the regularities or "laws" that bind ideas together, and it requires an awareness, beyond the particular ideas in and of themselves, of the relationships among the ideas and between the ideas and yourself. Such wisdom understands the structures of knowledge and its changeable particulars. Yet the wise person will not become disoriented.

Wise persons are sensitive to nuance, to shades and subtlety. They reflect on the accumulation of many experiences against which any given hunch or trial can be evaluated mentally. Some of the special flavor of wisdom is conveyed in Pascale and Athos's discussion of Japanese management approaches. The day-to-day experiences are regarded as an important learning laboratory for acquiring wisdom. These everyday experiences are valued more than the formal, substantive learning of the business school. The Japanese value long, experience-rich careers that feature a slow climb up the company ladder, a process that engenders a long-term, whole-organization perspective. They also value a thoughtful, gradual approach to achieving change—that is, an outflanking of organizational obstacles, rather than a head-on attack. Instead of "using dynamite," they aim to trace a way around the obstacle with a light touch (1981, pp. 113-130).

We consider wisdom to be "quality knowing." It is knowing; knowing the limitations to what one knows, and knowing and valuing what others know. It also involves knowing what you knew in the past and how this has been rearranged, modified, and enlarged over time as new learnings enter your perspective or as earlier valued knowledge is ousted.

Our thinking about the connection of knowledge and wisdom is enriched by a consideration of Lewis's discussion of skill (along with knowledge, values, action and style). Style is the component that gives the enactment of skill its unique, individual, quality. Style distinguishes each person's particular stamp on an action. According to Lewis, style is characterized by its attractions: the beauty or lack of beauty of the product, simplicity, coherence, clarity, precision, balance, harmony, warmth and color of the human involvement. Style changes over time and is influenced by natural processes of maturation that alter it; yet it is also consistent, in that it is recognizable as a particular personal way of doing something (Lewis, 1976).

The wisdom component of competent supervision is qualitative. It has to do with the richness of personal experiences and the knowledge and skill of the supervisor in knowing how to place this elaborated experience at the service of others.

## RESPONSIVE PROVISION

We have noted the many challenges that influence the practice of the competent supervisor. The three elements that make up competent and imaginative supervisory performance are influenced by, and can influence, the nature of responsive provision as it is expressed at the agency level of service delivery. We will now turn to a consideration of the characteristics and dynamics of responsive provision—the second component of the community mandate—and to how these are interrelated with the dimensions of the competent supervisor.

The nature of service provision in the United States is a topic for continuous analysis, discussion, and debate. Regardless of ideological differences, there is general agreement that the essence of social welfare is "government-protected minimum standards of income, nutrition, health, housing, and education for every citizen, assured to him as a political right, not as charity" (Wilensky and Lebeaux, 1965, p. xii). We have chosen to incorporate these societal concerns under the umbrella of *responsive provision,* a historical imperative rooted in the Constitution's expression of concern for the general welfare. Speaking for the profession of social work, Charlotte Towle cast this as "the imperative of enlightened society to respond to 'common human needs'" (Towle, 1957, p. 1). We shall consider the processes and outcomes of the struggles over responsive provision as the background for our specific construction of this component of the community mandate.

## Shifting Forces Affecting Responsive Provision

As background for understanding the community mandate, it is necessary to consider various influences, three of which we highlight: historical cycles, political perspectives, and futurists' scenarios. Each of these forces has affected and continues to affect what the community thinks that organizations should be about.

*Historical cycles.* Public and private interest in the general welfare of all persons has involved cycles of activity that can be characterized as initiating and expanding, reacting and contracting, reflecting and regrouping, repeated over time. Various historical examples come to mind. In the mid-19th century, the advocacy of Dorothea Dix led to humanizing institutional provisions for the mentally ill by a number of states. This trend was countered by President Pierce's veto of proposed national legislation to mandate responsive provision of mental health care in all states. The veto was based on Pierce's opposition to any legislation that would transfer responsibility from states to the federal government (Dobelstein, 1980). This veto became a precedent that lasted until the federal initiatives under the New Deal of President Franklin D. Roosevelt. Similarly, within the settlement-house movement to meet needs of low-income persons and new immigrants (Addams, 1910/1961), the efforts of program initiators and service workers were later countered by restrictive immigration laws. This reactionary response was further reinforced by the Palmer raids on locations presumed to be the spawning grounds for immigrant anarchists (Leuchtenburg, 1958). More recently, during the same period that the Supreme Court approved hiring quotas to redress institutional racism, there was a retreat from court rulings giving priority to justice in juvenile proceedings (Axinn and Levin, 1982).

In sum, we have experienced cyclic pursuit of responsive provision characterized by initiative and expansion in the 1930s and 1960s and a mix of reaction and contraction and reflection and regrouping in the 1950s and 1970s. The pattern seems to vary by decades, with the exception of the 1940s, during which period the nation was primarily concerned with fighting World War II. If this pattern persists, we anticipate that the world economic crisis of the 1980s will produce a retreat from federal initiatives in favor of states' rights, voluntarism, and individual responsibility. Evidence of this is already apparent in President Reagan's proposal for a "New Federalism" (Gramlich and Laren, 1982). It would not be until the 1990s that we anticipate any reaffirmation of the imperatives of federal guarantees for essential levels of minimum provision responsive to the rights and needs of all citizens.

*Political perspectives.* Perspectives on responsive provision usually are associated with one of three major philosophies of political and social action—conservative, liberal, or radical (Galper, 1975; Longres, 1981; Dluhy, 1981). The conservative philosophy supports actions designed to recreate social arrangements of the past. It reflects commitments to returning to the *way things were*. With regard to responsive provision, conservatives believe that social problems are a consequence of individual failures, not of the limitations of social or governmental systems. Frequently, conservative initiatives focus on reducing the role of the federal government in guaranteeing responsive provision. Systems, institutions, and processes of daily living should not be tampered with, but when problems exist, individual responsibility for change in attitudes and behavior should be reinforced. So, in the face of structurally induced unemployment, affected individuals should take the initiative in developing new knowledge, skills, and career options that will make them employable once again.

A second philosophy, liberalism, has been dominant during most of the intervening years from the New Deal to the present. Those identifying with this philosophy support initiatives targeted at improving existing conditions to make them more positive for particular citizens or population groups. This viewpoint reflects commitments to *incremental reform*. The liberal approach to responsive provision is one of minor corrections to system imperfections that create social problems for people. To achieve the fine tuning of existing systems, it is assumed that the federal government has the responsibility to provide necessary guidelines and resources. A gradual incremental approach is adopted on the basis of a policy of minimizing any major disruption or major restructuring of existing systems, institutions, and processes. For example, to reduce the level of poverty among single-parent mothers, day-care programs should be provided that would enable these mothers to work.

Radical initiatives emphasize organizing and mobilizing collective action to alter social institutions or structures that are oppressive or inequitable. These initiatives reflect commitments to fundamental *reorganization* and *redistribution* of resources. Social problems are conceptualized as by-products of nonresponsive or malfunctioning systems. Radicals are critical of federal government initiatives in behalf of responsive provision, since they hold that the government primarily mirrors an economic system controlled by, and serving the interests of, the dominant classes. Restructuring systems, institutions, and processes of daily living is believed to be imperative if the society is to achieve equity and justice for all its members. For example, to overcome the problems of institutional sexism (e.g., higher pay for men than for women when both are doing the same work), women's consciousness-raising activities should be organized. Consciousness raising would be the first step in preparing women for political and economic activism.

*Futurists' scenarios.* Shifts in political and economic interests often coincide. Such shifts affect not only political and economic policies, but also the social policies that influence the social and psychological well-being of individuals and entire population groups. Several contemporary analyses of these shifts have forecast that the period between now and the beginning of the 21st century will be characterized by turbulence and uncertainty, conditions that will influence the imperatives for responsive provision. These shifts have been captured in three metaphors:

1. The "sea-changes" in demographics, technology, and economic productivity (Drucker, 1980)
2. The "third wave" of high technology and communications (e.g., microprocessors) and changed social arrangements (e.g., altered family structures and sex roles, the mutual support and self-help movements, the consumer movement), crashing against the "second wave" thinking born of the industrial revolution (Toffler, 1980)
3. The "world turned upside down," in which individuals search for self-fulfillment and deeper commitments to personal relationships and common survival, in contradiction to the older traditional ethic of self-denial and deferred gratification (Yankelovich, 1981).

Such dynamic metaphors are consistent with the processes of the kaleidoscopic world we discussed in Chapter 2. Such shifts on the currents of turbulent times mean that social workers must be even more vigilant in protecting and advocating for responsive provision (see Note 3). This is essential if the disadvantaged, powerless, and oppressed are to enter the mainstream and participate in the betterment of the human condition.

### The Supervisor's Place in Achieving Responsive Provision

As supervisor or supervisee, you will need to relate to the shifting imperatives of responsive provision by fulfilling your role—the provider—in the web of institutional arrangements that comprise the social services delivery system. Responsive provision—reflecting legislation, policies, regulations, and the activities of other organizations—is expressed through three basic elements: the service arranger, the service provider, and the client system (Savas, 1981).

The *service arranger* is the sponsor of the service. In this capacity, the arranger may assign the provider to the client or the client to the provider. Service arrangers can be a unit of government (local, state, or federal), a voluntary association, or the client system itself. *Service providers* deliver the services to clients. Providers can be governmental organizations, private organizations (voluntary associations, profit or nonprofit organizations), or in the case of self-help organizations, the clients themselves, as in Alcoholics Anonymous. *Client systems* are those who directly receive material benefits or social services. Clients can vary from individuals, groups, and neighborhoods, to specific target populations such as the poor, mentally retarded, minorities, elderly, and so forth.

As a member of the provider system, you will be directly affected by shifts in the policies, regulations, and financial allocations of the service arranger(s). The network of services in your community will expand and contract in number of services, types of program focus, and routes of access. These adjustments will influence the options available to you and your agency's clients in meeting needs. Your agency will be affected in at least three areas: target population(s), program goals, and methods of intervention. The consequences of these changes in arranger-provider priorities and commitments will challenge your imagination and competence. The challenge will be manifest in the ethical contradictions between valued, personal practice principles and impersonal, external determinations of amounts, types, and strategies of provision. A typical issue in this regard is routinization versus individualization of client services. For example, in a children's service within a mental health agency, you might have to contend with a requirement that all children referred from public schools be administered standardized intelligence and psychological tests, regardless of need. Many social work professionals have struggled valiantly to overcome the harmful, dehumanizing effects of a captor-captive system (Rhodes, 1979). These efforts have ranged from trying to minimize means tests for provision, to advocating for the least restrictive service arrangements for the disabled. They have pursued initiatives that would prevent us all from becoming "prisoners of benevolence" (Glasser, 1978). Yet the shifting political economy of responsive provision requires continual vigilance in analyzing and taking a stand on impending alterations in provision.

As a supervisor you will need to develop a framework for critical analysis that includes assessment of the impact of these alterations on clients, agencies, the social work profession, and the human conditions of the broader society (for examples of such frameworks see Longres, 1981; Cox, Ehrlich, Rothman, and Tropman, 1974). Recognizing your place in the scheme of responsive provision raises to conscious awareness the political realities that must be addressed in creating a more enlightened public concept of provision. Such awareness and critical analysis are necessary if we are to avoid the serious consequences of inattentiveness to the politics of services. Inattentiveness to the political realities of human services has frequently resulted in helping professionals who function as human managers (shufflers and controllers) rather than as responsive providers of human services (Wolfensberger, 1972). The development of social welfare programs has involved concern for the role and rule of government, what government may and may not do for its citizens. The challenge has been and continues to be one of designing and implementing social policies, programs, and services that are decent and caring without being coercive (Gaylin, 1978). We shall turn now to a focus on resources, needs, and skills as central supervisory concerns that affect responsive provision.

*Resources.* The United States is a heterogeneous society. Its cultural, religious, political, social, and economic belief systems frequently clash over issues of how to allocate resources in achieving the goals of social welfare systems. Resource provision and allocation is a reflection of the goals of the larger society for itself and of society's views of itself and its various members (Axinn and Levin, 1982). Three types of resources are involved: program, people, and strategy resources (Lauffer, 1979). Program resources are defined as the services and programs (cash, in-kind, noncash services) available to those in need. People resources include the availability and degrees of involvement of administrators, supervisors, direct service workers, volunteers, self-help groups, and social support systems in distribution of program resources. Strategy resources are defined as the means available for the development and implementation of program and people resources. Program-related strategy resources include money, facilities, equipment, and supplies. People resources include education and training, political influence, personal energy, professional status and expertise, and public support for the arrangers, providers, and clients. Decisions about these resources have implications for economic development, political organization, and social stability.

Traditionally, the United States has valued the private sector over the public, and individual choice over collective choice. It has resisted the redistribution of resources that is inherent in responsive social welfare provision (Galper, 1975; Dobelstein, 1980; Axinn and Levin, 1982). Often the argument has been that the use of resources for social welfare involves too great a cost. Here, cost is based not only on the absolute expenditures for social welfare, but also on the opportunity costs—resources used for social welfare that could be applied to some alternative production process, for example, defense spending (Gray and Gray, 1981). This concept of opportunity cost is often phrased as a negative force in choosing among options. Yet, in Chapter 8, we shall offer a positive alternative to this view and develop its significance for supervision.

Budgetary constraints, increasing demands for the benefits of responsive provision, and a reawakening concern for national security constitute the centerpiece of debate about the development and distribution of resources. Recurring periods of inflation and recession add urgency to the debate about choices in allocations of resources in the arranger-provider-client network. These resource questions related to social welfare center around the combination of the following five options (Savas, 1981): governmental services; government contracts and grants; vouchers; free market and voluntary associations; and self-help.

Governmental services have emerged as the most common approach. Public funds have been allocated to those governmental units through which government employees provide services (such as public assistance). An increasingly popular option has been government contracts and grants. Under this type arrangement, the government supports the delivery of specific services to particular client populations through a grant or contract mechanism. Private nonprofit organizations become the provider under this arrangement (for example, Title XX (1976 Social Services title added to Social Security Act) contracts with community mental health centers).

Vouchers, free market and voluntary associations, and self-help are newer options. Vouchers subsidize clients and permit them some choice in meeting needs on the open market. These vouchers support the use of particular services by specific target groups; examples include rent vouchers, food stamps, tuition credits, and Medicare and Medicaid cards. Under the free market and voluntary-association approach to resource allocation, the client arranges for services and selects the provider, usually a private voluntary organization, which is then paid directly by the client. Self-help relies on the initiative of client systems to develop their own service organizations. These self-help organizations provide services that may be funded through grants, affiliation agreements, and/or fees. These three options (in contrast to the first two) would reduce the scope of government involvement in social welfare.

It is likely that demands for greater efficiency and effectiveness in service provision in the public sector will have profound consequences for social service agencies. These demands are likely to produce pressures on social agencies to reorganize in a network of large comprehensive generic services and smaller separate specialized services. The trends toward declassification of social service personnel categories are an example of the consequences of these cumulative pressures. Instead of employing workers with specialized training at the master's level, workers with bachelor's degrees are being employed for front-line service in meeting client needs. The preponderance of governmental resources are directed toward the large public agencies—for example, general hospitals, mental hospitals, and umbrella departments of human resources, including economic security, social services, and public health. Such organizations are frequently the target for criticism by clients, professionals, and the public. Yet initiatives for greater responsiveness in provision to meet needs will probably have to come from these organizations, because of their monopoly of financial and human resources.

Given that most social workers are employed in these settings (see Chapter 6), the role of the supervisor becomes pivotal. As a supervisor, you will use the qualities of leadership, dignity, and wisdom to achieve desired outcomes with the available resources, to meet client needs, and to ensure the development and application of skills consistent with responsive provision. These qualities are essential to your identification of opportunities for creativity, social innovation, and change in organizing and delivering needed services and benefits. As you can see, we argue for a strong relationship between leadership and resources. Continually raising the "what ifs" about resource options is necessary to understanding and acting on the consequences and implications of various resource patterns. Your leadership qualities will assist you and your supervisees in analyzing the consequences and identifying possibilities for strategic interventions to influence shifts in values, priorities, and dominant vested interests.

*Needs.* Typically, need is defined as the lack or deficiency in something useful or necessary to satisfy the requirements of daily living. Common needs include money, employment, access to opportunities, knowledge and skills for problem solving in managing personal affairs, and appropriate psychological resources for growth through learning, adaptation, and change. Definitions of need can be based on statistics, research, case records, surveys, or political vested interests (Dluhy, 1981). A central concern is who defines the needs that will be met through the social welfare system. As we have seen, the institutional system is made up of arrangers, providers, and clients. The perspective adopted will obviously have much to do with the what and how of provision. Arrangers will be influenced by political factors in defining need. Providers may be influenced by methodological preferences or biases in their definitions. Clients will differ in their definitions, depending on their overall political, social, and economic position in society.

When thinking about needs, a critical conceptual distinction to recognize is the one between private troubles and public needs (Mills, 1959). Private troubles occur within individuals or their immediate relations with others. Public issues transcend individuals, their inner lives, and their immediate situations. These issues are concerned with the institutions of society, and they may threaten the values of the general public. A private trouble would be the stress experienced by unemployed persons and their families. The attention would be given to reducing stress, promoting self-esteem, and building confidence in searching for other work. This particular personal trouble may be symptomatic, however, of a larger public issue, for example, the highest unemployment rate since World War II. Despite the social issues involved in many private troubles, it is the private troubles and not the social issues that usually receive the primary attention of helping professionals. The persistent danger in our society is the laundering of public issues into private troubles without recognizing the inseparability of troubles and issues.

Several examples can be noted to illustrate the dangers involved. In the area of unemployment, it is argued that people who want to work can work; yet public issues of massive unemployment and discrimination on the basis of race, sex, and age are critical determinants. With regard to the dangers of nuclear power plants, many critics have been accused of hysteria. Yet when accidents occur (for example, Three Mile Island), the response may be crisis intervention for nuclear accident stress, rather than tightening construction standards. Similarly, the residents of the Love Canal area were treated for physical and emotional disorders associated with proximity to toxic wastes. Still, wastes continue to be dumped near residential areas. Finally, some public officials explain divorce as a consequence of inadequate personalities, although the trends show a rapidly increasing divorce rate among highly diverse social groups. For divorce as a public issue, we might explore the relationship between changing sex roles and marital stability; for divorce as a private trouble, we might seek to increase the number of marital therapists. Differences in definition and response to both private troubles and public needs are significant to the quality of life for all of us.

Whether this distinction is recognized and adhered to in practice will be a determining factor in the relationship between resources and needs. If needs are actually related to public issues but are treated as private troubles, all the best efforts of direct service workers interacting with clients on the person level will be invalidated (Wolfensberger, 1972). Equally important will be the question of goodness of fit between resources, skills, and needs. Public issues generally require action and the expansion of resources and opportunities, while private troubles necessitate initiatives directed at adaptations to the economic system, adjustment of specific details in the individual's environment, and/or individual counseling (Longres, 1981). It is important for both supervisors and supervisees to be aware that failure to make this distinction results in limitations on resources and satisfaction of needs.

Examining the dynamic nature of responsive provision involves considering not only the potential for meeting needs, but also the harm that might result. For example, requiring AFDC mothers to work might improve their job skills, but this does not address harm that might be done to the socialization needs of their children. It has been suggested that only "those programs might be adopted that seem to be the least likely to make things worse" (Glasser, 1978, p. 146). Factors to consider might include the right to manage your own destiny, the right to control your own body, the right to come and go freely, the right to free speech, association, petition, counsel, access to information, and due process (Glasser, 1978). Moreover,

> the extent to which potential beneficiaries are viewed as claimants, recipients, or clients suggest not only the intent of the program but also the extent to which eligibility factors will be deterrent or invitational. (Axinn and Levin, 1982, p. 2)

The challenges involved in meeting needs include a reconciliation of the tensions inherent in respecting rights while not ignoring needs—in making allowances for individual autonomy while fulfilling social obligations (Rothman, 1978). As a supervisor, you will probably want to be aware of the practice implications of the distinction between private troubles and public issues. This includes your concern for dignity as evidenced by a greater search with your supervisees for opportunities for client participation in specifying and prioritizing needs. Also, it will involve continuous assessment of the goodness of fit between resources, needs, and skills and the pursuit of interventions appropriate to public issues as well as those related to private troubles. Part of your responsibility will be to safeguard against the abuses of the unequal power in the arranger-provider-client system of provision.

*Skills.* Skills are the particular behaviors necessary to perform the tasks required to meet needs. With regard to responsive provision, the issue is to ensure the presence of skills appropriate to the various intervention methods that address needs. There are two questions for you, as supervisor, to consider in addressing this issue:

1. Are the social workers on this agency's staff sufficiently skilled to achieve satisfactory results in applying resources to needs?
2. Are there adequate arrangements (e.g., in-service, educational leave, teaching function of supervision) for service providers to continue developing their knowledge and skills?

Organizational arrangements as reflected in structure, location, and staffing also influence the development and use of skills in serving clients and the community. (For detailed consideration of organizational arrangements and effects, see Chapter 6.) For the supervisor, the skill component of responsive provision relates directly to wisdom. It will be particularly useful for you to become adept in determining what to ask, when, and of whom, thus bringing wisdom to bear on skills, resources, and needs.

*Awareness and flexibility.* The predominant mindset that has governed arrangements for responsive provision has been one that assumed that the future would be a continuation of the present—perhaps with different priorities but the same basic pattern. In our earlier discussion of the world as kaleidoscope, you have seen that a more pertinent assumption in thinking about today and the future would be *uniqueness*—the random event and fluctuating structures. Responsive provision within this kaleidoscopic world view demands a strategic mentality (leadership), one of watchfulness for probable sources and targets of greatest change. Such strategic watchfulness will enable supervisors and supervisees, in partnership with clients and the public, to capitalize on the opportunities of the unforeseen and unforeseeable. Supervisors and supervisees are the pathfinders leading the way in innovating new and different opportunities for tomorrow.

As a supervisor, you will need to develop in yourself and your supervisees, the skills related to "maintaining pivotal readiness" (Middleman, 1979) and asking probing questions. Pivotal readiness is another way of thinking about strategic watchfulness, since it implies alertness and a strategic strike capability for moving in a variety of directions as opportunities are created or revealed:

> An emphasis of pivotal anticipatory readiness suggests valuing one who is prepared to move in any direction and who has a generalized, poised concern for such tasks as getting information, communicating, seeking feedback about his impact, keeping options open, looking ahead, living with ambiguity, and realizing in advance that there will be some situations in which he will have to fail. (p. 35)

Central to these concerns for the supervisor and supervisees is developing skill in asking questions. It has been suggested that the most critical skill for social workers is asking the right questions rather than attempting to give the right answers (Rein, 1970). Some strategic questions come to mind as illustrations: Would a different deployment of my strengths as a supervisor, those of supervisees, or of the agency produce different and better results? What is the potential of program X or method X in satisfying the mandates of responsive provision? Or to anticipate the flows within the world as kaleidoscope,

> What performance capacities do we have to add to exploit the changes, the opportunities, the turbulence of the environment—those created by demographics, by changes in knowledge and technology, and by the changes in the world economy? (Drucker, 1980, p. 65)

The incremental development of welfare state programs has tended to burden agencies with responsibilities for past, present, and future promises that conflict with one another and constitute a severe drain on scarce resources. This is reflected in many goals that once developed in response to the demands of a particular time period, but that today remain only as hopes, rather than having been achieved. Similarly, some objectives that are pursued have either been demonstrated to be impractical or have been largely achieved (Patton, 1978). It has been suggested that in times of turbulence and scarcity the critical question becomes, "If we weren't in this already, would we go into it knowing what we *now* know?" (Drucker, 1980,

p. 44). This is a particularly difficult question for any organization, but is especially problematic in social agencies that are need-oriented in the pursuit of equity and justice. All too frequently we have examined our efforts and the results produced and concluded that what was required was greater effort and more money to support these efforts. Now and in the foreseeable future—given turbulence and scarce or diminishing resources—we may have to consider viable alternative approaches, to identify changes in the arranger-provider-client configuration that might produce greater results. Additionally, it will be important to continually reexamine the mix of resources and skills, and to change it if this would accomplish agency and client goals as defined by needs.

The community mandate is expressed not only through the competent supervisor (and all other staff) and responsive provision; it is also manifest in the dynamic organization. We shall turn now to a discussion of the elements of the dynamic organization.

## THE DYNAMIC ORGANIZATION

The dynamic organization component of the community mandate is grounded in the perspective of organizations as open systems, a perspective that is also consistent with the kaleidoscopic world view. This perspective provides a useful framework for understanding and working within the social service agency. The demands on the competent supervisor and the uncertainties of responsive provision are part of the way of life in the social services. Continuity in participation by clients and workers, quality and quantity of services to clients, and internal and external linkages are either enhanced or diminished by these organizational circumstances.

In terms of supervision, we believe these organizational concerns can be translated into a triad of pragmatic imperatives that must be addressed: stability, effectiveness, and adaptability. Stability concerns variables that the organization seeks to control in achieving and maintaining integration. Effectiveness concerns constraints that must be faced in terms of the process and outcome of service delivery. Adaptability involves the contingencies that must be met in the internal or external environment. These issues constitute imperatives for the dynamic organization if it is to persist and satisfy expectations as a component of the community mandate. We shall address each one separately and link each to the competent supervisor, to responsive provision, and to the functions of supervision.

### Stability

Traditional organizational theory has typically addressed survival issues in terms of standardization of tasks, coordination of work units, and general execution of rules, regulations, and procedures (Katz and Kahn, 1966; Thompson, 1967). The concern is for using and sustaining resources, integrating the work of production and service subunits, matching goods and/or services to clientele, and maintaining balance and consensus among competing internal and external interests. Thus, this particular aspect of organizational persistence emphasizes the efficient use of resources, rather than effectiveness per se.

From our perspective, the survival issue has a somewhat different focus. In terms of competent, imaginative supervision, organizational concerns for stability are defined in terms of integration of people and resources. The focus is on the supervisees and the dynamic organization. In part, the issues include meeting worker needs, maintaining commitments, reducing conflict and tension. These issues are pertinent to sustaining the performance of workers and the organization in serving client needs—both within limits of organizational and staff capability and within the surrounding context.

Several organizational scholars have asserted that an organization that is surrounded by a turbulent environment will increase behavior directed toward maximizing survival, with a corresponding decrease in goal-oriented behavior (Emery and Trist, 1965; Terreberry, 1968; Mileti and Gillespie, 1976; Hall, 1972). Given the numerous sources of uncertainty that social service organizations must address, such organizations would appear to be at high risk for disruptions to organizational continuity. Typically, responses to threats to survival involve greater emphasis on conformity with rules and regulations, more concern for numbers served than for quality of services, and less tolerance for flexibility in the ways supervisors and supervisees do their work. In addition to these responses, social service organizations may have to contend with the threats posed by declassification of personnel, across-the-board cuts, and layoffs. The cumulative effects of these threats and responses have consequences for supervisors and supervisees. There are the tensions associated with threats to job security and the tendency for competition among workers to increase in efforts to protect their jobs. Supervisors and supervisees alike are affected when professional commitments to quality conflict with organizational demands for quantity. Threats of across-the-board cuts and layoffs can contribute to supervisors and supervisees feeling devalued. The interaction of tension, conflict, and devaluation can lead to lack of trust among workers, as well as between workers, supervisors, and those higher up in the organization. If these issues are not addressed, they usually magnify the threats to organizational survival that produced these conditions in the first place.

Essential to the stability of an organization is the willingness to cooperate, the ability to communicate, and the existence and acceptance of purpose (Barnard, 1938). At the core of these organizational dynamics is the continuing commitment of participants, a balance of inducements and contributions (Barnard, 1938; March and Simon, 1958; see Note 4). As a competent, imaginative supervisor, you can meet these stability issues by exercising dignity in relationships with your supervisees, as well as by demonstrating sensitivity to the needs component of responsive provision. This will require your attention to the whole person and your valuing of supervisees in terms of their needs, potentials, and contributions. For the supervisor, we see the imperative of stability in the dynamic organization as a matter of integration. Integration includes attending to the personal and interpersonal aspects of the work and maintaining a sense of purpose. When you are a supervisor, integrative work will involve you in confronting stress and conflicts that could lead to isolation; in intervening to limit the personalization of organizational issues; and in reducing inappropriate competitiveness. Also, integration will require that you initiate practices that promote interdependence, cooperation, and communication. In Chapter 5, in detailing the integrative supervisory functions of humanizing, managing tension, and catalyzing, we shall address concerns for stability, dignity, and needs.

## Effectiveness

We live in an age of accountability (Newman and Turem, 1974; Lewis, 1972). Accountability has been defined as the probability that people and organizations will be responsive to mandates of legitimate authority or influence (Lipsky, 1981). Essentially, the focus is on relationships—individuals, groups, and organizations are always accountable to someone. In the social services, the concept of accountability is very complex. It can be assessed in terms of worker and organizational responsiveness—for example, to target populations, to individual client needs, or to other social agencies. Also, it can involve assessment of worker performance in response to organizational goals, objectives, and expectations. In addition, it may require considering the relationship of the organization to funding sources, governmental units, and the general public. For professionals, there is also the concern for relationships to professional associations in terms of norms, values, and ethics. Because social service organizations are primarily public entities, work with people, and apply methods with outcomes that are indeterminant to varying degrees, all these variations on accountability are critical concerns. For our purposes, we shall define these concerns in terms of the effectiveness imperative for the dynamic organization. Specifically, we shall identify the particular aspects of effectiveness that fall within the purview of supervision.

Effectiveness is the result of ongoing, changeable interactions among resources, worker knowledge and skills, organizational goals and objectives, and client needs. The way in which these factors are balanced and integrated in delivering services contributes to an organization's overall pattern of effectiveness (Miringoff, 1980). This conceptualization makes it mandatory to distinguish quantity and quality. Pressures to document effectiveness in terms of outcomes have frequently resulted in misplaced emphasis on quantity. It is a fallacy to assume that one can infer quality from measures of quantity. Given the variability in client characteristics and responsiveness, differential worker knowledge and skills, lack of specificity in goals, and indeterminancy in methods, quality is not reducible to quantity. Attention must be given to matters of difficulty, periodic review of worker performances, adjustment of performance criteria, adjustments in knowledge and skill related to altered goals and different client needs, and the role of values in service delivery.

Qualitative measures of effectiveness are meaningless without differentiation among levels of difficulty (Lipsky, 1981). At the organizational level, there are differences between voluntary and involuntary clients, socialization and resocialization services, social-control goals and social-change goals. Desired outcomes may require vastly different services because of the difficulties presented. A similar problem exists at the worker level. Evaluations of effectiveness would need to address whether working with neurotic individuals is comparable to working with psychotic individuals, or whether helping a family deal with child abuse is different from helping a family adjust to the "empty nest" syndrome.

Many agencies evaluate worker effectiveness through periodic assessment of performance with standardized forms. It is assumed that these assessments will provide the basis for retrospective sanctions that will modify future behavior. The problem is such standardized assessments do not take account of the unique particulars of a worker's situation. Moreover, there is the matter of fairness. Quality service involves openness to possibilities and to the use of judgment "in the moment" to introduce fresh thinking and flexible action. Effectiveness is often determined by standards of what others think they would have done or what should have been done, independent of the specifics of the situation. This approach assumes that an agency can standardize the responses it prefers (Lipsky, 1981). Yet this contradicts the notion that workers should have the opportunity to use unique and fresh approaches. What is needed is an approach that balances agency preferences and client needs. Client needs, however, will be a primary concern in social service organizations. The extension of public trust depends upon reciprocal accountability to people as individuals when they are encountered in the course of service delivery (Lipsky, 1981).

We have explored the shifting nature of responsive provision and the rapid change in knowledge and methods applied to meeting human needs. For workers, these shifts and changes will require parallel flexibility. Effectiveness must take account of the presence or absence of action by administrators, supervisors, and workers to develop their knowledge and skills and relate these to newly emerging methodologies. Expectations and responses must be examined in terms of consistency or inconsistency with professional norms and ethics. Combining all these concerns makes it necessary to adopt an orientation to effectiveness that goes beyond cause-effect simplicity. Such an approach will address how these factors interact, both with one another and with the uncertainties of internal and external environments. Both program effectiveness and personnel effectiveness must be evaluated.

The competent, imaginative supervisor has a central role in assuring the effectiveness of supervisees. We define this role in terms of process and product concerns. Process refers to developing and applying methods of service delivery that are ethical, caring, and responsive to the dynamics of human interactions. Product issues concern the outcomes expected in terms of agency, clients, and the profession. Also important are the adequacy of worker knowledge and skills for the effort required, as well as the fit between worker capability and client needs. Process and product concerns require negotiating performance criteria, giving feedback, and assessing the results. This approach, which can lead to the identification of gaps in knowledge and skills, is pertinent to ongoing professional development and to the protection of values and ethical standards in practice.

Two other matters directly related to effectiveness are attending to developing and maintaining skills associated with responsive provision; and sharing your wisdom as a competent supervisor. These matters will involve your creating an environment that encourages exploration, innovation, and experimentation with fresh approaches. Structuring events for individual or group learning of new knowledge and skills is yet another aspect of extending your wisdom to supervisor-supervisee interactions. In your role as supervisor, effectiveness is related directly to the attained wisdom of your supervisees and to the process and product of your agency. In Chapter 5, we elaborate the functions of evaluating, teaching, and career socializing as the central aspects of supervisory practice related to effectiveness.

### Adaptability

The preceding discussion of responsive provision referred repeatedly to the concept of uncertainty. We noted that such uncertainty has different sources that overlap and interact to produce positive and/or negative consequences for the organization and its participants. Our purpose has been to demonstrate that the dynamic organization must constantly change by adapting to environmental uncertainties. Since organizations need resources and legitimacy to persist, they are subject to continuing shifts in goals and priorities. Goals and priorities may be supplanted or supplemented, modified or deemphasized, depending on organizational and environmental contingencies (see Note 5). For the dynamic organization to persist, internal and external adjustments to such uncertainties must be made if the organization is to adapt in ways that contribute to stability and effectiveness.

It has been suggested that the organizational problem of "stalemate" emerges when the organization ceases to adapt to changes in goals, environment, or both (Hirschhorn, 1978). Stalemate is the result, first, of a failure to adapt structures and actions to change in goal or environment, and second, of collusion on the part of organizational members to deny this aspect of reality. Since goals and environments are inherently ambiguous or unstable, and since change is occurring more and more rapidly, professionals are increasingly dissatisfied with organizational settings. This dissatisfaction arises from lack of opportunities for development and adjustment. Thus, stalemate is a serious problem that makes adaptability an imperative for the dynamic organization.

The environmental press for adaptability is reflected in interactions among, and reactions to, six common priorities in social service organizations. These priorities include: expansion of the number of clients served; improvement of the quality of present programs and services; increase of staff morale; minimization of service costs per client; development of new programs and services; and increased accountability to funding sources (Finch, 1978, p. 392). The choice of one or more of these priorities for emphasis is likely to involve both internal and external linkages. Adaptation of internal and external interdependencies in pursuit of these priorities creates additional contingencies that make adaptability even more necessary. Critical to the outcome is the degree of congruence between perceptions of administrators, supervisors, and supervisees regarding choices and initiatives to ensure adaptability. For example, if staff perceive that morale issues are being ignored out of deference to other issues, adaptability may be hindered. In periods of contraction in responsive provision, these adaptability issues become paramount in the activities of supervisors (see Note 6).

For a competent, imaginative supervisor, the challenges of adaptability are numerous. Your knowledge of the priorities and values of internal and external constituencies is important for identifying problems and choosing which ones to address from the position of supervisor. For achieving adaptability, your capability as well as that of your supervisees and of the entire organization will influence the choices available. Questions of what to change, when to change, and how to change must be confronted. Flexibility in balancing internal and external demands is essential. Identifying or creating opportunities in the internal and external field of forces will help you navigate and negotiate your way through the conflicting expectations. This will require the mental and emotional toughness to help supervisees and the organization "slough off" outmoded structures or practices that result from the external constraints on autonomy and discretion (Drucker, 1980). The dynamic, adaptable organization anticipates and searches for such options before crises result. Such anticipation and searching is the responsibility of people in the organization. As a supervisor you will directly encounter adaptability demands in terms of resources and leadership. In particular, the "transforming" character of supervisory leadership is the vehicle for relating effectively to both supervisees and the organizational environment. By exercising creative, flexible leadership you can help to release the potentials of others in meeting the needs that are affected by adaptability demands.

The dynamic organization is involved in multiple interactions with its internal components and its external environment. These interrelationships must be simultaneously analyzed and acted on by administrators, supervisors, and supervisees. Supervisory leadership extended to supervisees and to the organization can facilitate this analysis and action. In addition, the focus of the competent, imaginative supervisor can be extended into administering, advocating, and changing—three adaptability functions that relate to internal and external linkages (see Chapter 5).

In conceptualizing the community mandate as it influences the professional social worker in the organization, we have described and illustrated the connections and reciprocal relationships among the competent supervisor, responsive provision, and the dynamic organization. The degree of emphasis among the components of the community mandate, and within each component, can be understood more fully if you are aware of the dialectical processes and uncertainty that characterize the life course of organizations. As additional backdrop for viewing the challenges to the professional in the organization, we shall turn here to an exploration of the life-course perspective.

## LIFE COURSE OF ORGANIZATIONS

In Chapter 2 we discussed three world views and noted that two (machine and lottery) emphasized rational, mechanical, closed-systems thinking, with the decline and demise of living systems being inevitable. These concepts have influenced thinking about formal organizations as relatively fixed structures with predictable processes of action. Yet our preference for concepts and actions that are consistent with a third world view, the world as kaleidoscope, leads us to acknowledge the importance of ideas suggested in the embryonic literature on the life course of organizations (Lippitt and Schmidt, 1967; Kimberly, Miles, and Associates, 1980; Krell, 1981). These ideas about organizational life course can be seen as a developmental model of organizations.

Human beings pass through a life course. This life course consists of birth, growth, maturity, decline, and death. Similarly, formal organizations are created, grow, mature, decline, and in some cases cease to exist, as with the widely reported collapse of small businesses (Boswell, 1973) and the disappearance of organizations created by President Lyndon Johnson's "Great Society" (e.g., Model Cities). Unlike human beings, organizations have the potential to persist indefinitely through a course of alternating stability and fluctuation. Products and services can be altered, personnel replaced, structures modified, administrative and methodological approaches expanded or contracted. Organizations are fluid and dynamic as they exist in time and space; they act and react. Similar to the conflicts and responsive adjustments called for in the individual life course, organizations experience crises and conflicts, although they demand responses of an administrative or organizational type.

> EXAMPLE: The March of Dimes faced a decision about whether or how to continue after development of the polio vaccine satisfied its original purpose. The decision was made to retain the name but to adjust the mission to include support for research and programs directed toward all disabling childhood diseases.

Such responses are indispensable if the organization is to meet the tasks of the present stage in order to move to the next.

### Creation

At the point of creation, an organization must decide what to risk and what to sacrifice in achieving viability (Lippitt and Schmidt, 1967). During the creation stage, an organization must consider what consumer needs are to be emphasized. The products and/or services must be desired by, and appeal to, the potential clients.

> EXAMPLE: In creating community-based residential services as part of a program for deinstitutionalizing mentally retarded individuals, the interests and needs of both the retarded and their families, as well as attitudes of the gen-

eral public, would be considered. Such considerations may lead initially to focusing on the moderately retarded who have good potential to develop additional skills required for semi-independent or independent living in the community.

This latter consideration reflects the importance of careful specification of the target population to be served by the new organization in order to minimize conflicting claims on its resources.

Additionally, a new organization must answer questions about what methods of production or service are to be emphasized and at what cost. Costs must be competitive with those of alternative organizational approaches to the same product or service. Methods need to be determined in the context of availability of personnel and skill resources.

> EXAMPLE: The costs for operating the community-based program would need to be competitive with those of other residential services, especially the large institutions for the retarded.

During creation, questions about how to establish a board and what kind, what to include in articles of incorporation, and what to include in the by-laws must be resolved. Typically, the creation stage is one of slow growth, as the organization concentrates on these issues, keeping an eye toward supportive and constraining forces in the environment (Krell, 1981). Supervisors in new organizations will likely encounter demands for balanced attention to leadership, dignity, wisdom, resources, needs, skills, and the imperatives of stability.

### Growth

During the growth stage, the organization needs to examine the appropriateness of its design for problem choosing, problem facing, and problem solving as aspects of continuity or survival. Typical issues include eligibility criteria, or emphasis on short-term versus long-term services. Balancing available resources against the demand for an organization's products or services will also be a growth issue.

> EXAMPLE: The community-based residence for the retarded may have to choose whether to grow despite limitations on resources and an unfriendly community, or to maintain its current level of operation at the risk of alienating supporters and those demanding inclusion in the program.

Part of this issue involves a second important consideration in the growth stage, the development and maintenance of a core of high-quality personnel. To grow may require additional education and training of the initial core staff, as well as the recruitment and employment of additional high-quality staff. Such efforts involve costs in terms of money and time. Costs in this area will often limit what can be done in other areas of growth, such as number of locations and number of different services. Also, the growth stage involves organizational consideration of what and how to review and evaluate, in order to receive the feedback necessary to continue meeting needs and responding to the initial community mandate. Determining current efficiency and effectiveness will be important in deciding direction and amount of growth.

> EXAMPLE: For the community-based program, one critical question may be whether to include outside persons in the process of evaluation. Careful selection of such external evaluators could contribute to additional support for the organization, if it is doing a good job.

Considering whether to change, and then deciding how to change, are growth processes that may determine the organization's uniqueness and flexibility. Supervisors in the growing organization will often find themselves emphasizing leadership and wisdom as they anticipate the future and as they attend to necessary ongoing development for themselves and their supervisees. Such emphases will be integrally related to issues of resource and skill requirements and the imperatives for effectiveness and adaptability in service delivery and in the internal and external conduct of organization members.

### Maturity

The mature organization is one that has demonstrated sufficient efficiency and effectiveness to earn legitimacy in the eyes of its backers and followers (Lodahl and Mitchell, 1980).

> EXAMPLE: Maturity in the community-based agency for the retarded might be indicated by: sufficient number of appropriate referrals; consistent budgetary support; successful completers greater in number than dropouts or reinstitutionalized clients; adequate level of community acceptance; and actively functioning board of directors, along with a process for orderly replacement of board members.

Such factors can be identified as indicators that the organization can continue to operate independent of the presence of the proponents and personnel who initially embodied the organization.

During the maturity stage an organization may review its original methods and target population to determine if diversification is appropriate and possible.

> EXAMPLE: After several years of successful advocacy, Councils for Retarded Children realized that all retarded persons needed their efforts. As a consequence, these organizations changed their name to Councils for Retarded Citizens.

Typically, mature organizations explore the availability of additional sources of funding that could minimize dependency on the original sources as well as support new initiatives or modifications in original methods and target populations. Or attention might be addressed to improving the personnel policies—to improving the reward system, as well as to providing for continuing professional development to better serve client and organizational needs now and in the future.

In general, the maturity stage emphasizes the review of prior plans and objectives, an update of policies and philosophy, and formulation of an ongoing plan for the future (Lippitt and Schmidt, 1967; Krell, 1981). Supervisory emphases in the mature organization will likely be on matters of dignity and wisdom, identifying any shifts in patterns of needs. These emphases parallel and will be propelled by the persistence imperatives for organizational stability and effectiveness, two imperatives that are the centerpieces of mature organizations.

### Decline or Demise

The possibility of decline or ultimate demise is a real one for organizations. While creation, growth, and maturity are usually sequential in the life course, decline can begin during, or can follow, any of these three stages. Evidence of declining organizations can be seen in public schools, where demographic changes and busing for desegregation have produced serious decreases in enrollments, leading to school closures. Other examples of decline are visible in government services, where eroding tax bases caused by unemployment result in cutbacks; and in the social services, where government funds have been cut or reallocated.

It has been noted that decline can be stimulated either by scarcity or abundance (Boulding, 1975; Scott, 1976; Whetten, 1980). Scarcity tends to produce cutbacks in the work force, budget, and/or clients. Examples of this can be seen in the tightening of eligibility for food stamps, and in the layoffs in public social service agencies. Abundance tends to produce stagnation, passivity, and insensitivity to worker interests and client perferences. During periods of abundance, organizations tend to overemphasize acquisition of resources and to neglect the development of political acceptance. This often leads to a lack of allies when support is needed.

> EXAMPLE: Many community mental health centers expanded rapidly with the availability of time-limited federal grants, but they minimized developing strong local supports; as a result, these programs suffered decline when the federal grants expired. Also, some criminal justice organizations experienced decline or demise when the emphasis shifted from incarceration to rehabilitation. These organizations gained or lost public funding, depending on which values they embodied. (Rothman, 1972)

Organizational responses to decline vary according to whether the attitude toward change among key organizational members is positive or negative. Negative attitudes tend to result in either defending or preventing initiatives, whereas positive attitudes tend to result in either responding to or generating initiatives (Whetten, 1980). Defending initiatives may involve appeals to demonstrating compliance with rules and regulations that represent efficiency, diligence, and productivity of workers. For example, many social agencies respond to proposed budget cuts by making detailed reports on size of caseloads, low error rates, and uncompensated overtime work by employees. Initiatives that are preventive include campaigns to generate public support, to influence client preferences, and to lobby for political influence and social policy changes that are favorable to the organization.

> EXAMPLE: A drug program with a recidivism rate of 100 percent responded to a proposal to terminate the agency by publicly accusing local government of abandoning its commitment to problems of drug abuse. In this case local officials felt obliged to continue the program despite its lack of effectiveness in producing the intended results. (Whetten, 1980)

Responding initiatives typically reflect acceptance that organizational reduction is inevitable, and such initiatives attempt to ward off further decline by quick responses to scarcity. For example, across-the-board cuts, cuts based on performance, and layoffs based on seniority may be quickly implemented to demonstrate that the organization is realistic and responsible in the face of changing circumstances. Generating initiatives may involve reorganization of programs, reallocation of personnel, innovations designed to replace one funding source with another, or plans to change clientele.

Whatever the organizational response to decline or demise, the best possible alternatives are seldom considered, since it is hard for most organizations to imagine alternatives that differ radically from the present reality (Downs, 1967; Whetten, 1980). Supervisors in organizations facing decline or demise are likely to be buffeted by simultaneous pushes and pulls for organizational stability, effectiveness, and adaptability. In such situations, they will need to demonstrate high degrees of leadership, dignity, and wisdom in relationships with supervisees and higher-ups. Moreover, they will need to consider imaginative yet realistic possibilities in adjusting to resource, need, and skill requirements.

We think that considerations derived from the life-course perspective are essential to both supervisors and supervisees in assessing where their agency has been, where it is now, and where it might be going. This perspective is of particular relevance to the context and history components of the foursome mentality. To assist you in making this assessment, we suggest you complete Appendix F, Organizational Life Course Profile.

## SOCIAL SERVICE ORGANIZATION
## LIFE-COURSE ACTIVITY CYCLES

Once created, organizations can prosper unchanged for decades; undergo one or more relatively dramatic changes in mission, structure, or both; or enter a phase of decline that, if unresolved, can result in absolute demise. The outcome of a social agency's progress in the life course is likely to be determined by how it deals with three problem cycles that affect organizational continuity. A discussion of social service organizations as open systems has suggested that these problem cycles of activity are capability, politics, and values (Miringoff, 1980). Each is related to the turbulent environments of social agencies and each represents a potential area of uncertainty. These problem areas overlap and interact in ways that may be beneficial or problematic for the social agency. We shall briefly elaborate each cycle and relate it to stages in the life course.

### Capability

Capability involves issues in matching service delivery resources with the characteristics of clients of the organization. It reflects the degree to which knowledge and skills of personnel can be mobilized and applied in implementing services required to achieve agency goals and meet client needs. Capability emphasizes concern for the pragmatic, the practical possibilities for fine-tuning methods and for deepening commitments to priorities. It is a matter of the *can*—what can actually be done, what can actually be achieved. The capability cycle involves considering how client and organizational problems can be addressed. This consideration includes assessment of the knowledge and skills of current personnel; comparing available resources to resources needed; and comparing current efficiency and effectiveness to what will be expected with the same, different, or additional service priorities. While this activity cycle may be triggered during any of the life course stages, often it will be most salient during the growth stage. Questions of whether to grow and in what directions (locations, services, target populations) are very much related to what *can* be done now and in the foreseeable future.

> EXAMPLE: Assume that the community-based program to deinstitutionalize mentally retarded adults has successfully dealt with issues of the creation stage. It now faces growth-stage issues that might include expansion of locations, expansion of services to current clients, and expansion to new target populations (such as institutionalized children or more severely retarded adults). From the capability perspective, *can* the agency do more than it is doing? Working with children probably will require more elaborate support systems in the community. The questions will be whether current staff can develop these additional supports in the community and whether current staff has the knowledge and skills required to work effectively with children. Equally important, can the agency deal with the costs of new programming (i.e., personnel and time commitments; additional education and training for staff)?

Within this cycle, the emphasis will be what can be done in terms of how much and how well. Concern for the *can* will require an assessment of what can be achieved, what can be gained, and what can be lost—for the agency, for clients, and for staff. As a supervisor involved with these concerns, you will want to take account of the knowledge and skills that yourself and your supervisees possess (wisdom). On the basis of this stock-taking, you can then work with supervisees and others to shape new approaches to what is possible (leadership), to identify worthwhile risks (dignity), and to participate actively in directing the capability—the *can*—towards organizational effectiveness.

### Politics

Politics in social service organizations involves issues of power and control in determining goals; determining priorities in providing benefits and services; calculating gains and losses in internal and external support for the organization; and balancing the organizational commitments necessary for survival. This problem cycle reflects the concern for balancing the internal and external control of the purposes of the organization—including latitude not only in determining what services to provide, but also in how to provide them within the constraints of the policies and regulations established by funding sources, governmental bodies, and boards of directors. Internally, political questions are concerned with the costs and benefits to individuals in accepting or opposing the wishes of peers, supervisors, and administrators. Externally, the political issues involve funding; expansion or contraction of numbers and types of services and programs; expansion or contraction in number of locations or facilities; conflicts among competing societal and community goals; and relative emphasis on efficiency versus effectiveness. Politics is essentially a matter of *may/must*—what *may* be done (the possible) within the limits imposed by goals, funds, and internal commitments of personnel, and what *must* be done to comply with policies, regulations, and efficiency-effectiveness criteria.

> EXAMPLE: In a "homelike" community-based residence for runaways, the goal may be to achieve reunification of the family by providing services that focus on individual and family-relationship issues. Yet the regulations require having plastic mattress and pillowcase covers, locking away cleaning supplies, and allowing cigarettes to be lighted only by counselors. In this situation, the agency will need to decide what it *may* do to counteract the distrust among clients while complying with the *musts* of the regulations. The agency *may* decide to offset the sterility of plastic covers by encouraging residents to decorate their living space with photographs, posters, drawings, or whatever would help them feel at home. Also, it *may* consider some form of group values clarification that deals with how and why the *musts* came to be, and with how these *musts* relate to the *may/must* dynamics of client relationships with peers and authority figures (such as parents, teachers, and counselors). To counteract the deviancy connotations of the restrictive regulations, the agency *may* decide to organize parent-child advocacy groups, as well as to take a risk in joining with community groups in a coalition to seek changes in the regulations.

Although the politics cycle may be triggered in any life-course stage, it is likely to be central in the maturity stage. Questions of how to maintain client and worker commitments to organizational goals, how to respond to pressures for alteration in goals and methods, and how to maintain support of the community and funding sources are all matters of politics—as well as critical concerns—in the maturity stage of an organization. In addition, organizations in the maturity stage usually review their efficiency and effectiveness, and this review will involve *may/must* considerations.

From the perspective of politics, the agency will need to emphasize concern for distinguishing which pressures it *may* ignore and which pressures it *must* respond to because important vested interests insist on response if they are to continue commitments necessary for the organization's survival. As a supervisor in the politics problem cycle, you will probably encounter the challenge of applying the combined influence of dignity and wisdom to the work, since politics may affect clients, supervisees, and supervisors alike. Also, supervisor and supervisee tasks related to stability and adaptability are likely to be predominant in this cycle.

## Values

Values are a significant part of social service provision in the United States. Values influence responsive provision, as previously indicated, and they are a critical component of the context (see Chapter 6). The values cycle in organizations involves the ideals of a society and the idealism of organizational personnel, which are translated into questions of *ought*—given identified needs and the ideals of society and the helping professions, what should be done. The value cycle has both internal and external sources of the *ought*. Each of the helping professions (e.g., social work, psychiatry, psychology) has a body of professional norms and ethics to guide practice. Members of particular professions are expected to conform to these standards in pursuit of an ultimate set of goals, such as equity and justice.

Moreover, external values are held by clients, funding sources, regulatory bodies, and the general community in which the organization is located. In the 1960s, the interplay of these values and a renewed spirit of idealism contributed to launching the "War on Poverty." Out of a consensus that something *ought* to be done to alleviate poverty in the United States, legislation was passed, funding was appropriated, and numerous service organizations were created to support work toward the ideal of defeating poverty. Within the broad brush strokes of these ideals, specific *oughts* were mandated—such as maximum feasible participation of the poor on governing boards set up to monitor programs serving the poor. Maximum participation as an *ought* reflected not only the ideals of democratic governments but the professional norms regarding client self-determination.

While values are a fact of life across the organizational life course, the values cycle will be especially significant in the creation stage. The idealism of the proponents and founders of a new organization is the cornerstone of creation. In considering the critical question of what to risk, the organization in the creation stage is likely to respond in terms of what *ought* to be done. Given the opportunity to start something new, which ideals *ought* to be appealed to as priorities in determining goals and methods of service? A productive decision about *oughts* will involve an assessment of which societal and community values can be appealed to. In building support for the commitments to the *ought* by the organization's founders, initial members, and clients, such an assessment is necessary.

EXAMPLE: In the creating of a community residential agency for the retarded, issues of what *ought* to be done can be cast in terms of societal values of self-sufficiency or constitutional rights in such areas as self-determination and opportunities to succeed. Appealing to these values helps support goals and services that the organization prefers (for instance, to foster social skills training, community living rather than institutionalization, and education and vocational training for sheltered or independent employment).

Specification of the *ought* is a significant part of the activity in the value cycle, and it includes interactions among the constituents of an organization and between them and the organization itself. Community norms, ideologies of service arrangers, attitudes and aspirations of client groups often combine with the values of organizational members in influencing a given organizational decision. As a supervisor, you are deeply involved with value issues affecting service delivery, particularly as these relate to identifying and meeting needs. When the value problem cycle is dominant, this will probably require you to orient your leadership toward keeping dignity issues in the forefront in working with supervisees and others. Also, concerns for the *ought* will influence the task emphases of you and your supervisees as you strive for effectiveness and adaptability.

## INTERACTION OF CAPABILITY, POLITICS, AND VALUES IN THE LIFE COURSE

Across the life course of an organization, there will be cycles of activity in which one of the problem areas is more dominant than others. We have suggested that in the creation stage, values—the *ought*—will initially be the dominant activity cycle. At the beginning of the growth stage, issues related to capability—the *can*—will predominate. Issues of politics—of *may/must*—will be first in priority during the maturity stage. Table 4-1 depicts the relationships between life-course stages and the activity cycles.

In our discussion of life-course stages, we noted the many uncertainties encountered by an organization that is in a stage of decline or facing total demise. With respect to the problem activity cycles of social service organizations, we call your attention to survival issues as the dominant concern in the decline stage. As depicted in Table 4-1, some shifting back and forth can be expected between capability issues (the *can* cycle) and the politics of the *may/must* cycle. Most organizations in this stage become deeply involved in the pragmatic issues of survival—maintaining resources or developing new ones; maintaining demand for its services either from the original consumer target population or from new ones; and ensuring the commitments of key personnel and key influentials in the community. Although some reiteration of ideals (the *ought*) may be expressed in terms of the social value of organizational goals and services, these are likely to be secondary to concerns for *can* and *may/must*. For the organization that has not satisfactorily addressed issues of decline and is facing the real possibility of demise, a strong appeal to values can be expected. The organization *ought* to continue because of the good it has done in the past and present, and the potential for doing more good. When these appeals have limited impact, then an organization may decide

TABLE 4-1    Social Service Organization Life Course Activity Cycles

| LIFE-COURSE STAGE | CORE ACTIVITY CYCLES | | |
| --- | --- | --- | --- |
| | CAPABILITY | POLITICS | VALUES |
| Birth | can | may/must | ought[a] |
| Growth | **can** | may/must | ought |
| Maturity | can | **may/must** | ought |
| Decline | **can?** | **may/must?** | ought |
| Demise | can? | may/must? | **ought?** |

[a] Boldface denotes the dominant problem activity cycle.

to stand on its original value commitments and terminate—rather than have termination imposed by others who do not share the same ideals.

The core problem activities in social service organizations have been described as cycles because of the tendency for one problem to peak and then diminish when another area emerges as dominant. For example, after a period in which ascendant values reflect initiatives for more enlightened responses to providing for needs of the disadvantaged or oppressed, there would likely follow a period of political adjustments for expanding provisions. This would likely be followed by a cycle of activity related to capability issues in meeting an enlarged mandate. Thus, each problem area produces activities for another in a dialectical process.

> EXAMPLE: The combined effect of Supreme Court rulings and civil rights activism was in the values cycle, which generated convictions that something *ought* to be done to ensure equal educational opportunities for children. These value considerations generated activity in the capability cycle—regarding what schools and the society *can* do, and how to do the *can* within school systems. The uncertainties in the capability cycle produced pressures for activity in the politics cycle, ultimately resulting in a determination that forced busing to achieve desegregation was part of the necessary response, a *must*. The interplay of *ought, can,* and *must,* in turn, led to environmental change, with the flight of many whites to the suburbs and with some the enrollment of white children in private schools. Uncertainty related to equal educational opportunity has not been resolved. The dialectical processes described above are likely to repeat themselves in some form as long as this issue remains a social and human welfare concern.

The turbulent environment of social service organizations can also produce shifts in dominance of the three problem cycles of capability, politics, and values. Often these shifts will be triggered by changes in the mandate for responsive provision. The uncertainties associated with responsive provision can stimulate activity in one or more of the problem areas which then becomes an impetus for the dialectical process among them all. Changes in attitudes or knowledge regarding clients are likely to generate activities related to capability and values. An organization's attempts to alter its goals and scope of services will generate political problems. Challenges to prevailing methods and their effectiveness in achieving desired outcomes for clients will produce value problems among the professions and between the organization and its clients. These, in turn, will require focusing on capability questions, and so the cycles go on and on.

## CONCLUSION

The focus throughout this chapter has been on several aspects of the professional in the organization. We have argued that in competent, imaginative supervision, it is crucial to consider these aspects. Further, these aspects have been examined from a developmental perspective as applied to organizations. Throughout the organization's life course, predictable stages and various task imperatives will face supervisors and all agency personnel. To draw these ideas together, the following linear diagram summarizes the key relationships among the central ideas developed in this chapter.

| COMPETENT SUPERVISOR | RESPONSIVE PROVISION | DYNAMIC ORGANIZATION |
|---|---|---|
| Leadership | Resources | Adaptability |
| Wisdom | Skills | Effectiveness |
| Dignity | Needs | Stability |

In Chapter 5 we describe nine functional imperatives that are components of all supervision. These imperatives direct the work and its inherent activities, and they form the centerpiece of our theoretical approach. In Chapter 6 we consider how they are connected with complex organizational contexts.

## NOTES

1. For example, supervisors need to regard the worker's welfare and development not merely because of their role as supervisors, but because the worker is a human being. Among the ethical obligations to workers that supervisors need to assure are a job where one can succeed; a job worthy of the person's preparation and training, even if impractical for the agency; a good start on the job; the resources and materials needed to do the work; the opportunity for growth and creative development; and a periodic evaluation of where the workers stand and how their work is perceived (Levy, 1973). Supervisors, according to Levy, need to assure workers just consequences (not necessarily favorable ones), fair advantages (not necessarily special ones), and opportunities that are safe from hazards (not necessarily preferential opportunities). These ethical supervisory actions reflect recognition of worker dignity in situations where it is clear that the worker and supervisor hold unequal power. It is the supervisor who must take the initiative in being considerate of the worker's dignity.

2. According to Reynolds, new teachers approach wisdom when they have "outlived the stage of expounding" or "the irresistible need to demonstrate their command of the subject matter by reciting it." Such teachers know how to keep preoccupation with subject matter from getting in the way of finding "the point of living contact" between each learner and the subject. They have translated into experience the intellectual concepts gained from lectures and reading. They have marshaled the subject matter into an orderly array; yet their real work

is scarcely begun until they discover the joy of developing the learning power of others. Wise teachers have grown alert to what the learners are thinking and feeling and are intrigued by the problem of translating the subject matter (now a secondary concern) into terms that let living people use it (1942/1965, p. 307). This description captures a type of "knowing" that we label *wisdom* in our thinking about the competent supervisor.

3. Drucker argues we are entering a period where "knowledge is becoming performance and this means rapid change" (1980, p. 56). Technological growth, social innovation, and social change are equally important on the horizon of the future. "It is highly possible that we can anticipate a period of rapid change in a great number of areas, regardless of the attitude of the public toward . . . change. Resistance to change may make it more expensive, but is unlikely to slow it down" (Drucker, 1980, p. 56).

4. Barnard (1938) and March and Simon (1958) argue that an organization will persist as long as it can offer to its members inducements that exceed the contributions it asks of them.

5. Patton (1978) noted that goals "are the product of a variety of influences, some of them enduring and some fairly transient. . . . Finally, it is clear that goals are multiple and conflicting, and thus the 'character' of an organization is never stable . . . (because) organizations pursue a variety of goals, sometimes in sequence, sometimes simultaneously" (p. 123).

6. As a result of shifts in priorities during periods of contraction, attention must be directed toward renegotiating the inducements to and contributions demanded of staff. According to Finch, "this appears to be especially critical in relation to those priority items that emerge as possible determinants of dissatisfaction, namely, increased accountability and an expansion of number of clients served" (1978, p. 398).

## REFERENCES

ADDAMS, JANE, *Twenty Years at Hull-House.* New York: 1910; rpt. Signet Classic, The New American Library, 1961.

ARGYRIS, CHRIS, "Learning Environment for Increased Effectiveness," in *Theories of Group Processes,* Gary L. Cooper, ed. New York: John Wiley, 1975.

AXINN, JUNE, and HERMAN LEVIN, *Social Welfare: A History of the American Response to Need* (2nd ed.). New York: Harper & Row, 1982.

BALES, ROBERT F., *Interaction Process Analysis: A Method for the Study of Small Groups.* Cambridge, Mass.: Addison-Wesley, 1950.

BARNARD, CHESTER I., *The Functions of the Executive.* Cambridge, Mass.: Harvard University Press, 1938.

BATESON, GREGORY, *Mind and Nature: A Necessary Unity.* New York: Bantam Books, 1980.

BECK, BERTRAM M., "Humanizing the Human Services," in *Toward Human Dignity: Social Work in Practice,* John W. Hanks, ed. Washington, D.C.: NASW, 1978.

BLAKE, ROBERT R., and JANE S. MOUTON, "Management by Grid Principles or Situationalism: Which?" *Group & Organization Studies,* 6, no. 4 (December 1981), 439-455.

BOSWELL, J., *The Rise and Decline of Small Firms.* London: Allen & Unwin, 1973.

BOULDING, KENNETH E., "The Management of Decline," *Change,* 64, no. 2 (1975), 8-10.

BOWERS, D.G., and S.E. SEASHORE, "Predicting Organizational Effectiveness with a Four Factor Theory of Leadership," *Administrative Science Quarterly,* 11, no. 11 (September 1966), 238-263.

BURNS, JAMES MacGREGOR, *Leadership*. New York: Harper & Row, 1978.

COX, FRED M., "A Suggestive Schema for Community Problem Solving," in *Strategies of Community Organization* (2nd. ed.), Fred M. Cox, John L. Ehrlich, Jack Rothman, and John E. Tropman, eds. Itasca, Ill.: Peacock, 1974, 425–444.

DAS, HARI, "Relevance of Current Organization Development Values and Assumptions to Scarcity Situations," *Group & Organization Studies*, 6, no. 4 (December 1981), 402–409.

DAVIS, TIM R.V., "OD in the Public Sector: Intervening in Ambiguous Performance Environments," *Group & Organization Studies*, 4, no. 2 (June 1979), 352–364.

DLUHY, MILAN J., *Changing the System*. Beverly Hills, Calif.: Sage, 1981.

DOBELSTEIN, ANDREW W., *Politics, Economics, and Public Welfare*. Englewood Cliffs, N.J.: Prentice-Hall, 1980.

DRUCKER, PETER F., *Managing in Turbulent Times*. New York: Harper & Row, 1980.

DOWNS, ANTHONY, *Inside Bureaucracy*. Boston: Little, Brown, 1967.

EMERY, F.E., and E.L. TRIST, "The Causal Texture of Organizational Environments," *Human Relations*, 18, no. 1 (February 1965), 21–32.

FIEDLER, FRED E., *A Theory of Leadership Effectiveness*. New York: McGraw-Hill, 1967.

FILLEY, ALAN C., *The Compleat Manager*. Champaign, Ill.: Research Press, 1978.

FINCH, WILBUR A., JR., "Administrative Priorities: The Impact of Employee Perceptions on Agency Functioning and Worker Satisfaction," *Administration in Social Work*, 2, no. 4 (Winter 1978), 391–399.

FLEISHMAN, E.A., "The Measurement of Leadership Attitudes in Industry," *Journal of Applied Psychology*, 37, no. 3 (June 1953), 153–158.

FRANKL, VIKTOR E., *Man's Search for Meaning*. New York: Washington Square Press, 1963.

FRIEDRICH, OTTO, "F.D.R.'s Disputed Legacy," *Time*, 119, no. 5 (February 1, 1982), 20–43.

GALPER, JEFFERY H., *The Politics of Social Services*. Englewood Cliffs, N.J.: Prentice-Hall, 1975.

GAYLIN, WILLARD, "In the Beginning: Helpless and Dependent," in *Doing Good: The Limits of Benevolence*, Willard Gaylin, Ira Glasser, Steven Marcus, and David J. Rothman, eds. New York: Pantheon Books, 1978.

GLASSER, IRA, "Prisoners of Benevolence: Power versus Liberty in the Welfare State," in *Doing Good: The Limits of Benevolence*, Willard Gaylin, Ira Glasser, Steven Marcus, and David J. Rothman, eds. New York: Pantheon Books, 1978.

GRAMLICH, EDWARD M., and DEBORAH S. LAREN, "The New Federalism," in *Setting National Priorities: The 1983 Budget*, Frank A. Pechman, ed. Washington, D.C.: The Brookings Institution, 1982.

GRAY, CHARLES M., and VIRGINIA H. GRAY, "The Political Economy of Public Service Options," *American Behavioral Scientist*, 24, no. 4 (March/April 1981), 483–494.

HALL, RICHARD H., *Organizations: Structure and Process*. Englewood Cliffs, N.J.: Prentice-Hall, 1972.

HALPRIN, A.W., and B.J. WINER, "A Factorial Study of the Leader Behavior Descriptions," in *Leader Behavior: Its Description and Measurement*, Ralph M. Stogdill, and Alfred E. Coons, eds. Columbus, Ohio: Ohio State University, Bureau of Business Research, Research Monograph 88, 1957.

HANKS, JOHN W., ed., *Toward Human Dignity: Social Work in Practice*. Washington, D.C.: NASW, 1978.

HERSEY, PAUL G., and KENNETH H. BLANCHARD, "Grid Principles and Situationalism: Both! A Response to Blake and Mouton," *Group & Organization Studies*, 7, no. 2 (June 1982), 207–210.

_____, *Management of Organizational Behavior: Utilizing Human Resources* (3rd ed.). Englewood Cliffs, N.J.: Prentice-Hall, 1977.

HIRSCHHORN, LARRY, "The Stalemated Agency: A Theoretical Perspective and Practical Proposal," *Administration in Social Work*, 2, no. 4 (Winter 1978), 425–438.

HOUSE, R.J., "A Path Goal Theory of Leader Effectiveness," *Administrative Science Quarterly*, 16, no. 3 (September 1971), 321–338.

KAHN, ALFRED J., *Social Policy and Social Services*. New York: Random House, 1973.

KATZ, DANIEL, and ROBERT KAHN, *The Social Psychology of Organizations*. New York: John Wiley, 1966.

KIMBERLY, JOHN R., "The Life Cycle Analogy and the Study of Organizations: Introduction," in *The Organizational Life Cycle*, John R. Kimberly, Robert H. Miles, and Associates, eds. San Francisco: Jossey-Bass, 1980.

KRELL, TERENCE C., "The Marketing of Organization Development: Past, Present, and Future," *The Journal of Applied Behavioral Science*, 17, no. 3 (July-August-September 1981), 309–323.

LAUFFER, ARMAND, *Resources for Child Placement and Other Human Services*. Beverly Hills, Calif.: Sage, 1979.

LEUCHTENBURG, WILLIAM E., *The Perils of Prosperity, 1914–1932*. Chicago: University of Chicago Press, 1958.

LEVY, CHARLES S., "The Ethics of Supervision," *Social Work*, 18, no. 2 (March 1973), 14–21.

LEWIN, KURT, RONALD LIPPITT, and ROBERT K. WHITE, "Patterns of Aggressive Behavior in Experimentally Created Social Climates," *Journal of Social Psychology*, 10, no. 2 (May 1939), 271–299.

LEWIS, HAROLD, "The Future of the Social Service Administrator," *Administration in Social Work*, 1, no. 2 (Summer 1977), 115–122.

_____, "The Structure of Professional Skill," in *Social Work in Practice*, Bernard Ross, and S.K. Khinduka, eds. Washington, D.C.: NASW, 1976.

_____, "Developing a Program Responsive to New Knowledge and Values," in *Evaluation of Social Intervention*, Edward J. Mullen, James R. Dumpson, and Associates. San Francisco: Jossey-Bass, 1972.

LIKERT, RENSIS, *The Human Organization: Its Management and Values*. New York: McGraw-Hill, 1967.

LIPPITT, GORDON L., and WARREN H. SCHMIDT, "Crises in a Developing Organization," *Harvard Business Review*, 45, no. 6 (November-December 1967), 102–114.

LIPSKY, MICHAEL, "The Assault on Human Services: Street-Level Bureaucrats, Accountability, and the Fiscal Crisis," in *Management Systems in the Human Services*, Murray L. Gruber, ed. Philadelphia: Temple University Press, 1981.

LODAHL, THOMAS M., and STEPHEN M. MITCHELL, "Drift in the Development of Innovative Organizations," in *The Organizational Life Cycle*, John R. Kimberly, Robert H. Miles, and Associates. San Francisco: Jossey-Bass, 1980.

LONGRES, JOHN F., "Social Work Practice with Racial Minorities: A Study of Contemporary Norms and Their Ideological Implications," *California Sociologist*, 4, no. 4 (Winter 1981), 202–215.

MARCH, JAMES G., and HERBERT A. SIMON, *Organizations*. New York: John Wiley, 1958.

McGREGOR, DOUGLAS, *The Human Side of Enterprise*. New York: McGraw-Hill, 1960.

MIDDLEMAN, RUTH R., "Quality Circles: People/Industry Panacea?" *World Wide Shipping/World Ports*, 45, no. 2 (April/May 1982), 1–4.

————, "Some Particulars of Urban Social Work Practice and Education, 1977," in *The Urban Mission*, Louisville, Ky.: University of Louisville, Raymond A. Kent School of Social Work, 1979.

MILETI, DENNIS S., and DAVID F. GILLESPIE, "An Integrated Formalization of Organization-Environment Interdependencies," *Human Relations*, 29, no. 1 (January 1976), 85–100.

MILLER, HENRY, "Value Dilemmas in Social Casework," *Social Work*, 13, no. 1 (January 1968), 27–33.

MILLS, C. WRIGHT, *The Sociological Imagination*. New York: Oxford University Press, 1959.

MIRINGOFF, MARC L., *Management in Human Service Organizations*. New York: Macmillan, 1980.

NEWMAN, EDWARD, and JERRY TUREM, "The Crisis of Accountability," *Social Work*, 19, no. 1 (January 1974), 139–147.

PASCALE, RICHARD T., and ANTHONY G. ATHOS, *The Art of Japanese Management*. New York: Simon & Schuster, 1981.

PATTON, MICHAEL QUINN, *Utilization–Focused Evaluation*. Beverly Hills, Calif.: Sage, 1978.

PERSKE, ROBERT, "The Dignity of Risk and the Mentally Retarded," *Mental Retardation*, 10, no. 1 (February 1972), 24–26.

REDDIN, W.J., *Managerial Effectiveness*. New York: McGraw-Hill, 1970.

REIN, MARTIN, "The Boundaries of Social Policy," in *Social Policy*, Martin Rein, ed. New York: Random House, 1970.

REYNOLDS, BERTHA CAPEN, *Learning and Teaching in the Practice of Social Work*. 1942; rpt. New York: Russell & Russell, 1965.

RHODES, GARY B., "Deinstitutionalization: A Normalizing Approach to Activating Formal and Informal Systems in Urban Areas," in *The Urban Mission*. Louisville, Ky.: University of Louisville, Raymond A. Kent School of Social Work, 1979.

ROSOW, JEROME M., "Human Dignity in the Public-Sector Workplace," *Public Personnel Management*, 8, no. 1 (January/February 1979), 7–14.

ROTHMAN, DAVID J., "The State as Parent: Social Policy in the Progressive Era," in *Doing Good: The Limits of Benevolence*, Willard Gaylin, Ira Glasser, Steven Marcus, and David J. Rothman, eds. New York: Pantheon Books, 1978.

————, "Of Prisons, Asylums, and Other Decaying Institutions," *The Public Interest*, 8, no. 26 (Winter 1972), 3–17.

SAVAS, E.S., "Alternative Institutional Models for the Delivery of Public Services," *Public Budgeting & Finance*, 9, no. 1 (Winter 1981), 12–20.

SCHOTTLAND, CHARLES I., ed., "Introduction," *The Welfare State*. New York: Harper & Row, 1967.

SCOTT, WILLIAM G., "The Management of Decline," *Conference Board Record*, 13, no. 6 (June 1976), 36–39.

SIU, R.G.M., *The Master Manager*. New York: Mentor, 1982.

STOGDILL, RALPH M., *Handbook of Leadership: A Survey of Theory and Research*. New York: The Free Press, 1974.

STOGDILL, RALPH M., and A.E. COONS, eds., *Leader Behavior: Its Description and Measurement.* Columbus, Ohio: Ohio State University, Bureau of Business Research, Research Monograph 88, 1957.

TERREBERRY, SHIRLEY, "The Evolution of Organizational Environments," *Administrative Science Quarterly,* 12, no. 4 (March 1968), 590–613.

THOMPSON, JAMES D., *Organizations in Action.* New York: McGraw-Hill, 1967.

TOFFLER, ALVIN, *The Third Wave.* New York: William Morrow, 1980.

TOWLE, CHARLOTTE, *Common Human Needs* (rev. ed.). New York: NASW, 1957.

WHETTEN, DAVID A., "Sources, Responses, and Effects of Organizational Decline," in *The Organizational Life Cycle,* John R. Kimberly, Robert H. Miles, and Associates. San Francisco: Jossey-Bass, 1980.

WILENSKY, HAROLD L., and CHARLES N. LEBEAUX, *Industrial Society and Social Welfare* (2nd ed.). New York: The Free Press, 1965.

WOLFENSBERGER, WOLF, *Normalization: The Principle of Normalization in Human Services.* Toronto, Ontario: National Institute on Retardation, 1972.

YANKELOVICH, DANIEL, *New Rules: Searching for Self-Fulfillment in a World Turned Upside Down.* New York: Random House, 1981.

ZALESNIK, ABRAHAM, "Managers and Leaders: Are They Different?" *Harvard Business Review,* 55, no. 3 (May/June 1977), 67–78.

# CHAPTER FIVE
# NINE FUNCTIONS
# OF SUPERVISORS

## INTRODUCTION

The particulars of organizational life that are central to contemporary delivery of social services constitute a set of imperatives for doing your work as a supervisor. In our earlier discussion of the dynamic organization, it was noted that the life of an organization, its vitality and viability, is related to its stability, effectiveness, and adaptability. Regardless of your personal convictions and preferences about social work in organizational settings, we believe that exploration of these particulars is essential to developing a realistic yet hopeful and responsive approach to competent, imaginative supervision. In depicting the dynamic organization as an aspect of organizational persistence, we have attempted to provide an initial response to a challenge issued several years ago:

> It is time for the social work profession, bureaucrats, and schools of social work to stop hiding their knowledge of bureaucracies. What we now need are new ideas, concepts, and models—in short, a new vision to reconstruct our working lives and new ways to relate to each other and those we serve."
> (Wasserman, 1971, p. 95)

## THE COMMUNITY MANDATE
## AND SUPERVISORY FUNCTIONS

Table 5-1 shows how the community's specification and sanction of certain services as the province for social work (community mandate) become translated into aspects of competence for the supervisor, for service provisions, for organizational

**TABLE 5-1    Relationships Among Dimensions**

| WORKER (COMPETENT SUPERVISOR) | RESPONSIVE PROVISION | DYNAMIC ORGANIZATION | SUPERVISORY FUNCTIONS |
|---|---|---|---|
| Dignity | Needs | Stability | Integrative<br>  Humanizing<br>  Managing Tension<br>  Catalyzing |
| Wisdom | Skills | Effectiveness | Service delivery<br>  Teaching<br>  Career Socializing<br>  Evaluating |
| Leadership | Resources | Adaptability | Linkage<br>  Administering<br>  Advocating<br>  Changing |

imperatives, and thus, for specific supervisory functions. As you will see, these functions are clustered in units of three that reflect three levels of concern for the imperatives of organizational persistence. For clarity and ease of understanding, we deal with each cluster of functions separately, although we recognize that they are all intimately intertwined—that is, as supervisor you may be engaging in two more of these functions simultaneously.

## INTEGRATIVE FUNCTIONS
## OF SUPERVISION

Social service organizations, like other complex organizations, pursue multiple goals and are pressured by the often conflicting demands of various groups whose support is important to organizational survival. To persist, an organization must maintain some degree of stability. Yet social service organizations are continuously confronting flows and ebbs in financial resources, shifts in political ideology of governmental decision makers, and unpredictable public attitudes that support welfare but demonstrate antipathy toward agencies and their services. In addition, there is the continuing discussion of whether social workers can fulfill their professional responsibilities in bureaucratic organizational contexts. For these reasons and those noted in Chapters 4 and 6, the organizational imperative of stability (or survival) often comes first in the life of any organization. If the organization does not survive, all else is inconsequential.

The perpetual uncertainty confronting the social service organization and the accompanying imperative for stability have many implications for agency staff. At a minimum, there are issues of worker morale and personal integrity, conflicts between stability and the pressures to meet increased demands. For supervisors, there are the challenges of responding to the pushes and pulls of forces in the agency, among the workers, and in the external environment. As a supervisor working in the middle, you will be directly involved in the crossfire of these various demands. Administrators will expect you to implement processes that focus on survival (for example, greater conformity to rules and regulations). At the same time, supervisees will be pressuring for additional resources to meet new demands and for a relaxation of rules in order to better meet increased client needs. In your practice as a supervisor, you will want to be sensitive to the consequences of your actions in maintaining worker commitments to clients, the profession, and the organization. In this sense, you are involved in continuously integrating human interests with organizational interests—an integration that contributes to the stability and survival of both the organization and the individual.

Many social workers are attracted to the social services out of a desire to apply a special competence in meeting human needs. Because social service work is such a human endeavor, focusing on intense, intimate relationships between workers and clients, the organizational pressures mentioned above have special significance. It has been noted that "the people who choose social work as a career—who seem to have the interests and qualifications necessary for working with people— tend to be more sensitive to these pressures" (Pines and Kafry, 1978, p. 502). In return for sticking with the tasks at hand and coping with these pressures, social workers often expect an organizational environment that acknowledges professional attributes and values. Such an environment would reinforce the code of ethics, ongoing professional development, valuing worker efforts, and independent as well as interdependent practice within the limits of specified roles and agency goals.

These factors can be thought of as minimally essential incentives for sustained worker commitments of knowledge, skills, and personal energies to a career of helping. To achieve organizational stability, these incentives will need to be integrated into the organizational scene. While many agencies and workers tend to persist and to prevail in attempts to meet client needs, too much is at stake for all involved to leave the balance between incentives and commitments to chance. As a supervisor, you become a pivotal person in integrating staff and organizational concerns for stability and survival.

In fulfilling your responsibilities as a supervisor, concern for dignity will be of prime importance. Your supervisees and their clients are precious resources, to be valued and nurtured as a part of the integrative process for achieving organizational stability. You will need to initiate actions to combat the sense of impotence, frustration, and failure that many workers experience in their efforts to help clients in the face of overwhelming odds and conditions that characterize nonprofit service organizations. Lack of attention to worker-level dignity issues may account for the findings of several studies. These studies noted that workers with the highest civil service examination scores or with the most professional education are often the ones who leave public agencies for private practice or other occupations (Wasserman, 1970; Mandell, 1973; Podell, 1967). As a supervisor, you can be forewarned of these possible reactions to organizational pressures by being sensitive to the development of the following symptoms:

1. Social *isolation* among members of the work force
2. Increased competitive attitudes and behaviors generated by concerns for *turf* and personal survival
3. A sense of *burnout* in some workers

A recent review of the literature on the impact of work conditions and organizational environments on social workers suggested that these factors are critical determinants of the symptoms mentioned above. In particular, it was noted that an organizational climate that recognizes workers when they perform well and helps them recognize this in themselves is essential to maintaining positive commitments to the work, the agency, and individual competence (Glicken, 1980). This suggestion reaffirms Kadushin's observation that "if social workers are to do their job effectively, they need to feel good about themselves and about the job they are doing" (1976, p. 202). He continues by noting that these concerns are a dominant aspect of supervision. Since service delivery is a thoroughly human enterprise where the methods and outcomes of helping are based primarily on human resources, it will be important for you, the supervisor, to protect as well as develop human dignity in the agency. You can address dignity at the worker level and stability at the organizational level by engaging in the integrative functions of humanizing, managing tension, and catalyzing.

### Humanizing

A national study of workers and their working conditions concluded that "what workers want most, as more than 100 studies in the past 20 years show, is to become masters of their immediate environments and to feel that their work and they themselves are important—the twin ingredients of self-esteem" (DHEW, 1973, p. 13). We have noted that many people enter the social services because of a desire to help others and a belief that social service work is meaningful. At the same time, we have noted it cannot be left to chance to maintain and enhance these commitments and beliefs. Initiatives to enhance the enabling aspects of organizational structures and processes, and to combat the constraining aspects, are essential for worker dignity and organizational stability. Management, in the person of the supervisor, has both the responsibility and the potential to create conditions that encourage and enable workers to feel that both the work and they themselves are important to the organization. Your words and actions as a supervisor are key aspects in the development and maintenance of such conditions.

Humanizing is the supervisory function related to personal and interpersonal aspects of the work. This function is central to creating and maintaining the conditions for working that promote human dignity and contribute to organizational stability. As you fulfill the responsibilities of this function in regard to the personal aspects of the work, your aim will be to help workers feel valued, needed, and central to the service delivery of the organization. On the interpersonal level, your concern will be to facilitate valuing others, being valued by others, and appreciating individual differences for their unique contributions to the work group and to service delivery. Since social service organizations are composed of diverse staff and clientele, you will want to develop sensitivity to personal and interpersonal work barriers. It is our contention that by attending to these aspects of the work, you will be able to generate psychological and interpersonal resources among supervisees. These resources will help supervisees mobilize the personal and technical energies needed for effective job performance.

It has been noted in the literature that organizational effectiveness depends upon the personal and interpersonal as well as the technical competence of the work force (Argyris, 1970; Glicken, 1980). Despite this recognition, there may be a tendency for bureaucratic structures and processes to overemphasize the technical to the neglect of the personal and interpersonal. This tendency is related to the bureaucratic emphasis on reinforcing and rewarding impersonality in relationships and a corresponding lack of concern for the worker as a whole person. Still, in studies of worker and supervisor-supervisee relationships, it has been noted that self-acceptance, shared meaning and valuing in interpersonal relationships, and the ability to utilize knowledge and skills and to express central needs are critical, both to personal satisfaction and to a continuing commitment to client and organizational interests (Kadushin, 1976; Pines and Kafry, 1978; Glicken, 1980). We shall address the supervisor's activities and actions within the humanizing function and relate them to these concerns.

*Encouraging self-acceptance.*   Self-acceptance is concerned with the extent to which workers have confidence and personal regard for themselves in meeting client and organizational needs. Feeling valued, feeling needed, and sensing that work is worthwhile are central aspects of self-acceptance among workers. As a supervisor, it will be important for you to be aware of your role in promoting supervisees' feelings of self-acceptance. Communicating a sense of caring and regard for the personal worth of workers can have a significant, positive impact on self-acceptance. Often, your supervisees will give their best effort and still be disappointed by the outcome. Unless you express your sense of understanding for the resulting feelings of frustration and your continuing sense of value for supervisees, they may become discouraged and withdraw from future tough assignments. The following experience is typical of those you might deal with in promoting self-acceptance and countering self-devaluation.

EXAMPLE: A supervisor has noticed that one of her workers, who has worked in AFDC for one year, seems withdrawn. He sits alone in his office more than in the past. The supervisor knows that this worker recently completed five months of persistent effort to arrange public housing for one of his clients, a mother and three children. This family has been living in a tarpaper shack. Just when the housing appeared to be arranged, the worker's client was denied housing because of a prior arrest for alleged pot smoking. Although the client was not convicted, the worker was unable to persuade the housing authority to accept this family.

What can the supervisor do? In response, typical commonsense remarks might include, "That's too bad. Maybe if you had tried . . . ," or "Don't worry about it, that's life." As a supervisor, you need to give a response that reflects "uncommon sense"—an openness to considering different explanations for the worker's behavior and different options in approaching him. From a humanizing perspective, you do not have information to confirm the supposition that the worker's withdrawal behavior and the client's dilemma are related. You can observe his behavior and acknowledge it. In this instance your initial approach might be to recognize your appreciation of five months of hard work. This may relieve any guilt or feeling of failure that the worker may be experiencing. Communicating that you have noticed and valued his work could lead to a discussion of his feelings and withdrawal behavior. Then you can act to further preserve his self-acceptance by noting that even when we do our best, there are no guarantees of success. Moreover, this may provide an opportunity for engaging in other supervisory functions. For example, an approach that makes clear that you value the worker may lead to using this experience as the basis for exploring alternative tactics with the housing authority (teaching function).

In general, you can reinforce self-acceptance by acting on the basis of information that can be verified; by limiting your attribution of cause or motive to what you observe; and by allowing room for supervisees to discuss attitudes, feelings, and behaviors in their own terms. Also, you can avoid threats to self-acceptance by carefully dealing with the rumors and innuendos that abound in bureaucracies. Your sensitivity to the negative consequences of accepting rumor as fact is very important to maintaining a work climate conducive to self-acceptance among workers.

Two examples may help you think more concretely about these aspects of humanizing.

EXAMPLE: A rumor circulating is that one of the clients at a residence for status offenders has had sexual relations with one of the workers.

This is a serious accusation. It is important to the well-being of the client, the worker, and the agency to determine the validity of the rumor. It might be natural to accept organizational concerns as a priority and suspend or terminate the worker on the basis of the client's allegation. But this would put the supervisor in a position of accepting rumor as fact and attributing unethical conduct to the worker. This is a supervisory dilemma you may encounter in one form or another in your practice. As the supervisor, you are accountable for what goes on. You have to be *for* the client, yet also be *for* the worker. Situations such as this one are delicate matters to address. They will require your sensitivity and decisiveness.

In this case, the supervisor invited the worker in for a private conference to share the rumor and to indicate that he would have to check it out. The worker claimed the rumor was just that and denied engaging in sexual relations with the client. In checking out the rumor, the supervisor determined that the worker had denied the client privileges for one week for assaulting another resident. This event occurred a few days prior to the beginning of the rumor. Also, the supervisor discovered that the client had made similar claims in the past whenever a worker had refused her advances or placed limits on her behavior.

What we can note from this is the value of a balanced, nonjudgmental supervisory approach to a serious matter. The supervisor's behavior demonstrates sensitivity to all parties involved and communicates a willingness to explore situations objectively before arriving at conclusions.

A second example concerns a less controversial issue, yet one that clearly illustrates the particulars of the humanizing function in supervisory practice.

EXAMPLE: The supervisor of a youth-services team has observed that every afternoon for the last three days, one of her workers has had his head down on the desk and appears to be sleeping.

While there are probably an unlimited number of possible explanations for the observed behavior and a similar unlimited number of supervisory responses, consider these two:

1. Supervisor: "What's wrong with you?"
2. Supervisor: "I have noticed you sitting with your head down for some time each of the last three afternoons and I am concerned."

At first glance, both responses seem possible for a supervisor. However, there is a critical difference between the two that has implications for worker self-acceptance and for the supervisor-supervisee relationship. Although the first approach appears to be straightforward, let us consider the matter of expression. The question reflects a negative judgment by the supervisor, as indicated by the word *wrong*. This is likely to generate a defensive response from the worker. As stated, the question may also suggest that the supervisor is accusing the worker of something. The question prematurely personalizes the response expected.

In the second response, the supervisor engages the worker by noting her own observation without any expression of judgment. The statement of an objective observation coupled with an expression of caring allows room for the worker to save face. This approach increases the possibility of a more open, less defensive discussion of the behavior with him. In essence, the supervisor is approaching the worker in a manner that shows sensitivity and personal regard for him. The worker's dignity is not questioned, as it is in the first approach. In the second approach, the statement "I am concerned" suggests that the worker is valued and needed.

*Encouraging interpersonal regard.* When considering interpersonal relationships as part of the humanizing function, you will need to remember the personal elements discussed above. In addition, you must consider the particulars of interpersonal relationships and how to affect them from the position of supervisor.

Certain characteristics have been identified as contributing factors in the development and maintenance of interpersonal relationships—both in our private lives and in our everyday work situations. Factors such as trust, caring, openness, and interdependence are essential to the kinds of relationships that are sought not only privately, between supervisors and supervisees, but also within an agency.

Trust can be established when the supervisor is consistent in word and action and follows through on commitments made to supervisees. In the work situation, trust includes allowing workers to perform their duties and tasks with a sense of confidence that you, as supervisor, will support their efforts. This is particularly important if you wish to facilitate the ongoing development of supervisees. You are extending the concern for worker self-acceptance to the development of the interpersonal aspects of the work.

Closely related to trust is the sense of caring that you demonstrate by investing your time and energy in behalf of supervisees and the work to be done. As workers come to the realization that your interest and concern for them in interpersonal relationships is genuine, their job performance is likely to be enhanced. They will be able to carry over the positive interpersonal supervisor-supervisee relationship into peer relationships and worker-client relationships. To illustrate the importance of trust and caring in supervisor-supervisee relationships, we can note the following report of a B.S.W. social worker in a residence for disabled adults.

EXAMPLE: A particularly memorable event occurred one afternoon, when a 24-year-old resident came to me to report that she had been raped the previous afternoon. This resident was borderline mentally retarded. Needless to say, she was terribly frightened and upset. I talked with her for some time and decided to call my supervisor at home, as it was after 5:30. He agreed with my plan of intervention and asked that I keep him posted. So, I contacted the resident's parents and husband and then notified my supervisor that the decision had been made to call the police and the Rape Relief Center.

While we were waiting for the police to arrive, my supervisor arrived on the scene stating that four-on-one seemed like rather heavy odds. He wondered if I might like to have some support myself. He was extremely helpful in working with the husband and the father while I focused on the resident, her mother, and the police. He stayed with us until 1:30 a.m., when the rape examination was finished at Community Hospital and the resident and her husband left for her parent's home. My supervisor's support, expertise, and expression of concern for me and confidence in my ability made the nightmare bearable.

In this example, the supervisor began by affirming the worker's strengths (the intervention plan) and then, recognizing the extreme interpersonal demands of this situation, made his own caring and personal energies available to the worker and her client. The worker experienced the situation as one of valuing her, trusting her ability, and caring about her as a person as well as a worker. These are examples of the types of interpersonal components of the work that are central to the humanizing function. In essence, by word and by action the supervisor contributed to the worker's self-acceptance and confirmation. His voluntary presence helped generate the psychological and interpersonal resources necessary to support both client and worker.

Openness is another factor that is necessary for the development of positive interpersonal resources at work and in relationships. By openness we mean sharing of ideas, opinions, feelings, and experiences. It involves recognition of the diverse talents of workers and variability in approaches to effectively dealing with clients, workers, and supervisors. As you carry out the humanizing function of supervision, you will need to be open to a variety of adjustments that reflect concern for supervisees as important resources. This can include flextime for workers with small children or for workers with other special caretaking needs at home. Caseload adjustments may be in order for some workers. Initially, new workers might be assigned fewer cases while they get oriented to the agency and to peer and supervisor-supervisee relationships. Or caseloads may be adjusted to provide unusual on-the-job opportunities for supervisees to develop additional knowledge and skills. When you recognize differences in the level of difficulty of cases assigned to various workers, you may make adjustments to demonstrate your open recognition of such differences and their impact on worker capacity to respond effectively. Finally, you may make adjustments in office arrangements. For example, you could respond positively to worker suggestions for a rotational schedule of time in the office to cover emergency intakes and to stay current on paperwork.

Being open to personal and interpersonal aspects of the work situation will help you and your supervisees in early identification of issues that might ultimately affect getting tasks accomplished. Such an approach will help you and your supervisees attain qualitative and quantitative goals of agency service without losing sight of the personal and interpersonal aspects of the work.

*Giving feedback.* Openness involves more than recognizing the uniqueness of your supervisees and making adjustments in the work environment to meet worker needs. Giving feedback is an additional aspect of openness that is important to the humanizing function. Feedback has been found to be significantly correlated with positive worker attitudes and performance (Pines and Kafry, 1978). We have previously noted that from the perspective of supervision, much of a supervisee's performance is invisible. This creates pressures for both supervisees and supervisors. For the supervisee, the pressure comes from experiencing too little of success—positive outcomes from the helping process either are nonexistent or develop only slowly. Moreover, the most frequently visible result may be perceived as a negative outcome—for instance, when clients return for more services because of new problems that they cannot resolve unassisted. Briar has pointed to the prevalence of a feeling of despair among practitioners, a feeling that nothing they do works (Briar, 1973).

For you as a supervisor, the pressure is to recognize the distinction between feedback that is formally mandated in terms of periodic performance appraisal (the evaluating function, discussed later) and personal feedback regarding the "little things." Such personal responses can make a difference in the attitudes and behaviors of your supervisees. This kind of feedback usually focuses on the work of supervisees and includes the sick worker, and so forth. In giving this kind of feedback, you help supervisees feel valued. In addition, your behavior sets an example for workers to emulate with one another. The combined effects of supervisory and peer feedback contribute to an atmosphere of appreciation and affirmation of individual and collective efforts on behalf of clients and the agency. In part, this helps to replenish the necessary psychological and interpersonal resources that your supervisees need to function effectively and to maintain commitments to the agency. The following example of feedback illustrates these ideas.

> EXAMPLE: Like most B.S.W.'s with little practical experience, I was unsure of my professional abilities and unaware of my strengths and weaknesses. I wanted help in objectively seeing what I did well and what I needed to work on, since it would affect my performance and motivation. My supervisor on the adult psychiatric unit of the hospital was very sensitive to this aspect of supervision. He complimented workers on things they did well. He praised very specific tasks at the time they were achieved and did not resort to general comments to everyone that "you did fine." I remember during my first month on the job I had noticed that a depressed patient did not talk to anyone. I decided to invite him for a walk outside on the grounds. Reluctantly, he went along. After about ten minutes of walking quietly together he stopped and said, "You know I am a carpenter and work outside most of the year. You are the first person to get me outside, and I have been here two weeks." When we returned to the unit, my supervisor noticed that the patient and I were engaged in conversation. A few minutes later, he came up to me and said, "That was very thoughtful of you to take the patient out and get him to talk with you. He has not talked to anyone on staff except the psychiatrist since he has been here. I would like you to work with him, since you seem to have gotten him started." I was so happy. From that point on I knew I could make it as a social worker.

As reported, this represents the ideal in the use and outcome of appropriate feedback. The supervisor gave specific recognition to the worker's accomplishment, at a fitting time, and in a way that communicated respect and valuing of the worker. Not only was feedback given, but a specific assignment was made that further reinforced the worker's belief in herself and the supervisor's confidence in her ability to help a client with whom others had been unable to relate.

One of the additional impacts of feedback relates to commitment. By recognizing and reinforcing your supervisees' feelings of value and competence, you can set the tone for them to initiate activity. It has been noted that the quality of service delivery is enhanced when workers assume responsibility that goes beyond what is delegated by the supervisor (Arndt, 1973). In the example, the worker took the initiative by inviting the client to go outside and getting him to communicate. Then she was reinforced by the supervisor, when he assigned her the case responsibility. Because she initiated a relationship that became formalized, she will be more likely to take initiative in the future. As a supervisor, when you recognize the specific accomplishments of your supervisees as they occur, you communicate your awareness of their performance as well as your commitment to encouraging their skills usage. The combination of your personal recognition and your recognition of specific skills can contribute a great deal to job satisfaction and worker dignity.

To establish and maintain a work environment conducive to openness and feedback, you will want to demonstrate your own ability to give feedback on yourself. In particular, you can effectively model openness by accepting responsibility for your own behavior, including mistakes and errors. Giving feedback on yourself will help supervisees feel comfortable about doing the same. The demands of service delivery and the metawork (activities that enhance the work but are aside from the work itself) of the organization result in individual mistakes or errors at all levels. It is important for you and your supervisees to be able to identify and acknowledge mistakes. Acknowledging that anyone can and will make mistakes or errors helps to depersonalize and universalize work issues in interpersonal relationships. Also, mistakes that are dealt with as they occur can be the basis for new learning that can be applied in future work situations.

Other types of issues may also be generated by your likes and dislikes for certain aspects of the supervisory role. Just as you might expect your supervisees to acknowledge parts of the job that they dislike and that affect their performance, so you should be prepared to do the same. When you identify and own up to personal and interpersonal vulnerabilities that have affected your performance, you demonstrate openness to yourself and to sharing critical self-assessments. Also, you display the security that is so important in achieving needed adjustments related to the humanizing function. Such behavior on your part, as a supervisor, may very well free up your supervisees to engage in the same kinds of personal and interpersonal assessments, and this can enhance the personal and interpersonal aspects of the work.

Giving feedback involves not only praise and publicly valuing good work but also constructive critical feedback regarding mistakes or inappropriate work behavior. Timely critical feedback is just as important as timely positive feedback. When one of your supervisees has made a mistake or an error in judgment, it is important for you to provide immediate feedback. If you wait until later, it may appear to your supervisees that you have stored up incidents with which to clobber them. Japanese managers tend to approach this type of feedback with an eye to saving face for those involved (Pascale and Athos, 1981). We think this makes especially good sense for supervisory behavior in the social services.

Deliberate face-saving with supervisees involves giving them constructive criticism in private. This approach avoids public embarrassment of the supervisee and demonstrates your caring about the supervisee as well as the problem. To illustrate the importance of saving face you can consider the following example from practice.

EXAMPLE: One day as I walked down a hallway past the training room toward my office, I overheard a worker yelling at a client about not following through on all tasks assigned at a prior group session. As I continued on to my office, the yelling continued and I was sure that others passing by overheard the worker. I decided to invite the worker in at the end of the day for a conference. I began by asking about the job-readiness group. The worker responded that some were making progress and others were not. After a brief discussion I mentioned that earlier in the day, when walking past the training room to my office, I had overheard some yelling at the clients. The worker explained that the yelling was a motivational technique used to get the clients going in being more assertive and persistent in doing tasks required in getting a job. I agreed that motivation was important and I shared my ideas on motivation and motivational techniques. Also, I noted that others who overheard the yelling might have thought we were mistreating our clients and that this was a serious concern. I indicated I would like to avoid doing things that might be misinterpreted by our clients or others involved with the agency. I then asked the worker if being yelled at was motivational for him. He looked away and sighed. I commented that getting clients who had never worked ready for a job was a tough assignment. He then opened up about how frustrating it was and how much he wanted all the clients to be successful. We explored approaches to increasing follow through that were more appropriate than yelling. At the end of the conference, he thanked me for not yelling about his yelling and for listening to his frustrations. He agreed to try different approaches and to be more aware in the future of any tendency to shout or yell at clients.

What is clearly apparent in this face-saving approach is that the worker is allowed to explain the behavior in question from his perspective. Then the supervisor notes alternative interpretations of the same behavior and suggests possible undesirable results. The worker is not attacked publicly or privately, but is made aware of the problematic behavior and options for its elimination followed by replacement with other more appropriate behaviors pertinent to the same desired outcome.

In summary, we have described, analyzed, and illustrated from practice the ways in which the humanizing function contributes to solidarity among supervisees and between supervisees and supervisor. This solidarity results from the supervisor's sensitivity to integrating the personal and interpersonal aspects of work with organizational requirements. The cumulative effect of the humanizing function is to enhance worker dignity, as well as organizational stability. Supervisor activities within the humanizing function include at a minimum:

1. Commending supervisees on specific action
2. Expressing publicly the valuing of the work of others
3. Making adjustments in the work environment
4. Openly pointing to or admitting own mistakes
5. Deliberately allowing supervisees to save face

### Managing Tension

Various research studies have suggested that uncertainties associated with work and the organization can produce tension, reflecting stress and conflict

(Kahn, 1981). Work that is characterized by uncertainty of success, underutilization of worker skills and abilities, and heavy demands for quantity can result in both stress and conflict, for supervisors and supervisees. In addition, when organizational environments involve responsibilities for both soluble and insoluble problems, impersonality in work relationships, and a routinization of activity, these factors interact with the work characteristics just noted. The result is considerable frustration for workers and supervisors (Austin, 1981). Moreover, in the social services, supervisors and supervisees are not only concerned with their own well-being, but they are also directly responsible for the well-being of others and are expected to be responsive to many people under continuous pressures of time and scarce resources. To maintain a climate of dignity and some degree of organizational stability will involve initiatives to minimize the negative and to nurture the positive aspects of these and other sources of stress and conflict.

Managing tension is the supervisory function related to using the power of supervisors and supervisees as a means of coping with stress and conflict. This function is critical in combating the deleterious effects of unresolved stress and conflict, both on worker dignity and on organizational stability. Stress may be related to ambiguity in performance standards and organizational goals, to the uncertainty in matching services to needs, and/or to the precariousness of resources available to the organization and its clientele. Conflict is usually related to the contradictory demands of clients, the agency, and the profession.

In the social services, stress and conflict are inevitable; in fact, they are productive at times. On the other hand, they may contribute to low morale and a sense of powerlessness among workers and clients. As you fulfill the supervisory responsibilities related to this function, your aim will be to help workers maintain a sense of control over their work and interpersonal relations; to recognize and use their power potentials, working from the lower positions in the agency; and to express as well as recognize diverse perspectives on common issues concerning workers, service delivery, and/or the organization. Attending to the stress and conflicts inherent in service delivery and the organizational context will help you and your supervisees develop approaches to utilizing the power of the lower-level members of organizations—access to and control over persons, information, and other resources (Mechanic, 1962)—for managing tension.

*Interpersonal tension.* It has been noted in the literature that organizational pressures for compliance with standardized rules and procedures in service delivery can produce feelings of frustration and powerlessness among workers (Pines and Kafry, 1978; Finch, 1981). These pressures are a source of tension in the typical social agency, whose direct service staff is characterized by diversity, and whose clients may represent a microcosm of the problems and aspirations of the whole society. The interaction of age, gender, education and experience, and ideologies can be sources of strength and competence if you recognize the value of diversity and help your supervisees to do the same.

Openly encouraging communication that may include diverse points of view will be important to you and your supervisees in early identification of possible sources of tension. By openly expressing your own opinions on agency, worker, client, and professional issues, you can create an environment for supervisees to feel comfortable in when they take risks by expressing their own ideas and feelings. When you encourage and support freedom of expression, you contribute to your supervisees' psychological sense of having command over thoughts and feelings about personal, interpersonal, or organizational issues.

It has been noted that polarization of conflict in a group can often be avoided by generating alternatives, focusing discussion on issues and feelings rather than individuals, and encouraging feedback among group members (Phillips, 1973). In such cases when supervisors have encouraged these behaviors, they have contributed to the sense of power of individual supervisees and of the group as a whole. When alternatives and specific action plans are generated, additional credence is given to the power of professional norms (e.g., consultation in decisions that affect individuals and their work; teamwork to increase the resources beyond those of a given individual). Also, the potential power derived from demonstrating interest and investing effort (Mechanic, 1962) is advanced by supervisee involvement, for example, in developing a specific in-service workshop.

Social work professionals encounter a multitude of demands from a variety of sources, including the clients, the agency, and the profession. To the extent that the demands from one source conflict with the expectations of another, stress is experienced and tension is aroused. Often the focus of agency procedures is primarily on task completion. While task completion is obviously necessary for stable, effective agency functioning, it will be important for you, as a supervisor, to consider the tensions accompanying the work as well as the tasks themselves. Many of the criticisms and angry feelings of your supervisees will be related to confusions and contradictions between agency expectations and supervisee responsibilities. It will be important for you, first, to create a supportive context in which the doubts, anxieties, and confusions that have precipitated these feelings can be shared, and second, to provide a structure in which approaches to their resolution can be discovered.

A second approach is also possible. You might pursue a mediating stance toward your supervisees. This is illustrated through the following situation in an institution for the care and treatment of the mentally ill and mentally retarded. This situation underlines the importance of your ability to assume a mediating position. This stance can often result in a compromise that is acceptable to you and your supervisees. It is important for you to take action that can reduce stress and conflict while still producing supervisee responses that satisfy your expectations and those of the agency.

EXAMPLE: The supervisor of the acute-care social work team sent a memo informing all workers that from then on, for patients ready for release, discharge reports were to be prepared two weeks prior to the discharge date. Previously, discharge reports had been submitted on the day of release. This new directive was met by opposition. Many expressed their dissatisfaction and anxiety about the impact this would have on services. The supervisor decided to hold a meeting to clarify the issues and attempt to reduce tensions. During a lengthy discussion, the reasons behind workers' concerns were expressed: mainly, work loads that were already too heavy, too much paperwork, and not enough time to comply with the two-week deadline.

The supervisor said it was difficult to evaluate plans that were not available prior to the date of discharge. Moreover, his secretary was overloaded and needed the two weeks to prepare the reports. At the same time, he expressed a willingness to consider alternatives that would balance both sets of concerns. After more discussion, they were able to compromise on a one-week deadline.

In such situations it will be important for you to recognize that managing tension involves not only reacting to stress and conflict, but also initiating action to prevent their escalation. In the illustration, the supervisor reacted to tension by calling a meeting and being prepared to mediate to avoid escalation. In general, we would suggest that you consistently act to develop an atmosphere of mutual respect where problems are confronted rather than covered up. Your goal is to surface any differences of opinion and work them through before they grow into major tensions. By utilizing differences of opinion to develop innovative approaches to supervisory, agency, and supervisee problems, you can help prevent tensions. Specifically building into your supervision the opportunity for ventilation or expression of feelings (especially anger) may be essential to developing an atmosphere that supports the constructive use of disagreements.

*Organizational environment tensions.*   As a supervisor, you will need to deal with stress and conflict that reflect tensions produced by the organizational environment (as contrasted with tensions produced by interpersonal sources). The nature of formal organizations builds in tensions that will constantly be of concern to you and your supervisees. Tensions arising from organizational sources will usually be of two types. One will be organizational-design decisions that conflict with service provision. A second type will be the conflict between organizational goals and individual supervisee goals. Tensions of the first type often will relate to increases in work loads, demands for quantity over quality, displacement of ends by means (e.g., workers spending more time on paperwork than in contact with clients), and organizational rules and procedures that inhibit appropriate service delivery procedures. Tensions of the second type often focus on issues of professionals in the bureaucracy, especially in terms of performance expectations or standards and worker discretion (see Chapter 6).

By developing creative approaches to distributing work loads, to balancing quantity and quality, and to handling less pleasant tasks, you can often reduce the tensions involved. As a supervisor, your own attitude and approach to these organization-based sources of tension are crucial. Research has shown that the emotional costs of such tensions include low job satisfaction, low confidence in the organization, a high degree of job tension, and behavioral responses of withdrawal or avoidance (Kahn, 1964). Your ability to look for creative ways to get the job done within organizational constraints will provide a model for your supervisees in combating the negative effects of these tension-producing organizational problems. Involvement of your supervisees in this effort can contribute to the creation of an esprit de corps that can aid in managing tension.

Introducing creative, flexible approaches to managing tension whose source is the organization may involve you in risk taking. You will need to use your judgment about where to draw the line between compliance with organizational demands and responsiveness to client, supervisee, and professional demands. There may be occasions where your decision on reconciling opposing demands will involve bending, modifying, or adjusting procedures. We can illustrate this response to detrimental organizational constraints on effective service delivery through the following situation in a county welfare agency.

EXAMPLE: Responding to public criticism of the efficiency and effectiveness of county government agencies, the county administrator established mandatory work hours for all county employees from 8:30 A.M. to 5 P.M. The director of the county welfare agency complied with this executive order and instituted these hours for all agency staff.

One of the programs of the agency provided youth services with a primary goal of delinquency prevention. Social workers in this program had worked mainly from noon to 8 P.M., since services were oriented to working with youth, teachers, and families after school and work hours. With the mandate for new working hours, the supervisor of this program directed his workers to comply.

After several weeks, it became apparent that these new hours were seriously limiting the ability of workers to do their outreach work and to meet their groups for teachers, youth, and parents. Because of the time constraints and the problems in continuing to meet groups according to the previous schedules, some youth and parents had dropped out. Also, some teachers were complaining about social workers making contacts during school hours more frequently than in the past, a situation that they found disruptive to their educational responsibilities.

The supervisor agonized over these dilemmas and took the situation to his immediate superior. He was told that the hours were mandatory and that the agency needed to comply in order to avoid further threats to its already precarious budget.

After thinking through possible options, the supervisor held a meeting with his workers at his home. He expressed understanding of their dilemma and explained the outcome of his conversation with his superior. He expressed his belief that relieving the situation involved risks for himself and for the workers. After discussing the pros and cons of continuing the program as it was or risking a modification, there was consensus that the needs of the clientele were worth taking risks. The supervisor then shared a plan for rotating work hours during the week so that there would always be office coverage. The plan also included "explanations" that would account for workers who were not in the office in the morning, so that they might work during the original hours. It was agreed to keep the adjustment of working hours confidential. Details for the rotation were worked out carefully, and the supervisor and workers mutually pledged to stand together if the adjustment was discovered and challenged by higher-level administrators.

Obviously the supervisor and the workers took a calculated risk. If discovered, they risked sanctions and reprimands in their personnel files. Also, they had to accept the possibility of their being dealt with through the use of coercive power, especially the possibility of increased close surveillance of their performance. These risks were balanced by appeals to normative power in the form of group consensus and approval of a plan for mutual aid and protection. Also, the power to withhold information as well as to collect information, and the power to document accountability despite the bending of a rule, provided the supervisor and the workers with some degree of countervailing power to that of the administration.

While this approach is probably one to be followed very cautiously, the facts as presented in the illustration warrant the actions taken. As a supervisor, you will need to exercise your professional judgment and not yield unnecessarily to the requirements of administrative convenience (Pruger, 1973). Your assessment in situations such as this one will involve your recognition that sometimes organizational procedures must be adjusted in order to achieve certain valued program goals. Such actions may be necessary to ensure that the organizational rules and procedures do not unduly restrict use of resources in meeting legitimate client or worker demands. As a supervisor, it will be important for you to develop the ability to distinguish "between that which serves the organization *and* the organizational mission, and that which merely serves the organization per se" (Kurzman, 1977, p. 430).

For managing the tensions produced by the organizational environment, one approach, not frequently explored in the literature, is the use of humor. Some level of tension is usually present for professionals in bureaucracies. At the same time, some irritations or stresses will have no immediate or lasting resolution. It is in such situations where the judicious use of humor, jokes, or storybook analogies and the ability to laugh at one's predicament can make the tension more tolerable. It has been suggested that use of humor and laughing at yourself are critical to maintaining your sense of self in environments that make heavy emotional demands or involve aversive environmental constraints (Goffman, 1959).

As a supervisor, you will want to recognize situations that present irresolvable tensions and to consider using humor to lighten up an otherwise tense atmosphere— whether among your supervisees or between yourself and supervisees. As a supervisor, you occupy a buffering position that includes responsibility for dissipating tensions among your supervisees before they escalate to the point of interference with work performance (Kadushin, 1976). In a review of occupational-stress studies, it was found that effective buffering of job stress and strain can alleviate tension, particularly physical tension, within the person (French, 1974). Humor is one buffer source available to you and your supervisees.

The following humorous story, used by a supervisor in a tense staff meeting, illustrates this approach.

EXAMPLE: As a supervisor, I was involved in a staff meeting called to discuss workers' complaints about a policy change that increased minimum workload assignments and committed each worker to one day per week of outreach work (including weekends) in the retirees program.

The meeting seemed to be moving from the usual griping toward acrimony, victim blaming, and name calling. So, I intervened to state that the feelings being expressed reminded me of a story appropriate to the issue at hand.

There was a man who saw a 100-year-old grandfather clock with a huge weight at the bottom. He watched that old clock having to push that weight back and forth and thought, "That's a terrible burden for such an old clock. It moves so slow." Obviously it was tiring to the old antique. So he opened the glass case and lifted the huge weight off to relieve the old clock. But the clock said, "Why did you take my weight off?" And the man replied, "Well I know it was a burden to you." But the old clock explained, "Oh no! My weight is what keeps me going!"

The workers smiled at the story. Some began to tell their own stories and to make other light-hearted comments in the spirit of understanding the reality and necessity of the service delivery burden while at the same time wanting to protect time for their own personal needs.

Situations such as this one are increasingly common in the social services as they are buffeted by reduced resources and increased demands. In this illustration, the supervisor used humor to relieve what might have become an ugly interpersonal and personalized atmosphere of attack and counterattack. It will be important for you to use humor appropriately to relieve tension-charged situations. But you will also need to avoid the mistake of substituting humor for action on serious issues related to clients, agency, and professional demands. Humor may be an appropriate means of relaxing your supervisees so that together you can address issues systematically—in the search for options, the development of commitments, and the implementation of action to resolve stress and conflict that endure beyond the immediacy of the felt tensions.

In summary, we have identified and described sources of stress and conflict that you and your supervisees can expect to encounter while working in the agency context. We have defined and illustrated from practice the supervisory function of managing tension. We have analyzed the importance of this function in contributing to a sense of power rather than powerlessness for yourself and your supervisees. In discussing illustrations of managing tension in supervisory practice, we have emphasized the importance of this function for preserving commitments to client, agency, and professional expectations that also support dignity for workers and the work. The cumulative result of managing tension at the supervisee level is to enhance supervisees' ability to use tension for development and change rather than circumvention, sabotage, and manipulation. Supervisor and supervisee feelings of power and self-management in tense situations are essential to maintaining organizational stability. Supervisor activities within the tension managing-function include at a minimum:

1. Encouraging diverse points of view
2. Helping others see something from a different perspective
3. Assuming a mediating position
4. Allowing time for ventilation or expression of anger
5. Bending, modifying, or adjusting a procedure
6. Using humor in tense situations

### Catalyzing

In Chapter 4, we mentioned the dilemmas faced by clients, workers, and agencies as a result of the tendency of society (especially policy makers and governmental service arrangers) to translate public issues into private troubles. To the extent that this occurs, social service workers and supervisors are expected to apply Band-aids to individuals and groups who are victimized by significant social problems, such as unemployment, racism, sexism, ageism, insufficient housing, and lack of health care. The resulting frustrations may lead to cynicism as well as physical, cognitive, and emotional overload (Wasserman, 1971; Pines and Kafry, 1978). During periods of reaction and contraction in the community mandate, public disillusionment and disenchantment with the social services magnify these pressures.

As a supervisor, you will need to be sensitive to these contextual influences on service delivery and on your supervisees. It will be important to initiate actions that can help supervisees feel competent despite these societal and organizational pressures. Maintaining a sense of dignity and worth for supervisees so that they may convey these same feelings to clients is an integral part of developing and sustaining integration of supervisees and the work. These actions are fundamental in fulfilling your supervisory obligations related to organizational stability. It has been noted that social service workers and supervisors highly value a work environment that provides stimulation in thinking about new ways to deal with old problems. This includes thinking in new ways about theory and practice, bringing new developments in the profession into the work group, and interacting with colleagues who through their curiosity, idealism, and enthusiasm stimulate renewed individual and group energy and commitment (Kadushin, 1976; Haynes, 1979; Glicken, 1980). Your actions as a supervisor can have a significant impact on supervisee curiosity, enthusiasm, and spirit of solidarity. When encouragement is given to a work environment and work relationships that involve the sharing of ideas and responsibilities, a sense of teamwork or interdependence can be developed. Such interdependence can contribute to freedom of self-expression, a greater sense of power, and more involvement in the agency; these, in turn, contribute to stronger morale and commitments to clients, peers, the agency, and the profession.

Catalyzing is the supervisory function that focuses on fostering interdependence or teamwork, and on building morale, and that is often related to the "new idea." In initiating the activities associated with this function, you will contribute to the maintenance of the implied contract linking individual, group, and agency goals. In social service agencies, the face-to-face work group is the place where, potentially, supervisees can satisfy their needs, influence the organization, and integrate personal goals with those of the group and the agency. We have chosen purposely the term *catalyzing* to label this function. Your catalyzing activities as a supervisor are analogous to those of a catalyst in the natural sciences and medicine. As a catalyst, you can speed up creative responses to issues and slow down negative or pathogenic processes (as in the catalytic converter in automobiles, which is designed to reduce polluting emissions). Moreover, in the world as kaleidoscope, catalyzing is an important element in the thinking and acting we have discussed.

The transforming and self-organizing potential of individuals and groups in the organizational context has been argued to be a function of supervisors and other administrators who assume the responsibilities of a catalyst (Zeleny and Pierre, 1976). As you fulfill the catalyzing function, your aim will be to make practice more exhilarating, to counter the stagnation that can occur in the life course of an organization, and to counter frustrations and cynicism that can result from the pressures for uniformity and predictability in delivering services that involve ambiguity and uncertainty. Rules and regulations are likely to increase as agencies come under greater surveillance by politicians, funding sources, and the public. But "mere condemnation of rules and regulations is a little like cursing the darkness, rather than lighting a candle: After the cathartic effect has worn off, no light has been shed on the problem" (Kurzman, 1977, p. 429). As a supervisor, you can act within the catalyzing function to stimulate supervisees to assert themselves and determine their own actions in these organizational structures and processes. In this way, interdependence is fostered and morale is enhanced.

*Fostering interdependence.* We have noted previously that the more complex and specialized the organization, the greater the importance of interdependence. In achieving agency goals, meeting client needs, and responding to an ever-fluctuating context, staff must be able to work together to pool their resources to produce results beyond the capacity of a single individual (Weber, 1972). At the same time, the integration of individual, group, and agency interests may be perturbed by stress and conflict—between individuals and the agency, between peers, between demands for cooperation and drives for competition, and between short-term and long-term objectives. As a supervisor, you cannot leave this integration to chance; you will need to balance concerns for independence and dependence with the imperative of interdependence.

Each of us as an individual needs to feel free, independent, and capable of doing things on our own at least part of the time. In most organizations, this is reflected by a climate of individualism and competition. In social agencies, this need is more often reflected in a push for autonomous practice. Yet at other times we need to be dependent, to have the right and the opportunity of placing ourselves in the care of others when our own resources are not sufficient. In social work, we recognize this need in terms of nurturing relationships and a nurturing work environment. Equally important to these needs is that of interdependence, which allows us to share our specific knowledge and skills with others in a collaborative way to produce good-quality decisions and good-quality outcomes. Still, it has been noted that social work supervision has frequently encouraged and perpetuated worker dependency, rather than independence and interdependence (Perlmutter, 1972).

In most contemporary social agencies, the need is for supervision that fosters interdependence. The recent attention to the "art" of Japanese management has emphasized that organizational survival is coming to depend critically upon how well people collaborate within complex organizations (Pascale and Athos, 1981; Ouchi, 1981). As a supervisor, you can play a catalyzing part in building inter-dependence by spurring the natural curiosity and creativity of your supervisees. It was noted long ago that interdependence is integral to the creative side of or-ganizations (Barnard, 1938). In the following example, we see how a supervisor fosters interdependence by supporting the curiosity and enterprise of two M.S.W. supervisees.

> EXAMPLE: In a large comprehensive-care center, numerous items of audio-visual equipment had been purchased over a number of years. The equipment was kept in storage, and usage was monitored by the director of operations and budget.
>
> One day two M.S.W.s who had seen the equipment in storage approached their supervisor. They asked about the purpose of the equipment. The super-visor told them that the equipment had been purchased for training and other clinical applications, but that it had been in storage since the training direc-tor's position had been eliminated. The workers explained that they were more curious than knowledgeable about AV equipment and possible applica-tions, but that they would like to experiment with it during spare time. The supervisor expressed his support and enthusiasm for what might result and arranged for the equipment to be checked out on a long-term basis to the workers.
>
> Over the following weeks, the workers began to "play" with the equipment, learning how to assemble and use it on their own. They held mock interviews and involved the supervisor in demonstrating the potential available. When other workers and supervisors questioned the supervisor about what was going on and expressed doubts or criticisms, the supervisor backed the workers for their initiative and encouraged others to join in.
>
> Once the workers felt comfortable with the equipment, they began to use it in their clinical work with groups and families. In addition, the workers offered informal training sessions on the equipment for other interested staff. These staff members began to use it in their work. The use was extended to a group in a prison setting and to assertiveness training, where clients were taped and then given visual playback and feedback. Over the course of several months, several worker groups formed to develop other uses for the equip-ment, and responsibility for the equipment was transferred from the director of operations and budget to the two workers and their supervisor.

This example documents not only the primary gain of enhanced cooperation between two supervisees, but also the secondary gain of an elaborated network of creative interdependencies among many supervisees and supervisors. Not only did the supervisor encourage his workers, but he also supported them in the face of questions and criticisms. Moreover, the environment of the agency was refreshed by creative endeavors. Also, agency resources were more fully utilized in ways that contributed to worker, client, and agency interests. In this case, the catalyzing ac-tivity of the supervisor in encouraging supervisees to pursue a special interest in-creased interdependence as well as new knowledge and training opportunities for themselves and others.

Molding individual and group interests into a cohesive set of relationships that produce valued results for clients, supervisees, and the agency is also a matter of supervisory concern. It has been noted that in Japan, management attends to these interdependency issues by relating to both technical and interpersonal skill domains of employees. In contrast, organizations in the United States tend to emphasize the technical to the detriment of the interpersonal, especially among line workers (Pascale and Athos, 1981). To offset this tendency in social agencies, it will be important for you, as a supervisor, to encourage staff in working together at meetings, in getting things done with peers, and in collaborating with you on various tasks. In this way, you will all learn to be resources to one another and to establish mutual recognition that for any given situation, the resources may reside with the supervisor, with supervisees, or in the combined forces of the two.

The following situation illustrates the benefits that can accrue to supervisors, supervisees, and the agency when the supervisor deliberately encourages staff collaboration on an important problem.

EXAMPLE: The community multiservice center had grown rapidly during the last three years. The growth had been so rapid that the initial job descriptions were no longer appropriate. As supervisor, I was continuously at odds with the new program director regarding my responsibilities and those of my workers. Attempts to negotiate a solution had been unsuccessful. One day, several of my workers stated that their frustrations had reached the breaking point. They offered to propose that new job and task descriptions be drafted and adopted for our unit. I was relieved by their offer and encouraged them to proceed, even though they had little experience in this area and I had reservations about the receptivity of the program director to such initiatives.

My workers pulled in their peers and developed a work plan to produce new job descriptions within one month. At the end of the month, they had developed basic descriptions and performance standards for themselves and for me. A delegation was chosen to accompany me to the program director. In this meeting I explained my workers' concern about conflict and ambiguity in job performance during the recent past. Then we introduced the job descriptions and standards as a possible option for our unit. To my surprise, the program director was very enthusiastic and asked my workers to draft basic descriptions and performance standards for all line and management positions in the agency. When these drafts were completed, he circulated them to all staff for feedback and changes.

At the end of the process when final copies were distributed for implementation, my workers were commended at an agency-wide staff meeting. For my workers and me, as well as for other staff, there was a sense of greater security about our responsibilities. The conflict and stress that had built up dissipated.

This example demonstrates the multiple benefits that can result when a supervisor applies the catalyzing function to work with supervisees on agency problems. The stimulus for catalyzing activity in this instance emerged from organizational change that had an impact on supervisee, supervisor, and administrator performance. While the supervisor recognized that problems existed, the initiative to address the problem came from supervisees. Then this initiative was encouraged by the supervisor. This sequence of events demonstrates that with respect to the catalyzing function, the initial stimulus can come from sources outside the supervisor. You will want to be cognizant of these possibilities as you perform daily supervisory activities, since the catalyzing function can trigger actions that are related to other supervisory imperatives.

Specifically, this situation involved the interdependence of agency, worker, and supervisor interests. By encouraging the workers, the supervisor increased the resources available to address the identified problems. As a result, potential for increased stress and conflict was reduced—an important contribution to maintaining worker dignity and agency stability. The outcome of job clarification and objective performance standards contributed not only to interdependence, but also to secondary gains in service delivery (performance standards for accountability within the evaluating function) and to linkages (improved understanding of roles and communication channels within the administering function).

Fostering interdependence also may require the supervisor to act to damp out threats to cooperative problem solving and decision making. In the catalyzing function, you will want not only to stimulate and encourage supervisees in using their curiosity and creativity in working together on common problems, new ideas, and special assignments; you may also need to discourage negativism in response to changes or proposals for new approaches to accomplishing the work. Effective catalyzing may require initiatives to counter the actions of those who would squelch the new, the unimaginable. Sometimes interdependence may be threatened by the biases and prejudices of individuals who disrupt collective action by discounting or suppressing differing views and approaches. When it is necessary to discourage the squelching of the new, you will want to approach this challenge not only from a catalyzing perspective, but also with sensitivity to the face-saving component of humanizing. Sticking to the issues, appropriately confronting "yes—but" reactions to the new, and saving face when necessary—these actions not only are important to effective catalyzing in terms of fostering interdependence, but they also contribute to maintaining and enhancing your supervisees' morale.

*Enhancing morale.*    Building and enhancing morale is complementary to your supervisory activities for fostering interdependence. Actions to build and enhance morale involve the fostering of positive feelings in supervisees—about the work they do, and about their roles and contributions as critical agency resources. Supervisees with high morale will feel a sense of purpose, maintain their commitment, and have confidence about the future (Davis, 1975). These are important to the stability of the dynamic organization, as well as to supervisee dignity and professional integrity in the context of social services—a context that tends to create morale problems.

Frequent work in crisis and other stressful situations and continued work with problems not easily resolved make it difficult for supervisees to feel confident about accomplishing work goals. The relatively low pay and status of social work also contribute to morale problems. As a supervisor, you will need to create a climate that contributes to productive supervisee morale in the face of these pressures. In your position, you will want to be open to new ideas and search for ways to encourage supervisee feelings of self-reliance and self-direction, as well as mutual aid and cooperation (Arndt, 1973). Between yourself and your supervisees, as well as among your supervisees, this involves, in part, initiating and encouraging interactions that function positively—to inspire, animate, and make exhilarating the shared capability and responsibility for competence and excellence in meeting your expectations and those of supervisees, clients, the agency, and the profession.

In the following situation, the supervisor is open to a new idea from a supervisee. By encouraging the new, the supervisor serves as a catalyst not only by showing respect for the supervisee, but also by enhancing morale through supporting self-direction and cooperative approaches to problem solving.

> EXAMPLE: As a supervisor of six workers, one in each of six nursing homes, I had noticed that one of my workers had seemed "down" recently. This worker had been in this nursing home for about six months. As a recently graduated M.S.W., he had entered the program with great enthusiasm and commitment to working with the elderly. To discover the source of his apparent low morale, I scheduled a conference to explore his concerns.
>
> At the conference he opened up immediately. He reiterated his strong commitment to serving the needs of the elderly residents in the nursing home. He described his accomplishments to date and emphasized that he had been trying to do the types of things a social worker should do in a nursing home. This was difficult because he felt obstructed by the medical staff and devalued as a professional. In discussing specific situations he had experienced, he noted that a real concern right now was lack of resident involvement in specifying their needs and the ways they could help one another. He commented that he wanted to form a resident council, but the idea had been scoffed at by some of the nurses.
>
> I encouraged him not to give up on his idea. I observed that resident councils had been successful in other nursing homes in stimulating greater resident participation. We discussed possible reasons for objections by nursing staff. I encouraged him to review the literature in this area and to develop a written proposal that he would share with me prior to introducing it to the home. Brightening up at my support and suggestions, he proposed to have a draft in one month.
>
> At the end of the month, he brought in a proposal identifying the needs he had observed, the objectives for a resident council, an implementation plan, and criteria for evaluating its impact. We reviewed the proposal and I asked him to present it to the other workers. It was determined that the directors of all six homes would be invited to a meeting to discuss the proposal and methods of implementation. As a result of this process, the council concept was implemented in three of the homes, including the home served by the worker who originated the idea. Despite the lack of uniform acceptance by the nursing homes, all my workers seemed to develop renewed energy from the experience. They requested that we use a part of staff meetings for presentation and discussion of new practice ideas.

This example highlights the benefits that can result from attending to potential morale problems as soon as you become aware of them. As a supervisor, your actions in response to low morale can turn an immediate downturn into a long-term positive upturn. The energy and ideas generated by enhanced morale, interdependence, and feelings of mutual support can then be directed toward better service delivery (i.e., teaching function). In a profession where monetary rewards and the ability to receive the satisfaction that comes from seeing tangible work results are often limited, conveying optimism about the ideas and actions of others is very important to maintaining positive work relationships and good morale.

Throughout our elaboration of the catalyzing function, we have noted the importance of this function for capitalizing on the creative resources of supervisees. Many times you will act to stimulate ideas presented in a preliminary rudimentary form, or you will encourage experimentation with new ways of doing the work, whether these new ways involve individual supervisees or interdependent patterns of collaboration and mutual aid. In addition to the responsive actions you may take as a catalyst, you also have the responsibility to offer new ideas or plans when such initiatives can enrich the work environment, foster interdependence, or enhance morale. The following example illustrates the value of supervisory catalyzing initiatives.

> EXAMPLE: As a supervisor of a newly organized team of public health social workers whose practice was often solitary because of responsibility for state-wide coverage, I decided it was important to establish a process at our regular team meetings to build solidarity and to buck up morale. My basic purpose was to help my workers become sensitive to each other's needs and to reinforce their analytic, problem-solving, and decision-making skills. My idea was to use part of the team meeting to generate worker interest in analyzing these processes as they occurred in the team meeting itself.
>
> At an early meeting, I offered my idea and a plan on how to put it into practice. My plan was to take the last 30 minutes to explore their feelings about what had transpired at both the cognitive and emotional levels during the meeting. I suggested as a beginning, a structured review organized into two parts with specific questions. For the emotional-process review, I suggested the following questions: How involved did you feel in the meeting? How did you feel about any decisions that were made? and How did you feel about how decisions were made? At the cognitive level, I suggested three additional questions: How clear were communications between myself and workers and among workers. How well were resources explored and utilized in analyzing and deciding about issues? and What problem-solving techniques were used in making decisions?
>
> My workers were genuinely interested in the potential of this format. Several of them expressed the need for feedback in checking out the work they frequently had to do in isolation from one another and from me. In accepting my idea, they also proposed a periodic review of this approach, including the introduction of case situations to be explored using the same questions. Also, interest was expressed in modifying the structure, the process questions, or both, whenever this became appropriate in the evolution of group cohesion.

As a supervisor, you will want to anticipate potential issues that might affect interdependence and morale. Moreover, you will need to generate ideas and actions in advance, rather than always being in a reactive position. It seems highly probable that this supervisor avoided some of the threats to interdependence and morale by offering a creative approach early on. In recognizing the benefits of catalyzing, you can initiate actions that contribute to an environment that supports the new and stimulates supervisees to do the same. Such an atmosphere can also support your other supervisory activities that relate to humanizing and managing tension. This interaction among the supervisory functions will promote feelings of dignity and competence and will maintain the proper balance in integrating individuals, group, and agency goals.

In summary, we have defined, analyzed, and illustrated the catalyzing function and its contribution to the supervisory imperative for integration of supervisees into the agency context. We have called your attention to the specialness of catalyzing, particularly to how it can capitalize on the creative energies and talents of supervisees. By attending to the possibilities you have for stimulating an invigorated approach to solving practice and agency problems, you can foster interdependence and enhance morale. The resulting climate is important to maintaining the integration of individual, group, and agency interests. Moreover, such an atmosphere of exhilarated, animated practice can contribute to a sense of competence and excellence. We believe the outcomes of the catalyzing function are often prerequisite to the effective discharge of the linkage functions of administering, advocating, and changing. Our argument is based on the necessity of open participation, self-reliance, risk taking, and a spirit of inquiry and innovation as essential to the activities involved in these three functions. Supervisor and supervisee interdependence and good morale are critical to maintaining organizational stability while meeting the imperatives of adaptability. Supervisor activities within the catalyzing function include at a minimum:

1. Encouraging supervisees to take on special assignments or participate in training opportunities
2. Encouraging supervisees to work together on a common problem
3. Discouraging "yes—but" responses to the new or to change
4. Encouraging new ideas
5. Conveying optimism about ideas or actions
6. Offering new ideas or plans

## THE SERVICE-DELIVERY FUNCTIONS

Continuing support and development of social agencies is predicated on the accountability of the profession to the public, of practitioners to clients, and of practitioners to the agency (Tropp, 1974). At the level of the dynamic organization, we have defined these concerns in terms of the effectiveness imperative. This involves expectations for demonstrating competence in applying knowledge and skill, responding to client needs in conformity with the value and ethical base of the profession, and demonstrating that performance is consistent with client and agency goals. As a supervisor, you will be involved in responding to these demands by engaging in activities that constitute the functional imperatives of service delivery.

It has been noted that many of the resources involved in service delivery are not the property of the profession but of the community (Perlmutter, 1972). As a consequence, social agencies, supervisors, and supervisees are significantly influenced by the responsive provision component of the community mandate. As a supervisor, you will need to be sensitive to and watchful for politically motivated initiatives that may cloud issues of adequate and effective service delivery. You and your supervisees will be confronted with the pushes and pulls of conflicting ideologies about the purposes of service delivery. These forces may manifest themselves in shifting emphases on problems of the individual, problems of social institutions and social structure, or problems requiring a blend of individual and institutional adaptation. It is apparent then, that "the community sometimes does not make clear what response it expects from agencies in the face of social problems. Workers ultimately have the task of making decisions in the face of poorly defined or even conflicting objectives" (Kadushin, 1976, p. 220). As a supervisor, you will need to support your supervisees in making choices within an ethical framework in order to meet their obligations to clients, the profession, the agency, and the public. Moreover, since most services are delivered within a bureaucratic context, you will need to devise opportunities for your supervisees to develop and enhance their knowledge and skills for engaging in the challenges of this reality (Finch, 1976).

Service delivery also is influenced by changes in the cultural, agency, and professional contexts (see Chapters 1, 4, and 6). With regard to cultural changes, there is an emerging emphasis on personal fulfillment in contrast to production for the sake of consumption (Yankelovich, 1981), and this emphasis is coupled with movements for mutual cooperation and self-help (Toffler, 1980). You and your supervisees may encounter these changes in client demands for greater participation in the service-delivery process—from problem definition to service planning to evaluation and feedback. At the agency level, changes are reflected in declassification and in a resultant increase in baccalaureate-level service providers. For you as a supervisor, these changes will require attentiveness to knowledge and skill development, career development, socialization into a social work professional value base, and performance contracting that emphasizes progressive personal and professional development.

Changes in the professional context have been stimulated by an ever-expanding knowledge base and a reawakening of interest in person-environment fit as a "new/old" approach to methods and skills (Maluccio, 1981). In part, these trends reflect one level of response to the quality issue, which is a dominant concern within the profession (Tropp, 1976). The quality issue involves challenges to the profession from within, regarding lack of innovation, continuation in the teaching and practice of methods whose relevance has been challenged empirically, and evaluative studies that have raised questions about agency effectiveness (Briar, 1973; Tropp, 1974, 1976). These changes and concerns are reflections of the recognition that as social work professionals,

We no longer have a monopoly, nor outstanding track record, on address-ing social problems and human relationships. Our singular excellence is questioned—by other professions, by paraprofessionals, by the influentials, by the community, and by a growing ethos that favors self-help enterprises. (Middleman, 1977, p. 4)

As you anticipate these demands and opportunities (i.e., knowledge and skills, cultural diversity, values and ethics, accountability) and engage in the supervisory functions related to service delivery, we believe it is essential for you to be aware of two types of practice errors. These errors are classified by research conventions as Type I (finding positive effects that do not really exist) and Type II (ignoring im-portant effects because they might not be statistically significant). Problems arising from such practice errors are identified by Jones (1979). For example, the serious damaging practice error for white workers with black clients is Type II. Practice errors of this type overgeneralize and lead to conclusions that there is no difference between blacks and whites, when in fact there *are* differences; such errors ignore between-group differences as if black culture had no special social reality. Super-visors' humanitarian or liberal perspectives may direct them to see all persons as simply persons. The practical consequences of the Type II errors—which can deny between-group differences as supervisors conscientiously focus on the uniqueness of each individual (the within-group differences)—lead to using inward-focused sen-sitivity approaches rather than cognitive, behavioral, outward-focused, problem-solving approaches, which would be more valuable for many blacks. In contrast, Type I practice errors occur when we dismiss a suspicion that a given intervention makes no difference, when in fact it really does *not* make any difference. Such errors are reflected, for example, by supervisors who persist in spending time and energy with certain staff even when they suspect their efforts are doomed despite their approach; or by workers who continue to stay endlessly with treatment groups, when helping the group members face and deal with the group's ending may offer the most growth-producing experience.

Despite the nagging pressures manifest in these conflicts, inconsistencies, and ambiguities, social work supervisors and supervisees need to continue to work to deliver the best and most appropriate services in meeting client, agency, and profes-sional expectations. As a supervisor, you can respond to the organizational impera-tive for effectiveness through your attention to the dynamics of service delivery—that is, to what services are delivered and how they are delivered. Your task will be to help your supervisees integrate the concern for *the what* with concern for *the how*. We have previously defined concern for the *what* as a reflection of product issues, and concern for the *how* as a reflection of process issues (see Chapter 4). Product concerns involve the assessing of supervisee performance in relation to agency goals, client needs, and public demands for efficiency and effectiveness. Process concerns involve developing and maintaining knowledge, skills, competence in the ethical, and the caring application of such knowledge and skills in the help-ing process.

For you as a supervisor, your emphasis in service delivery will be to help your supervisees provide effective services compatible with client needs, agency goals, professional values, and public accountability. At the worker level, you will contribute your wisdom as a competent supervisor to developing and protecting the wisdom of your supervisees in an environment of mutual sharing and cooperation. This will include encouraging inquiry, innovation, and risk taking in developing and applying knowledge and skill to new approaches to the work. The integration of wisdom and skill with ethical considerations will contribute not only to practice efficacy in meeting client needs, but also to the effectiveness imperative of the dynamic organization. You can address wisdom at the supervisee level, skills at the responsive provision level, and effectiveness at the organizational level by engaging in the service delivery functions of teaching, career socializing, and evaluating.

For reasons elaborated in Chapter 1, we view teaching and career socializing as two supervisory functions with which you possess (and need to use) more discretion than you have with other supervisory functions that are more circumscribed by day-to-day agency routines. We will briefly address these functions below, but they will be given more special and detailed consideration in Chapter 7. The evaluating function will be dealt with here in detail, as were the integrative functions in the earlier part of this chapter.

### Teaching

In Chapter 1, we noted that part of the historic specialness of social work supervision has been its educational function. It has been a means of enhancing the professionalism of social work, and it has shaped the socialization of direct service workers so that professionalism in bureaucratic contexts has been maintained. At the same time, we observed that in contemporary social agencies, the educational function has disappeared from supervisory practice. While we share in the lament over this reality, we still believe that you have the responsibility and the opportunity as a supervisor to promote professionalism in the workplace by attending to the ongoing development of your supervisees. By sharing your wisdom in response to the developmental needs of your supervisees, you can contribute to their competence in handling agency, client, and community problems.

Teaching as a supervisory function is defined in terms of knowledge and skill development. The emphasis is on concepts, theory, research, skills, and practice strategies and tactics. We exclude from the teaching function the activities related to basic orientation and updating on policies, procedures, and regulations. Even though some observers include these latter activities in the teaching-training supervisory responsibility (Austin, 1981), we see them as elements of the administering function. Given the increasing complexity of service delivery and its contexts, and the volume of daily pressures you and your supervisees encounter, teaching and learning should be viewed not as backbreaking additional burdens, but as opportunities for professional renewal of self and others.

In initiating teaching activities, you will want to be open to both formal and informal approaches—whether to develop new knowledge and skill or to enhance and maintain prior knowledge and skill. Given the scarce resources, time pressures, and increasing demands for quality and quantity in service delivery, you will need to think strategically about opportunities to contribute to ongoing professional development as an essential component of the work. You will need to look for, as well as create, possibilities for developing knowledge and skill that are linked to effective job performance. Stated differently, the goal of your teaching activities should be to maximize the full professional potential of your supervisees. Ongoing attention to developing supervisee potential is essential to enhancing worker confidence, competence, and wisdom. In particular, wisdom can be thought of as the capacity for responsible self-directed learning and practice by your supervisees. It has been suggested that supervisory teaching can contribute to enhanced professional practice if it attends to the knowing, feeling, and doing components of service delivery (Gitterman, 1972). At the knowing level, you will want to be sensitive to the development of knowledge concerning the impact of sexism, racism, ageism, and classism on clients, supervisees, and the agency. At the feeling and doing levels, you will want to consider interpersonal relationships, interpersonal skills, strategies and tactics for change, and internal and external networking related to organizing and advocating for clients, supervisees, the agency, and the professions.

To fulfill your teaching obligations, you will want to use your own wisdom as well as the wisdom of supervisees in making choices about content, format, and method. As a supervisor, you are in a position to assess the capabilities of all your supervisees (evaluating function) as a means for identifying common learning needs. This includes both needs related to working with clients and the community and needs emerging from the interactions involved in doing the work. For example, we would call your attention to teaching possibilities identified in your integrative-function activities. In this area, we noted opportunities not only for both in-the-moment teaching but also for teaching that requires a more structured format. We believe that needed teaching activities may emerge from your involvements with any of the other functions. These needs may be identifed, and then they can be satisfied by teaching activities that you and/or your supervisees plan and initiate. You should also consider drawing on the expertise of other persons in the agency or in the community, if this will enhance the ongoing development of yourself and your supervisees.

*Formal activities.*  We define formal teaching activities as those based on predetermined content, as identified by you or your supervisees. This approach is most appropriate when dealing with abstract or complex concepts, theory, research, or methodology. The time required for these teaching activities often will exceed that required for other approaches. This reflects the effort required to plan, organize, and prepare for the activity. The teaching/learning activities themselves may require varied amounts of time. In some instances, you will be able to use staff meetings for this purpose; in others, you may need to arrange a special time for an in-service event during or after working hours, to provide enough time for the learning experience to have meaning and impact. The following example is an illustration of a supervisor-initiated formal teaching activity conducted at a staff meeting.

EXAMPLE: As a supervisor in a community mental health center, I had noticed that during periods of crisis or peak client demand, my workers had some problems related to cooperation and interdependence in case coverage. Similar problems also were apparent in staff meetings, where a few workers dominated the meeting without awareness of the impact this was having on the morale of the whole group. I decided to develop a teaching/learning experience for use at a staff meeting.

I began the staff meeting by sharing my thoughts on the importance of cooperation in case management and office coverage, and then I presented several options for increasing our effectiveness in this area. As I talked, I was unwinding string from a ball of twine and wrapping it around my hand. When I was finished, I passed the ball to the first worker who spoke up; I asked her to do as I had done with the ball of twine. When she stopped speaking, she passed the ball to the next worker who spoke. This process of passing the ball and winding the twine continued as different workers engaged in the discussion.

At the beginning of the last half hour of the staff meeting, I summarized the concerns that the workers had expressed about the options for increasing cooperation and mutual assistance in case management and office coverage. Then I asked them to visually examine what had happened with the ball of twine. After a pause, my workers began to talk all at once. One noted that we were all connected to each other by the string, and he defined this as illustrating the importance of group cohesiveness. Another commented that it was not possible for any one person to move without affecting others. Yet another noted the differences in the amount of twine wrapped around the hand of each; he observed that a few had talked a lot, whereas others had talked very little, perhaps only once. Following this reporting out, I summarized the experience by noting that we were interdependent in doing our work, and that too much or too little participation had a limiting effect on the use of ourselves as resources in getting the work done. I noted the importance of sharing as reflected by our being tied together, and linked this to case management and office coverage.

As an outgrowth of this experience, a subgroup formed to develop a plan for more cooperative case management and office coverage by workers. It was also my observation that at future staff meetings there was a much more balanced degree of participation, as those who had previously dominated talked less and encouraged the more reticent workers to talk more.

This illustration reflects the creativity you can apply in drawing on your wisdom as a competent, imaginative supervisor. This supervisor blended didactic and visual presentation methods with an inductive process at the end to fully involve the participants in their own learning. As a supervisor, you will want to incorporate into your teaching variations that are responsive to different learning styles (e.g., learning by hearing, learning by seeing, learning by doing) and that enhance the active involvement of learners in their own development of knowledge and skills.

It has been noted that when persons formulate their own learning needs, help to discover learning resources, and decide their own course of action, then significant learning is maximized (Rogers, 1979). The acquisition of knowledge and skill, whether the recognition of a pattern, the attainment of a concept, or the development of practice wisdom in using a particular method, is an active process. So, learners should be regarded as active participants in the knowledge- and skill-getting process. This includes selecting what is to be learned, transforming information to fit their abilities and context, and applying the newly acquired knowledge or skill in appropriate situations (Bruner, 1973). As a supervisor, it will be important for you to encourage and support your supervisees as active adult learners. This will require your recognition of the supervisees' ability to identify needs, resources, and approaches to teaching/learning requirements in their ongoing development.

As a corollary to being involved in the planning and development of teaching activities and resources that they need, supervisees can also plan and present some content themselves. Many times some of your supervisees may have special knowledge or skills that would be of benefit to their peers. This special information may be the result of extensive self-directed study, independent participation in continuing-education offerings outside of work time, or attendance at professional conferences. By encouraging such initiatives, you reinforce the supervisees' ownership of responsibility for their learning, recognize their special talents, and extend the resources available for fulfilling the teaching function. The following example from practice offers one illustration of this approach.

> EXAMPLE: One of my workers had recently attended a statewide retreat sponsored by NASW. At this retreat, one of the workshops he attended focused on various approaches to recording. Since I recognized a need for my workers to develop additional competence in case recording, I invited this worker to discuss what he had discovered at this workshop. After he described what had been covered, I asked his help in sharing this information with his peers. He agreed to develop a plan for what he could present at a special staff meeting. When he submitted the plan, I agreed to arrange for duplication of materials he would need for his presentation.
>
> At the special staff meeting, the worker gave a brief overview of research on recording and the latest approaches discussed in the literature. Then he involved me in sharing my perspective on the changes that appeared important in improving our individual and group effectiveness in case recording. Following my remarks, my worker then guided us through the handouts that illustrated various approaches and the strengths and limitations of each. He then broke us up into two small groups to apply the material to our situation.
>
> Following this small group activity, he involved all of us in developing a preliminary design for future use in case recording by workers. Over the next several staff meetings with the worker as teacher/facilitator, we developed a case-recording procedure. This procedure included criteria for assessing service outcomes, worker accountability, and a time structure for regular timely completion of recording without detracting from other aspects of the service-delivery work.

*In-the-moment activities.* An important approach to the teaching function involves spontaneous supervisor activities related to the learning needs of supervisees. We call these *in-the-moment activities* to capture the importance of supervisory alertness to situations that provide opportunities for sharing information and insights—related, for example, to new knowledge, to skill, or to alternative applications of current knowledge and skill. If you recall a situation presented in this chapter's discussion of the humanizing function, in which a supervisee was frustrated and disappointed from inability to move a client into public housing, you can recast this as an opportunity for the in-the-moment teaching. In this instance, assuming you were the supervisor, you could review the strategy and tactics utilized with the supervisee, and then you could explore modifications or alternatives that you believe might be tried in similar situations in the future. Your teaching content might include assertiveness techniques, advocacy techniques, or using internal or external network resources to bring pressure to bear on uncooperative agencies or professionals.

Other in-the-moment teaching activities can be initiated during staff meetings or in individual or small-group conferences with your supervisees. These activities may relate to the particular learning needs of all, a few, or only one of your supervisees. For example, you might imagine that you were the supervisor in the agency where supervisees planned and arranged for the teaching of group skills. At staff meetings following this learning experience, you might watch for and call attention to appropriate use, nonuse, or misuse of skills covered during this teaching/learning event. In this way, you emphasize prior learning, in the moment, as a reminder and reinforcer of the knowledge and skills included in previous teaching activities.

In-the-moment teaching also may include activities by you, the supervisor, that can be defined as coaching. In-the-moment identification of learning needs that can be met through coaching can occur in staff meetings, individual or group conferences, or informal discussions. In coaching, you present information or demonstrate a new activity, skill, or behavior that your supervisees want and need to learn in order to enhance their professional competence and service effectiveness. After introducing or demonstrating the new activity, skill, or behavior, you help the supervisees practice the new approach until it has been internalized—just as a basketball coach might do in helping a player learn a more effective technique for shooting free-throws. The following situation represents an illustration of coaching as an element of the teaching function.

> EXAMPLE: As a supervisor in a program for displaced homemakers, I had become aware from self-reports in individual conferences and from the most recent performance evaluation that one of my workers was having difficulty managing her responsibilities for paperwork, client appointments, and community outreach for job development and placement. I decided to initiate teaching related to time management at our weekly conferences.
>
> When we met in conference, I shared the basic principles for effective time management, including making weekly time schedules and daily updating to reflect priorities. I asked her to keep a record for a week on how she spent her time each day. The following week, we reviewed her results and noted time-wasters that could be eliminated. I showed her how to make a plan for the following week, including setting priorities. I suggested she do this each Friday and discuss it with me near the end of the day on Fridays. Also, I showed her how I updated my weekly plan at the beginning of each day in order to accommodate newly emergent priorities.
>
> Each day for two weeks, I spent 15 minutes with my worker at the beginning of each day to prompt her when necessary in setting and prioritizing

daily goals. On Fridays, we reviewed her achievements for the week and her plan for the following week. By the third week, she reported (and I confirmed by my own observation) that she had made consistent progress in effectively developing and implementing weekly and daily plans with a resultant improvement in balancing paperwork, client counseling, and community outreach.

In this situation, the supervisor identified a need with the worker and then coached her in a new structure and new behavior related to increasing her effective job performance. Coaching also might be used to improve recording, to develop skills in reading and interpreting computer printouts, to use the computer for information storage and retrieval, and so forth. While it will often be a time-intensive activity, it does represent considerable potential in helping supervisees learn specific, concrete practice activities, skills, and behaviors.

*Sharing activities.*   Obviously some degree of sharing is present in the teaching/learning activities already discussed. We identify sharing as a unique approach, in the sense that sharing activities are similar to consultation as it was conceptualized in Chapter 1. Such sharing can be content-centered or person-centered, depending on the primary focus of the teaching/learning process. Such sharing can involve a teaching/learning process between supervisor and supervisees or peer teaching/learning among supervisees. The choice is a matter of expertise and purpose. Supervisor-supervisee sharing for the purpose of teaching can occur in individual or small-group settings. Supervisee-supervisee sharing can occur in informal discussions or in case-review presentation and in a follow-up, interactional, consultative process.

The content for sharing activities can be drawn from articles, books, and prior practice experiences that can be utilized in the further development of knowledge, skills, and approaches that may help improve job performance. As with other teaching activities, emphasis can be given either to content related to common learning needs or to the unique needs of an individual or a small group of supervisees. In using this approach to teaching, you may want to develop sharing activities that involve joint supervisor-supervisee responsibilities for the teaching and learning. Through the sharing model, such an approach will increase ownership in and commitment to teaching/learning activities. As a supervisor using this approach, you will have a primary responsibility to structure a goal-directed teaching/learning process to enhance competence.

We believe supervisees are more likely to learn, to analyze and conceptualize, and to take risks with new practice or theoretical possibilities when they are involved in an active, cooperative teaching/learning activity, as represented by the sharing mode. It will be important for you and your supervisees to mutually agree on structure, content, and process. These are important considerations for ensuring that such sharing is actually a teaching/learning experience, in contrast to a general bull session. The latter activity is more appropriately useful for the humanizing and tension-managing functions.

In summary, we have defined, described, and illustrated various approaches to activities subsumed within the teaching function of supervision. We have called your attention to being open to a range of activities from formal to in-the-moment directive teaching/learning situations, to sharing in a consultative, collaborative mode. We have emphasized the importance of alertness to teaching/learning possibilities as they arise, rather than operating exclusively from a predetermined teaching agenda. Moreover, we have encouraged you to employ your wisdom, competence, and imagination in using yourself and your supervisees as resources for teaching/learning activities. By attending to the possibilities of the teaching function, you can contribute to your ongoing development and that of your supervisees—in meeting the supervisory imperatives for professional development, in enhancing quality of the product and process of service delivery, and in advancing the organizational imperative for effectiveness. Supervisor activities within the teaching function include at a minimum:

1. Presenting, discussing, or describing concepts, theory, or data
2. Inviting a speaker on a topic to present information or teach skills
3. Planning for staff to present some content
4. Coaching supervisees in new activities, skills, behaviors
5. Sharing or circulating articles, books, reports, and studies

### Career Socializing

Much has been written about the dilemmas facing professionals who must deliver services within the predominantly bureaucratic context of practice. Quality and quantity in service delivery depends on the initiatives of supervisors and supervisees in addressing the tensions and conflicts that arise from the pushes and pulls between the professional culture and the organizational culture. (Expectations based in the organizational culture are identified in Chapters 4 and 6.) The organizational culture often values hierarchical decision making, conformity to rules and regulations, loyalty, and accountability, sometimes with an emphasis on quantity over quality.

The professional culture emphasizes particular values and norms to guide actions in the delivery of service. In general, these values reflect beliefs about the importance of the service being provided, and about the knowledge-based authority of the profession. Norms represent expectations for performance in service delivery, including appropriate conduct when working with clients, peers, superiors, subordinates, and the community (Heraud, 1970; Finch, 1976). Thus, those who identify with the professional culture share a group identity and a common set of values (Lubove, 1965). Identification with the professional culture helps to hold in place and perpetuate norms and values via the socialization of workers into the profession. In social work, these values and norms relate to conduct as a social worker, responsibility to clients, responsibility to colleagues, responsibility to the agency, responsibility to the social work profession, and responsibility to society (NASW, 1981).

In order to achieve the product and process objectives of service delivery, it becomes significant to identify with and internalize social work values and norms. Assuming that workers are competent in their delivery of service, there is still a concern for whether they possess a sufficient orientation to social work values and ethics to apply them consistently in service delivery (Levy, 1979). When workers enter the service-delivery work context, they have already been conditioned in work attitudes and habits by two or more decades of work- and career-related experiences in school, with family, and with friends (Perlman, 1968). Choosing employment in the social services is only a partial reflection of values. Other considerations may include conditions in the job market, financial needs, preparation, and marital and family concerns (Golan, 1981).

We have already noted the increasing diversity in characteristics of the service-delivery work force. In a typical agency, there will be various proportions of supervisors and supervisees holding M.S.W. or B.S.W. degrees, and B.A. or M.A. degrees in other disciplines, as well as paraprofessionals whose main qualification is life experience. Given the variability in primary socialization, education, and life experience among workers, it can be expected that they also will exhibit considerable variability in the identification with and application of social work values and ethics. As a supervisor, you may encounter supervisees with strongly held attitudes toward minority groups, welfare recipients, racism, sexual preferences, crime and delinquency, ageism, sexism, and so forth (Kadushin, 1976). As a supervisor, you will be a key person in guiding your supervisees to develop and apply the values and ethics of social work. In your efforts in this area, it will be important for you to approach supervisees not only in terms of their particular jobs in your particular agency, but also in terms of their career development and enhancement.

Career socializing as a supervisory function focuses on the core issues of the social work profession's survival. We define the function as career socializing in order to capture your supervisory responsibility to help your supervisees develop a value and ethical base that is meaningful to all practice contexts. So, your efforts to support continuing development of professional values and ethics for yourself and your supervisees should include concern not only for development in the current job and agency, but also for development appropriate for other jobs in service delivery, whether in your service agency or in other agencies (Levy, 1973). Activities related to career socializing involve those designed to promote continuing development of knowledge about the social work profession as well as professional values and ethics. It is not enough for you to develop your identification with professional values and ethics; you will need to assist your supervisees in this process as well. In attending to the career-socializing function, you will be contributing to the establishment and maintenance of the conditions in which quality and quantity service delivery can be achieved.

*Career development.*   As a supervisor, you will find it important to be sensitive to the variations in developmental needs of your supervisees. This will depend on their respective career stages. New supervisees in their early to mid-twenties will be preoccupied with settling into the position and applying their entry-level knowledge and skills (Golan, 1981; Gehring and Baker, 1982). At this stage, you will want to encourage them and assist them in examining their practice from the perspective of social work values and ethics. Supervisees in their late twenties to mid-thirties who have some experience are likely to be looking for opportunities to develop their practice competencies and value base, with an eye to advancement and promotion. At this stage, you will want to assist them in pursuing opportunities to further strengthen existing competencies and develop new ones appropriate to future goals.

Supervisees in their mid-thirties to mid-forties are likely to be reexamining their values in relation to their present position in the agency, pursuing other positions in the agency or in a different agency, or considering options for using their service-delivery competencies in other careers (Gehring and Baker, 1982). With these supervisees, you will want to be supportive of their reflective self-examination and assist them in considering options within the framework of their professional values. In working with supervisees in their mid-forties or beyond, you will want to be responsive to their developmental needs to solidify the strengths in their performance and to modify the negatives. Also, you will need to be responsive to their adjustment to physical changes associated with growing older as well as to assist them in making initial plans for retirement (Gehring and Baker, 1982). It will be important for you to base your activities in this area on an understanding of the changing needs of individual supervisees at different career stages.

> Each worker has an external career related to exploring occupations, entering first job, gaining promotion and some form of tenure or seniority, acquiring a responsible position, and preparing for retirement. The internal career parallels the external with such stages as personal self-assessment and exploration, developing occupation self-image as a worker, developing self-concept as a co-worker and peer, managing success and failure, handling feelings of seniority or "having made it" which is sometimes referred to as the achievement crisis, acquiring a new sense of growth and maturity, and learning to accept the aging process and deacceleration. (Austin, 1981, p. 273)

*Making ethical choices.* From the perspective of the professional culture of social work, both what you and your supervisees do and how you do it are based on values. Assuming that all parties have competence in the requisite knowledge and skills required for service delivery, ethical conduct is determined by consistency between what you and your supervisees are supposed to do and what is actually done. In this sense, making ethical choices represents values in action (Levy, 1979). The dilemma for you and your supervisees will involve making judgments when the professional culture conflicts with the organizational culture. It has been observed that workers and supervisors often cope with this dilemma by consciously or unconsciously developing patterns of accommodation. The dilemma is more intense when there is high professional identification and low organizational identification, or when identification with both is low (Finch, 1976). As a supervisor, you will be

challenged to develop and maintain a strong sense of identification with professional values, concomitant with ethical conduct that reflects identification with
the quantity and quality demands of the organizational culture. The following
example demonstrates supervisory action based on professional value premises.

EXAMPLE: As a supervisor of a child-abuse and child-neglect unit in a large
public agency, I was aware of the importance of pursuing opportunities to
increase the awareness of the community about the needs of abused children
and abusive families. One day I received a call from the president of the local
chapter of the Jaycees. He asked me to speak at one of their luncheon meetings. I explained that I would prefer to send my most experienced worker,
a woman who had years of experience with abused and abusive clients, as
well as specialized knowledge and skill attained through attendance at workshops and conferences. The president replied that he would prefer a male
speaker. When I asked why, he explained that a male would have more prestige and credibility with the membership. I stood my ground and emphasized
that choice of a speaker should be based on professional experience and competence, not gender. He replied that he was afraid a woman might take a
softer approach to the problem. Noting that such views in the community
represented a stereotype that needed to be dispelled, I reiterated my position
that the best choice was to send the most qualified person. In the end, he
accepted my female worker as the guest speaker.

The choice made by this supervisor reflects identification and conduct consistent with the value of preventing and eliminating discrimination against any
person or group based on personal characteristics, condition, or status (NASW,
1981). At the same time, this action on the part of the supervisor also responds
to social work value commitments to expand opportunities for all persons—especially those who are members of a disadvantaged or oppressed group. Sexism is a
major issue in our society, in the profession, and in social agencies. In spite of the
fact that social agency personnel are predominantly women, they are underrepresented in key decision-making roles and are often paid less than men at all levels
of job responsibility (Perlmutter and Alexander, 1977). Moreover, sex-role stereo-
types may account for the fact that employers give females less encouragement
to pursue opportunities to develop new knowledge and skills (Sutton, 1982). As
a supervisor, you will want to take actions that reflect your sensitivity (and enhance
that of your supervisees) to identifying and combating discrimination—whether in
service delivery to clients, in agency personnel practices, in the profession, or in
the community. This may involve exposing yourself to unpopular but ethical
actions as illustrated below.

EXAMPLE: When I was supervisor of a foster-care team, my staff was made
up of all white workers, although nearly half of our client population was
black. Owing to the size of caseloads, the administration granted me another
worker position. The Personnel Office referred four applicants, three white
and one black. As was my usual practice, I involved my workers in interviewing and making recommendations on priorities for hiring. Following the interviews, my workers rank-ordered all three whites ahead of the one black. Their

justification was based on the fact that the whites had more experience than the black applicant, who had just received her M.S.W. In spite of their rankings, I ranked the black candidate first and was successful in getting her hired.

My workers were very unhappy with my decision. At a staff meeting, I decided to deal with this issue directly. I pointed out that the black applicant was the only applicant with an M.S.W. and that our client population was nearly 50 percent black. Also, I pointed out that few black workers were employed in the whole agency. I then discussed our professional responsibility to promote opportunities for members of minority groups and other disadvantaged populations. After a candid group discussion, we mutually agreed to devote time at the next staff meeting to minority issues and our professional responsibilities consistent with support for professional values and ethical conduct.

Once again we see a supervisor making decisions that reflect professional values. As a supervisor, you will want to take risks and support your supervisees in doing the same when affirmative-action issues arise. Studies have called attention to the small black representation in middle- to higher-level agency positions, as well as to the fact that more opportunities exist for black social workers in public as compared to private agencies (Perlmutter and Alexander, 1977). In addition, "although minorities—blacks especially—are overrepresented as clients in the total social agency population, particularly in the public sector, minorities are underrepresented as professional staff, both in educational and agency settings" (p. 438). In a society characterized by many instances of institutional racism, it is an ethical imperative for you and your supervisees to take actions, even if unpopular, that directly challenge racism in service delivery, in agency personnel policies, in the profession, and in the community.

For you as a supervisor, an equally important area of concern related to ethical conduct involves the actions of your supervisees in their work with clients. It is incumbent on you to help supervisees to consciously examine their practice in the light of professional standards and norms. This process of deliberate, focused self-examination will advance both individual development and agency and client purposes. The following example from practice illustrates supervisory action to increase a supervisee's awareness of professional standards and norms.

EXAMPLE: As a supervisor at a day treatment center for juvenile status offenders, I actively encouraged my workers to arrange for recreational outings with their clients off campus in order to enhance peer relationships as a component of the program's treatment philosophy.

The day following an outing, one of my workers came to me expressing concern about a statement made by one of the youth who had attended the outing. The youth reported that they (and the worker in charge) had gone "skinny dipping." I assured this worker I would follow up on the report.

When I called the worker who supervised the trip in to discuss the outing, I asked him for his view of how the activity had worked out. He explained that everyone had a good time. He added that one of the participants had stripped and jumped in the river and everyone, including himself, had followed. I asked if he had any reservations about what had occurred. He explained that it was all in good fun.

In response, I called his attention to the fact that our clients had many problems without inviting more by skinny dipping in a public spot. He looked down and replied that he didn't think it would hurt anyone. I noted that as a professional, he was expected to demonstrate good judgment and be an appropriate adult role model for the youth. I added that the community standards would not support skinny dipping in public, nor would the values and ethics of the profession. He commented that he had not thought about the situation in those terms, only in terms of the youth having fun and his acceptance by them. We used this event as the basis for further discussions of professional standards related to work with clients. The standards we agreed to explore further included overidentification with clients, developing relationships that conflict with the best interests of clients, and the need for discretion in applying values, knowledge, and skill to the helping process.

In this situation, the supervisor took the initiative to act in the interest of the professional standards, client interests, and the image of the profession and the program. As a supervisor, you will want to encourage high professional standards among your supervisees. This will include helping them to become consciously aware of values and ethics in making choices in their work with clients, their peers, and the general public. A mutual effort on the part of you and your supervisees is necessary to establish awareness as well as diligence in upholding the values and ethics of the profession. In this regard, it will be important for you to become aware of the prior socialization experiences of your supervisees; this awareness can serve as one approach to identifying areas for priority emphasis within the career-socializing function.

*Enhancing commitments to social work values.* We noted earlier that the social services are buffeted by shifts in public attitudes, varying priorities of funding sources, and changes in target populations and their needs. Also, we noted that problems encountered by supervisors and supervisees in their efforts to meet demands for quality and quantity in service delivery are often compounded by agency policies and procedures, by the delivery of services in "host" settings that may be dominated by the culture of other professions or disciplines, or by a lack of community understanding of social work perspectives on social issues and client concerns (see Chapters 1 and 4). In addressing these issues, it will be important for you and your supervisees to consistently engage in activities that support professional social work values and ethics as an essential component of enhancing commitment to social work value perspectives.

Given that professional development is a continuous process and that socialization into the social work profession is problematic for reasons noted earlier, it will be important for you to take advantage of every opportunity that arises for you to help your supervisees distinguish social work values and beliefs from those of other professions and disciplines. You and your supervisees share in the responsibility of espousing and defending the culture of the profession as one aspect of promoting professional identity and recognition of social work as a profession. This involves distinguishing social work values and beliefs from those of other professions, as illustrated in the following example.

EXAMPLE: One day one of my workers came to me very upset about a decision made by one of the staff psychiatrists at the mental health center. She explained that she had been working with a female client who was very depressed. The woman had recently been abandoned by her husband, and she was left with responsibility for three children with no income and no family nearby. My worker explained that she had been trying to develop a day-care arrangement that would allow her client to search for a job. When she came to work that day, she discovered the psychiatrist had referred the client to the inpatient unit at a general hospital. The children were being placed in temporary foster homes. The worker stated that she simply could not understand this decision.

After empathizing with her feelings, I noted that this was an example of the differences between social work and psychiatric perspectives on meeting the needs of some clients. We reviewed the assumptions of the medical model, including inpatient services where the use of medications as part of treatment could be monitored. Then, I contrasted this with the social work belief in least restrictive forms of service. I supported her efforts and encouraged her to convey her difference in perspective to the psychiatrist as an initial way of beginning to create a different working relationship in service delivery.

Frustrations such as these occur frequently in various agency contexts. Sometimes, you will have to address agency policies that conflict with social work beliefs. At other times, you will have to use encounters with other more dominant professions as opportunities for expressing and defending social work values. These value-related problems are often a reflection of a broader problem for social work—a lack of public recognition as a profession, and a lack of understanding of the profession's values and ethics. In order to address this broader dimension of career socializing, you and your supervisees must accept responsibility for interpreting the social work perspective on social issues and client concerns as situations present themselves to you.

In summary, we have defined, elaborated, and illustrated the career-socializing function of supervision. By attending to this function, you can advance the development of your supervisees, the agency, and the profession in promoting ethical conduct based on social work values. In providing for the ongoing development of your supervisees, you are enhancing the products and processes that define service delivery. At the same time, for administrators, members of other professions and disciplines, and the general public, you are expanding their awareness of social work values and ethics—as they relate to effective services and as they relate to the well-being of the whole society. Supervisor activities within the career-socializing function include:

1. Encouraging supervisees to grow in the job and/or grow out of the job
2. Making choices or decisions based on a value issue
3. Taking ethical stands, even if unpopular
4. Acting in relation to staff behavior out of regard for professional standards and norms
5. Challenging agency policy that conflicts with professional imperatives

6. Asserting or distinguishing a social work belief from the orientation of another profession
7. Encouraging self and supervisees to interpret a social work perspective on social issues, the profession's image, or client concern, to others in the community

### Evaluating

The effectiveness imperative for the dynamic organization involves accountability for quality and quantity in service delivery. This accountability exists in several areas. In the agency context, the concern is the accountability of supervisors, supervisees, and the agency for services rendered in relation to services needed and promised. Demands for accountability (in terms of assessing effectiveness of performance, services, and outcomes) arise from many sources. The broad consumer movement has reinforced client demands for quality and quantity in service provision. The emphasis is on offering and delivering services that are qualitatively appropriate and acceptable. In this sense, effectiveness is a matter of performance rather than of professional certification or status (Posavac and Carey, 1980). The social work profession also has recognized accountability by its focus on quality as a core issue in service delivery (Briar, 1973; Tropp, 1974, 1976; Miller, 1971; Newman and Turem, 1974; Kadushin, 1976; Austin, 1981). Professional concerns for quality include setting job-specific standards that are reviewed and adjusted periodically; balancing qualitative and quantitative assessments of performance and outcomes; and measuring the impact of services on clients and the community. Funding sources also have fueled the drive for accountability, in order to make allocation decisions based on objective information (as a counterbalance to the pleading of special, vested-interest groups). These demands have been further reinforced by federal and state demands for accountability with regard to the use of public funds for service delivery.

The test of accountability lies in the assessment of several dimensions of service delivery. One is assessing whether services are delivered effectively, efficiently, and humanely. Another is the extent to which professional knowledge and skill are applied competently and ethically in the provision of service. A third relates to the delivery of services requested and needed by clients. Finally, accountability includes the assessment of ongoing professional development and the periodic recertification of professional qualifications (Tropp, 1974). The cumulative assessment of service delivery along these dimensions provides the basis for determining effectiveness. At the same time, it is important to note that these assessments do not guarantee effectiveness; rather, they only indicate that the providers demonstrate good intent in their application of the available and appropriate professional competencies in the delivery of services. "All that can be asked for in effectiveness in any human service profession is that a person performs well enough to meet reasonable expectations, with the best available knowledge and skill, under given circumstances" (Tropp, 1974, p. 142).

Evaluating, as a supervisory function, focuses on developing and instituting ways to assess practice performance, worker impact, and service outcome. Employee performance evaluations are at least an annual activity in most human service agencies. Yet both supervisors and supervisees often approach evaluation as an unpleasant activity (Wiehe, 1980). We can identify several probable reasons for, and consequences of, avoiding conscientious and systematic evaluation of job performance. Some of the unpleasantness and resistance related to evaluating supervisors and supervisees may stem from agency reliance on formal, standardized evaluation instruments that may neither reflect the particulars of job responsibilities nor contain provisions for noting improvement in specific practice competencies. Interrelated to these possible problems are concerns that the evaluations are not very useful in supporting opportunities for continuing professional development, promotions, or merit increases. Yet to avoid active involvement in systematic evaluation is to reinforce reliance on more informal, subjective evaluation.

In the agency context, administrators, supervisors, supervisees, and clients are engaged, consciously or unconsciously, in making informal assessments of the performance of others. Often these informal assessments are reflected in the valuative connotations of verbal and nonverbal communication. Your challenge as a supervisor will be to work with your supervisees and others in the agency to promote positive attitudes toward evaluation processes that support both ongoing professional development and enhanced quality and quantity in service delivery.

In practice terms, evaluating job performance should involve the objective assessment of an employee's quality of performance and quantity of accomplishment on the job during a specified period of time (Kadushin, 1976). A number of commonly recognized methods for evaluating performance are available to you and your supervisees. Those mentioned most frequently in the practice literature include rating scales, essay comments, critical incidents, checklists, and results-oriented formats (e.g., management by objectives, and job-performance analysis) (Wiehe, 1980; Austin, 1981).

Rating scales specify ranges of performance qualities and characteristics related to job responsibilities and expectations. As a supervisor, you assess supervisee performance by checking a box, placing a mark along a continuum, or circling a number or letter assigned to each performance indicator. The following example illustrates one performance indicator that uses this approach.

A. *Openness*—the willingness to risk enough to learn.

| Openly resists any risk | Risk only with unusual support | Average risk taking | Usually risks in order to learn | Actively seeks opportunity to risk in order to learn |
|---|---|---|---|---|

The essay format for evaluating performance is based on written statements in answer to questions regarding strengths and limitations; sometimes, also, it includes prescriptions for ongoing development. The following questions typify those that might be included in an essay format for evaluating performance.

1. In providing services to emotionally disturbed adolescents, what are the employee's strengths and limitations?
2. How skillful is the employee in dealing with crises such as suicidal situations, rape crises, physical abuse, and so forth?

The critical-incident format involves systematic recording of specific examples of especially good or poor performance as they occur. The following critical-incident statements are reflective of this approach.

A1. Good performance—supervisee observed escorting the most withdrawn patient on the ward outside for a walk.
B1. Poor performance—supervisee screamed at resident for spilling glass of water.

A supervisor who uses checklists for evaluative purposes works from a list of statements, checking those that describe the performance of a given supervisee. The supervisor checks only those statements that appropriately reflect the supervisee's actual performance. Examples of statements that might appear on such a checklist appear below.

1. Establishes and maintains effective collaborative relationships with professional peers.
2. Empathizes with clients without overidentification.
3. Adheres to professional social work standards in maintaining client confidentiality.

The results-oriented approach to evaluating job performance involves rating achievement in terms of quantifiable, measurable objectives established in advance. The objectives may be established by the supervisor, the supervisee, or both. The following standard rating format illustrates the type of objectives that might be established in using this approach.

Objective 1—To increase from 4 to 8 hours per week the average number of hours spent making home visits to natural parents of children in foster care. (Circle one.)

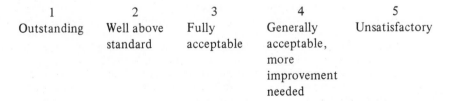

| 1 | 2 | 3 | 4 | 5 |
|---|---|---|---|---|
| Outstanding | Well above standard | Fully acceptable | Generally acceptable, more improvement needed | Unsatisfactory |

Each approach has strengths and limitations. You and your supervisees should choose an approach reflecting a format and process that capture the particulars of service objectives, job assignments, and your ongoing professional development in the agency context. As you carry out the evaluating function of supervision, we encourage you to adopt an approach that will: provide for giving direction to activities to improve performance; identify teaching/learning needs related to self, relationship, task, and content competencies (see Chapter 7); support promotional and merit considerations; and document quantity and quality of performance in relation to the accountability expectations of agency, program, and supervisor and supervisee.

*Supervisee performance.* In approaching the evaluation of your supervisees, it will be important for you to emphasize evaluation as a process for directing attention to the effort and competence of your supervisees. Also, evaluation will be important for assessing the impact of their performance on clients, peers, supervisor, and the agency, and for assisting supervisees in their ongoing, systematic professional development. This emphasis will require you and your supervisees to consider both verbal and written assessments; to engage in the mutual development of job-performance standards linked to both product and process, in service delivery as well as in professional development objectives; and to assess and evaluate quality of performance and quality of accomplishment at least every six months (and where necessary and feasible, more often). So, we are defining your activities related to the evaluating function as ones that go beyond typical evaluative practices in social agencies. If evaluations are to have both meaning and impact, they must be conducted often enough to incorporate changes in client populations or client needs, changes in service priorities and job assignments, and changes in supervisee competencies (those that have occurred and those that require further development or enhancement).

The following example illustrates the use of performance assessment that is close in time to a supervisee's specific action. This type of performance evaluation complements the more formal, systematic, periodic evaluation procedures (Delbecq and Ladbrook, 1979).

> EXAMPLE: As a social work supervisor on a psychiatric ward of a large state hospital, I believed it was important for me to give performance feedback to my workers whenever I observed appropriate or inappropriate behavior toward patients.
> One morning as I walked onto the ward, I noticed considerable activity in the day room. Upon entering the day room, I observed one of my workers talking to a patient who was threatening patients and staff with a chair. He was speaking in a calm tone of voice and acknowledging the feelings of this patient, who was newly admitted to the ward. He waved security personnel away as he approached the patient in a slow steady pattern. After 15 minutes, he had persuaded the patient to lower the chair and accompany him to a quiet place to talk. Later in the morning, I pulled this worker aside and praised him for his use of a calm, empathetic approach in engaging the patient. I specifically noted the skills I had observed him using in dealing with a troubled patient in a tension-filled situation. Also, I commended him on his nonthreatening rather than physical-coercive approach to calming the patient and eliminating the threatening behavior.

This situation illustrates the timely verbal assessment of a supervisee's performance. It is important to note that this assessment was based on the supervisor's observation of a supervisee's behavior in a specific situation. The assessment focused on particular skills and recognized the good judgment of the worker in choosing one approach over another. In your own practice, you will want to emphasize evaluative communications which are based on observation of situation-specific use of skills and which recognize the consequences of selecting a particular approach from a range of alternatives (Austin, 1981; Maier, 1976).

In approaching activities associated with the evaluating function, it will be important for you to involve your supervisees in the mutual development of goals and expectations to be emphasized during the specified time period. It will be especially important for you to orient new supervisees to this evaluative approach. New supervisees may either expect or have prior experience with the more traditional standardized annual review of performance. Early involvement of new supervisees in reviewing performance expectations will encourage positive attitudes about the evaluation process. In addition, it will be necessary that you and your supervisees mutually establish the basic performance objectives and standards that will be used in determining the decision about movement from probationary to permanent status.

In your evaluative activities with new as well as experienced supervisees, you will want to accept, at a minimum, the responsibility for including expectations and criteria related to working with clients, working in the agency context, and working on developing and increasing specific knowledge and skills related to the supervisee's needs for professional growth. These developmental needs should be defined in the context of your agency's service-delivery expectations, as well as in terms of the supervisee's career aspirations. The following example illustrates a supervisor-and-supervisee conference focusing on developing goals and criteria for the next performance evaluation.

EXAMPLE: In meeting with my worker to follow up on her most recent evaluation, I shared my emphasis on helping her to develop the areas of performance and assessment criteria to be used at her next evaluation. Then she shared her feeling that this evaluation process had more value for her than the standardized evaluations she had experienced in other agencies.

We began by exploring her current responsibilities and the needs of her clients, who included foster children, foster parents, and the natural parents of these children. She stated that she felt the need to improve her skill in assessing family functioning, as well as her knowledge and skill related to permanency planning. In addition, she agreed that she needed to work on devoting a greater percentage of her time to work with the natural parents. Then I noted my assessment, in the previous evaluation, of her performance in the area of timely submission of service plans, case notes, and monthly statistical reports. She confessed that she usually left paperwork to the last minute because of her preference for focusing on client needs. In response, I pointed out to her that service delivery involved both services and records. I called her attention to the importance of prompt submission of accurate statistics, since these were used in budget allocations.

Next, I translated these major job-performance issues into a set of statements that included criteria for improvement and basic steps to be followed in achieving these objectives. We identified literature she would study on family assessment. In addition, I agreed to observe a home visit to give her feedback on her application of knowledge and skill following a period of self-study. To assist her in improving her competencies related to permanency planning, I suggested she consult with another of my workers who had demonstrated considerable competence in this area. Also, we agreed to a weekly review of her progress in more timely and accurate submission of records and statistics.

This approach illustrates the considerable mutual effort of supervisor and supervisee in developing and implementing performance objectives central to quality and quantity in service delivery. The evaluation format includes both supervisee and supervisor assessments of what should be emphasized in the period between now and the next evaluation, as well as the steps required to demonstrate acceptable improvement. The content reflects a blend of supervisee needs, supervisor expectations, and the agency requirements. In your evaluative activities, you will want to leave room for including performance objectives that reflect the necessary competencies, and the standards to be accomplished, in working with clients, working within the agency, and working with the community. Also, you will need to consider objectives that are related to growing in the job and growing out of it.

Obviously, if the evaluative process in setting performance expectations with supervisees is to make a difference—both in the development of the supervisee and in the quality and quantity of service delivery—equal effort needs to be devoted to preparing and sharing written feedback with the supervisee before the evaluation conference. On the basis of the realities of most social agencies, we believe that a useful approach for you to follow is a combination of a rating form and written comments that amplify and note, where possible, specific instances of supervisee behavior that led to a particular rating. Moreover, the written feedback should include suggestions for a prescriptive plan that could become the basis for establishing the performance objectives to be emphasized during the following evaluation period. Also, we believe supervisees should be encouraged to complete their own self-evaluation prior to the conference. To support the development of supervisee confidence and competence in a more self-directed practice, it is important for supervisees to be skillful in evaluating their own performance in order to initiate self-correcting processes without being solely dependent on you, the supervisor, for such feedback.

*Supervisor performance.*  In order to enhance the credibility of performance evaluation, we believe it will be important for you to regularly solicit evaluative feedback on your performance (in addition to self-evaluation and evaluation by your supervisor). Given the interdependencies involved in the planning, implementing, and evaluating of service delivery (supervisee performance and client outcomes), your performance will have a significant impact on the performance of your supervisees, which, in turn, will affect agency achievements in the quality and quantity of service delivery. Moreover, in many agencies, your supervisees will be in a better position than your supervisor to provide substantive evaluative feedback, both on the quality and quantity of your performance and on its impact on their performance.

To help you establish an approach to self-evaluation and supervisee evaluation of your performance, we suggest you might start with a focus on the activities associated with the nine functions of supervision, as well as those associated with the design of supervision (see Chapter 7). You could list these activities and then recast them in a format consistent with the rating-scale format. Periodically, you could share the activities you will be working on with your supervisees in an effort to enhance your own competencies. At the same time, you could make the rating form available to your supervisees so that they can observe and reflect on your performance over a specified period of time. Then, prior to the supervisee evaluation of your performance, you could ask them to complete the rating scale, as well as to supply written comments on areas of supervisory performance that they would like you to emphasize more. Depending on your relationship with your supervisees, you can choose whether to receive their evaluations individually, in a staff meeting, or a combination of the two. We would expect hesitancy on the part of supervisees when you initiate this aspect of the evaluating function. It is highly improbable that any of them will have ever been encouraged to participate in a systematic, formal evaluation of their supervisor. Also, you may be uneasy about the initiation of this process. We think the best way to deal with discomfort or resistance is to openly discuss, with your supervisees, your responsibility to evaluate them and your belief that the responsibility should be shared and reciprocal.

*Program performance.* We have developed a formative approach to the evaluative function. Formative evaluations emphasize developing performance objectives, assessing performance based on these objectives, and giving feedback that can be used by supervisors and supervisees to improve effectiveness and efficiency in various service-delivery competencies (Delbecq and Ladbrook, 1979). The formative approach emphasizes evaluations for the purpose of improving the development and ethical application of the knowledge and skills of your supervisees and you in meeting client, agency, profession, and public demands for effective and efficient service delivery.

Formative evaluations also apply to assessing program performance. The focus of this type of program evaluation is on improving plans for services and/or their delivery, improving program and service efficiency, and identifying changes necessary to improve client outcomes (Posavac and Carey, 1980). A thorough discussion of evaluating program performance is beyond the purview of this book. Still, we believe you and your supervisees have a responsibility to familiarize yourself with the various designs and techniques used to evaluate program performance (see, for example, Franklin and Thrasher, 1976; Epstein and Tripodi, 1977; Posavac and Carey, 1980).

In many social agencies, little, if any, evaluation activity will be focused on program performance. Given the absence of information about client outcome, any information that you can gather on program performance can be of benefit to you, your supervisees, the agency, and the clients. As a supervisor, it will be important for you to analyze any existing evaluative studies of your agency, its programs and services. In the absence of such studies or reports, you may choose to conduct a simple study of your own design. The following example demonstrates one possibility available to you in gathering some basic information on program performance.

EXAMPLE: As a supervisor in a mental health center, I was increasingly concerned about public criticism of lack of impact of the services the center provided. These concerns were magnified by the expressed disappointment of my workers with the results of their service-delivery efforts. Since the agency had not conducted any systematic evaluations of program performance and did not have the financial resources to develop and implement a comprehensive evaluation study, I decided to initiate a client-satisfaction survey among clients served by my team.

After giving considerable thought to the factors to be included in this survey, I shared my ideas with my workers at a specially called meeting that focused on the design and implementation of such a survey. I explained that client participation was to be voluntary and based on informed consent. Moreover, survey data would be aggregated in order to ensure anonymity and confidentiality. Following these opening remarks, I encouraged my workers to brainstorm with me regarding the clients to be surveyed and the questions to be included.

As a result of this meeting, it was agreed that we would survey clients who were terminated from our program during the past three months. The questions were to focus on degree of client satisfaction along the following dimensions: crisis services; individual counseling; group-work services; family and marital counseling; treatment plan responsive to problems and needs; worker responsiveness to client requests and ideas; and changes made as a result of services provided. I prepared a draft of a survey, including these items. Then, I circulated it to my workers for their editions and modifications. Following this process, I prepared a final draft of the survey.

During the following month, my workers and I administered the survey by phone to clients who gave voluntary informed consent. Eighty-five percent of the potential client respondents agreed to participate in the survey.

When all the surveys had been completed, I collected them and remained after regular work hours to compile all the data on a master form. I had previously arranged with the computer services department to have the data processed by computer. The analysis of the client satisfaction data produced an overall satisfaction rating of 70 percent. An item-specific analysis revealed that clients wanted more and better group work and family counseling services. My team and I used this information to plan teaching/learning experiences designed to increase our competencies in these areas. In addition, the entire analysis was written up. This report was shared with the executive director, the medical director, the program director, and the board. A brief summary was released to the media. As a result of our efforts, the administration initiated steps to design and implement additional client surveys.

Although client-satisfaction surveys are an insufficient basis for making definitive statements about program performance, they are helpful as one element. In this situation, the survey results were used to plan specific professional-development activities, and they served as a stimulus for additional agency involvement in assessing program performance. As reported, the survey results could be expected to partially counter public criticism.

In summary, we have defined the evaluating function of supervision in terms of supervisee, supervisor, and program-performance assessments. We have described and illustrated various approaches that you can take in working with your supervisees to set goals, to establish performance objectives and assessment criteria, and to give evaluative feedback with simultaneous concern for self, client, and agency expectations related to quality and quantity in service delivery. Also, we have encouraged you and your supervisees to look for possibilities to study the outcomes of service delivery in your agency. By attending to the evaluating function, you can advance the ongoing performance improvement, as well as the development and enhancement of practice competencies. Ongoing improvement and development of people and programs is critical in meeting the effectiveness imperative of the organization. Supervisor activities within the evaluating function include, at a minimum:

1. Offering verbal assessment of supervisees' or other person's work
2. Helping develop performance goals – in the areas of self, supervisees, program, and service
3. Providing written feedback on performance to supervisees
4. Reviewing performance expectations with new supervisees
5. Soliciting feedback on and reviewing own performance
6. Conducting or analyzing studies of program performance–work conditions, program impact, client needs, client satisfaction, and so forth

## THE LINKAGE FUNCTIONS

The contemporary social agency can be described in terms of both internal and external networks of relationships. All of these are critical to developing and maintaining commitments and resources essential to service delivery. Internally, you will need to be knowledgeable about the interrelationships among policies, rules and regulations, procedures, programs, and services. You will want to consider your options for acting to resolve inconsistencies and conflicts that are detrimental to your supervisees, clients, and the agency.

At the level of internal human resources, you will need to assess the number and nature of relationships between administrators, program managers, supervisors, and supervisees. Depending on the setting, you will want to consider the relationships among members of different professions and disciplines. Then, on the basis of your understanding of these various interpersonal relationships, you will want to take actions that are appropriate to your position as supervisor and that can enhance cooperative, productive relationships. Also, you will want to attempt to influence competitive, conflictual relationships in directions that will be more beneficial in working with clients, working within the agency, and working in the community.

In addition to the dynamic relationships among internal forces, you, your supervisees, and your agency will be affected by the broad network of external forces involved in the social services. The multiple constituencies of the social services will vary for different agencies. In general, these constituencies include the media and civic organizations, funding agencies, governmental bodies, professional associations and unions, client-interest or client-advocacy groups, other social service organizations, and business and industry (Slavin, 1980; Martin, 1980). Media coverage, competition for funds, personnel, and clients, and legislative and regulatory initiatives are important forces that pressure the agency. As a consequence, you and your supervisees will experience these pressures in your work related to service delivery. You may recognize the impact of these forces in terms of stress and conflict, threats to interdependence and morale, or disruptions related to the product and process of service delivery. From the supervisory position, you will want to influence and direct these forces, which have a direct impact on you and your supervisees.

At the level of the dynamic organization, we have defined concern for these forces as central to the adaptability imperatives of the agency. The agency will need to develop and implement a variety of approaches that provide for flexibility in maintaining and enhancing constructive internal and external forces. Similarly, the agency will need to develop an array of approaches that can then be used in reducing and redirecting internal and external inconsistencies and conflicts toward stability and effectiveness across the organizational life course (see Chapter 4). The counterpart of the organizational imperative for adaptability is the supervisory imperative for linkages. Linkages involve both internal and external considerations.

At the worker level, as a competent supervisor you will employ leadership in working with and through others to mobilize and direct resources toward coordinated, effective, and efficient services. You can address *leadership* at the supervisee level, *resources* at the responsive provision level, and *adaptability* at the organizational level by engaging in the activities that comprise the linkage functions: administering, advocating, and changing. We shall address supervisory responsibilities related to each function, beginning with administering.

### Administering

In Chapter 1, we noted that throughout the historical development of the social work profession, the administrative function was recognized as one of two central components of social work supervision. The traditional conceptualization of the administrative function of supervision focused on directing, coordinating, enhancing, and evaluating supervisees (Kadushin, 1976; Austin, 1981). From this perspective, the supervisor was an extension of and a link to agency administration. Given the pressures arising from the multiple constraints and demands identified throughout this book, and the turbulent environment of contemporary service delivery, we believe a narrower view of the administrative function is necessary for competent, imaginative supervision.

The planning, directing, and coordinating of the work effort involves distinct concerns related to linking supervisee, client, and agency resources in the context of the internal and external forces that affect service delivery. As we noted in our earlier elaboration of the integrative and service-delivery functions, enhancing and evaluating supervisees involves numerous considerations that are not strictly managerial, and that, in many instances, may be in conflict with a hierarchical, managerial perspective. If there is no conscious awareness both of existing differences and of the importance of some degree of differentiation, we believe that lumping together several of these nonmanagerial functions within the administrative function is likely to result in their being ignored or in their being given less than equitable emphasis in comparison with other functions. As a supervisor who must link your supervisees to internal and external forces, you will find it important to differentiate your administrative responsibilities—that is, to see them as separate from, yet complementary to, the other eight functions.

The administering function of supervision is related to activities of planning, decision-making, and workload management, as demanded by the service-delivery situation. We see the central core of this function as planning, organizing, and making decisions about allocating work assignments. This involves delegating authority and responsibility, as well as monitoring the completion of assigned work that is acceptable in quality, quantity, and timeliness. Additionally, you will need to coordinate your work and the work of your supervisees with other internal agency members and activities related to service delivery. Doing this will require attention to patterns of horizontal and vertical communication. All these activities are essential to linking together persons and tasks in order to realize supervisor, supervisee, client, and administrative purposes related to service delivery.

Quality and quantity in service delivery is a matter of both individual and group effort. It will be important for you, as a supervisor, to be knowledgeable of the workload requirements and the strengths, limitations, and special interests of your supervisees in order to effectively organize and allocate responsibilities. Such responsibilities typically include standards for time, quantity, and quality. In addition, these activities and cooperative relationships within the agency require shared information. It is in this sense that you will want to initiate activities to access, organize, and disseminate information essential to the work of your supervisees. In order to accomplish this, you must enhance the communication network for sending and receiving information within the agency.

*Workload management.* As a supervisor, you share in the responsibility of the agency for assuring quality and quantity accomplishment related to policies, program goals, and client needs. In practice, you will be expected to initiate activities to make sure that the work for which you and your supervisees are responsible is accomplished. These activities will need to include planning, organizing, and assigning work in conformity with what your supervisees can manage effectively.

One important approach to planning, coordinating, and directing the work is delegation. By delegating as an approach to managing workloads, you will emphasize supporting your supervisees in using their unique, individual competencies (Kadushin, 1976; Austin, 1981) and their knowledge and skills. In addition to enhancing supervisee competencies, delegation can also improve both the quality of job performance and your effectiveness as a supervisor (Austin, 1981). Effective delegation will require that you give clear communication on the substance of the assignment. It will also require you to involve your supervisees in mutual determination of the authority and responsibility required for task accomplishment and that you and your supervisees carry out the responsibilities assigned (Gilmore, 1979). The following example illustrates task delegation related to service-delivery needs.

EXAMPLE: As a supervisor of a geriatric placement team in a psychiatric hospital, I was responsible for workers who followed up on the implementation of discharge plans for elderly patients. One day, the medical director approached me with a request that my team prepare a resource file on alternative community living arrangements for elderly patients. He expressed his concern about the increasing census of elderly patients who were scheduled for discharge, but who had no place to go. He felt that the development of such a resource file would make it possible for other hospital staff to assist my workers with arranging placements.

Being aware that one of my workers had been involved in a number of advocacy groups concerned with the quality of nursing homes and minihomes, I called her in to discuss the development of a resource file. We reviewed the nature of community placements required by our elderly patients and mutually agreed on the categories of living arrangements that would need to be included in the file. Then I asked her to accept authority and responsibility for developing the resource file. She agreed to the assignment, but noted that she would need help with her regular work in order to have time to identify and organize resources. I explained that I would prepare a plan for the redistribution of some of her work among myself and the other staff.

We agreed that she would prepare a plan and timetable for the development of the resource file, and that we would review these before she began the task itself. She agreed to have a plan by the end of the week. So we scheduled a conference time for Friday afternoon. During this conference, we finalized her plan and mutually agreed on an initial time frame of two weeks, with an understanding that we would adjust the deadline if more time was necessary to ensure a comprehensive, high-quality resource file. We established a schedule of meetings to review her progress and identify any resources or assistance she might need. I agreed to make available whatever assistance I could offer.

To complement your use of delegation, you will need to attend to interpreting agency goals, policies, and procedures with your supervisees. Moreover, you will want to follow up on these interpretive activities by translating these expectations into assignments, tasks, and activities for which your supervisees are accountable. Through interpretation and translation, you and your supervisees will be able to mutually identify service-delivery priorities that need to be reflected in managing workloads. Directly involving your supervisees in interpreting, clarifying, and translating agency goals, policies, and procedures into work plans and assignments will contribute to agency efficiency and effectiveness. It will also influence the quality and quantity of job performance by you and by your supervisees. This approach is essential if you and your supervisees are to understand where the agency is going, how you fit in as a group, and what your responsibilities entail. The following example illustrates this aspect of the administering function.

> EXAMPLE: As a supervisor in adult protective services within a state social services department, I was concerned with the implications that the new adult services legislation had for me and my workers. This legislation mandated 24-hour coverage in order to deal with emergency situations.
> I called a staff meeting to review the legislation and interpret the implications for workers and supervisors. I explained that we would need to develop a rotational schedule in order to comply with this mandate. None of my workers were pleased with this policy, but two of my unmarried workers volunteered to share the initial coverage of evening and early morning hours. I accepted their offer and suggested that we jointly plan a system of coverage with specific assignments for each worker the first month. Also, I suggested that we jointly review this plan at the end of the month in order to make adjustments that would improve the plan and maximize the performance of each worker. Although none of my workers were excited about this new responsibility, all of them actively participated in the planning and made specific commitments to carrying out their assignments.

Your aim in delegating, interpreting, and translating policies, procedures, and assignments is to manage workloads so that the specific knowledge and skills of your supervisees are utilized in relation to client, agency, and supervisee needs. It has been noted that supervisees and clients are often brought together without the careful balancing of knowledge, skills, and needs that is required in the uncertain pursuit of human welfare and development. By organizing and structuring activities so that flexible delegation, support, and consideration of supervisees are demonstrated, you will induce less frustration and resistance among your supervisees (Epstein, 1973).

A frequent source of conflict and frustration in social agencies is the expectation for timely and accurate completion of essential paperwork. Often, supervisees feel that demands for paperwork interfere with their primary interest in and commitment to direct client contact, work with peers, and work with other agencies and professionals in the community. At the same time, the agency will expect you, as a supervisor, to take whatever steps are necessary to ensure that you and your supervisees complete whatever quantity of paperwork is required and that the quality of the work is good.

Since paperwork is a fact of life in service delivery, it will be important for you to devote periodic attention to the values of paperwork, as a part of interpreting agency expectations to your supervisees (Wilson, 1980). The timely completion of essential paperwork is important to the budget process. As a result of legislative mandates and funding-source requirements, records and statistics are an important indicator of accountability; records also reflect accountability to clients. Current, accurate records can be used with clients in reviewing what your supervisees have done, how they have done it, and how these activities are connected to client needs and responses. Moreover, records, reports, and statistics provide documentation of service plans, actions, and results. This documentation can be used by you, your supervisees, and the agency in making workload adjustments and planning assignments that will contribute to the ongoing development of practice competencies. Another value in keeping paperwork current is the benefit to you or other supervisees who have to deal with clients when the supervisee of record is sick or unavailable. Finally, timely and accurate completion of forms and records can be a major factor in the early determination of client eligibility for services and benefits.

*Information processing.*   Paperwork represents one form of communicating that is vital to planning, organizing, and coordinating work flow. Quality and quantity of service delivery is dependent, in part, on the processing of information by you and your supervisees. When supervisors, supervisees, and administrators talk about communication problems, they usually are concerned with the problem of getting too little relevant information, too late. In addition, they may be deluged with a flood of irrelevant or inaccurate information (Gilmore, 1979). As a supervisor, you will want to take the initiative to improve processing and communicating relevant information related to managing and accomplishing service delivery assignments, activities, and tasks. Your activities in this area may include actions to develop communication networks and enhance the communication of written and verbal information. We will briefly illustrate each of these activities.

> EXAMPLE: As one of two family service supervisors in a county welfare agency, I was aware that the other supervisor and his workers were making disparaging comments about my workers to others in the agency as well as in the community. These comments appeared to be based on a misunderstanding of an innovation we had recently introduced in our work with the natural parents of children in foster care. On the basis of my study of literature in this area and an informal appraisal of our success rate in reuniting families, my workers and I had decided to institute seminars on parenting skills and normal child development. The other supervisor and his workers believed we were doing this at the expense of performing other service delivery responsibilities.
>
> To avoid negative repercussions for myself, my workers, and our clients, I decided to initiate a plan to open up communication between the two teams. My first step was to prepare a report summarizing ideas gleaned from the literature, as well as the results of my informal appraisal of the outcomes of our basic services. I followed this with a detailed plan of how we were managing this innovation while still meeting our regular service-delivery responsibilities. I shared this with my team and asked for their input, indicating that I wanted to distribute this document to the other supervisor and his

team. After incorporating ideas suggested by my workers, I prepared a cover memo explaining my interest in sharing what we were doing in an open fashion. Then I invited them to schedule times to sit in on these seminars.

A few days after I circulated this memo and document, I scheduled a meeting with the other supervisor. I discussed what we were doing and invited his feedback. He explained that he and his team were worried that our innovation would end up increasing their caseloads. Moreover, they were afraid that if this innovation was successful, it would make them look bad to administration and clients. I asked if he would like me and some of my workers to attend one of his staff meetings to further interpret what we were doing, how we were doing it, and how we were covering our other regular responsibilities. After some reluctance, he agreed to such a meeting. As a result of this opening up of communication, my workers and I were asked to work with this team in setting up a similar program.

From this example, we can see the value in taking a risky initiative to improve the communication network among supervisors and supervisees who work with similar clients in the same program area. An inherently conflictual situation that could have disrupted service delivery was resolved by sharing accurate information—both in writing and verbally. Crucially, this communication not only was precise but also was relevant to the quality and quantity of service delivery and to the planning, organizing, and coordinating of workloads.

As a supervisor, you are likely to receive a large volume of written information on a regular basis. It will be important for you to organize your time so that you can review and prioritize this information in a prompt, orderly manner. This individual information processing may involve agency reports, computer printouts, policy and procedural changes, budget allocations, and incoming mail and memos. You will need to determine which of this information is relevant to your responsibilities, to your supervisees, and to yourself. By attending to these information-processing responsibilities, you will be able to improve the dissemination of relevant information to those who are or may be affected by it. The following example illustrates the processing and dissemination of relevant information.

EXAMPLE: As a foster-care supervisor, I received quarterly computer printouts on service activity for all foster-care teams in my district. In reviewing the latest printout, I discovered that my team had recorded the highest volume of activity of any team in the district. Moreover, we also had achieved the highest rate of permanency plans, including more family reunifications than terminations and placement for adoption.

Having reviewed these data, I called a meeting of my team to share this information. We reviewed the reports and used them to analyze current assignments and identify services that appeared to be the main contributors to this volume of activity and level of success. On the basis of this discussion, we determined to assign even more priority to the Parents' Club that we had established for natural parents.

In this section of the chapter, we defined the activities associated with the administering function, and we differentiated them from other activities traditionally assumed to be components of this function. Calling your attention to the imperatives of workload management and information processing, we described these aspects of administering and illustrated various approaches to initiating activity related to each. We emphasized the importance of involving your supervisees in the planning, organizing, assigning, and coordinating of workloads and in the communication of information relevant to quality and quantity of service delivery. Our illustrations reflect the results that can be achieved by employing your leadership in developing and utilizing resources. By attending to the administering function, you can promote linkages among your supervisees, linkages between yourself and your supervisees and others in the agency, and linkages between information processing and the quality and quantity of service delivery.

Supervisor activities within the administering function include, at a minimum:

1. Delegating tasks related to service goals
2. Interpreting and translating agency goals, policies, and procedures into assignments, activities, and tasks
3. Monitoring the timely completion of essential paperwork (case notes, recording, reports, statistics, eligibility certification forms, and so forth)
4. Taking the initiative to affect or enhance communication networks, both written and verbal
5. Accessing and reviewing information (agency reports, computer printouts, budget allocations, mail, memos, and so forth)
6. Disseminating information relevant to the responsibilities of supervisees and others

### Advocating

Fairness, equity, and justice have been and continue to be key concepts in the social work profession and in the ethics of service delivery. Essentially, the concern has been expressed in initiatives to obtain and guard the rights of people (Middleman and Goldberg, 1974). In a review of the literature on organizational and bureaucratic behavior, it was determined that there is increasing concern for the equitable treatment of employees (especially minorities and women) and for the ways in which organizational structures and processes can be modified to increase fair and just outcomes (Gummer, 1978). Given the scarcity and vulnerability that typify the social, political, and economic realities of social services, inequities and injustices are likely to arise and persist as a consequence of the pressures and interactions of internal and external forces. These forces include legislation, policies, resources, and the actions of those responsible for interpreting needs and social goals and translating them into service delivery.

Advocating, as a supervisory function, is defined as action to push issues of concern to supervisees and/or supervisors upward and/or outward in the service-delivery system. In social agencies, there are frequent complaints of by-passing the chain of command, discrimination, and inequitable or inconsistent application of policies and procedures as these affect workers. As a supervisor, you will want to engage in activities necessary to plead, defend, or espouse the cause of supervisees as well as your own cause. Sometimes your activities will require that you function as a political tactician in intervening to rectify decisions and actions that disadvantage, mistreat, or misserve your supervisees and that interfere with their effective fulfillment of quality and quantity service delivery (Brager, 1968). Sometimes your activities will be more those of supporter and adviser. If need be, you may represent your supervisees in dealing with internal or external individuals and groups or organizations that adversely affect their performance as well as their commitment to service delivery (Briar, 1967). In many instances, your basic concern will be to protect your supervisees (and yourself) and other supervisors from reprisals resulting from having acted as advocates (NASW Ad Hoc Committee, 1969). In your role as a supervisor, your activities will include identifying issues of fairness, equity, and justice; defining the forces involved; and developing strategic plans for pleading, defending, and espousing supervisee/supervisor causes.

*Internal.*   As a supervisor, you may encounter issues that appear to affect a particular supervisee, but that have implications for all your supervisees. When these internal issues arise, it will be important for you to take appropriate initiatives to remove the organizational barriers that are detrimental to the well-being of your supervisees, and in turn, deleterious to service delivery to your target client population (Patti, 1974). The following example illustrates one approach to defending a *particular* supervisee, while at the same time espousing an ethical principle in support of *all* supervisees who might be similarly affected in the future.

EXAMPLE: As a supervisor of a child-abuse team, I have been concerned about the public criticism of my workers as well as other workers involved in working with abused children and abusive parents. Recently, one of my workers had been devoting extensive efforts to obtain the permanent removal of a child repeatedly subjected to serious abuse by her parents. The family had hired an attorney, who had succeeded in delaying action on my worker's petition for removal.

Two weeks ago, I opened my morning newspaper and read that this child had been rushed to the emergency room the previous evening, but that she had died from burns caused by scalding water. The following day, the media carried reports questioning the adequacy of my worker's services and efforts to protect the child. One day later, I received a memo from the director, indicating my worker had been suspended by the administration in response to demands from county commissioners.

I read the memo in disbelief. I called my worker, expressed my regrets about the precipitous action, and conveyed my confidence in the quality and quantity of services she had given to the child and the family. I asked her to come in to discuss the situation. During our meeting, we mutually agreed that some response was necessary. We began by reviewing the investigative report and her follow-up activities that had led to the petition. We pulled the case file together and prepared a written summary of the specific interventions that she had made.

When I had this documentation together, I requested a meeting with the director. At this meeting, I conveyed my concern and disappointment about the suspension of my worker. The director explained that he and the agency were under enormous pressure. I said I was aware of the pressure and the negative media image of our program. This, I explained, was part of the reason I wanted to meet with him. I expressed my feeling that my worker had been tried and judged in the media. I added that the suspension which resulted looked very much like "blaming the victim." Then, I reviewed the summary of my worker's services. I also showed him the extensive written documentation in support of my summary. I urged him to call the attention of the media and public officials to the meaning of the documentation, as well as to the responsibility the court had to shoulder for this tragedy. I pointed out that without a reversal of the suspension, not only would my worker suffer, but the morale of my other workers was likely to be lowered. Moreover, I wondered if we were starting a precedent that we would be expected to follow every time something unfortunate happened to one of our clients—especially if the media latched onto this fact. I suggested that he could reinstate my worker at the same time he appointed a review committee, including media persons and public officials, to conduct a thorough, impartial review of the situation.

Two days later, the director called me to announce that he had reconsidered the suspension. A study committee would be established, but my worker would be assigned to another program area, pending the outcome of the review.

This example illustrates a number of important ideas for you to consider in initiating advocacy activities from your position as supervisor. First, a deliberate, thorough review of the issue was conducted with the affected worker. This allowed the supervisor to determine what documentary support was available, as well as what particular issue to emphasize. Second, the supervisor took the issue to the person originating the communication. Third, this supervisor took an issue affecting one particular worker and interpreted the case in the interest of all workers, agency image, and possible impact on service delivery. Given the strong probability of resistance to your advocacy efforts (Patti, 1974), it will be important for you to consider strategic steps such as these.

Other issues may arise that are more specifically tied to supervisory issues for yourself and other supervisors. Again, the strategic planning before acting will be important in these advocacy situations as well.

EXAMPLE: About two months ago, my agency directed all supervisors of its group homes to spend some time every week making contact with and giving presentations to community groups including churches, Jaycees, Junior League, other voluntary associations, neighborhood organizations, and so forth. These efforts were initiated to counter negative attitudes among the public and the media regarding the group homes for emotionally disturbed children that were located in various city neighborhoods. Since this new assignment involved working some evenings and weekends, we were promised compensatory time if we kept accurate records of dates, times, groups contacted, and places of meeting.

At the end of the first month, I submitted a request, including documentation of my overtime work, to the personnel manager for one-half day of comp time. My request was denied with a notation that I should accumulate more time before submitting a request. Although the denial seemed inappropriate, I decided to wait until the following week to submit another request.

During the interim, some of my peers told me they had experienced similar denials. When I submitted my next request and it also was denied, I decided to get together with the other supervisors to compare experiences and decide what to do next.

During this meeting most of the supervisors expressed frustration about the breakdown in our agreement with the administration. We decided to prepare a report that combined the documentation of our PR work for the agency, a summary of our requests, and the denials by Personnel. Then, I took this to our program manager, and following a discussion, she agreed to contact Personnel. As it turned out, Personnel had denied our comp time because this policy did not apply to everyone, and the personnel manager was afraid of repercussions among other supervisors and workers if they found out. After some delay, our program manager succeeded in getting us the comp time we were entitled to.

This example also reflects the steps we outlined above in terms of an orderly, documented, and universalistic approach to redressing the denial of entitlements based on an agency procedure. In addition, it illustrates the importance of initiating advocating activities at the lowest hierarchical level that could achieve the desired objective (Middleman and Goldberg, 1974). In other words, this supervisor and his peers initiated the advocacy process with regard for the chain of command, rather than going directly to Personnel.

As a supervisor, you may on occasion become aware of inequitable or unjust personnel practices, or of service-delivery policies and procedures that are actually or potentially detrimental to staff members who possess certain ascribed characteristics (e.g., of race, gender, or age). Such policies and practices can have a negative impact on staff relationships and staff-development opportunities, as well as on the quality and quantity of service delivery. When such policies and practices become known to you, you may want to initiate advocating activities to correct the inequities before they have a detrimental impact on staff and service delivery. When you make a decision to pursue activities of this kind, it will be important for you to develop a rationale emphasizing the positive impact on service delivery that would result from changes in personnel policies or other service-related policies and procedures. Advocating on behalf of service delivery is likely to be given more credibility by administrators than is advocating that gives primary emphasis to your self-interest or that of your supervisees (Patti, 1974). One approach to this type of advocating would be the development and dissemination of a position paper focusing on the policy, procedure, or practice in question. An example of when this approach would be useful would be an agency with a majority of minority clients but very few minority supervisors or supervisees. Similarly, you might use this approach in an agency where the majority of supervisees are women but where few women are in supervisory or other key decision-making positions.

*External.*   External forces include the quality and quantity of media coverage of social issues and social services, shifts in the balance of power among vested-interest groups, ideological shifts related to allocation of resources and service priorities, and changing social policies at the federal, state, and community levels. Singly, or in combination, these external forces can have significant consequences for your agency and its clientele and for the service-delivery responsibilities of supervisors and supervisees. It will be important for you to establish linkages with the external forces that affect your agency, its clients, and in turn, you and your supervisees.

The public media (e.g., newspapers, magazines, radio, and television) can often have a significant impact on the quality and quantity of service delivery. Often the attitudes of government officials and the public toward social issues, the clients of social agencies, and the providers of social services are shaped by media coverage. Typically, the media present the negative, the sensational, the controversial, rather than positive, caring stories on human need, dignity, and the benefits to clients and the whole community that derive from quality and quantity in service delivery. We believe it is important for you and your supervisees to develop a plan for reaching out to establish positive working relationships with members of the public media that have the largest following in your community. Such contacts will lay the groundwork for you and your supervisees to more effectively advocate with the public media for more balanced coverage of emergent issues, policies, or problems that affect you, your supervisees, and your agency.

Other externally focused targets for advocating might include community groups, legislative committees, governmental task forces, internally based but externally focused action groups, and external action groups. In making decisions to initiate these advocating activities, it will be important to select issues that are of concern to you and your supervisees and that will affect the quality and quantity of service delivery. The following example illustrates one approach.

EXAMPLE: As a social service supervisor in one of the more progressive nursing homes in my community, I was aware of the fact that state licensing and regulation of nursing homes did not require a social services component. As a result, many homes had no social workers on staff, and only a few used social work consultants.

In preparation for the next legislative session, the state representative from my district had scheduled a community forum to discuss issues for the upcoming session. Given our knowledge of the needs of nursing home residents, my workers and I decided to attend this forum to advocate for a change in licensing to require social services in nursing homes.

We prepared statistics on the number of nursing homes and number of residents as well as profiles of the social service needs of residents. Also, we prepared a list of other states with licensing requirements for social services.

At the meeting we presented our information and disseminated copies of a written summary of our position and rationale to all those in attendance. Also, we offered to make ourselves available for consultation, testifying, or additional presentations of our position on this change in licensing regulations.

In this instance, the supervisor and workers used an opportunity organized by someone else to present and advocate for a change in regulation affecting service delivery. Moreover, they used the helpful technique of identifying and defining the issue in a way that could be linked to a rationale that was likely to win positive responses to the target issue. It is important to recognize that in the environment external to the social service delivery system, there may be competing, conflictual advocacy forces at work. You can strengthen your position and the likelihood that your position will win positive consideration, if you develop your case in a framework that will be easy for the target to accept; that allows for saving face; and that supplies a rationale that can be used by the target to justify a positive response to your position (Middleman and Goldberg, 1974). Finally, in the approach taken by this supervisor and her workers, the strategy used in going public with an offer for further involvement could be the foundation for the development of an action group. Your efforts at advocating will be strengthened if you look for ways to link strategies and issue-oriented interest groups together.

In summary, we defined, discussed, and illustrated various approaches and strategies to be used by you and your supervisees when you engage in activities that are part of the advocating function. We noted the importance of your identifying and analyzing internal and external forces that can adversely affect your job performance and that of your supervisees. Using this identification and analysis, we presented options available to you in linking up with these forces to plead, defend, or espouse supervisor and/or supervisee causes related to quality and quantity of service delivery. By attending to your responsibilities associated with the advocating function, you can demonstrate your leadership in mobilizing and/or enhancing internal and external linkage resources; this, in turn, will contribute to meeting the organizational imperative for adaptability. Supervisor activities within the advocating function include at a minimum:

1.   Taking a stand on behalf of supervisee(s)
2.   Taking a stand on behalf of self and other supervisors
3.   Developing a position statement and expressing or disseminating it
4.   Initiating contacts with public media
5.   Participating in community events to enlighten or influence attitudes about and commitments to proposed changes in policies, regulations, and procedures
6.   Joining with action groups (internal and external)

### Changing

According to our preference for the kaleidoscopic world view, the challenge for social agencies and their members is to harness and direct the forces and processes of change in an effort to improve job performance, quality and quantity of service delivery, and the linkage of internal and external forces. At the same time, we are aware that the organizational imperative for stability (survival) is often interpreted as a mandate for resisting or controlling change through damping out alternatives to the status quo. Unfortunately, such efforts can often produce an organizational condition of stalemate (Hirschhorn, 1978) typified by inertia and entry into the life-course stages of decline or demise. Still, we believe that the view of social agencies as dynamic structures reflecting continuous patterns of order out of chaos is the one most pertinent to competent, imaginative supervision.

Changing, as a functional imperative for supervision, is defined as modifying agency structures and processes from the bottom up. We believe that organizational functioning in relation to quality and quantity of service delivery can be improved by the persistent, focused activities of supervisors and supervisees. Since change is a constant in social service agencies, it will be important for you, as a supervisor, to be sensitive to impending changes and their probable consequences, as well as to identify needed changes not yet imagined by others. Although many social workers express the need for organizational change, they often tend to avoid taking action to bring it about, because of perceived lack of legitimacy for such initiatives (Patti and Resnick, 1972). At the same time, the NASW Code of Ethics not only legitimates but demands initiatives by supervisors and supervisees to bring about change in agency policies, programs, and procedures that are barriers to the quality and quantity of service delivery to clients (NASW, 1981). Moreover, we believe that your "inside" knowledge of clients and their needs, of the day-to-day consequences of policies and procedures, your working relationships with other professionals, and your practice competencies, are a plus in directing organizational change from the bottom up.

In approaching the changing function, it will be important for you to consider the basic concepts of organizational change. First, it will be important for you to determine what type of change is in order. Changes from within may be procedural, programmatic, or basic (Patti, 1974). Procedural changes focus on modifications of rules, regulations, and relationships that influence day-to-day activities of supervisors and supervisees. The aim of such changes is to improve coordination of service-delivery work and/or to improve the use of resources. An example would be efforts to improve methods of interdepartmental referral. Programmatic changes focus on innovations or modifications in methods and services in order to more effectively address client needs and agency goals. An example might be the introduction of behavior modification techniques into a child-guidance center. Basic changes focus on fundamental transformation of an organization's purpose or structure in order to accomplish a different set of goals. An example might be the reorganization of a juvenile delinquency agency into a social planning and social policy agency.

An equally important set of considerations relates to the scope of changes. Scope may range from the level of a team of supervisor and supervisees (component), to an entire department, division or program area (subsystem), to the total organization (system) (Patti, 1974). The larger the scope of change, the more difficult the task and the more likely it is that the forces of resistance will mobilize (Holloway and Brager, 1977). In considering organizational change, it will be important for you and your supervisees to examine the interrelationships between type of change and scope of change in order to more effectively focus your initiatives and define the sources and potency of resistance. (For more detailed consideration of these concepts and their relationship to strategies and tactics of changing social agencies from within, see Brager and Holloway, 1978; Resnick and Patti, 1980; Pawlak, 1976; Resnick, 1978).

Regardless of the type and scope of change, you will need to be prepared to anticipate resistance. In working for change from the bottom up, there are several typical sources of resistance. One source is likely to be your supervisor, who may not feel that change is possible without direction from the top down. As noted earlier, there is resistance that is related to uncertainty about whether it is legitimate to promote and direct needed changes. For you and your supervisees, the magnitude of this uncertainty will be influenced by such factors as job security and fear of reprisal and disapproval. Also, you and your supervisees may resist your responsibilities for working for organizational change from within, because of your concerns for time, energy, and competency (Resnick and Patti, 1980). While we recognize these very real concerns, we do not believe that resistance should be used as an excuse for avoiding your responsibilities to bring about needed changes in the interest of quality and quantity services.

From our perspective, your activities related to the changing function will be primarily related to procedural and programmatic types of change within a scope defined by component and subsystem levels. To increase your probability of success, it will be important for you to follow a number of basic steps, regardless of the type or scope of change. These steps reflect the principles of the action-research model for change (Lewin, 1948; Corey, 1953; French and Bell, 1978), as conceptualized for human service organizations (Resnick, 1978).

The first step for you and your supervisees is to identify the problem area that will be the target for change. It will be important to decide whether the type of change is procedural or programmatic and whether the scope is at the component level, the subsystem level, or both. Second, you will want to translate the problem into a goal to be achieved. Steps 1 and 2 involve gathering and analyzing information related to the problem and to possible sources of resistance, as well as involving those who are affected by the problem and support the goal. Next, you will want to select, plan, and initiate your approach to change. In this step, you should be guided by your consideration of the approach that is most likely to achieve the goal with the least resistance. Finally, after selecting and implementing your approach, you will want to evaluate the process and the outcomes as a guide to planning, structuring, and initiating future change activities. We shall illustrate some approaches to procedural and programmatic change that reflect these concepts.

*Procedural.* For changing procedures that affect services to clients, one approach is to review current as well as anticipated routine operating procedures that affect your supervisees and their clients. The following example illustrates this approach.

EXAMPLE: As a supervisor in a county welfare agency, I was concerned about a newly adopted procedure related to certification of eligibility for financial assistance. The new procedure required that applicants have a social security number before they could be certified.

I called a meeting with my workers to explore with them my concerns and to elicit their experiences with this procedure. They reported that many of their clients did not have a social security number. Moreover, they noted that getting a new number could take up to three months. They felt it was unfair to eligible clients to have to withhold assistance checks for that period of time. We agreed that it was unlikely we could speed up the process at the social security office. After discussing the pros and cons of various modifications of this procedure, we decided to recommend to our division director that the procedure be modified to allow certification of eligibility based on client documentation from the social security office of application for a new number.

Before presenting our recommendation, we surveyed other financial-assistance supervisors and workers to gather statistics on the numbers of clients being disadvantaged by this procedure. When we had compiled this information, we prepared a written analysis of the data and our corresponding recommendation for procedural change. The supervisor then presented this information and proposal to our divisional director at a divisional meeting. The director agreed to take our proposal to the agency director. Within a month, the procedure had been modified in accordance with our recommendation.

As a supervisor, you will also, on occasion, have to adopt a more confrontive, adversarial approach.

EXAMPLE: As a supervisor in an alcohol and drug treatment program, I had written a grant for primary prevention through drug education in the public schools. The grant was funded with considerable agency fanfare. I was encouraged to proceed with the steps required to launch the program. When my work was completed, the program was transferred to one of the program managers for adolescent services, which in effect eliminated my involvement and severely restricted any participation by my workers.

I decided to confront my program manager with the lack of fairness of this decision. But I determined to present the issue in terms of its likely impact on the future efforts of others to write grants to fund needed innovations in programs and services. During the meeting, I explained both my personal frustration as well as the probable spillover effect throughout the agency. He replied that only program managers could serve as project directors, and since there had been no prior objections, he discounted my position on spillover. I pressed the issue but was told there was nothing which could be done.

At the next program-level staff meeting I raised the issue again. Many supervisors joined in with my protest of this decision. When the program manager was unresponsive, some of us suggested that we thought the executive might respond differently. In the face of this pressure, my program manager finally agreed to take it to the next meeting of all program managers with the director.

*Program.* The steps and approaches we have defined and illustrated regarding procedural changes also apply to many possible issues and goals related to program change. When considering a program change at the subsystem level, you will want to follow the pattern illustrated in the financial assistance example. For example, if you were a supervisor in a fairly traditional mental health clinic in which poor clients received inadequate services in comparison to their needs, you would want to define the problem, document it with statistics on the needs, and collect information on approaches to serving this population as practiced by other mental health centers, including funding. On the basis of these steps toward change, you might then propose a new outreach program to impoverished neighborhoods in an effort to assist poor clients in using your agency's services. You would then follow this proposal through the system in a manner appropriate to your agency context, yet parallel to the process in the financial assistance program.

There may be occasions when you, as a supervisor, observe the need to implement an innovative idea of your own at the level of your own supervisees and their clients. An example of this approach follows.

EXAMPLE: As a supervisor in a primary care center, I was aware of the extensive demands on my workers for services to families where there were indications of child neglect. Our emphasis up to now had been on individuals, marital, and family counseling. Yet my review of records indicated to me that we were not being as effective as we wanted to be.

I called a meeting of my workers to discuss this concern. In this discussion, we identified major problems in these families, related to lack of understanding of normal child development as well as to limited parenting skills in disciplining the behavior of their children.

I took this information and launched my own study of alternative approaches to serving clients caught up in the problems of neglect and abuse. Also, I arranged for consultation from the family relations center at the local university. When I had explored the problem and alternatives, I designed a plan for parent-education groups to be tried out by myself and my workers.

I scheduled a meeting with my workers to share with them my efforts to gather information and come up with a new approach. I explained that given their concerns about client needs related to child development and child discipline, as well as the size of our workload, I had developed a model for parent-education groups. After much discussion, we divided into pairs, with each pair responsible for developing basic content on topics related to child development and discipline (developmental stages, nutritional needs, low-cost nutritious meals, nonphysical discipline, and other topics).

When we had the information together, we circulated the ideas and added my input and input from all my workers. Then I worked out a reorganization of workload in order to accommodate this new service. Also I designed a simple evaluation form to collect feedback from participating parents. As a result of this innovation and client feedback, we redefined these groups as parent groups, since these parents felt using the word *education* implied they were ignorant. The evaluation also showed that we were maintaining a higher level of service activity.

This example illustrates the steps involved in a systematic approach to program change at the component level. Equally important, it suggests the possibility for instituting changes to close gaps in service delivery to clients without adding resources or eliminating or reducing other services. This is an important consideration in approaching program change in a scarcity context. In this situation, activities related to the changing function are then linked to the administering function (work-load management). In your practice as a supervisor, you will want to be alert to these same considerations and possibilities within your agency and its context.

In summary, we have defined, described, and illustrated activities associated with the changing function. In particular we have called attention to types of change, scope of change, and action steps important to changing organizations from within and from the bottom up. These approaches and processes call for your leadership in developing, nurturing, and using your resources, those of your supervisees, those of others you must link up with to reduce resistance and advance the change initiative. Your selection of type and scope of change should be guided by your analysis of the relationships between current organizational operations and the quality and quantity of service delivery. By attending to the changing function, you can contribute to the development of yourself, your supervisees, the agency, and its clients. Moreover, so doing, you will be carrying out your supervisory responsibilities related to the organizational imperative for adaptability. Supervisor activities within the changing function include at a minimum:

1.  Encouraging review of standard operating procedures
2.  Implementing useful suggestion of another staff person (supervisee or supervisor)
3.  Differing with and confronting a superior
4.  Collecting and providing information about other approaches, thinking, programs, and data related to closing gaps in service delivery
5.  Implementing an innovative plan or idea of your own

## CONCLUSION

In this chapter we have defined, discussed, and illustrated the three goal imperatives for supervisors—integration, service delivery, linkages—and their corresponding relationships with the three organizational imperatives—stability, effectiveness, adaptability. For each of the goal imperatives, we defined three functional imperatives. We related each functional imperative to elements of the competent-supervisor and responsive-provision components of the community mandate. Specifically, we argued that the integrative functions of humanizing, managing tension, and catalyzing are connected with the dignity focus of the competent supervisor and the needs focus of responsive provision. For the service delivery functions of teaching, career socializing, and evaluating, we made corresponding connections to wisdom and skills. Finally, for the linkage functions of administering, advocating, and changing, the connections were made to leadership and resources.

The varying threes of the nine functions of supervision represent the pattern of patterns in the world as kaleidoscope. We have identified, as a beginning, several approaches and activities for you to use in practicing each function. Also, we have illustrated supervisor and supervisee behavior related to the practices associated with each function. We are sure you have already thought of other examples and will continue to do so in your continuing development as a supervisor. In this way your practice will contribute to the pattern of patterns of competent, imaginative supervision, and amplify change processes that may have been set in motion by your encounter with the nine functions.

Throughout this chapter we have noted the varying impact of different contextual factors on issues confronting supervisees, supervisors, and agencies. In Chapter 6 we shall elaborate the special organizational context of social work practice.

## REFERENCES

ARGYRIS, CHRIS, *Intervention Theory and Method: A Behavioral Science View.* Reading, Mass.: Addison-Wesley, 1970.

ARNDT, HILDA, "Effective Supervision in a Public Welfare Setting," *Public Welfare,* 31, no. 3 (Summer 1973), 50–54.

AUSTIN, MICHAEL J., *Supervisory Management for the Human Services.* Englewood Cliffs, N.J.: Prentice-Hall, 1981.

BARNARD, CHESTER I., *The Functions of the Executive.* Cambridge, Mass.: Harvard University Press, 1938.

BRAGER, GEORGE A., "Advocacy and Political Behavior," *Social Work,* 13, no. 2 (March 1968), 5–15.

BRAGER, GEORGE, and STEPHEN HOLLOWAY, *Changing Human Service Organizations.* New York: The Free Press, 1978.

BRIAR, SCOTT, "Effective Social Work Intervention in Direct Practice: Implications for Education," in *Facing the Challenge: Plenary Session Papers from the 19th Annual Program Meeting,* Scott Briar, et al., eds. New York: Council on Social Work Education, 1973.

――――, "The Current Crisis in Social Casework," in *Social Work Practice,* Scott Briar, ed. New York: Columbia University Press, 1967.

BRUNER, JEROME S., *Beyond the Information Given.* New York: W. W. Norton, 1973.

COREY, STEPHEN, *Action Research to Improve School Practices.* New York: Bureau of Publications, Teachers College, Columbia University, 1953.

DAVIS, LOUIS E., "Readying the Unready: Post-Industrial Jobs," in *A Contingency Approach to Management Readings,* John W. Newstrom, William E. Reif, and Robert M. Monczka, eds. New York: McGraw-Hill, 1975.

DELBECQ, ANDRE L., and DENNIS LADBROOK, "Administrative Feedback on the Behavior of Subordinates," *Administration in Social Work,* 3, no. 2 (Summer 1979), 153–166.

DEPARTMENT OF HEALTH, EDUCATION, AND WELFARE, *Work in America.* Cambridge, Mass.: MIT Press, 1973.

EPSTEIN, IRWIN, and TONY TRIPODI, *Research Techniques for Program Planning, Monitoring, and Evaluating.* New York: Columbia University Press, 1977.

EPSTEIN, LAURA, "Is Autonomous Practice Possible?" *Social Work,* 18, no. 2 (March 1973), 5–12.

FINCH, WILBUR A., JR., "Declining Public Social Service Resources: A Managerial Problem," unpublished paper presented at the Annual Program Meeting, Council on Social Work Education, 1981.

_____, "Social Workers Versus Bureaucracy," *Social Work*, 21, no. 9 (September 1976), 370–375.

FRANKLIN, JACK L., and JEAN H. THRASHER, *An Introduction to Program Evaluation.* New York: John Wiley, 1976.

FRENCH, JOHN R.B., JR., "Person-Role Fit," in *Occupational Stress*, Alan McLean, ed. Springfield, Ill.: Charles C. Thomas Publisher, 1974.

FRENCH, WENDELL L., and CECIL H. BELL, JR., *Organization Development* (2nd ed.). Englewood Cliffs, N.J.: Prentice-Hall, 1978.

GEHRING, DONALD, and CAROL E. BAKER, "Life Cycle and Staff Development," unpublished paper presented to The National Association of Student Personnel Administrators, Region III, Louisville, Ky., 1982.

GILMORE, THOMAS, "Managing Collaborative Relationships in Complex Organizations," *Administration in Social Work*, 3, no. 2 (Summer 1979), 167–180.

GITTERMAN, ALEX, "Comparison of Educational Models and Their Influences on Supervision," in *Issues in Human Services*, Florence W. Kaslow, and Associates. San Francisco: Jossey-Bass, 1972.

GLICKEN, VIRGINIA, "Enhancing Work for Professional Social Workers," *Administration in Social Work*, 4, no. 3 (Fall 1980), 61–74.

GOFFMAN, ERVING, *The Presentation of Self in Everyday Life.* New York: Doubleday, 1959.

GOLAN, NAOMI, *Passing Through Transitions.* New York: The Free Press, 1981.

GUMMER, BURTON, "The Social Responsibilities of the Organization: Fairness, Equity, and Justice," *Administration in Social Work*, 2, no. 4 (Winter 1978), 489–493.

HAYNES, KAREN S., "Job Satisfaction of Mid-Management Social Workers," *Administration in Social Work*, 3, no. 2 (Summer 1979), 207–217.

HERAUD, BRIAN J., *Sociology and Social Work.* Oxford, England: Pergamon Press, 1970.

HIRSCHHORN, LARRY, "The Stalemated Agency: A Theoretical Perspective and a Practical Proposal," *Administration in Social Work*, 2, no. 4 (Winter 1978), 425–438.

HOLLOWAY, STEPHEN, and GEORGE BRAGER, "Some Considerations in Planning Organizational Change," *Administration in Social Work*, 1, no. 4 (Winter 1977), 349–357.

JONES, DARIELL L., "African-American Clients: Clinical Practice Issues," *Social Work*, 24, no. 2 (March 1979), 112–118.

KADUSHIN, ALFRED, *Supervision in Social Work.* New York: Columbia University Press, 1976.

KAHN, ROBERT L., *Work and Health.* New York: John Wiley, 1981.

_____, ed., *Organizational Stress: Studies in Role Conflict and Ambiguity.* New York: John Wiley, 1964.

KURZMAN, PAUL A., "Rules and Regulations in Large-Scale Organizations: A Theoretical Approach to the Problem," *Administration in Social Work*, 1, no. 4 (Winter 1977), 421–431.

LEVY, CHARLES S., *Social Work Ethics.* New York: Human Sciences Press, 1979.

_____, "The Ethics of Supervision," *Social Work*, 18, no. 2 (March 1973), 14–21.

LEWIN, KURT, *Resolving Social Conflicts*, Gertrud Weiss Lewin, ed. New York: Harper & Brothers, 1948.

LUBOVE, ROY, *The Professional Altruist.* Cambridge, Mass.: Harvard University Press, 1965.

MAIER, NORMAN R.F., *The Appraisal Interview: Three Basic Approaches.* La Jolla, Calif.: University Associates, 1976.

MALUCCIO, ANTHONY N., ed., *Promoting Competence in Clients: A New/Old Approach to Social Work Practice.* New York: The Free Press, 1981.

MANDELL, BETTY, "The 'Equality' Revolution and Supervision," *Journal of Education for Social Work,* 9, no. 1 (Winter 1973), 43–54.

MARTIN, PATRICIA YANCEY, "Multiple Constituencies, Dominant Societal Values, and the Human Service Administrator: Implications for Service Delivery," *Administration in Social Work,* 4, no. 2 (Summer 1980), 15–27.

MECHANIC, DAVID, "Sources of Power of Lower Participants in Complex Organizations," *Administrative Science Quarterly,* 7, no. 12 (December 1962), 349–364.

MIDDLEMAN, RUTH R., "A Teaching/Training Specialization with the Masters Curriculum," unpublished paper presented at the Annual Program Meeting, Council on Social Work Education, 1977.

MIDDLEMAN, RUTH R., and GALE GOLDBERG, *Social Service Delivery: A Structural Approach to Social Work Practice.* New York: Columbia University Press, 1974.

MILLER, IRVING, "Supervision in Social Work," *Encyclopedia of Social Work* (16th issue), Vol. 2. New York: NASW, 1971.

NATIONAL ASSOCIATION OF SOCIAL WORKERS, *Code of Ethics.* Washington, D.C.: NASW, 1981.

NATIONAL ASSOCIATION OF SOCIAL WORKERS AD HOC COMMITTEE ON ADVOCACY, "The Social Worker as Advocate: Champion of Social Victims," *Social Work,* 14, no. 2 (March 1969), 16–21.

NEWMAN, EDWARD, and JERRY TUREM, "The Crisis of Accountability," *Social Work,* 19, no. 1 (January 1974), 139–147.

OUCHI, WILLIAM G., *Theory Z.* Reading, Mass.: Addison-Wesley, 1981.

PASCALE, RICHARD T., and ANTHONY G. ATHOS, *The Art of Japanese Management.* New York: Simon & Schuster, 1981.

PATTI, RINO J., "Organizational Resistance and Change: A View from Below," *Social Service Review,* 48, no. 3 (September 1974), 361–383.

PATTI, RINO J., and HERMAN RESNICK, "Changing the Agency from Within," *Social Work,* 17, no. 4 (July 1972), 48–57.

PAWLAK, EDWARD J., "Organizational Tinkering," *Social Work,* 21, no. 5 (September 1976), 370–375.

PERLMAN, HELEN HARRIS, *Persona: Social Role and Personality.* Chicago: University of Chicago Press, 1968.

PERLMUTTER, FELICE, "Barometer of Professional Change," in *Issues in Human Services,* Florence W. Kaslow, and Associates. San Francisco: Jossey-Bass, 1972.

PERLMUTTER, FELICE, and LESLIE B. ALEXANDER, "Racism and Sexism in Social Work Practice: An Empirical View," *Administration in Social Work,* 1, no. 4 (Winter 1977), 433–442.

PHILLIPS, GERALD M., *Communication and the Small Group.* Indianapolis: Bobbs-Merrill, 1973.

PINES, AYALA, and DISTA KAFRY, "Occupational Tedium in the Social Services," *Social Work,* 23, no. 6 (November 1978), 499–507.

PODELL, LAWRENCE, "Attrition of First Line Social Service Staff," *Welfare in Review,* 5, no. 1 (January 1967), 9–14.

POSAVAC, EMIL J., and RAYMOND G. CAREY, *Program Evaluation: Methods and Case Studies.* Englewood Cliffs, N.J.: Prentice-Hall, 1980.

PRUGER, ROBERT, "The Good Bureaucrat," *Social Work,* 18, no. 4 (July 1973), 26–32.

RESNICK, HERMAN, "Tasks in Changing the Organization from Within (COFW)," *Administration in Social Work,* 2, no. 1 (Spring 1978), 29–44.

RESNICK, HERMAN, and RINO J. PATTI, eds., *Change from Within: Humanizing Social Welfare Organizations.* Philadelphia: Temple University Press, 1980.

ROGERS, CARL R., *Freedom to Learn.* Columbus, Ohio: Charles E. Merrill, 1979.

SLAVIN, SIMON, "A Theoretical Framework for Social Administration," in *Leadership in Social Administration: Perspectives for the 1980's,* Felice Perlmutter, and Simon Slavin, eds. Philadelphia: Temple University Press, 1980.

SUTTON, JACQUELYN A., "Sex Discrimination Among Social Workers," *Social Work,* 27, no. 3 (May 1982), 211–217.

TOFFLER, ALVIN, *The Third Wave.* New York: William Morrow, 1980.

TROPP, EMANUEL, "The Challenge of Quality for Practice Theory," in *Social Work in Practice—Fourth NASW Symposium,* Bernard Ross, and S.K. Khinduka, eds. Washington, D.C.: NASW, 1976.

————, "Expectation, Performance, and Accountability," *Social Work,* 19, no. 2 (March 1974), 139–148.

WASSERMAN, HARRY, "The Professional Social Worker in a Bureaucracy," *Social Work,* 16, no. 1 (January 1971), 89–95.

————, "Early Careers of Professional Social Workers in a Public Child Welfare Agency," *Social Work,* 15, no. 4 (July 1970), 93–101.

WEBER, SHIRLEY, "From 'Separation' to a 'Turned on' Model of Services," *Social Casework,* 53, no. 10 (December 1972), 593–603.

WIEHE, VERNON R., "Current Practices in Performance Appraisal," *Administration in Social Work,* 4, no. 3 (Fall 1980), 1–11.

WILSON, SUANA J., *Recording.* New York: The Free Press, 1980.

YANKELOVICH, DANIEL, *New Rules: Searching for Self-Fulfillment in a World Turned Upside Down.* New York: Random House, 1981.

ZELENY, MILAN, and NORBERT A. PIERRE, "Simulation and Self-Renewing Systems," in *Evolution and Consciousness: Human Systems in Transition,* Erich Jantsch, and Conrad H. Waddington, eds. Reading, Mass.: Addison-Wesley, 1976.

# CHAPTER SIX
# THE SPECIALNESS
# OF SOCIAL WORK'S
# ORGANIZATIONAL
# CONTEXT

## INTRODUCTION

In Chapter 3 we identified the mentality that is necessary when you move into the role of supervisor. This mindset, like it or not, is required because you now have authority (power) over other people. We considered elements that contribute to the competency and imagination of a supervisor, to the dynamic characteristic of an organization, and to responsive service provision. These elements, along with the ever-present context, flow from the community sanction or mandate for the services of social workers, and they comprise the backdrop for your professional assignment.

## HISTORICAL AND ORGANIZATIONAL CONTEXTS

Three of the four components of the community mandate were discussed in Chapter 4. The fourth, *context*, is the central issue in this chapter. We shall view the context pragmatically by asking you to visualize yourself within an organization, as supervisor or supervisee, and to imagine some of the patterns and elements that will affect your work. As we described in Chapter 1, an important distinction of supervision in social work derives from its origins in an organization-based profession—

one that arose within agencies. These were small organizations patterned after the simple entrepreneurial businesses known to members of the agency's board of directors; or they were collegial groups of residents who lived in settlements with a head resident as the chief executive officer.

In the 1930s public social service agencies under federal, state, and city auspices evolved, and private agencies grew gradually larger and more complex. In both settings, a supervisory practice based on social work values and knowledge was elaborated. At this time, these agencies, public or private, offered social services as the primary service, and those were the services that the clients came for. Perlmutter (1982) described the agencies up until the 1960s as stable, and the social work profession as infused with feelings of pride, satisfaction, and expansion, where promotion to supervisor was a reward for being a good practitioner.

Just as we examined some of the forces that have contributed to a special "social work supervision" as compared with developments in other professions, so now shall we examine some of the influences that make the context in which you work special.

### The Movement to Diversity

From the mid-1950s on, social workers moved into diverse organizations and fields of practice; and members of other professions began practicing in social agencies and other areas previously "reserved" for social work. Today, services tend to be offered through multidisciplinary delivery systems. Diverse professions and orientations provide the technical know-how, and they also provide considerable public and professional "guild" controversy as to what *is* or *should be* the most valued technical know-how.

This development was initiated when the pressures and personnel needs for the War on Poverty, the mental health initiative for community-based services, the activities of various rights groups in the 1960s and '70s, the hopes for the Great Society, and subsequent national political and economic missions arose. All of these served to diminish seriously the supervisory tradition and continuity experienced by social workers. New ideologies and new professions appeared, for example, psychiatric nursing, clinical psychology, community psychology and psychiatry, applied sociology, expressive therapy, counseling, pastoral care, and human resources. Meanwhile, newly accredited B.S.W. degree programs grew to exceed 300 by the early 1980s, with graduates seeking entry-level positions as professional social workers; two-year community colleges flourished and graduated personnel ready to enter various service fields or enter baccalaureate programs; and many more social work schools developed doctoral programs.

The older distinctions between "private" and public organization faded since all organizatons grew more dependent on federal, state, and municipal support and on insurance systems as the "patrons" for services in the expanding service industries. Health and human service systems have become more businesslike as a result of fluctuating social policy, and as a result of contracted services that were purchased and monitored by systems more remote geographically from an agency, yet more controlling of the substance and extent of services and their "assured" quality.

During these times a burgeoning group movement arose and challenged more traditional psychiatric approaches. Group work was eagerly adopted by psychologists and social workers, and it also included another alternative to all professional helpers: the self-help or mutual-helping groups, particularly the single-issue service types. Such self-help groups now number three-quarters of a million, and they involve over 15 million participants; the Department of Health and Human Services predicts that their number will double by 1990.

Varieties of "different" organization types arose and flourished aside from or alongside of the more orthodox delivery systems. These "alternative systems" (see Note 1), attuned to the massive societal-change initiatives of the times, could respond to populations with needs not served through the "officially" sponsored programs (e.g., feminist, black or Hispanic mentalities; gay or lesbian mentalities; ex-mental-patient mentalities). Some were responsive to needs viewed as illegal (e.g., draft avoidance, abortion assistance), to politically partisan missions (disallowed within ordinary professional neutrality norms), to challenges of prevailing, dominant theory (e.g., disease and deficit views of persons), and to professionalism itself (e.g., its power, mystique, and privileges).

In some instances these alternatives have survived. Some have become new organizations now, with different persons holding the power positions; others have been incorporated—made legitimate by new legal determinations—and are components of the "regular" service organizations. Others have "died" through their own internal power struggles, through inability to meet funding and accountability requirements, or simply through the exhaustion of central leaders.

In any case, the role analogs (or self-views) we described (Chapter 1) as pertinent to the organization-based worker (coach, counselor, conferee) may be augmented by additional ones spawned in the more recent times. We might find the entrepreneur (coach or counselor—teacher or treater), the copartner (self-discoverer with help-seeker), and missionary (helper so long as particular values or orders are followed). Moreover, not only do practitioners view service seekers differentially (clients, patients, consumers, customers), but they view the organization variably, as Reish and Ephross described (1983). The organization may be viewed as the setting where professionals practice; as determiner of what practitioners may (or may not) be able to do; as an obstacle that conflicts with "professional" activity; or as change target equal in importance to practitioners' service work. Between career specialization in graduate social work education and the work assignment, the match is disjointed, or only approximate, since each component shifts and revises its way of organizing things. For example, a recent study of a major school of social work found that one-third of its recent graduates were primarily using a "method" of practice in which they had not specialized.

In view of these various shifts within the broader societal context, within the profession and in other professions and professional preparations, it is not surprising that the format and processes of supervisory practice are also in flux. Supervision in organizations tends to be mainly administrative, not educative as we have reviewed, and it is based mostly on organizational fiat, requirements, and custom, rather than any particular practice theory or supervisee developmental learning needs. As social workers have moved into different settings, different accountability systems are at work. At the same time, other professions, following the example of law, medicine, and business, have become based in the complex organizations, and the supervisory and accountability situation for social workers drifts toward systems characteristic of other professions.

If there ever existed a "social work agency" where all the professionals were similarly trained, where all had a common ideology, knowledge base, and socialization experience, and where a M.S.W. social work tradition and orientation prevailed, such a place currently is a rarity. Social workers will need to hold their own conceptually alongside supervisors from other disciplines and professions. They will need to contribute know-how derived from their own rich professional heritage, and at the same time they must collaborate with and accommodate to the traditions, knowledge, and insights of others.

The social work profession's claim for a unique supervisory structure and practice now seems lost in the process of its own organizational development. Social workers supervise in diverse ways—there is no single predominant "social work way" of supervising. The work force has grown diffuse; diverse practice approaches, especially in group and family practice, have proliferated in agencies; and well-argued attacks on "traditional" supervision in the journals of the 1970s are abundant. In group therapy, for example, workers are "supervised" most often through performing a co-leadership role with another worker, often their supervisor (Middleman, 1980). Family treatment supervision may require a one-way screen and telephone hook-up with a supervisor who watches the action live and flashes in directives to avoid therapeutic blunders. For those practitioners who need supervision of their clinical work in order to fulfill certification and licensure requirements, most likely they must contract and pay for this supervision themselves, aside from the work place.

While there may be no one comprehensive theory for supervision, practitioners who are supervisors still seek to enhance their knowledge and skills. New learnings are sought from occasional attendance in workshops, which usually deal with a particular technical area currently fashionable (important?), for example, time management, burnout, management by objectives, transactional analysis. For the most part, the working knowledge base for supervision is extrapolated from whatever supervisors have learned during their earlier social work professional education, and from the practice wisdom gained through on-the-job experience in their agency. This base may be extended through individual study of books from a literature mainly produced by theorists from diverse disciplines outside of social work—business, psychology, administration, sociology, management, training, the therapies, and so forth—and conscientious supervisors pursue this study on their own initiative.

### The Current Context of Social Work Practice

We asked that you visualize yourself within an organization as context. Hardcastle and Katz's manpower survey (1979) of social workers who were members of NASW found that 70 percent of their respondents were based in agencies and 45 percent of that group worked in the public sector. According to our analysis of the preliminary findings of the 1982 NASW membership survey, which will form the base on an ongoing data bank of the Association (NASW, 1983), 86 percent of the respondents were agency-based, and 46 percent of them worked in the public sector. The profession remains basically salaried, rather than entrepreneurial.

We had "felt" that the profession was becoming more entrepreneurial, possibly less based in organizations. These assumptions were made from the realization that resources have been withdrawn from many public-sector agencies, that programs and positions have been devastated by diminished financial support (because of purchase of services contracts with "private" agencies), by less available grant money for social programs, and by a national antisocial, political retrenchment policy. We saw some social workers moving into private practice or group practice in collaboration with other professionals, and we observed increasing numbers of practitioners obtaining licenses, vendorship status, and credentials that could make them less dependent upon particular agencies for employment. We knew social workers were moving into new practice arenas, such as industrial social work, banks' trust divisions, and real estate firms. And we speculated that the profession may be engaged in a sponsorship shift, in part a necessity for survival, in part a shared broadspread disillusionment among many in the service industries and in corporate business and industry as well. Such disillusionment, we believed, was largely related to the impersonality and cumbersomeness of complex systems.

The new data more than confirmed our suppositions about entrepreneurship, despite the mainly organization-based practice auspice. Twelve percent listed private practice as their primary employment and 10 percent listed it as their secondary (part-time) employment. Taken together, these figures suggest that one-fifth of NASW members now have some experience and identification with private practice. It may be that many of those 10 percent working part-time or moonlighting in addition to their primary position are en route toward this arena, as their clientele increases and as vendorship offers more insurance coverage for their specialty.

As we reviewed the data of organization-based practice to assess our focus on middle-level organization practice (our special interest), we found ourselves confined to the questionnaire's category system of *supervision* and *management/administration*. This categorization did not neatly fit our tastes, since the latter category covered, we think, a wide range of possible spans of influence. Nevertheless, the requirement for respondents to identify themselves (whether via organization-determined job titles or own self-perception) is interesting in its own terms. Among the respondents, 7 percent identified supervision as their primary employment, 20 percent management/administration. Among those who were supervisors, 58 percent were in the public sector, 42 percent in the private sector, while those in management/administration were distributed almost exactly opposite: 57 percent in the private sector, 43 percent in the public.

When we analyzed the distribution of *supervisors* by practice areas, we find that most supervisors work in the area of children and youth, followed in rank order by mental health, medical or health care, and family services. Taken together, 75 percent of *supervisors* work in these four practice areas, out of a category system of 16 possible practice areas. The distribution for *management/administration* is nearly parallel, with 62 percent working in one of these same four practice areas. The largest number is in mental health, followed in order by medical or health care, children and youth, and family services. We think it is important to note the high percentage of *supervisors* and *management/administrators* working in the multidisciplinary mental health, medical or health care settings.

We also compared the gender distribution and the white versus nonwhite ethnic (Black, Hispanic, Asian, American Indian, Alaskan native and other) distribution with respect to direct service and middle-level and administrative distributions. Among all respondents 69 percent were female, 31 percent male; 89 percent were white and 11 percent nonwhite ethnic. Comparing the gender percentages between total members and supervisors, the proportions are nearly identical: 66 percent female and 34 percent male supervisors. In terms of management/administration and total membership responses, men are disproportionately represented (49 percent male, 51 percent female). With regard to the racial, ethnic distribution of supervisors and management/administration, we find the distribution between whites and nonwhite/ethnic groups equivalent to that in the total survey population (87 percent white, 13 percent nonwhite ethnic).

Finally, whereas *supervisors* are roughly two-thirds female and one-third male, *managers/administrators* are roughly evenly male or female, and the *supervisory/managerial* roles of white and nonwhite/ethnic groups approximate their distribution among the total respondents. When we examined the distributions for direct service workers, we found that 76 percent are women; and that 65 percent of the white respondents and 58 percent of nonwhite/ethnic groups are direct service workers.

### A Contextual Approach to Supervision

In our approach to supervision, we will try to be responsive to the emergent aspects of supervision as required by the changing agency and organization scene—the many variable circumstances and other uncertain, unstable realities that characterize the complexity of the current world (to the extent that we, or any one, can make sense of it). Other discussions of supervision and field instruction remain important also for functioning within the complexity of this realm (see Note 2).

In Chapter 7 we shall present four intervention orientations that supervisors may use to guide their approach. These orientations may offer a diversified set of alternatives responsive to the changing contexts of service delivery, the different goals that need to be pursued, the relation of these goals to the structures and processes needed to reach them, and the variety of techniques now available to select. Although we have highlighted certain key supervisory functions (our conceptual preference) in Chapter 5, there is room for creative selection in the particulars of supervisory design—so as to match your special circumstances, setting, experience, and preference. These various elements might be viewed as possibilities for your work—as kaleidoscope, with patterns comprised of aspects that shift and turn according to the emphasis you give to any particular feature. As suggested by our earlier analysis foursome, the emphasis you select will be determined by *supervisor* and *supervisee*, with their *history*, and their shared *contexts*—a matter we will explore further in Chapter 7.

Despite the various shifts we have identified in the current diversification of social work practice, the profession and its supervision, as our data reveal, remain basically salaried, lodged in organizations. Our consideration of *context*, therefore, leads us to place most emphasis on the organization: the purpose of organization; organizational goals; different organizational structural patterns and dynamics; and the ways in which social workers' "homes" both resemble and differ from the general category *organization* (which often means the for-profit organizations most characteristic of U.S. mainstream culture).

At the outset, it seems important to state up front two of our basic assumptions:

1. You are most likely at work in a bureaucratic organization, and this arrangement will affect the quality of service delivery (and your work) more than your client-focused skills or those of other workers and supervisors.
2. Your organizational "home," whether a public or private service organization (or alternative service system), is quite different from the for-profit organizations that have spawned most of the organization literature.

Let us explore these assumptions as they influence the context and texture of supervision. We shall consider (1) organizations in general, (2) bureaucracies as a major type of organization where most social workers work, and (3) some of the special differences between human service organizations and for-profit organizations. It seems increasingly important for all social workers to understand organizations (their context) as much as they do their clients—both realms are exceedingly difficult to "know."

## THE PURPOSE OF ORGANIZATION

As we have seen in Chapter 4, organizations seek to be stable, adaptable, and effective. They, along with their personnel and resources, exist to meet a need for a product, service, or combination of both. They may be incorporated for profit or not for profit. The general purpose of organization is the direction and control of human activity. Human energy, material, time, and spatial arrangements are organized so that goals may be realized with maximum effectiveness and efficiency. The goals themselves and the resources needed to meet these goals are complex and extensive, and achieving them requires pooled knowledge and concerted action. Organization is the answer to meeting these requirements.

There is little room today for a Robinson Crusoe orientation, a self-sufficiency mentality in the workplace, because of the complex support elements that must be marshaled for any activity or service provision. In fact, it even has been suggested that solo practitioners *pretend* an organization when offering family therapy by telephoning an imaginary team during a session and holding an imaginary consultation discussion regarding next therapy moves (Hoffman, 1981). In this way "the team" is supposed to convey the therapist's connection to a support system, give the illusion of several opinions, and thus impress clients with an apparently extended knowledge (power) base. The solo practitioner constructs an "organization" so as to extend and add legitimacy to his or her impact, a ploy which may be questioned from an ethical standpoint as a form of client deception.

Some persons believe that organization of energy and material in time and place was first demonstrated by the building of the pyramids in Egypt. The pyramids represented a vast communal effort in which the goal was beyond the achievement of individual members of the society and transcended the subsistence needs of the community. A line of authority was developed from the top down, and a highly complicated task was organized into work that required only simple repetitive skills. Perhaps the pyramid structure of bureaucracy can find its roots here, in a 5,000-year-old heritage of this organization literally for pyramid building. Following this type of hierarchy, the most typical organization type has been the pyramidal or classical bureaucracy. This pyramidal structure usually is viewed negatively as a dehumanizing environment, but *bureaucracy* is not inherently negative. We put the connotation (value) onto the term. The main concern is what is to be organized and what roles and rules are developed to meet the goals. What if these were framed so as to generate creativity? What if the purpose of the organization is innovation, and structures are developed to ensure time for thinking, room for collaboration and stimulation? Then we would find that the seemingly rigid, dehumanizing pyramidal hierarchy would be deployed toward actualizing an opposite ambience—flexible, humane, creative experience.

In organizations, authority and control can be centralized or decentralized. With centralization, resources can be focused more easily, and the chances of undesirable actions and consequences can be reduced through control of what is thought to be negative. For example, computerization of records brings closer centralization and control to organizations. Gaps, mismanagement, and potential mischief of many varieties can be spotted and attended to speedily; yet the possibility exists for increased focus on minutiae, leaving lessened energies for attending to complex, serious distress. With decentralization, the energy, flexibility, and innovativeness of the organizational subunits are increased, but so is the possibility of runaway, undesirable, counterproductive, cross-purpose activity. Organization involves a trade-off:

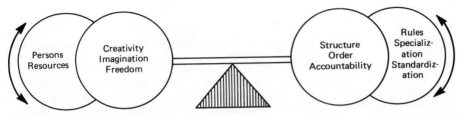

Organizations usually offer certain "standing orders" that aim to reduce the amount of personal supervision necessary and at the same time increase the likelihood of achieving coordinated action. The price for this? Routinization of work, standardization of responses, and erosion of areas for individual judgment. Despite these probabilities, we believe that an understanding of certain key components of organizational life, plus deliberate mastery of some organization-related skills, will give a supervisor more degrees of freedom and room for innovation than may have been imagined. For example, a major pitfall many supervisors fall into is assuming agency policy from everyday practice (that is, from precedent), rather than exploring the real necessity for a given decision or judgment, or researching what *is* a fixed policy.

### Organization Goals

As you look at your organization (or ones you have known), think first of its goal or mission. Of course, the organization may have more than one goal, may have several that may even conflict with one another, may be unclear about its goals or may be changing them. We list some examples of organization goals at a general level. Can you place your organization within these goals (or compose a general goal of your own to encompass your organization's intent)?

1. Influencing particular persons, families, groups, communities
2. Influencing others' (or society's) reactions to any of the above entities
3. Influencing both the particular entities (item 1, above) and others' reactions to them
4. Allocating, distributing, or redistributing resources (financial, health, mental health, education, cultural, aesthetic)

As you consider your organization's goals, you also think of your place as supervisor within the total service delivery arrangement. This arrangement may be described as follows, according to the "quadrant" model of practice proposed by Goldberg (1974) and Middleman and Goldberg (1974):

> The supervisory role is mainly concerned with Quadrant D — dealing with others (nonseekers of service) out of a concern for particular persons. (This also applies to the consultant, trainer, manager, administrator). Some supervisors may also do Quadrant A work — dealing directly with persons, groups, or families who have a problem or need, in order to help them meet their

needs. (A-type involvement happens when you carry some cases or co-lead groups directly as part of your supervisory approach.) This is also the focus of the supervisees when they are the frontline workers. Sometimes you may be engaged in Quadrant B-type work: working with some clients, for example, a committee of senior citizens, to plan an event for all senior citizens in your community. And at times, C-type involvement, dealing with non-seekers of service out of a concern for a category of clients, may be your emphasis—lobbying, fund raising, policy development, and so forth.

### Organization Structure

Let us assume you have considered these purposes and found a place within this schema for your organization. Now we will examine other ways in which organizations have been described. All organizations need mechanisms for differentiating and integrating the work. These mechanisms and the processes they generate are often at odds with each other and in tension. The integration is accompanied through some type of supervisory and accountability structure. Typically, this is bureaucratic and hierarchical, usually accomplished via the "pyramid," with persons under the supervision of someone at the next higher level. Less frequently, there is a matrix arrangement, where subordinates may need to report to two different specialists. When we look at organization vertically, we think in terms of hierarchy (i.e., what needs to be integrated). But organizational structure may also be viewed horizontally, so as to reveal how the organization has been differentiated by units and to pinpoint what needs to be coordinated. The issues involved—which, in combination, comprise complex organizations—are those of integration/differentiation and coordination.

Since the most prevalent form of organization in Western culture *is* the bureaucracy, and since our primary mentality is *up*-down (with *up* meaning better, higher, more important), we shall first look at the bureaucracy vertically. Later, we shall return with a sideways glance at horizontal spread.


## BUREAUCRACIES: A VERTICAL VIEW

Table 6-1 shows five vertical schemes for viewing bureaucracies. (For further discussion of bureaucracies, see Note 3.) Each scheme shows the levels that need to be integrated. According to our scheme, we see (1) workers—those who do the basic work with the clients; (2) supervisors—middle-level staff who link workers and administrators; (3) administrators—those at the top who make the strategic, long-range decisions; (4) staff specialists—consultants such as researchers, planners, accountants, and attorneys, whose work is related to design and control of the work; and (5) support staff—those who provide indirect services or handle information-processing chores.

It should now be apparent that you might find a social worker in any one of these key organizational parts, depending upon the purpose of the organization.

**TABLE 6-1   Hierarchical Schemes**

| PARSONS ←AND→ | KATZ AND KAHN | KOUZES AND MICO | MINTZBERG | MIDDLEMAN AND RHODES |
|---|---|---|---|---|
| *Top* | | | | |
| Community institutional (administrators) | External environment | Policy | Strategic apex | Administrators |
| Managerial (managers) | Internal operations | Management | Technostructure Middle line Support staff | Specialists Supervisors Secretaries |
| Technical (front/line/ supervisors) | Service delivery | Service | Operating core | Workers |
| *Bottom* | | | | |

For example, in a family and children's agency, social workers probably are workers, supervisors, and administrators. In these agencies, the major services provided are social services. By history and tradition, children's services are social work "turf," and they remain among the few arenas still dominated by the social work profession. However, in the mayor's office, where the major purpose is city administration and governance, or in the housing authority, whose major purpose is provision of housing, social workers might be part of the specialist staff—that is, one group among the specialists whose work is related to social components within the administrative or housing-authority domains and purposes. And in the employee-assistance department of an automotive plant, the social workers could be part of the support staff—that is, as part of the personnel services, they could provide an indirect service such as counseling or family treatment to the auto workers.

These five organizational parts (or types of organizational participants) are important to the functioning of all organizations. As we shall see, these components will enable us to distinguish different types of organizations. We need to point out that any given organization may not have these five components represented by "live bodies." Nevertheless, the functions would hold for any organization. At times certain functions (specialist, support, supervisory) might be carried by the administrator, or they might be purchased as needed, on a contract basis.

Figure 6-1 depicts our stylized view of the "organization as a person," with its five types of participants. Following Mintzberg's analysis, the size and salience of these five groups of participants (or organizational parts) lead to a conceptualization of five different kinds of bureaucracies:

The simple structure
The machine (classical) bureaucracy
The professional bureaucracy
The divisionalized bureaucracy
The adhocracy

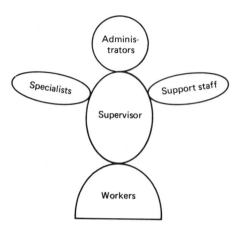

**FIGURE 6-1.**
**Five types of organization participants.**

Thus, we shall employ our *5-by-5 Rule:* Five types of participants (or organizational parts), rearranged and elaborated differentially, result in five types of bureaucracies. Now we shall look at some of the distinctions and advantages of these types of bureaucracies and relate them to social agency types.

### The Simple Structure

In Figure 6-2 we find the *simple structure*, with a small administrative head on a large body of workers. Within the profit sector, the simple structure's heyday was the late 19th century, when times were ripe for small innovative enterprises run by the founder with a tough autocratic mentality. Most organizations start out with this type of simple structure, and they grow with age into the other bureaucratic types, such as the *machine bureaucracy*. An exception to this general pattern is the partnership or coop, which may become a *professional bureaucracy*.

The simple structure is the organization in infancy, since most of these organizations begin with only a top administrator and the workers and with few or no supervisors (the services of specialist or support staff being purchased if and when needed). The organization is small, lean, and flexible. It works well in simple, dynamic environments, even those with extreme negative pressures. The administrator supervises the workers directly and coordinates the work. Such structures can outmaneuver the big bureaucracies. A parallel in the business world would be the small entrepreneurial company whose founder is in the driver's seat, closely related to all that happens. In the social agency arena, the early agencies such as the Charity Organization Societies and settlement houses, with their strong directors and cadre of workers would be examples of this kind of organizational structure. Today, examples of simple bureaucracy might include pilot projects or relatively small organizations, such as a planned parenthood clinic, a sheltered workshop, or a nutrition center.

### The Classical Bureaucracy

The second illustration in Figure 6-2 is the typical stereotype of a bureaucracy, named *machine* bureaucracy by Mintzberg because it should function like

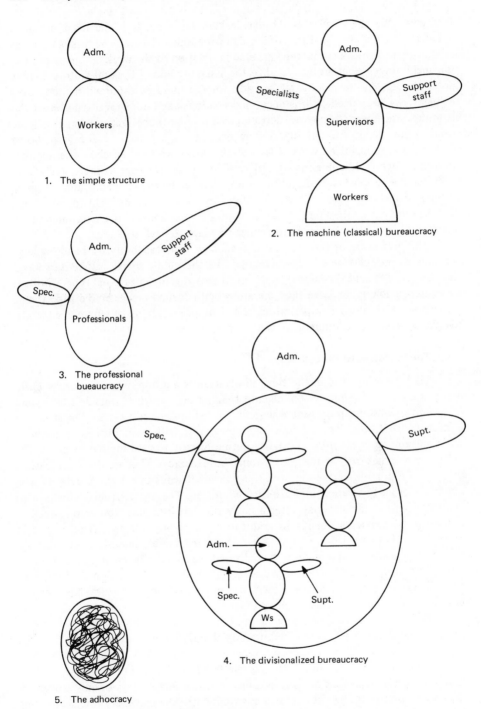

1. The simple structure

2. The machine (classical) bureaucracy

3. The professional bueaucracy

4. The divisionalized bureaucracy

5. The adhocracy

**FIGURE 6–2.  Five types of bureaucracies.**

clockwork. We shall call this the classical bureaucracy. It is the most prevalent organization type, the "mature" offspring of the industrial age. The primary characteristics of this organization type are standardization of the work and mass-production technology. Whether we visualize the assembly line of General Motors, the ten millionth Big Mac served by McDonald's, or the hundred thousandth food-stamp recipient, we see speed, consistency, and economy as the major attributes of this structure. And these features are accompanied by highly specialized jobs, usually demanding low skills for dull operations that produce masses of alienated, bored workers doing routinized work. Classical bureaucracies need an elaborate administration, a huge middle-line managerial staff to oversee the core workers, and a large specialist and support staff. Emphasis is upon rationalizing, analyzing, and designing systems that bring standardization, efficiency, and economy. This cumbersome organization—fat in the middle—depends on a stable, consistent environmental demand for its products. It is slow to change or adapt to new situations.

The usefulness of the classical bureaucracy is its capability for handling large amounts of products or services. Agencies like the public social welfare bureaucracies, the prisons, and the mental hospitals fit into this organizational type. They are structures that rely on a vertical hierarchy with formal power at the top, a large managerial staff, and an ample specialist and support staff, all of whom need a relatively unchanging environment for the system to work.

### The Professional Bureaucracy

The operating core in the third illustration is a group or professionals. Ordinarily, they are educated in schools and training organizations outside this system (e.g., universities and professional schools, workshops and institutes). The structure is decentralized, and the decisions and power rest with each professional who is working semi-independently and fairly autonomously toward the service goals. The skills are standardized in the professional bureaucracy. That is, there are certain things to be done in certain approved and licensed ways in certain situations. The operating procedures are complex but standardized. The professionals know how to identify client needs and may offer a fairly standard response "program," such as task-centered casework, family-life education, or group therapy. This does not mean that all is spelled out—only that there *are* some emphasized practice approaches "packaged" and ready to be delivered. As long as the environment is fairly stable, the professional bureaucracy does its job well. There are a limited number of possible response interventions, which can apply to problem situations so long as nothing too strange or extraordinary happens.

This structure requires a large support staff to assist the professionals and to perform the simple routine jobs required by them. However, there is little need for supervisors or specialists. The professionals have a great deal of control over their own time and work, and they feel a certain freedom in relation to their work. Professional bureaucracies are not distinguished for their adaptability or innovativeness; they work well in stable yet complex environments. The university, the accounting firm, and the general hospital are examples of this type, as are a city's Veterans Administration, a child-guidance clinic, and probation department.

### The Divisionalized Bureaucracy

The divisionalized form is a hybrid organization of recent vintage. It aims to mix bigness with adaptability to environmental shifts and to avoid the uniformity and dullness of the classical bureaucracy. Thus, organizations that grow large are split into divisions—parallel operating units loosely linked by a central administration. As we think of this bureaucratic type, we can imagine the multiversity, the large hospital system, the international unions, and government itself.

This structure resembles the *professional bureaucracy* with its loose linkage of units; here, however, the units are divisions, rather than individual professionals. A division's internal structure is mainly like the classical bureaucracy, a format Mintzberg argues is most easily responsive to pressures from "central office"— pressures that stress technocratic controls, measureable goals, and top-down decision making. Upper-level administration is still in control, and the administrator of each division still has much power; this format does not decentralize power. The divisionalized form is a partial structure superimposed on a different internal structure, thus allowing for both a certain amount of division autonomy and self-direction within an overall system of accountability and control.

Centralizing administration concentrates the power in a small group; certain specialist services such as legal advice are part of the central office. While there may be different operating procedures, staff deployment, priorities, and so forth among divisions, there are common accounting and reporting systems that effectively standardize outputs and worker performances in this type of bureaucratic organization. This kind of structure allows organizations to add and subtract divisions or, in other words, adapt to new conditions and spread the outreach, responsiveness, and risk. At the same time, this discourages risk taking and innovation, since division heads tend to watch each others' divisions and compete for importance. Adding and eliminating divisions and services deflects but does not eliminate the adaptability problem faced by the classical bureaucracy. Organizations can become obese, and power can be concentrated in a few hands when there is more input than output—a prevalent occurrence in big business. Since bureaucratic standardization is the output (product, service), the control through measurement of performance is difficult when the coin or profit is a human situation rather than quantity of money; and the temptation to ignore social costs in favor of divisional competition is cause for concern. The "bigness" principle that the divisionalized organization exemplifies can be seen in such nonprofit agencies as the community mental health center and its satellites, divisionalized family service offices, and the health center of a university.

### The Adhocracy

The final illustration in Figure 6-2 is the newest organizational form—a form that suits the new industries of our age, such as the aerospace industry, petrochemicals, think-tank consulting, computer development, film making. These organizations require a structure that encourages innovation and flexibility. To achieve this, all structural elements are diminished as much as possible. The adhocracy is a group of sophisticated specialists who form and re-form into project teams according to the tasks required and the talents of particular persons. The project team is a fluid entity that exists only so long as a particular problem needs attention.

The adhocracy refuses to accept the supposed necessity of standard operating procedures of most organizations, such as consistency in output, control by administrators, unity of command, and strategy that comes from the top. Instead, the power constantly shifts, and coordination and control occur through informal communication and interaction among the experts of the team, who make mutual situational adjustments as needed. Moreover, distinctions between the planning and design work as something separate from the operations and production are eliminated, as teams and project members work together in ever-shifting relationships. Such "think-tanks" work well provided they do not coexist with other structures in the same organization, in which case they tend to become elite "camps" or to sabotage the work of the ongoing structure and units. For example, in one organization an administrative committee made up of heads of division units met regularly to plan and recommend priorities and procedures to the administrator. A special ad hoc committee with different staff convened itself to deal with an external crisis. While this extra "brainpower" and planning were valued at first, it soon became apparent that the ad hoc committee was hard to disband and, in fact, was interested in attending to matters that the administrative committee had previously dealt with.

Adaptability is the emphasis in the structure of the adhocracy. Therefore, the structure is complex in its shifting fluidity. The organization is effective within complex, dynamic environments and situations where ambiguity is prevalent. Mintzberg identifies two types of adhocracies: operating and administrative. Typical of the first type is the consulting or advertising firm, which works on specially designed innovative projects in contract with clients. These firms aim to treat each client problem as a unique one to be solved creatively through a tailor-made approach. Such a problem-by-problem approach is in contrast with that of the professional bureaucracy, which would respond with a "ready-made" or standard solution to fit the request. In the adhocracy, experts cooperate with one another so as to develop a unique response, whereas in the professional bureaucracy, persons autonomously apply standard skills and programs that may or may not fit the particular situation. The administrative type of adhocracy, typified by NASA or the Rand Corporation, undertakes projects on its own behalf. Within its structure are both administrative and operating parts. The administrative part is devoted to design work and uses the project-team experts; the operating component focuses on executing the ideas, and it needs standardized, often automated tasks, with the more typical bureaucratic rules and controls.

Adhocracies aim to impart a democratic rather than bureaucratic spirit to the work place, and they are "in" these days. They feature "expertise, organic structure, project teams and task forces, diffused power, matrix structure, sophisticated and often automated production systems, youth, and dynamic, complex environments" (Mintzberg, 1981, p. 113). They are not known for efficiency, and they need lots of supervisory personnel, depend on costly liaison devices for communication, demand much time for processing information, and generate internal conflicts and pressures. Within the social agency terrain, there are few adhocracies. Perhaps our closest approximation would be the special research and demonstration projects funded to explore a program or situation. In addition, some of the projects of entrepreneurial consultation and organizational development may at times follow an adhocracy approach.

In all of these five types of organizations we find certain common structural elements. These elements include: specialization of tasks; formalization of procedures; indoctrination and training mechanisms; delegation of power both downward (vertical decentralization) and outward to nonmanagers (horizontal decentralization); action-planning and performance-control systems; grouping of units; liaison devices to facilitate communication; and a span of control for the supervisors or managers. In Table 6–2 we compare the five organizational types along five structural features: goal-compliance mechanisms, decision-making mechanisms, task requirements, environmental fit, and response to the unexpected.

## BUREAUCRACIES: A HORIZONTAL VIEW

Bureaucracies may be differentiated by the units to be coordinated. Making some adaptations to social work's organizations from Mintzberg's general differentiation scheme (1979), we suggest the following differentiation possibilities:

By profession or discipline (social workers, psychologist)
By work process and function (counseling unit, personnel)
By time (intake, treatment, discharge, follow-up)
By client (age groupings, problem types)
By output (typed reports, filled prescriptions, meals)
By place (catchment area, district)

In a given organization, one or more of these differentiation schemes may be operative. For example, you may find a counseling unit that is divided further according to ages served or treatment versus discharge. As you consider your organization's structure (or another you have known in the past), can you place it within this typology? As we imagine any of these differentiating systems, we are thinking horizontally and are visualizing divisions spread out within an organization.

## ASSESSING THE WORK CLIMATE

We have reviewed diverse purposes and structures of organizations, so that you could begin to "find" your agency and conceptualize some of its features, assets, and limitations as an organization type. This is a major prerequisite for informed

**TABLE 6-2** 5-by-5 Organizational Patterns

| STRUCTURAL FEATURES | ORGANIZATION TYPES | | | | |
|---|---|---|---|---|---|
| | SIMPLE | CLASSICAL | PROFESSIONAL | DIVISIONAL | ADHOCRACY |
| Goal-Compliance Mechanisms | In-person direct control | Rules, regulations, direct supervision | Professional norms (code of ethics), standards of skill levels | In-person direct control within divisions, plus central office directives and monitoring | Mutual adjustment and control via in-person exchanges |
| Decision-Making Mechanisms | Centralized in administrator | Hierarchical, via chain of command, plus delegation out from chain to non-managers (limited) | Loose linkage to administrator; horizontal decentralization, much autonomy | Limited, vertical delegation | Selective delegation down and out from administrator to team members |
| Task Affinity | Nonstandardized | Standardized | Standardized yet complex | Mix of standardized and nonstandardized | Nonstandardized |
| Environmental Fit | Simple and dynamic | Simple and stable | Complex and stable | Simple and stable plus diversified locations and services | Complex and dynamic |
| Response to the unexpected | Deals with | Ignores until a crisis | Redefines to suit methods | Develops new units, functions | Deals with |

supervisory practice. Also, we have questioned the suitability of bureaucratic organization for the needs of people-oriented services. This is important, because your supervision probably will take place in an organization. Epstein (1973) emphasized this point and lamented social work's preoccupation with psychological states more than organizational dynamics as "an historical error" (see Note 4); Wasserman's research (1970) on careers of master's graduates in child welfare, and Middleman and Goldberg's discussion (1974) of organizational "metawork" highlighted the effect of context on direct service opportunities (see Note 5). The issues raised now about organizations' impact on services go far beyond interpersonal transactions with colleagues and superiors, or time spent on metawork in the "social work agency." As we have described, they are issues of the complex context for practice, the bureaucracy, diversity in personnel and professional education, reluctant public commitment, reduced resource provision, and much more.

After describing various organizational dynamics, we suggested that organization is not inherently negative, but that it is necessary for marshaling the complex requirements of service delivery. We explored bureaucracies in terms of their vertical hierarchies and horizontal divisions, each structure aiming to standardize a particular element of the work, so as to make it more controlled. In terms of standardization and bureaucratic types, the following elements are standardized:

| SPECIALIZED STRUCTURE | STANDARDIZED ELEMENT |
| --- | --- |
| Simple | Communication |
| Classical | Tasks |
| Professional | Skills; methods; operating procedures |
| Divisionalized | Product or service |
| Adhocracy | Norms for innovation |

First, it is important to appreciate the profound influence your organization can have upon all that you will be able (allowed) to do. You will need to consider your organization in its similarity to bureaucracy types, and also its individuality. Not only is your agency its own unique operation, but also it shares with other nonprofit organizations certain differences from the corporate-sector organizations. These important differences need to be explored.

Bureaucracies, especially the huge aging ones of current times, are increasingly seen as questionable organizational arrangements for person-focused enterprises. To offset the obstacles to goal achievement that any of the five organization types faces in delivering human services, Cohen and March (1974), Aldrich (1978), and others proposed "loose coupling," rather than any hierarchy—a format where units are only minimally connected. Another approach to participative management, which features quality circles, is imported from Japanese management practices and offers a different organizational profile (Middleman, 1982). Quality circles emphasize decentralized decision making through the development of a network of small problem-solving groups of front-line workers who identify, analyze and deal with quality problems in their area. They are a part of popular awareness now;

many books attempt to explore "the Japanese mind," and TV and the newspapers highlight Japanese ways regularly, as the West attempts to understand Japan's economic successes. Many Western firms are importing Japanese ways and even some service bureaucracies, as we seek to humanize the workplace and its productivity. Nevertheless, the huge cultural and economic/political gulf between Japanese and American ways, as reported by Middleman (1983; 1984), makes such attempts highly questionable, especially for human service systems.

We are now ready to look more carefully at the human service systems (HSOs), to explore their differences from mainstream, corporate organizations, and to highlight some of their special complexities.

## BUREAUCRACIES AND HUMAN SERVICE ORGANIZATIONS

Figure 6-3 presents graphically many of the influences affecting the context of your supervision, which is most likely in multidiscipline service organizations. In this illustration, the supervisor and workers are embedded within the total agency work group which, in turn is affected by other forces. These forces are separated only arbitrarily. In reality all influences and forces transact with one another, are intermeshed. Likewise, the two lists are artificially separated so that you can "see" them more easily. In varying degrees of "pitch," all these forces are likely to be more or less strident and impactful.

Whether the typical bureaucratic format was congenial to the needs of medical services was questioned by Jaques (1976). In fact, he saw the hospital as inimical to the free development of ideas and the intimacy of the confidential doctor-patient relationship. Similarly, Farris and March state that bureaucratic agencies' effects on social work result in "the direct opposite of the practice norms needed for mutuality of relationship, holistic concern and flexibility" (1982, p. 94). Weisbord (1976) explained that the main problem with medical centers is the disjunctive functioning of their three internal systems: the governance, task, and identity systems. These criticisms are being raised as to the usefulness and appropriateness of the bureaucracy for social, health, and other programs.

A straightforward discussion of the mismatch between organizational purpose and actual practice is described by domain theory (Kouzes and Mico, 1979; 1980). Kouzes and Mico see human service organizations as inherently ridden with conflict. The HSOs include hospitals, mental health centers, social agencies, schools and universities, police departments, nursing homes, and other similar systems. Domain theory proposes three domains in the service organizations: policy, management, and service. These domains operate through different sets of governing principles, success measures, structural arrangements, and technologies (refer to Table 6-3). For example, the policy domain operates more or less as a mini-political-system would (i.e., representatives vote, follow Robert's Rules of Order, and aim to reflect the views of a larger constituency). The management domain, on the other hand, mirrors business and industrial management norms, with top-down, linear

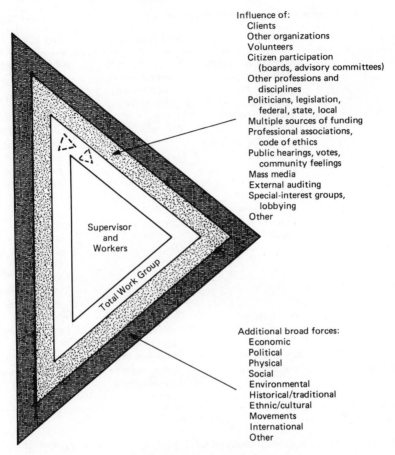

Influence of:
Clients
Other organizations
Volunteers
Citizen participation
(boards, advisory committees)
Other professions and
disciplines
Politicians, legislation,
federal, state, local
Multiple sources of funding
Professional associations,
code of ethics
Public hearings, votes,
community feelings
Mass media
External auditing
Special-interest groups,
lobbying
Other

Supervisor
and
Workers

Total Work Group

Additional broad forces:
Economic
Political
Physical
Social
Environmental
Historical/traditional
Ethnic/cultural
Movements
International
Other

**FIGURE 6-3.  Context.**

determinations and other no-nonsense processes. The professional domain embraces
a third set of principles, which feature autonomy and self-determination. As these
three different systems move in their diverse ways, the resultant dynamics make the
organization inherently incongruent, disjunctive, and discordant. These differences
and the others outlined in Table 6-3 lead us to repeat our second basic assumption:
that your organizational "home," whether a public or private service organization,
differs greatly from the for-profit organizations that have been most studied; and
that you must understand the differences as well as the commonalities. For instance, most nonprofits have an external auditor who is not on the payroll of the
agency. This fact makes the agency especially vulnerable to public opinion that
might not be in the client interest. Additionally, supervisors in social service agencies may not be able to reward good performance with bonuses or other favors.
The motivation for performance excellence is mainly a matter of conscience, not
extrinsic rewards.

TABLE 6-3   Domains of Human Service Organizations

| DOMAIN LEVEL | POLICY | MANAGEMENT | SERVICE |
|---|---|---|---|
| Governing Principle | Elected or appointed representatives of community; consent of governed; voting | Hierarchical control and coordination; businesslike rationality | Autonomy; self-regulation; Code of ethics |
| Success Measures | Equity; just, impartial, fair policy decisions | Efficiency; effectiveness | Quality of service; good standards of practice; process concerns |
| Structure | Representative; participative | Bureaucracy | Collegial |
| Work Modes (Decision Making) | Voting; negotiating; bargaining | Linear techniques and tools | Individualized, specific client-related problem solving. Indeterminant technologies. |
| Norms | Debate; public disagreement | Conformity to rules and procedures | Individuality, nonconformity |
| Focus on Environment | Demands from the political realm | Changes in the technological and economic sector | Changes in the cultural realm |

Adapted from Kouzes and Mico (1979), pp. 449–469.

In line with these general assumptions, both about the pervasive influence of the organization and the workplace climate on all that you may do, and about your organization's distinctiveness from the for-profit organization, we direct your attention to the following questions:

1. What purposes have you identified as major, as minor?
2. What structures predominate? What mechanisms for integration and differentiation do you notice?
3. What patterns exist as supervisory mechanisms? Individual? Team? Group? Consultative?
4. What other disciplines and professions are in your agency? How is the power distributed among specialty groups? What is the relative position of the social work profession in relation to others? Is there a pecking order? If so, how would you identify it?
5. Do you notice any turfs, empires, or camps? Is social work a "visitor" in this organization, or an old, entrenched inhabitant? Is it welcomed or unwelcomed? By which other professionals or workers?
6. If there are teams that involve various disciplines, is the work *interdisciplinary* (i.e., does each member represent and aim to stay within the boundaries of

his or her particular knowledge or role contribution)? Or is the work *trans-disciplinary* (i.e., are members expected to move beyond the theory and role of any one discipline and to aim for a new synthesis and posture)?

7. What is the discipline of the person chairing the team meetings? Does this suggest anything to you?

After answering these questions and considering your organization in these specific aspects, it is important to begin to think of your workplace in terms of certain qualities common to nonprofit organizations.

### Some Features of the Nonprofit Service Organization

Understanding the common elements of organizations provides you with a conceptual map of your work terrain. The information discussed in this section will help you to understand your practice context and to see certain values, ideas, and actions as endemic to your organization type, rather than as idiosyncrasies of particular persons. As a result, you will be able to concentrate your energies on the most tractable aspects of your assignments. However, while social agencies and all the nonprofit service organizations are similar to the for-profit organization in some respects, there are key differences. Research findings and theory from the general organizational literature cannot be applied to nonprofit organizations without the recognition that these may be inapplicable to the nonprofit sector—an area that has been largely ignored, so far as theory development and organizational intervention strategy go (Martinko and Tolchinsky, 1982).

Certain distinctions characterizing human service organizations have been described (Hasenfeld and English, 1974). To highlight the contextual difference that supervisors will face in their work, we have selected three key aspects of the nonprofit organization: *agency and professional vulnerability, a scarcity heritage,* and general *cultural difference*. We believe these factors combine to make the context unique and complex.

*Vulnerability.* Certain aspects of the complexity of the nonprofit public sector organization were captured by a frustrated organizational development consultant who tried to use his organizational knowledge and skills with a public welfare organization (Davis, 1978). He found that, unlike business firms, the social agency's external environment, with its multiple funding sources, is determined (whether through taxation or charitable contribution) by fickle public opinion that is influenced by self-interest, diverse values, special interest groups and lobbies, consumer reactions, public hearings, voting patterns, mass media propaganda, and so forth. Where social programs and responsibility are concerned, the shifts and fluctuations of public sentiment and resources—whether dealing with legislation at federal level, the state level, or the local level—parallel a gigantic ping-pong match. Perlmutter (1982) called this type of vulnerability the "precarious purpose"—an organizational constraint that may confound any attempt to establish orderly plans and policies. Not only do social agencies deal with society's most complex, intractable social problems, but they also must do so with delivery systems that are unstable.

In these organizations, as Perlmutter observed, it is impossible to work with the assurance and support of a steady, ongoing working structure. More likely, one's preparations and strategies, no matter how carefully and systematically developed, may become obsolete within a brief time span. In delivery systems where emergencies and crises are commonplace and instability is the byword, budget cuts, leadership shifts, reorganizations, social policy changes, and new regulations make a shambles out of even the best-laid plans. In order to survive in such vulnerable organizations whose purposes are eternally precarious, Perlmutter prescribes, for staff at all levels, a consciousness-raising diet that she calls "a process of empowerment." This process emphasizes interpretation and education, so that staff members understand that the problems they face are reality-based and not a result of personal inadequacy. Such a process involves cognitive restructuring, so that problem definition is recast in *structural* rather than in individual terms—an approach proposed by Middleman and Goldberg (1974) for viewing client problems and social work in general.

The precarious purpose, the programmatic instability, and the hardly sincere commitment to human well-being, in social policy at a national level, have left a legacy of fluctuation in terms of social programs. Perlmutter described these radical social policy shifts of the past two decades as moving from an emphasis on service effectiveness in the 1960s, to an emphasis on efficiency (accountability) in the 1970s, and then to the RIFS (Reduction in Force), mammoth cuts, and phase-outs of the 1980s (which we call service effacement). The vulnerability of social service organizations can be illustrated in this way: (1) Pressures are generated by multiple, uncertain goals that are stated in terms of politically phrased, often fuzzy objectives, the achievement of which is to be reported to diverse sources. (2) Vague programs and performance criteria, plus rigid regulations and procedures, are handed down. (3) Services are delivered through politically and nonpolitically appointed administrators who are backed up by multiple service specialties with varied ideological identifications. (4) Finally, all of these factors are to be mobilized within shifting policy directives that at first accented *effectiveness*, subsequently *efficiency*, and then *effacement*.

A second kind of vulnerability relates more to the social work profession than to the organization. Social workers have multiple accountability: to the client, to funding sources, to the community, to the profession, to their superior, and to their own selves. Many others would like to control what social workers may or may not do. What the social work professional may do is often determined by citizen participants on boards and advisory committees, or by professionals from other backgrounds who are at the helm of the particular organization. According to Boehm:

> No other profession is less free than social work from being directed by the laity or from being deprived of self-determination regarding the nature of its professional functions and the manner in which it discharges them. (1965, p. 644)

These same sentiments more recently were expressed by Lewis as follows:

> More often than not, social workers have less to say about how their skill, as a resource, will be used, than do many comparable professions. Since most allocations of this resource are made through the budgets of social agencies (public and private, sectarian and non-sectarian), decisions reflect the preferences of community leaders of various persuasions regarding what social workers should do far more than the workers' own sense of what they can and want to do. (1982, p. 184)

Lewis describes social work as a "socialized profession" where the practitioner works for agencies and must be understood as a functionary of an organization where "much of what she must know and do is influenced by where and for whom she works, by the tasks she is expected to perform, and by the recipients of her service" (p. 30), plus community restraints and deprivations that severely limit workers' "opportunities to achieve at the level of their known capacities" (p. 89). Despite professional status that carries certain values, ethical imperatives, professional norms and rules of conduct, and standards for service delivery, social workers and social programs are constrained by multitudinous laws, rules, regulations, guidelines, policies, and procedures. All of these delimit the areas for initiative and independent judgment that social workers should be accorded.

Controls on professional actions are unqiue to social work, Toren (1972) explains, because in practice social workers give away something that is not their own—that is, the community's material goods. However, the internal resources of a professional person (specific knowledge, skills, and ethics) are less controllable by outside agencies than the concrete resources that social workers dispense (pp. 65-67). Social workers deal with both material and informational/relational resources. Thus, a traditional cause of tension has been conflict between accountability for the treatment, on the one hand, and the financial components of social services, on the other hand. This tension has been described in social work circles as therapeutic versus administrative requirements, "nurturant" versus "demanding" functions (Toren), or professional versus bureaucratic norms. In any event, it is obvious that the determination of results or accountability in the realm of relationships (i.e., treatment) demands a system of evaluation and measurement that is different from the mechanisms of accountability and measurement in the fiscal, more concrete realm. In one instance, the measures would be qualitative, in the other, quantitative (see Note 6). The major source of tension is between bureaucracy's need for centralized decision making, control, and efficiency, and professional norms of autonomy, quality in relationships, and individuality. Moreover, social work's value base calls for equality and collegiality, nonhierarchical structures, and participative management; yet the organization's reality results in centralization of authority, power differentials, and emphases on standardization and uniformity. Mandell (1973) describes a move against these organizational constraints, a move accentuated by various rights movements of the 1960s, as "the equality revolution in supervision." She claims that the search for autonomy and independence from organization restrictiveness, rather than a desire for more money or prestige, was what led many practitioners to leave social agencies in favor of private practice. Mandell's finding is similar to Cohen's assessment (1966) that private practitioners aspired to professional and not merely financial goals. Also, in a 1975 study of NASW members, 67 percent of private practitioners sampled expressed a desire to escape agency constraints (Wallace, 1982, p. 26).

*Scarcity heritage.* Another difference between the nonprofit and the profit organization is the scarcity mentality that has dominated the nonprofit sector. We suggested that this vulnerability was connected with the distribution of others' resources; now we must add that these resources have always been in short supply. Except for a relatively brief period in the 1960s, when national attention and resources were deployed in the War on Poverty, the organizations that were home base for social workers have operated under a stringency aura. A scarcity mentality has, in the 1980s, arrived at the door of the corporate, for-profit firms in mainstream U.S.A., a realm that has enjoyed more or less continuous growth and expansion since World War II. This mindset is quite familiar to the non-profit organizations, where there were always fewer resources than persons or situations in need. Like the "old woman in the shoe," there was always too much to do and too many mouths to feed. A make-do atmosphere prevailed.

The scarcity mentality of the nonprofit organization can be likened to the persistent fearfulness of the child of the Great Depression. In both instances, the view of the world and thus, the way of interacting with others, is nonexpansive and testy, cautious and conservative. With limited, inadequate resources, the organizational focus is almost totally on operations (delivery services), with little funding for research and development, for planning or retrospection, for thinking time as opposed to doing time at the front-line level. Hence, a major orientation is present-focused, often in a crisis-to-crisis mentality, as opposed to either future or retrospective vision. This lack of future vision is demonstrated by nonprofit agencies' negligible investment in research. The situation can be compared to the dilemma facing the profit-sector automotive and electronics companies, as U.S. firms compete at a disadvantage with Japanese counterparts; one important difference is illustrated by the amount of investment in research and development by each nation in 1980—Japan: 6 percent; United States: 1 percent (Brown, 1981).

Administrators of social service organizations face pressures of an uncertain funding plus a typically suspicious, hostile, investigative press eager to make the most of system fraud. These pressures can be relieved partially by transmitting them downward through the organization hierarchy to the middle-line supervisors. Indeed, the literature describes the supervisor as a buffer (Kadushin, 1976) or a shock absorber between administration and workers. The notion here is that somehow this Janus-like supervisor, looking both toward administration and toward workers and clients, could diffuse these tensions. Instead, what typifies the nonprofit, scarcity mentality, in the main, is a lineup of vertical levels characterized by mutual suspicion, frustration, and even hostility, with little communicative exchange and a subtle inner belief that each level is letting the others down. The atmosphere is not beneficent in a scarcity climate. Hard work and "good deeds" do not pay off; openness and trust are not valued. Organizational survival needs take precedence over human needs. If the pie is smaller, conflict increases and there are more win-lose situations, rather than win-win situations. The situation places supervisors in a "middle-management bind," according to Austin (pp. 32-35)—a conflict comparable to industry's conflict between the statuses and roles of the shop steward and the foreman. That is, the steward's advocacy and mediator roles are attuned to worker satisfaction and motivation, while the foreman's roles of rule enforcer and monitor are geared toward management's need for efficiency and productivity.

The scarcity mentality is rapidly becoming a scarcity reality, not only for the nonprofit agency, but for the profit sector as well. The 1980s reveal a faltering economic system for the industrialized nations of the world. Perhaps the nonprofit sector is more experienced with the hard realities that currently face all organizations. Some of the probable features of scarcity situations in days to come include: decreasing services and positions, especially in the middle-management realm; eliminating in-service training and staff development opportunities for employees; reducing the number of organization goals with a redefinition of priorities and fewer program alternatives. Further, organization structures will need to be modified to minimize and absorb uncertainty by altering the control and reward systems, and increasing attention to communication processes while trimming and standardizing more of the services. More concern will be accorded to meeting crises and survival needs with more top-down decisions and less participation by workers, and this trend will result in less room for compromise or concessions. Finally, it seems there will be less risk taking, less attention to workers' developmental needs, and more concern with enforcing harmony and consistency to meet the threat of external pressures. These belt-tightening probabilities will demand conceptual clarity in supervisors, so that they can understand the roots of these processes and dynamics; and meeting these issues will demand competence, organization-sensitive skills, and imaginative alternative strategies. We shall consider these requirements in the balance of this book.

*Cultural difference.* The final differentiating concept highlighting the distinctions between the nonprofit and for-profit organizations is Lewis's notion (1975) of the nonprofit organization as a part of a "different culture." Cultural difference has been a useful concept for understanding minority individuals and groups whose background and traditions are unlike those of the dominant mainstream values. Practitioners are familiar with this concept and understand such differences through acquisition of specialized knowledge and examination of practice experiences. Because of this, they are able to work with sensitivity and skill. We believe an equal case can be made for appreciation of cultural difference in macro terms—that is, in relation to the profession and many of the organizations that sponsor its services. And we see the relevance of this cultural difference to the form of traditional social work supervision in contrast to the supervision practices of business, psychiatry, medicine, psychology, and other professions.

Farris and Marsh (1982), drawing on Habermas (1973), describe social work as a "foreign body" within mainstream marketplace capitalism. By this they mean that its values place human dignity and need ahead of profit—either corporate (agency) profit or individual (practitioner) economic gain. In social work's embrace of such ideas as full employment, guaranteed income, adequate medical coverage for all, accessible and decent housing, and a fairer distribution of resources, decision-making options, and opportunities, the mission of the profession historically has gone against the grain of the dominant cultural values. Thus, the profession's values are culturally different from mainstream capitalist values and from most other profession's values (as also is social work's concern for social well-being). These values have never been popular. Social work has championed and been identified with minorities, and because of this, the profession has been scapegoated along with the minorities it knows so well.

The concept of an entity (a foreign body) at odds with and peripheral to the priorities of the mainstream (profit, growth, expansion) suits social work and its clients, in that cost, rather than gain, is involved. Other foreign bodies (those forming the inactive portion of the population in market terms) include: children, students, the unemployed, those receiving annuities, welfare recipients, women working in the home, and criminals. All these populations, like social work itself, are costly and yet structurally necessary for capitalism to work. The tension generated is between human rights and profit. The demands of human needs and rights are an irritant to the short-run calculations of the profit sector. They are like a grain of sand in the eye—something bringing a tear that needs to be extruded so far as the profit-economics mentality goes. Yet this same grain of sand in an oyster may be nurtured to become a pearl—a thing of value and worth in the long run. It is this stance that has characterized the social work profession and its value base, norms, ethical imperatives, and traditions—a mentality concerned with social costs and human loss.

At the organization level, social workers care about fairness more than efficiency (Lewis, 1975) and about the well-being of clients more than the maintenance of an agency (Weissman, 1982). As Weissman described, a flaw in the business-oriented management of the large public agencies during the 1970s was the absence of a value base related to social reform and client need. He cited Avigliano's description of business technology's emphasis as being an efficiency mentality with negative effects on services:

> Money and manpower were poured into information systems, without necessarily meeting the needs of families and individuals . . . (Program Evaluation and Review Technique) PERT does not eliminate poverty; (Management By Objectives) MBO does not prevent mental illness or retardation; flow charting does not stop the aging process; computerization does not eliminate despair; accurate check amounts do not stop inflation; zero-based budgeting does not prevent or alleviate marital conflicts. (Avigliano, 1977, cited in Weissman, 1982, p. 162)

The point here is not that business techniques, efficiency, and accountability are unimportant. It is, rather, that issues of value and purpose (which at times run counter to the efficiency motif) are *most* important. It is a quality-quantity or means-ends issue that haunts us here.

Our listing of qualities that make nonprofit organizations unique is lengthy. We have described vulnerability to the environment and have discussed the elements that contribute to this vulnerability in social service organizations. These include: diverse interested parties to satisfy, unstable resource provision, precarious purposes, external audits, monopoly of certain services with more-or-less captive clients, and inability of supervisors to offer tangible rewards for performance excellence. Other differences cited by Lewis (1975) include the following notions:

> Success is when you are no longer needed, not when the product (service) remains a necessity.
>
> Since clients are unlikely to take their business elsewhere, there is no competition that may spark efficiency.
>
> Organizations seek to attract the most difficult to serve, perhaps the most costly to serve.
>
> The cost of service is rarely carried through user payments, and the client's threat of nonpayment or quitting causes little disturbance to the system.
>
> Given the limited resources that the organizations have, inefficiency may be important because to the extent that all who qualify or need a service actually know about it and come to use it, the system might be overwhelmed.
>
> Efficiency is measured by unit service cost, rather than by profit.
>
> Managers have limited internal choices to make in trying to lower unit costs without damage to services.

As Lewis notes, "They may hire less costly staff, require more productivity of staff, limit waste, give less to each client, choose only the clients who need less . . . or control intake in order to manage with the available resources, but this would not necessarily control unit costs" (1975, p. 617).

Human service organizations have limited power over hiring, firing, pay, and promotion, and this further weakens administrative and supervisory clout. Staff is diverse: Some are career civil servants, some are political appointees, and many have their professional, vocational, and ideological ties to a particular specialty. Consequently, the alliances are not neat and tidy. Politics, civil service specifications, and commitments to previous program ventures, moreover, further confound and complicate goal determination. In fact, goals may remain ambiguously phrased for the protection and survival of the organization. A crucial cultural difference described by Kouzes and Mico is in the area of power and control (see Note 7).

We think human service organizations and other nonprofit agencies are inherently tension-ridden, and in Chapter 5 we suggested that managing tension is a key supervisory function. Here we emphasize that the tension that goes with the position of supervisor should be viewed as an organizational given, a fact of the very structure of the nonprofit organizations and their difference from business organizations. This structural view of tension differs from one that sees tensions as if created by individual workers, as personality clashes, lack of motivation, stress, and burnout that workers, helped by the "good" supervisor, are encouraged to deal with in themselves. We prefer the view of organization tensions as a systems issue, not as mainly a worker issue, and in Chapter 8 we shall propose system-based strategies to respond to such tensions.

These special dynamics and processes of nonprofit agencies make the already cumbersome classical or professional bureaucracies slow to move and adapt to environmental shifts and client need. They comprise some of the major frustrations that beset workers and supervisors as they try to remain freshly responsive to the many varieties of pain, hurt, anger, and frustration comprising the daily diet of organization life. As we shall see, the strategies and skills required to cope with such a context represent as much, or more, challenge as do the skills of working with the client.

## CONCLUSION

We have cited some of the special circuitry of the organizational landscape that you, more than likely, will inhabit as worker or as supervisor. This has been done to emphasize the impact that this context will have on your practice. We see these aspects, less evident in other professions' experience or in private practice, as both hazard and challenge. These context issues have also spawned a unique brand of social work supervision—traditional or educative supervision—a supervision where agency personnel took seriously the obligation to guide and assist supervisees' ongoing professional (and personal) development. Kadushin (1976) describes supervision's "special importance" in social work and offers thirteen reasons for this difference (pp. 23-38). Some of these we have described as aspects of organizational context: vulnerability, scarcity, and cultural difference. Other elements in Kadushin's analysis connect more with the profession than its habitat: its limited sanction by the community; the inability of its national professional organizations to guarantee professional conduct and competence; the limitations of social work's knowledge base and technology; the distinctive personality characteristics of social work recruits; and the profession's predominant femaleness, which, in combination with the other elements, may make workers more willing to be supervised (directed and supported) by others.

We tend to attribute the specialness of supervision in social work to other emphases internal to the profession's development—to the profession's origins and organizational arrangements, which we have explored in this chapter and in Chapter 1. Our main point about supervision today is this: *Educative supervision, for all practical purposes, has disappeared from the organizational landscape.* In Chapter 1 we looked more closely at the specialness of social work supervision, a brand of supervision that always had to be concerned with the context, and that was an organization-determined supervisory practice. There was never the "luxury" of a practice that concerned itself only with the clinical side of helping. In this sense social work supervision has differed from supervision in psychiatry or psychology. And there was never the value base that permitted an exclusive focus on the organization's productivity, on numbers served, on efficiency; here, social work supervision differed from supervision in business and commerce. In this chapter, we have reviewed the specialness of the context of social work supervision—especially the specialness of the human service organizations, which constitutes an additional complicated contextual influence. It is to these matters relating to helping workers learn about doing their tasks with compassion, quality, and impact—to matters of teaching—that we turn in Chapter 7.

## NOTES

1. See Miller and Phillip (1983) for an extended discussion of alternative systems.

2. See Kadushin (1976) and Munson (1979) for reviews of traditional supervision and issues; Austin (1981) for theoretical and technical material important for the managerial aspects of the supervisory role; Shulman (1982) for a comprehensive description of a mediating orientation and interactional skills; and Wilson (1981) and Shaefor and Jenkins (1982) for helpful materials related to the technical and substantive issues involved in student supervision.

3. Parsons (1960) described three system levels: technical, managerial, and community or institutional; this formulation was also favored by Katz and Kahn (1966). The technical level is comprised of front-line supervisors and workers who monitor and deliver services. The middle level are managers who structure, coordinate, and monitor internal operations. At the top are those who attend to organizational goals: stability and adaptability. This hierarchy concerns service delivery, internal operations, and connection to the external environment, and it is peopled by various supervisors, managers, and top administrators who integrate, monitor, structure, and coordinate. Kouzes and Mico (1979/1980) called these three levels the service, management, and policy domains, and they proposed that there are inherent tensions between these levels in human service organizations. Mintzberg (1981) proposed an organization comprised of five parts: operating core, middle line, strategic apex, and (adding two additional components to the middle level) technical and support staff. The Middleman and Rhodes typology draws on Mintzberg's and adapts it to complex systems in terms more familiar to social work.

4. Epstein described the error as follows:

> [It] fails to take into proper consideration the fact that the structure and processes of an organization such as a social agency decisively determine the work climate in terms of aims, quality of practice, distribution of power and authority, and behavior of staff and clients. The individual's aims and practices and the character of his interpersonal transactions with peers and supervisors are determined by the organizational context, not the other way around . . . organizational structure and process are so powerful that supervisory practice must focus its major attention on them. (1973, p. 6)

Wasserman (1970) concluded that the professional knowledge and skill base of early career graduates was of little use in the work situation where structural constraints dictated the decision-making process.

5. Middleman and Goldberg (1974) examined the amount of time spent on organization-inspired work—metawork, or work about the work—and other contextual issues. They discussed involvement *about* services to clients (which is not *with* clients in a face-to-face situation): all the informational red tape plus supervision, the record-keeping and accounting systems, case conferences, staff meetings. According to a massive nationwide time study of the Family Service Association of America that was conducted in the early 1950s and replicated almost identically in the early 1970s, metawork accounted for 73 percent of agency time and client contacts for only 27 percent. In one private children's agency, only 19 percent of the time spent by staff

was with clients; 81 percent of work time was taken for supportive activities (dictation, phone calls, record reading, interview preparation, conferences, meetings, court hearings, and travel). These data were based on findings gathered in the most sophisticated, professionalized agencies, where the social workers were M.S.W.s and followed what was thought to be the most informed practice theory and supervision for high-quality service.

6. Other discussions of professional-bureaucratic strain are offered by Austin (1981), Heraud (1970), Toren (1972), Finch (1976), and Munson (1979).

7. Kouzes and Mico (1979) describe power and control issues as follows:

> In the business and industrial world, managers are for the most part in control of their organizations. Through discretionary use of reward systems, structural arrangements, leadership behaviors, information systems, task assignments, and people, managers can maintain control over the differentiation and integration of their systems. Managers in HSOs do not have nearly the same degree of control. The Service Domain, preferring to set up mechanisms to regulate itself, opposes attempts by Management to reduce the degree of autonomy and personal discretion among Service personnel. The Policy Domain is also outside the control of the Management Domain. In fact, the system is designed the other way. The Management Domain is ultimately accountable to the Policy Domain. Yet frequently managers perceive policy makers encroaching upon their domain, attempting to administer programs, not just make policy. The Management Domain resists this tactic. Since independent decisions made in each domain impact upon the others, each struggles to maintain its integrity and seeks to balance the power in the system. Adversary relations frequently develop. Rather than seeing themselves as collaborators attempting to work toward a common purpose, the domains often find themselves in a struggle for control of the HSO. (p. 460)

## REFERENCES

ALDRICH, HOWARD, "Centralization Versus Decentralization in the Design of Human Service Delivery Systems: A Response to Gouldner's Lament," in *The Management of Human Services,* Rosemary C. Sarri, and Yeheskel Hasenfeld, eds. New York: Columbia University Press, 1978.

AUSTIN, MICHAEL J., *Supervisory Management for the Human Services.* Englewood Cliffs, N.J.: Prentice-Hall, 1981.

AVIGLIANO, JOHN, "Position Paper for Workshop on Deprofessionalization," paper presented at the Annual Meeting, Pennsylvania State Chapter of the National Association of Social Workers, 1977, quoted in Harold H. Weissman, "Can Clinicians Manage Social Agencies?" *Social Casework,* 77, no. 3 (March 1982), 162.

BOEHM, WERNER W., "Relationship of Social Work to Other Professions," in *Encyclopedia of Social Work,* Harry L. Lurie, ed. New York: NASW, 1965, 640–648.

BROWN, CHRISTOPHER, "How Japan Does It," *Time,* March 30, 1981, 54–60.

COHEN, MICHAEL, "Some Characteristics of Social Workers in Private Practice," *Social Work,* 11, no. 3 (April 1966), 69–77.

COHEN, M.D., and J.G. MARCH, *Leadership and Ambiguity.* New York: McGraw-Hill, 1974.

DAVIS, TIM R.V., "OD in the Public Sector: Intervening in Ambiguous Performance Environments," *Group & Organization Studies,* 4, no. 3 (September 1978), 352–364.

EPSTEIN, LAURA, "Is Autonomous Practice Possible?" *Social Work,* 18, no. 2 (March 1973), 5–12.

FARRIS, BUFORD, and JAMES MARSH, "Social Work as a Foreign Body in Late Capitalism," *Journal of Applied Behavioral Science,* 18, no. 1 (1982), 87–94.

FINCH, WILBUR A., "Social Workers Versus Bureaucracy," *Social Work,* 21, no. 5 (September 1976), 370–375.

GOLDBERG, GALE, "Micro-Level Intervention: A Frame of Reference and a Practice Model," *Journal of Education for Social Work,* 10, no. 3 (Fall 1974), 25–29.

HABERMAS, JURGEN, *Legitimation Crisis,* T. McCarthy translator. Boston: Beacon Press, 1973.

HARDCASTLE, DAVID, and ARTHUR J. KATZ, *Employment and Unemployment in Social Work.* Washington, D.C.: NASW, 1979.

HASENFELD, YEHESKEL, and RICHARD A. ENGLISH, "Human Service Organizations: A Conceptual Overview," in *Human Service Organizations,* Yeheskel Hasenfeld, and Richard A. English, eds. Ann Arbor, Mich.: The University of Michigan Press, 1974.

HERAUD, BRIAN, *Sociology and Social Work: Perspectives and Problems.* New York: Pergamon Press, 1970.

HOFFMAN, LYNN, *Foundations of Family Therapy.* New York: Basic Books, 1981.

JAQUES, ELLIOT A., *A General Theory of Bureaucracy.* New York: Halsted Press, 1976.

KADUSHIN, ALFRED, *Supervision in Social Work.* New York: Columbia University Press, 1976.

KATZ, DANIEL, and ROBERT L. KAHN, *The Social Psychology of Organizations.* New York: John Wiley, 1966.

KOUZES, JAMES M., and PAUL R. MICO, "How Can We Manage Divided Houses?" in *Middle Management in Mental Health,* Stephen L. White, ed. San Francisco: Jossey-Bass, New Directions for Mental Health Services, no. 8 (1980), 42–57.

_____, "Domain Theory: An Introduction to Organizational Behavior in Human Service Organizations," *Journal of Applied Behavioral Science,* 15, no. 4 (October-December 1979), 449–469.

LEWIS, HAROLD, *The Intellectual Base of Social Work Practice: Tools for Thought in a Helping Profession.* New York: Silberman Fund and Haworth Press, 1982.

_____, "Management in the Nonprofit Social Service Organization," *Child Welfare,* 54, no. 9 (November 1975), 615–623.

MANDELL, BETTY, "The 'Equality' Revolution and Supervision," *Journal of Education for Social Work,* 9, no. 1 (Winter 1973), 43–54.

MARTINKO, MARK J., and PAUL D. TOLCHINSKY, "Critical Issues for Planned Change in Human Service Organizations: A Case Study and Analysis," *Group & Organization Studies,* 7, no. 2 (June 1982), 179–192.

MIDDLEMAN, RUTH R., "The Quality Circle: Fad, Fix, Fiction?" *Administration in Social Work,* 8, no. 1 (Spring 1984), 31–44.

_____, "An Holistic View of Quality Circles," Program of the 27th Annual Conference: Society for General Systems Research, v (1983), 535–545.

_____, "Quality Circles: The People/Industry Panacea?" *World Wide Shipping/ World Ports,* 45, no. 2 (April/May 1982), 1–4.

_____, "Co-Leadership and Solo-Leadership for Social Work with Groups," *Social Work With Groups,* 3, no. 4 (Winter 1980), 39–50.

MIDDLEMAN, RUTH R., and GALE GOLDBERG, *Social Service Delivery: A Structural Approach to Social Work Practice.* New York: Columbia University Press, 1974.

MILLER, HENRY, and CONNIE PHILIPP, "The Alternative Service Agency," in *Handbook of Clinical Social Work*, Aaron Rosenblatt, and Diana Waldfogel, eds. San Francisco: Jossey-Bass, 1983, 779–791.

MINTZBERG, HENRY, "Organization Design: Fashion or Fit?" *Harvard Business Review*, 59, no. 1 (January/February 1981), 103–116.

————, *The Structuring of Organizations*. Englewood Cliffs, N.J.: Prentice-Hall, 1979.

MUNSON, CARLTON E., "Authority and Social Work Supervision: An Emerging Model," in *Social Work Supervision*, Carlton E. Munson, ed. New York: The Free Press, 1979.

NATIONAL ASSOCIATION OF SOCIAL WORKERS, "Preliminary Report on NASW Data Bank, 1982 Membership Survey." Washington, D.C.: NASW, June 1983.

PARSONS, TALCOTT, *Structure and Process in Modern Societies*. New York: The Free Press, 1960.

PERLMUTTER, FELICE D., "Caught in Between: The Middle Management Bind," paper presented at the Annual Program Meeting, Council on Social Work Education, 1982.

REISCH, MICHAEL, and PAUL H. EPHROSS, "Worker and Agency in Textbooks —Images of Which Reality?" *Social Casework*, 64, no. 8 (September 1983), 394–405.

SHEAFOR, BRADFORD W., and LOWELL ED JENKINS, eds., *Quality Field Instruction in Social Work*. New York: Council on Social Work Education and Longmans, 1982.

SHULMAN, LAWRENCE, *Skills of Supervision and Staff Management*. Itasca, Ill.: Peacock, 1982.

TOREN, NINA, *Social Work: The Case of a Semi-Profession*. Beverly Hills, Calif.: Sage, 1972.

WALLACE, MARQUIS E., "Private Practice: A Nationwide Study," *Social Work*, 23, no. 3 (May 1982), 262–267.

WASSERMAN, HARRY, "Early Careers of Professional Social Workers in a Public Child Welfare Agency," *Social Work*, 15, no. 3 (July 1970), 94–101.

WEISBORD, MARVIN R., "Why Organizational Development Hasn't Worked (So Far) in Medical Centers," *Health Care Management Review*, 1, no. 2 (Spring 1976), 7–17.

WEISSMAN, HAROLD H., "Can Clinicians Manage Social Agencies?" *Social Casework*, 63, no. 3 (March 1982), 160–167.

WILSON, SUANNA J., *Field Instruction: Techniques for Supervisors*. New York: The Free Press, 1981.

# CHAPTER SEVEN
# THE DESIGN
# AND REDESIGN
# OF SUPERVISION

## INTRODUCTION

In this chapter we shall review the arrangements you can make to guide you and your supervisees in your collaboration toward competent service delivery. This will entail a design process on your part, a process of constructing approaches to supervision that fit both the needs of the supervisees and the requirements of the organization. Your design for supervision will spring from the application of a *foursome mentality* as you seek to understand the whole situation. It is *me* (supervisor), looking at *it* (supervisee), with our *shared contexts* (organization and its others), and *history* (all that has preceded our interaction, plus current and future aspirations). Within these four transactional components, some of the complexities that will help you determine what you will do are the following:

### THE DESIGN FOR SUPERVISION

*Supervisee*—previous training, experience, cognitive style, attributes
*Supervisor*—training and experience, interpersonal style, intervention theories, values, beliefs, world view
*History*—past, present, and future prospects of situation
*Context*—organization, administrators, expectations, requirements, regulations, service tasks, client expectations

**TABLE 7-1  Summary of Teaching/Learning Events**

| LEARNING EVENT | GOAL | GOAL DETERMINED/ EVALUATED BY | FOCUS | UNIT OF ATTENTION |
|---|---|---|---|---|
| Supervisor teaching as Coach | Service delivery and learning | Mutual contract | Activities; tasks | Individual (group) |
| Counselor | | Mutual contract | Deliberate use of self in relationship | Individual |
| Conferee | | Mutual contract | Diverse roles in relation to tasks | Group, team sometimes individual |
| Training | | Trainer; Faculty | Any specified content | Class, institute, workshop |
| Consulting | | Consultees | Specific problem; staffing of cases; specialties | Individual (sometimes team, group) |
| (Administering)[a] | | Agency | Rules and regulations | Individual and team |

[a]Administering is included because some teaching is involved; in this text, it is considered as a supervisory function separate from the teaching function.

All of these elements impinge upon your supervisory situation and become a kaleidoscopic configuration requiring a diversified approach to supervising. The realities of today's supervisory scene lead us to observe that anything short of an eclectic, versatile supervisory capability will miss the mark. The complexities of your context, your terrain, will undoubtedly shift in form and substance, even as we seek to capture their essence. So we shall offer neither blueprint nor road map. Perhaps what we can offer is like a mechanized golf cart with a sensitized *you* in the seat: a you who, having teed off, are now more alert to jump aboard, see where you landed, avoid the sand traps and marshes, approach the obstacles—slowly or speedily—or back up before another move. We shall identify certain key components that become the figure of importance, according to your imaginative judgment of *what* should work *when here,* with *this/that person.*

In this chapter we shall propose a way of viewing these four elements to obtain a useful intervention orientation with specific supervisees. In fact, we will describe four orientations that will form some order to your assessment of where the worker needs to start out with you. We suggest that you imbue your supervisory design with a nondogmatic, accommodative stance, a tailor-made construction, so as to match your approach to the needs and requirements of the situation

| RHYTHM OF ENGAGEMENT | DEGREE OF CHOICE FOR LEARNER | HIERARCHY STATUS | EXPECTATION FOR USAGE |
|---|---|---|---|
| Specified: regular as required and determined by supervisor | Negotiated and variable | Superior/subordinate | High |
| Specified: regular as required and determined by supervisor | Negotiated and variable | Superior/subordinate | High |
| Specified: regular as required or determined by either party | Negotiated and variable | Collaborative | High |
| Time-limited; one-shot, one day, etc. | Variable: active to passive involvement | Power of knowledge | Variable: motivation of learner to content's applicability |
| Episodic; as needed or regular and planned | Variable: as needed by individuals; or planned meetings of team | Peer/colleague; or senior to junior staff | Take it or leave it |
| Regular | None | Superior/subordinate | Must comply |

and of each supervisee. This will be more effective than an approach that stems only from your preference, prior habit, or predispositions. By agreement with the supervisee, it will be rather simple to shift from one perspective to another and back again according to the arranged needs and goals for supervision at a particular time in the supervisee's career. These orientations are flexible enough to include a variety of techniques and technologies (many of them common to several emphases)—e.g., written process recordings, role play, an empty-chair procedure. But these technical aspects are the tail, and so, they should not wag the dog. Each orientation will help you be consistent and reliable in what you do with any given person. The various ways of accomplishing your supervision goals will be apparent if you have a clear grasp of your intended approach or frame of reference. Still, an ordered approach needs to be balanced by flexibility and fluidity. In this way, you can connect with the diversity and diffusion you will encounter in today's organizations.

In addition to selecting your supervisory orientation as a frame of reference, you will need to follow some system of progression, some process, in your work with each supervisee. We shall offer a process plan, the Action Cycle, which can help you recognize several phases of your supervisory work.

Table 7-1 summarizes the material presented in Chapter 1, which aimed to review past and current supervisory practices and other teaching/learning opportunities (training, consultation) operative in today's workplace. Recall that Chapter 1 concluded that today's supervisor *shares* the teaching responsibility with those who conduct other teaching/learning opportunities; that the particulars of the expanded domain of the knowledge and skills of social work practice are spread broadly (in literature, and in standards and conceptual frameworks developed by the profession itself); and that the supervisor of the 1980s is mainly an *administrator of the learning experience*—planner, coordinator, and sometimes teacher.

With such a perspective, you can devote more concentrated attention (and possibly time) to the part of the overall nine-function supervisory assignment that is the focus here, i.e., *direct teaching.* One aspect of your direct-teaching emphasis (through what you talk about and how you role-model professional behavior) has been simplified to some extent by the work of task forces concerned with professionalism in NASW, in CSWE, and in the broad manpower area by federal and state government—all such bodies aiming to clarify tasks and performance levels.

## SOCIAL WORK TASKS AND WORKER PERFORMANCE LEVELS

Starting with the 1960s, increased attention and intensive work have been focused upon specifying the activities and tasks of social workers and others in human service organizations, and upon defining the skills and abilities that workers need in order to function in various positions. The impetus has been political, economic, and intellectual. In 1973 the NASW, as part of its standard-setting function, published a policy statement (*Standards for Social Service Manpower*) that described a six-level hierarchical classification system (two preprofessional and four professional) for service-delivery positions (Alexander, 1975). Subsequently, professional practice levels (basic, specialized, independent, and advanced), were elaborated in the *NASW Standards for the Classification of Social Work Practice* (NASW, 1981). In this document, the levels of competence in social work were based on the following factors: knowledge, responsibility, skill, situational complexity, social consequences, client vulnerability, and social purpose (p. 7).

The NASW also initiated other activities to develop, monitor, and validate competence certification and standards (e.g., NASW, 1977; Middleman, 1981b). In addition, Civil Service Commissions during the 1970s were concerned with state licensure, testing, and competence. Manpower deployment in the social work profession, as well as the appropriate educational requirements for the different levels (positions), has been a continuing concern (Dinerman, 1975). Among the persistent issues facing the social work practice and education communities are generalist and specialist knowledge and skill requirements; curricula foci for paraprofessional, B.S.W., and M.S.W. educational programs; career continua (ladders and lattices); and issues of differentiation and declassification (retrenchment of classifications) among the various job levels. These issues also have great importance for other professions and personnel in health and human services, for politicians, and for the community at large.

In addition to the push toward specifying professional standards, two other forces have had a strong influence (at least until the current conservative political moves) on federal, state, and local job reclassification systems, and the selection, promotion, and training of personnel. These forces are the goals of the EEOC (Equal Employment Opportunity Commission), and the affirmative action goals stimulated by Title VII of the Civil Rights Act. Pressures to specify the differences among various positions stem from many sources, including (but not limited to) the following: slurs aimed at the social work profession by politicians and others in employment systems; economy moves; encroachment of paraprofessionals and others from related professions and disciplines on social work's historic domain; licensure requirements; the move by social work to qualify for third-party vendorship in national health insurance programs; and, in short, the gradual, increased complexity and specialization in all systems of "modern" living.

Differentiating among different service-delivery jobs is a complex intellectual task that has occasioned enormous commitment of resources and energy by those who study professions. One approach of promise is job analysis (see Fine and Wiley, 1971; Primoff, 1975). This complex research process of examining the actual tasks of practitioners in various practice arenas is presently being pursued by the NASW in a national study of its membership. The need for such an analysis has long been recognized. For example, Meinert's review (1976) of the literature in three major social work journals concludes that the articles mainly advised social workers on what they *should* do, rather than indicating what they actually *did* (p. 156).

A valuable intellectual contribution to understanding social work practice comes from Lewis's analysis (1976; 1982). Lewis describes four components of skill: knowledge, action, values, and style—a useful framework in its own right. Then he explores each of the components of skill, differentiating among these at three levels: the preprofessional or technician, the professional or master, and the advanced professional or expert. For example, in the knowledge area the preprofessional follows rules and directives, the professional follows propositions and practice principles, while the advanced professional utilizes various theoretical formulations. Comparable differentiations are made within the action, values, and style areas (1982, p. 162).

## COMPETENCE IN PRACTICE

We have chosen *competence*, rather than *skill*, as a central concept. As we discussed in Chapter 2, we see competence as a combination of both knowledge and skills, performed in accord with some predetermined standard, when and where needed. We stressed the in-action aspect of a combined knowledge/skills approach and shall continue to consider knowledge and skills collectively in this chapter as we pursue the elements of a supervision design. We are concerned with demonstrated knowledge and skills (i.e., performance) by workers and by supervisors. Because of this, we see no real need to attempt to separate the underlying knowledge from skill so far as our approach to the design process is concerned.

We believe, though, that it will be helpful to separate what the supervisor needs to possess (in the domain of knowledge and skills) from what the supervisee needs to know and do. While these two knowledge/skill domains (i.e., the supervisor and supervisee domains) share certain commonalities, there are also differences. We do not assume that the supervisor will come to know what is necessary for adequate performance in the supervisory role simply by "serving time" as a front-line worker in the agency and observing the supervisors doing their work. We do not believe that becoming a supervisor should be a reward for competent, loyal performance at the direct-service level (i.e., that the good worker will make a good supervisor—an orientation that has prevailed in the past). Different competencies are required of a supervisor, and some of these may be at odds with some of the requirements for direct service. Nor do we favor the point of view that there should be all-purpose supervisors (or managers) educated and trained for this role (i.e., specialized entirely in background toward mastery of content and skills to direct or facilitate the work of others). We think substantive understanding of workers' tasks and dilemmas, empathy at the relationship or interpersonal level, and credibility as a supervisor come from experience and familiarity with the basic service-delivery tasks. How long or how extensive this front-line experience needs to be is an open question.

For both supervisor and supervisee assignments, we see the requisite competence (knowledge and skills) in terms of four components derived from aspects of the work. These components may be thought of as follows:

> *Task competencies*—related to the specialized activities through which the core functions of a position are actualized
> *Context competencies*—related to the actions required by a particular organization, program, or population
> *Relationship competencies*—related to the person part of the work and the process aspects of a job, involving how you accomplish your aims
> *Self competencies*—related to self-awareness and self-understanding, to insight into your own behavioral patterns and affective sensitivity, so as to deal consistently and sensitively with others

We shall explore each of the competency areas (task, context, relationship, and self) that face supervisors and supervisees separately, starting with those of supervisors, and finally show their interrelatedness in Figure 7-3. You will note that these components are depicted as a triangle so as to convey graphically the interrelatedness among the elements of each component within a figure which, in itself, signifies the most stable yet variable, dynamic view of a set of forces.

## Supervisor Competence Domain

Starting with the *task competencies*, which derive from the nine functions elaborated in Chapter 5, we see in Figure 7-1 the general functions, and in Table 7-2, selected examples of particular activities (which could be further subdivided into countless actions). The listing is virtually endless; it is also continuously in flux, with new particulars appearing on the horizon yearly and others dropping

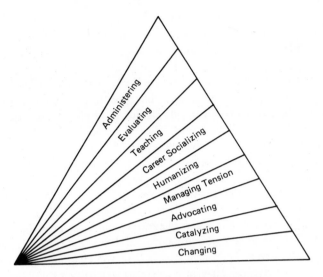

**FIGURE 7-1. Supervisor task competencies.**

into oblivion or fading away. These specific content and activities, encompassed as task competencies, are the easiest learned and the easiest forgotten. They are essentially technical; and much as any technical knowledge or skill, they require an intellectual learning process plus practice for mastery. Task competencies comprise the bulk of in-service training and continuing-education workshops, because it is relatively easy for trainers to break down knowledge and skills into bits and pieces and to put them together in variable time slots, whether of two hours or two days. Task competencies may be presented in educational or training programs, but they may also be acquired through various do-it-yourself modes, such as reading,

**TABLE 7-2   Task Knowledge and Skills Required of Supervisors: Some Examples**

*Administering*—budgeting; cost accounting; quality assurance; PERT; MBO; grant writing; marketing; public relations; functional job analysis; priority setting; chairing meetings

*Advocating*—lobbying; persuasion; presentations; debating; the legal system

*Changing*—force-field analysis; surveys; network development; coalition development; dynamics and processes of groups; research design; data analysis techniques

*Teaching*—role play, simulation, goal setting, learning contracts; cognitive style; learning; specific content areas such as neurolinguistic programming, transactional analysis, hypnosis

*Career socializing*—competence assessment; ethics; time management; life goals

*Evaluating*—needs assessment; program evaluation; monitoring systems; information-tracking systems; quality assurance; computers; research methods; objectives development

*Managing tension*—negotiations; bargaining; exchange theory; stress innoculation; relaxation techniques; conflict management; power; burnout; assertion training

*Catalyzing*—nominal group technique; Delphi technique; brainstorming; creativity; human potential; the brain; motivation

*Humanizing*—communication; values clarification; affirmative action; life-career planning

hearing audio tapes, watching videotapes, or watching successful supervisors in action. As with anything new, a self-imposed "learning campaign" is needed, which includes vigilance, time, attention, and motivation.

*Context competencies.* These competencies are bridging ones; that is, they are the knowledge and skills that relate the core functional areas to actions that will be needed in a particular organization. For example, a supervisor most likely could move from a community mental health center to a residential treatment center for alcoholics and could draw upon general competencies related to evaluating, humanizing, or managing tension. Still, there would be certain differences among settings, populations, and fields of practice that would require specialized knowledge and skills in order to manage well. These context competencies arise from the demands of the workplace. They deal with the populations served, with the policy, legal precedents and components of the system of service, with the routines, rules, accountability requirements, and roles within the programs and organization, with service approaches used (or avoided), and with the "secrets" and taboos of the operation. They also relate to structuring the work, scheduling, making job assignments, and other requirements that may be unique to any particular setting. Mainly, these competencies are learned on the job. They have been described as "practice wisdom" and should not be minimized, for they often spell the difference between the retrenchment "casualties" and "survivors" when push comes to shove.

Also vitally important for organizational success are the political strategies and tactics, the "wheel and deal" maneuvers, so well mastered by the organization person. These subtleties involve an informational and behavioral set of components that defy cataloging. They may be acquired through the personal investment of a mentor who "adopts" a particular novice, which speeds up the acculturation process. Or the culture may be partially acquired independently through careful mastery of agency manuals, and documents about policy and procedures. Otherwise, it seems to be learned by osmosis through careful monitoring of others' actions and inactions, noticing key patterns and aspects of organizational life. Considerable information about populations and service-delivery approaches may, of course, be learned from attending relevant workshops and classes, through reading, and other individualized routes. Much as with task competencies, these context competencies shift and change with the times and the organizational personnel involved.

*Relationship competencies.* These are the people-based or process competencies. They are intimately related to the task and context know-how. Relationship competencies deal with *how* you do what you do. They include both outcome and instrumental knowledge and skills, according to the task. For example, if the task is one of helping clients with their interpersonal relationships, socialization, or general well-being in the world of human affairs, helpers should have mastered these competencies themselves. In this sense, relationship competencies have comprised the major emphasis in professional social work education, at least to the mid-1960s, when the main method learned in professional education was casework. Now, these competencies commonly are referred to as clinical skills. They are, in this connection, task-related ends in themselves for a profession concerned with persons' achievement of potential and meaning. Knowledge and skill in relationships is a primary social work concern. It is learned informally as part of growing up and is more formally attended to through professional education. For social work, relationship competencies are also part of the value base and Code of Ethics; they have a vital place in the ideology and mission of the profession.

Relationship competencies have an instrumental value at the supervisory, workplace level. That is, they affect the way any of the nine supervisory functions are accomplished. The relational knowledge and skills condition your success in the workplace with supervisees, with colleagues or peers, and with superiors. Use of these competencies determines how you "get along" and accomplish your purposes in all forms of interaction. For example, in the functional areas of changing or advocating, there are relationship as well as task and context aspects. These supervisory activities may be conducted so that the actions are perceived by others as supportive or as assaultive.

We have no special supervisory category of "supportive function;" any function may be supportive or not, depending upon the effective use of relationship competencies by the supervisor. In this sense, they are *outcome* competencies. Primarily, these people-based or process competencies, a long suit for social workers, are what makes social work supervision different from supervision in business and industry. This concern for the other and for the process is precisely what is now being "discovered" by business professors. This concept is described as "the soft levers of influence" and is characteristic of Japanese management style, in contrast to U.S. ways (Pascale and Athos, 1981).

Although the do-it-yourself movement has produced many books and tapes about social skills, relationships, and the like, relationship competencies are *not* learned through reading or other vicarious means; this distinguishes them from the task and context competencies. They depend upon experiences of deep emotional involvement with people, and they grow out of developing positive feelings and confidence about yourself and others. They demand affective complexity and versatility plus cognitive processing and intellectual grasping of the emotional experience —a synthesis of emotional and intellectual processes. These experiences may be had in professional education (practice class and field work), in therapy, in encounter and sensitivity groups, and through other formal and informal means, such as workshops, training institutes, and other continuing-education opportunities.

At the supervisory level, relationship competencies involve consideration and sensitivity to others. These competencies include such specifics as being accessible, explaining one's actions, being responsive, and representing and respecting others. Mastery of these competencies requires the "light" and "heavy" touches as needed, resiliency, and a host of steady, reliable ways of engaging with others with compassion and feeling. Conceptual material that will help one to understand and attain relationship competencies includes theories of learning and development, of giving and receiving help, and of persons in environments, as well as the philosophy and values concerned with world view.

*Self-understanding.* The final area of competencies concerns self-awareness and self-understanding. Perhaps this should have been addressed first, since it is involved in all the other three areas, especially relationship competencies. It is basic to all competencies in any profession concerned with the human condition and direct involvement with people. Social workers are concerned with self-understanding throughout their careers. Learning about the self starts in early infancy and proceeds through family interactions, childhood socialization experiences, young adulthood, and each subsequent phase of the life cycle. The "teachers" are parents, Sunday-school leaders, peer groups, friends, and others who directly affect you through their reactions and interactions. As is the case with relationship competencies, this area is more experiential than academic and involves insight and affective sensitivity. Insight is concerned with knowledge of your interpersonal behavior patterns. Affective sensitivity is concerned with awareness of emotions that occur during interpersonal interactions. Self competencies are prerequisite to consistency in relationships with others. Assumedly, understanding and "knowing" themselves will enable supervisors to keep personal uncertainties from getting in the way of being with and for the other.

These self competencies are important for every person, and most important for those who aim to use their relationship with others as an instrument of service, as with social work. Self-understanding contains elements of personal philosophy and purpose. It embraces a system of values, beliefs, and regard for your own and others' place in the world. As is the case with relationship competencies, the self competencies are informed by the profession's Code of Ethics. Ordinarily, self-knowledge may be approached formally as part of your professional education, through class and field experience, or through other informal developmental experiences. In the organization, these competencies are comparable to what have been described as "adaptive skills" (Fine and Wiley, 1971). Examples of these include self-management in relation to authority, impulse control, attention to personal appearance, use of time and self-pacing, and dealing with routine.

## Supervisee Competence Domain

As we claimed, some areas of required knowledge and skills are the same for supervisors and supervisees, and some areas are different. Both need task, context, relationship, and self competence, but as Figure 7-2 reveals, it is the task area that differs most. There will, of course, be certain shifts in emphasis in the context area, since the "same" context will look and be "different" for each role level. Certain aspects of the seemingly same context will have added salience, according to where *you* are in the hierarchy. Moreover, evaluating is conceptualized as a task competence for supervisors, since it is a generic area of knowledge and skill that supervisors *must* be able to understand and initiate wherever they work. But in the supervisee assignment, knowing how to comply with the accountability and organizational reporting mechanisms for the particular agency is better viewed as part of context. Clearly, the major change and new learnings reside in the set of task competencies demanded by each role. The elements of the relationship and self competencies are essentially the same.

Shulman (1982, pp. 165-166) drew upon Schwartz's formulation (1964) of professional performance as comprised of (1) professional practice, (2) professional

FIGURE 7-2.    Task competencies for supervisors and supervisees.

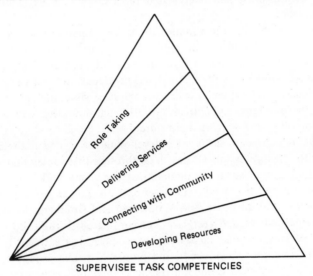

SUPERVISEE TASK COMPETENCIES

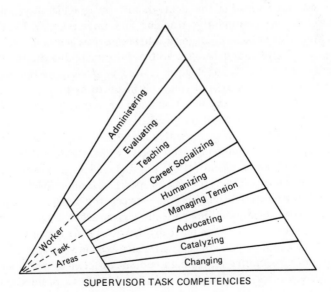

SUPERVISOR TASK COMPETENCIES

impact, (3) job management, and (4) professional learning. He further described core practice skills as being those of communication, assessment, relationship, and problem-solving, and he saw social-change skills as central to the impact area. Considering Shulman's formulation within our conceptual scheme, we propose the following: problem-solving, assessment, and changing skills fit into our task area; communication and relationship skills fit our relationship and self areas; and job-management skills fit within our context area. The learning skills are related to each of our four areas, since all areas (competencies) are deepened and broadened through the commitment and energy that practitioners devote to ongoing professional development.

Figure 7-3 highlights the commonalities (self, relationship, and context) that are basic to the work of all practitioners and the part of your professional assignment as supervisor which diverges from the task imperatives of supervisees. At the supervisory level, your focus for distinctive knowledge and skills requisites will be on the nine functions (Chapter 5), while for the supervisee, the task arena is encompassed by four functional imperatives: role taking, delivering services, connecting with the community, and developing resources.

*Role-taking* competencies involve developing the stance and related activities associated with the professional roles; it is through these roles that a worker can deal with others according to the demands of the client work, the delivery work, and the norms of the profession and organization (i.e., as conferee or counselor, broker, mediator, and advocate; see Middleman and Goldberg, 1974, pp. 54-80). Competencies needed for *delivering services* are related to the following activities: establishing relationships, making assessments, delivering treatment (via individual, group, or family approaches), evaluating progress, making referrals, terminating, and conducting follow-ups. Competencies in *connecting with community* involve these activities: understanding the demographic, geographic, psychological, and cultural facets of the community; reaching and interacting with others whose presence and interests impact on organizational objectives and facilitate the achievement of those objectives; and being a visible, informed advocate for the community's interests and needs. Competencies related to *developing resources* include: determining what resources exist or may be made to exist, planning ways to encourage the setting of priorities and articulation of resources, and involving others in the development and creation of resources.

Of course, other than those presented, there are many different ways to categorize knowledge/skills requirements and social work activities [for example, see Fine and Wiley (1971) and Austin (1981, pp. 312-329)]. Moreover, the variety of possible work arenas makes any overall proposal hazardous. Our aim here is to identify in general terms the relationship between the supervisor and supervisee domains, rather than to propose dogmatically a given schema. Our focus in no way negates the important distinctions made by Lewis (1976) concerning differences in how you work and how you conceptualize and explain your way of determining what you will do—*qualitative* rather than content differences which were conceptualized as degrees of skill: advanced professional (expert), professional (master), and preprofessional (technician) (pp. 11-12).

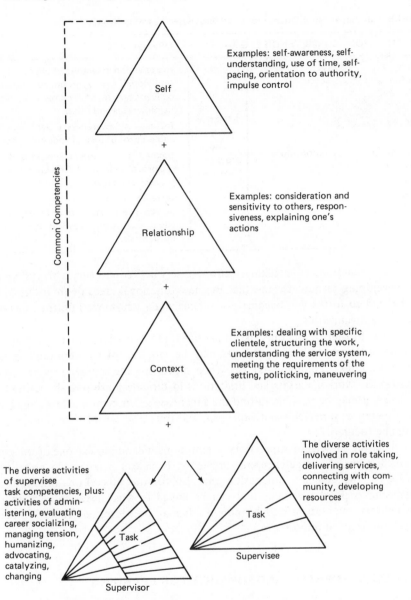

Examples: self-awareness, self-understanding, use of time, self-pacing, orientation to authority, impulse control

Examples: consideration and sensitivity to others, responsiveness, explaining one's actions

Examples: dealing with specific clientele, structuring the work, understanding the service system, meeting the requirements of the setting, politicking, maneuvering

The diverse activities involved in role taking, delivering services, connecting with community, developing resources

The diverse activities of supervisee task competencies, plus: activities of administering, evaluating career socializing, managing tension, humanizing, advocating, catalyzing, changing

**FIGURE 7-3.  Overview of supervisor and supervisee competencies.**

After you compare the areas that workers and supervisors have in common (context, relationship, self), you can examine particularly the distinctions in the task requirements for both levels (see Figure 7-3). You can also observe the uniqueness and the likeness in type (or content) of the competencies comprising worker and supervisory tasks. In Figure 7-3 we have embedded the worker task requirements in a corner of the supervisor task competencies to suggest the nested relationship between these two sets. That is, we assume the supervisor can perform the

**TABLE 7-3  Supervisory Orientations and Supervisee Learning Needs**

| ORIENTATION | COMPETENCIES | GOALS | OBJECTIVES |
|---|---|---|---|
| Skills/ information | Task | | Increase understanding of client (individual, family, group, community), delivery system, environment; master helping skills and roles. |
| Self | Self | Effective services and supervisee learning | Increase self-awareness, insight, sensitivity, and control of own purposeful behavior. |
| Transaction | Relationship | | Increase understanding and skills of the reciprocal self/other transaction, the process, the impact. |
| Pattern | Context | | Increase use of planning, strategies, and power within total system of service: client, colleagues, superiors, and other influentials. |

supervisee functions (role taking, delivering services, connecting with community, and developing resources), and that the new functional areas (administering, evaluating, and so forth) will become your focus when you move into the supervisory role in the organization.

Two further points must be emphasized: (1) According to any given agency's purpose, different task competencies may be required of workers (and certainly different context requirements). (2) When supervisor and supervisee work together to assess the worker's assets and limitations in the relationship, task, context, and self areas, it may be possible to find the supervisee's dominant and less known areas of competence; supervisee and supervisor can thus plan where their initial energies should be focused.

Each of these four supervisory orientations will emphasize one of the knowledge/skill (area-of-competence) requirements. Each can become the point of departure for the designed supervision and also for the supervisor's orientation for supervising—a point for focus that can be linked to what needs to be learned, so that delivery imperatives and learning needs may be addressed. Table 7-3 depicts the relationships of importance.

## THE DESIGN EMPHASIS AND SUPPORTS FOR LEARNING

We believe we have simplified matters, first, by directing your attention to the task differences in supervisory and worker job requirements; and second, by suggesting that for supervisor and for worker, the knowledge/skill requirements of context, relationship, and self are essentially comparable. While no one can ever "finish" learning in any of these areas, this conceptualization should help the supervisor to begin by focusing on the major substantive content areas—that is, where each supervisee needs to start in order to do the work.

The determination of what the supervisee needs to know and do in order to meet the demands of the job is of first importance, since agency tasks and needs come first. The second concern is the worker's learning needs and interests in instances where the supervision is provided through agency auspices. Of course, where the supervisory arrangement is contracted by practitioners with a consulting supervisor aside from the job (e.g., for certification or special licensing requirements), the supervisees will determine their learning priorities, which may or may not place organizational goals first. But no matter how important gaining certain competencies may be, these may not be acquired if the supervisee is not willing to work at them. The supervisee's motivation and interest are necessary for any supervisory plan "to work."

Later in this chapter we shall describe four supervisory orientations, each with its particular focus and objective—with *knowledge and skills* development, *self-awareness* development, the *transaction process* enhancement, and strategic impact in the overall service *pattern*. All of the models share the ultimate goal of effective services delivery through refinements and learnings by the service staff. While in principle any of these may represent your initial orientation, your start-up approach will be through the *skills/information model* focused on the task and context competencies, since the organization-based practitioners will be concerned with the success of the agency tasks.

As we consider designing the supervision, we can simplify matters by proposing that only two of the nine supervisory functions will vary in any fundamental way in relation to the persons you supervise. This may come as a surprise. Hopefully, this awareness will enable you to concentrate major energies in the *career socializing* and *teaching* areas, where differentiation can make some difference. The other seven aspects of your work as supervisor—administering, evaluating, humanizing, managing tension, catalyzing, changing, and advocating—are quite important but are ongoing and constant, no matter whom or how many you supervise. These functions ordinarily accompany the role of supervisor as agency staff members. The creative, diversified potential of the other two functions, career socializing and teaching, will receive special consideration now. Both are closely connected with the educative function of supervision, which, as we contended in Chapter 1, has virtually disappeared from most present-day organization-based supervision. Perhaps our treatment of career socializing and of teaching in the discussion of supervisory designs will enable the interested supervisor to become more *intentionally* educative in approach.

In this discussion, we have frequently referred to learning. We tried to indicate just where the four different types of practice competencies are learned, formally and informally. Learning, we propose, unites both teaching and career socializing, since these supervisory functions deal with a learned acculturation process that includes values, feelings, attitudes, information, and behavior. We suggest that values, feelings, and attitudes are "caught," and information is "taught." Behavior (actions) are a result of the combined learnings. The supervisor plays a key role in both the "caught" and "taught" arenas.

### Career Socializing

As we have described, career socializing deals with conveying the values, ethics, and code of behavior of the social work profession, as well as the particular norms of behavior that fit a given agency. It is linked closely with context, relationship, and self competencies, since it deals with values, attitudes, conduct, and behavior in relation to the self, others, the profession, and a particular agency. For a full appreciation of what is involved in career socializing, let us expand the conception of "career" in light of the complexities of context discussed in Chapter 6. You may think of several careers and how they mesh with one another. Social work (or nursing, or psychology, or accounting) is a career. But one person may have several simultaneous careers, such as organization member, parent, citizen, and so forth. We have expanded the conception of career beyond the social work professional career because (1) you may be supervising persons from other backgrounds or disciplines with their varied careers, and (2) all persons have several career paths.

The main contribution a supervisor may make to the career socializing function with supervisees is through helping them understand and appreciate the origin of values and behaviors. This is especially true when there may be conflicts between the "messages" of different careers. For example, the agency career message to the social worker in the hospital might be that the client must be discharged immediately, while the professional message might be that more time is needed for the client to make decisions about living arrangements. Beyond imparting understanding about career socialization and working on balancing discordant career messages, the supervisor has a role in helping supervisees become and live out what they truly aim to become.

Career socializing deals with attitudes and feelings, many of which are laid down early in your life and resist modification. Maier, who was concerned with the development of a professional self in the context of the field instructor/student relationship, describes the process of identification as basic to attitude change. We think this holds for the supervisor/supervisee relationship as well. Maier sees attributes related to "what I am to be" (e.g., accepting, less anxious, self-aware, empathetic, professional) as important, but as secondary to acquiring knowledge, practice capability, and effective service delivery. They are consequences that develop out of a constellation: a combination of specific information (cognitive knowledge), behavioral competence (behavioral acquisition), and identification with the value transmitter (affective attachment) (Maier, 1981). It is through close identification with the supervisor, described as "the weathering of many practice and learning crises together at 'the front lines' of practice" (p. 16), that the supervisees *catch* these qualities and attitudes, from how the supervisor *is*.

Because of this close working proximity between supervisee and supervisor, the supervisor is a powerful influence, a role model, who conveys qualities and general prescriptions as well as specific practices and procedures. This type of learning is akin to the informal learning described by Hall (1959). It is learning by watching others. It is out of conscious awareness, a learning of gestalts—that is, of patterns through modeling and imitation, with no knowledge of the rules or elements, or any overt learning at all.

As the supervisor and supervisee experience the shared calamities and vulnerabilities of the agency hurly-burly, a subtle process of identification operates, through which the supervisor's attitudes and behaviors are picked up by the supervisee. This process of attitude change and reinforcement is made possible when the object of identification is salient or especially significant to a person (Kelman, 1958). This situation may exist in the supervisor/supervisee relationship, especially when the supervisor is competent, attractive, and of the same professional background. In this way, values and attitudes are "caught" during the supervisory relationship.

The supervisor will need to devote deliberate attention to this identification process and be especially sensitive to the difficulties that may confound or work against this role-modeling process when discipline-based or personal attributes (gender, race, age) may separate supervisee and supervisor. In this sense, the differences in backgrounds between the supervisor and supervisee will pose special conditions to consider with respect to career socializing. For example, if the supervisor comes from a background in social work and the supervisee from personnel and guidance or expressive therapies, it is obvious that the "caught" learnings will *not* happen "out of awareness"; they will be deliberately acquired to the extent that the supervisee sees their value. The role-modeled learnings may be impeded for males when supervised by females and vice-versa, since many subtle behaviors that may be out of the supervisor's own awareness may offend the supervisees, rather than attract them to emulate the supervisor. And it is obvious and well documented that in supervisory situations where white, black, Latino, or any mixed combination of supervisor-supervisee backgrounds prevail, world views and value stances will diverge at points. The "desirable" values and actions of both viewpoints will need to be respected in their difference, and these values and actions will probably demand self-conscious reflection as much as they require out of awareness assimilation.

Career socializing is an ongoing learning process. It will occur as you carry out the particulars of your other functional imperatives. It is appreciated from *how* you do the work, for example, from your efforts in the realms of humanizing, managing tension, and evaluating.

### Teaching

The teaching function presents the supervisor with great challenge. The "trick" here is to match the supervision to both the needs of the agency and the needs of the supervisee. This can be complicated by the complexities of the workplace demands (context), by past and future prospects for all persons involved, by the broader societal realm in matters of social policy and provision, and by the inherent diversity among supervisees. There is much opportunity for you as supervisor to demonstrate competence and imagination in the construction of your supervisory approach through individualizing a design for each worker, or grouping workers with comparable needs, learning style, and interests.

Teaching is not confined to the supervisees' knowledge/skills requirements in the task area alone (role taking, delivering services, connecting with community, and developing resources), since any of these components of practice must also involve *evaluation* (which is a context competency for supervisees). There is evaluation of the substance of the work, and evaluation initiated by the organization—statistics, records, and other paperwork required to meet external monitoring systems. Documentation of the work and other requirements for accountability to external funding sources and various local, state, national, and professional communities are on the increase. Moreover, pressures arise from legal or bureaucratic fiat, from consumer sensitivity, from increased emphasis upon and need for third-party payments (especially in health and mental health systems), and from review and monitoring requirements.

Considerable teaching is necessary for supervisees to learn these procedures (the right and wrong components involved in the evaluating and monitoring systems) and for them to understand these aspects of practice in that particular agency. Professional Standards Review Organizations (PSROs) set guidelines affecting diagnostic activities and other professional standards, and all of these demand mastery of the tasks associated with such accountability requirements. We have arbitrarily separated the teaching demanded by these activities from the examination of teaching that is to follow, since these aspects are central components of the administering function and are essentially directive, with little room for variability or choice in terms of right-or-wrong performance. There may be differences in the way these requirements are presented (e.g., with visual aids or through other specialists' promotional and training devices, which may clarify what is "told"). But in this chapter's discussion of teaching we shall emphasize the areas that present more latitude and discretion. (For further information on the content particulars of the managerial aspects of the work, as well as some ways these may be structured and conveyed, you may wish to review the materials emphasized by Austin, 1981, and to consider these areas when we discuss didactic teaching.)

The relationship between teaching and learning is not intimate. As we have seen with career socializing, much is learned that is not deliberately taught. Alternatively, much that is taught is not learned. The most we can claim is that supervisors *intentionally* teach certain content in certain ways that they consider important. They teach contents they have the know-how to present, and are content domains sufficiently described and conceptualized so as to be communicable to others. To the extent that something is learned by the supervisee, the supervisor probably accelerated and augmented what the worker might have learned naturally, though more slowly. Through applying focus, emphasis, and selective judgment as to what is critical or important for the supervisee to know at a given time, the supervisor contributes by selecting, sequencing, and simplifying the learning tasks—that is, the supervisor plans a design for instruction. Various principles can guide the sequencing of content. You should move from concrete experiences to more abstract ones, from simple to complex situations (to the extent that this can be known in advance), from separated facts to their connection with integrating principles or relationships, from what supervisees know to what they need to know, from either specific to general or general to specific instances, and in the case of teaching a process, from beginnings through middle phase, to endings.

## Learning

Let us consider learning further before returning to teaching and the design of instruction. Learning is a constructive process and, ultimately, it remains within the control of the supervisee. It is the supervisees who will (or will not) use what the supervisor provides for their own learning and who will integrate the new learnings in some meaningful way into their existing frames of reference. The supervisor may assist in this process but certainly does not determine its outcome.

The methods and techniques of the supervisor may lead to learning but need not do so. Learning is a complex process and is as difficult to understand as is personality. There is no grand theory to account for how one learns. Rather, there are many competing theories and many types of learnings—for example, intellectual skills, verbal skills, cognitive strategies, motor skills, attitudes, feelings, and values (Gagné and Briggs, 1974). Additionally, there are nonverbal information-handling skills and interactional skills.

Learning theorists in psychology mainly have followed either behavioral (stimulus-response) or cognitive (stimulus-organism-response) orientations. The former view learning as habit acquisition through trial and error, while the latter consider it to be the acquisition of increasingly complex cognitive structures that lead to insight, understanding, and problem-solving. Regardless of theoretical orientation, the learning that accompanies service provision under supervision involves having a direct experience and then drawing back to think and talk about the experience and about the related cognitive material, feelings, meanings, perceptions, and values that accompanied the experience. These understandings may lead to correctives in behavior, attitudes, and thinking; they may be connected with other comparable experiences past or concurrent; and they may be modified, readied for future use.

Kenneth Boulding claimed that nothing succeeds like failure. Most educational theorists of the 20th century would agree with the theory that we learn from our mistakes, and this would hold for the behaviorists as well as those influenced by Dewey or Piaget. Knowledge of the results of your actions helps you correct and change what you do another time. You learn or acquire adaptive behavior when confronted with problems, and you apply knowledge and skill to meet the problem at hand. Learners are active and make mistakes; but they want to avoid mistakes and make sense of things. Such learning comes from risk taking, becoming self-critical, and becoming confident about the possibility of improving their knowledge and skills in a responsive, supportive learning environment. There are various beliefs and theories about the "best" way for learners to find out about their "errors" (e.g., being told directly in advance, or watching "correct" enactments, or making ad hoc decisions in the moment, seeing their consequences, and determining next steps out of these trials). In addition, there are differences of belief as to who is in charge of the learning experiences that happen for supervisees: supervisee or supervisor. These differences are all the more complicated by the fact that supervisees may be learning at the expense of real live persons—clients, just as the supervisor learns out of experiences with live persons—supervisees. Clearly, client needs and interests must take precedence over supervisee learning needs; yet learning needs contribute to the service. A balance must be found, for both service and learning needs must receive attention.

In any case, the supervisor mainly serves to speed up learning that is already within the reach of the supervisees. The primary learning will always belong to the supervisees in time and place. The supervisor may inspire the supervisees' interest, but it is the supervisees, themselves, who will construct their own inch-by-inch ascent toward practice competence. In this regard, McKeachie's observations are instructive and poignant, coming after a lifetime of research devoted to searching for the most effective teaching method and arrangements (e.g., class discussion, lecture, class sizes, amount of student participation in decisions). He concludes he was looking at the "wrong" thing in his study of student-centered teaching. All the observations and measures were in the classroom; yet the attention should have been on the most student-centered aspect, "studying—an activity in which the student controls the time, place, and method of procedure" (1980, p. 86). Just as the most student-centered variable is *studying*, so is the most worker-centered variable in the learning of practice competencies: *motivation* to work at perfecting involvement with others through trials, assessment, corrections, and retrials. But since it would be difficult to dissect this learning, we shall at least examine the teaching process.

No amount of charisma, "magic," or method to the madness will divert the mystery of learning into one of gifted teaching. Supervisees deserve a supervisor's interest in how they learn best, in what their particular cognitive style may be. They deserve a supervisor who knows different approaches to presenting information, exposing them to opportunities for learning—a person who is versatile and comfortable with various supervisory emphases. To this end, we shall introduce these elements that will condition how you design your supervisory approach in the teaching function:

Components that differentiate teaching approaches, learning preferences, and learning environments

Issues and points of choice that will affect your planning

Four supervisory orientations

An Action Cycle to guide your teaching

Five general educational principles

## DETERMINING YOUR TEACHING APPROACH

In our discussion of the educative function of social work supervision (Chapter 1), we identified its historical emphases, especially the "traditional" insight- and growth-focused emphasis that was important as social work developed as a profession. Subsequently, we distinguished the roles of coach, counselor, and conferee as analogs that may be linked to your way of *teaching*.

We see the coach, counselor, and conferee roles as linked to the supervision orientations (see Table 7-4), which were identified as *skills/information, self, transactional process,* and *pattern.* Three of these—*skills/information, self,* and *transactional process*—are orientations that social work shares with other mental health professions, since these focus primarily on the client/practitioner interaction. (For social workers, however, the *skills/information orientation*—which focuses not only on practice requirements but also on organization-related requirements—is broader than the analogous requirement for knowledge and clinical, interpersonal, and communicative skills in psychiatry, psychology, and counseling.) It is the *pattern orientation* that is most unique to social work, especially organization-based practice, since its focus is not only on the clients but also on the organizational dynamics and impinging forces affecting delivery systems, and because it introduces planning and strategizing as central facets of the intervention, plus an expanded expectation for systems change.

The teaching roles of coach, counselor, or conferee each give you, as supervisor, an area of legitimate power as a base of influence, because you *are* the supervisor. In addition, you have the supervisees' expectations of certain *expert* power—that is, you are supposed to know certain particulars as a part of the teaching role's focus. These bases of power are elaborated by French and Raven (1968) and Raven and Kruglanski (1970). This is true in terms of any supervisory orientation, as illustrated in Table 7-4.

**TABLE 7-4  Supervision Orientation, Roles, and Bases of Power**

| ORIENTATION | ROLE | POWER/INFLUENCE |
|---|---|---|
| Skills/Information | Coach | Legitimate: As supervisor<br>Expert: In activities and tasks |
| Self | Counselor<br>(sometimes Coach) | Legitimate: As supervisor<br>Expert: In conscious use of self |
| Transactional process | Counselor<br>(sometimes Coach) | Legitimate: As supervisor<br>Expert: In reciprocal impacts |
| Pattern | Coach<br>Conferee<br>Counselor (rarely) | Legitimate: As supervisor or team leader<br>Expert: In strategies, tactics, and impact |

These power bases will be discussed further when issues of power and control are considered. For now, we wish to identify the two main "advantages" that supervisors hold: (1) legitimated power conferred by the organization through its structural arrangements, and (2) the power of knowledge—expert power—and the way you use it. These power differentials will affect the hierarchical distance between supervisor and supervisee. For coach and counselor, the distance is distinctly superior/subordinate, a master/learner hierarchical distance. In the conferee role, there is less distance (despite the supervisor's expert knowledge and skills), since the role requires collaboration, shared differentiated tasks, and more peer involvement among supervisees. Coaching accents telling, identifying, directing, modeling, and presenting a clear picture of desirable outcomes in terms of skills and information acquisition. Counseling may involve telling, or asking and guiding, via indirection. On the other hand, conferring makes possible the use of many stances, including those related to coaching, counseling, collaborating, consulting, and exchanging.

As you plan your teaching approach, you should *not* determine what you should do or how you should be from your recollections of how you were supervised, nor from your unexamined but preferred practice orientation (school of thought, preferred therapy or service delivery formulations), nor even from observation of the ways of other supervisors in the organization. What you determine to do with each supervisee should evolve from your own analysis of the situation, which will be comprised of the following components:

1. Your own knowledge, skills, abilities, and preferences—that is, what you know and know how to present; and how "teachable" the content domain is in terms of its conceptualized components
2. An assessment of your supervisees' backgrounds, prior learning experiences, interests, gaps in competencies
3. The expectations and requirements of the particular work assignment in your organization
4. An assessment of the past, current, and ongoing influences on and prospects for you, the supervisees, and the organization.

This analysis will be determined mutually at the outset of your engagement with each supervisee; probably in a one-by-one individual conference you seek to determine (1) *what* should work, (2) *when, here, now, with this person,* and (3) *how well* both of you arrive at mutual expectations of the competencies to be achieved.

If you conceptualize the knowledge/skills requirements of any job in terms of task, self, relationship, and context, as we suggest, your decisions of where to begin will be guided by two factors:

1. The worker task competencies (role taking, delivering services, connecting with community, and developing resources) and the context competencies (e.g., how to follow the rules, procedures, and accountability records in this organization) will gain first attention. These are the elements needed for successful functioning in a particular organization in order to meet the expectations of the job.

2. Your joint analysis will also reveal which among the *task, self, relationship,* and *context competencies* may be most familiar to the supervisee from prior learning experiences. This will serve to suggest how long or how intensively you need to concentrate on the *task* and *context* competencies. You will determine when you might diminish entirely your teaching plan with a seasoned, well-prepared supervisee, perhaps shifting to a consultative arrangement. Or you may renegotiate a supervisory teaching focus beyond the immediate demands of the presenting professional assignment and responsive to the in-depth learnings requested by the supervisee. These two priorities pertain to organization-based supervisory teaching, where the organizational needs come first. In instances of contracted supervisory arrangements for certification, specialty, or licensing requirements, which the supervisee may initiate, the supervisee's requested learning needs come first.

### Educational Values and Theories

There is increased recognition in the social work literature that the knowledge and techniques required to perform the teaching part of supervision effectively should be derived from the realm of educational theory. For example, Gitterman (1972) and Gitterman and Miller (1977) describe supervision in terms of educational theories. Kadushin identifies six principles to guide the educative task (1976); Shulman (1982) devotes a chapter to issues of teaching and learning; Morton and Kurtz (1980) link learning theory with assessment, planning, instructional techniques, and design; and Gross (1981) focuses on instructional design as the area needing the social worker's most deliberate attention in order to make the teaching work.

Your teaching plan (or instructional design) must raise questions of your own values, beliefs, and power orientation as you contemplate what you will do. A part of your internal dialogue might sound like this:

> What is my basic self-view vis-à-vis supervisees: expert? coinquirer? colleague?
> How can I build on and add to the strengths the supervisees possess, even when their ways differ from my own?
> How much choice (power) will I or can I allow the supervisees in arranging the teaching/learning situation?
> What will be my preferred teaching style?

These matters of theory and practicality, of the potential dilemma posed by variability in supervisees' learning styles, and of the responsibility you hold in the organization for competent service delivery will infuse our consideration of instructional design. First, we will consider "good" practice (a value preference) and educational theory as components of *your preference.* Then, after we review some of the differences among supervisory teaching approaches, we shall return to matters of power.

The issue of "good" practice and how to teach it introduces an overwhelming array of possibilities. Regarding individuals, groups, families, and communities, there is no lack of intervention approaches, schools of thought, and explanatory theories that are prized operative orientations; and all of them are applicable to the four basic service task competencies that supervisees will need (role taking, delivering services, connecting with the community, and developing resources). This explosion of information—from academia, from social work's knowledge/skill base, from the mental health and organizational development professionals, and from the training institutes—forms a rich background. Social work supervisors have developed their professional stance, primarily an eclectic one, from their own learning experiences. So it is tempting, though dogmatic and constricting, to seek to develop a clone of one's self.

In former times, when supervision paralleled casework practice, the transfer of learning from the supervisory experience to the help-offering situation was more direct. It was an essentially talking, one-to-one, learning experience whose content and dynamics were similar to the worker-client relationship. This situation may still apply in psychoanalytic supervision, where one must be analyzed before one can be psychoanalyst to others. But for social workers, especially those in organizations, their own personality structures are not dealt with as a prerequisite for helping others face their own situations. According to one study of clinical supervision in community mental health centers, "staff seem to prefer an active, available supervisor who provides advice when necessary, encourages self-directed thinking and problem-solving, and helps staff members assess the role of their personal feelings in clinical work" (Cherniss and Egnatios, 1978, p. 222). Even when the focus of the supervision is on self competencies or relationship competencies, the focus is not on resolving the personal problems of supervisees or restructuring their personalities, but on helping them become more in touch with themselves and others through service delivery.

Consider the fear of the violin student contemplating study with a different, esteemed teacher, knowing that such a move would involve a breaking down, an unlearning of all previous technique, and a beginning again from scratch. Comparable concerns apply to learning helping skills and modes of service provision. Your supervisees may come to you with fears that they will have to start all over again and conform to your ways of valued practice. The challenge facing you and the supervisee is to seek the common ground of the known competencies, to identify these and reassure their value, while seeking to discover through your mutual efforts, what is most important for them to learn.

In determining your preferred content and educational goal, Axelrod's typology of teaching approaches will be informative (1973). From an extensive survey of university teachers, Axelrod distinguished between didactic and evocative approaches. In a *didactic* stance, the objectives are clear, easy to formulate, and known at the outset by supervisor and supervisee. The goal is mastery of a definite body of information or acquisition of skills, with emphases on cognitive knowledge (memorization) and skill mastery through repetition and practice. Skill is not dependent on reasoning. That is, it should become an automatic or semiautomatic response without reflection. Problem solving is not emphasized, since this would get in the way. The emphasis is on learning to do, not learning about. Where a body of information is to be learned, the emphasis is on transmission, on direct presentation and memorization of facts and generalizations, rather than through discovery or inquiry. In these situations, the instructor is the ultimate authority and has this motto: "I will transmit the *right* skills and information."

The second basic orientation, according to Axelrod, is *evocative*. This approach relies on stimulating learning through inquiry and discovery on the part of the learner. The emphasis is on *discovery* of what is known in the realm of practice by you and others. According to what gains most emphasis—the content to be learned, the instructor, or the learner—four evocative subtypes are identified:

1. *Principles-and-facts instructor*—Such an instructor focuses on principles, concepts, and other kinds of content, is concerned with systematic coverage of what needs to be learned, and aims to inform learners directly about certain key information and issues as well as to provoke them into added learning through their own inquiry and discovery. This instructor's motto is, "I teach what I know."

2. *Instructor-centered*—These instructors see themselves as models and are less concerned with covering the content systematically than sampling selected content to demonstrate the way an expert deals with problems. Here, the motto would be, "I teach what I am."

3. *Learner-as-mind*—With these instructors, the emphasis is on *how* the learner acquires knowledge, not *what* they know. That is, the emphasis is on process. There is no attempt at complete coverage of a content area. Samples are selected and organized so that learners can perform complex intellectual operations to develop ease in a variety of intellectual skills (e.g., verbal; analytic; rational; movement from problem formulation to analysis of data to solutions). Here, the motto would be, "I train minds."

4. *Learner-as-person*—These instructors focus on whole-person development, including the totality of individual growth, not only "the mind." The learner is viewed as a person with intellectual, emotional, aesthetic, and other developmental potentials—all inseparable. An emphasis in this learning orientation is on peer-group interaction. The motto of this instructor is, "I work with learners as persons."

Axelrod arrived at these orientations empirically through questions that are pertinent to the supervisory situation. For example, do you have in mind an ideal learner? Do you think that all supervisees should change similarly as a result of your supervision? Or do you have different expectations for each learner? Should learners who reach your goals change in the same way? Are you concerned with cognitive knowledge only, or also with affective insights? With process or only outcome? Is there attention to the irrational, nonrational, and nonverbal as well as the rational—to engaging as well as to talking? Other questions dealt with characteristics of the learning situation: Who decides what happens? How much emphasis is placed on learner-to-learner communication? How much lecturing? Who initiates the discussions? How much role modeling do you do? How much are cooperative projects encouraged among the learners?

Extrapolating from Axelrod's research on formal classroom teaching, we may pose questions applicable to teaching in supervision. For example, is there a definite set of ideas and skills that must be learned that permit only a certain given "right" approach? If so, you are in a didactic stance. Much of the skills training (and the accountability reporting) are conveyed in this way—*didactic instruction.* Or do you lean more toward an evocative stance? If so, your emphasis is on the presentation of concepts and principles to be learned within the first month, by the sixth month, and so forth—*principles and facts instruction.* Perhaps you have extracted certain key concepts and competencies and are content to cover a selected sampling of these using yourself as role model. Through role plays and discussion of selected cases, you convey your approach to practice—*"good practice," supervisor-modeled instruction.* Or are you mainly interested that supervisees learn problem solving, developing the analytic, observational, and assessment skills to meet immediate and emergent situations? In this way, they may enhance their own reasoning skills and discretionary choices in current and new instances—*supervision as mind instruction.* Or, finally, is your preference the total learning gestalt of values, reasoning, feeling, and action as experienced with you, other learners, superiors, and clients? This may be achieved by setting up conditions for learning through supervisory and peer-group exchange—*supervision as person instruction.*

Axelrod's analysis reveals five different approaches to teaching: a directive, *didactic* stance that leaves no room for deviation from what has been decided in advance as "correct" instruction, and four *evocative* orientations that aim to involve the learners in elaborating and embellishing the teacher's content. These five educational philosophies are not posed as better than one another; effective teaching can occur in each orientation. They represent differences in values and preferences about what is important to learn and how it should be taught. Probably you will evolve your own main preference, which may change during the course of your professional career and seasoned experience in supervising. Also, you may shift between didactic and evocative approaches from time to time according to the particular aspects of the work to be learned. Didactic (expository) and evocative orientations, with their transmission-versus-discovery teaching goals, are well-known approaches in the education literature. The applied-training literature ordinarily is less differentiated and uses only didactic and experiential categorizations, a dichotomy we shall now briefly review.

*Training approaches: didactic and experiential.* Axelrod's four evocative types of teaching could be collapsed into the experiential category in the training literature. The concepts *didactic* and *experiential* in this context refer to how the trainer (or supervisor) *acts,* more than they refer to the *outcome* of the learning. As we have seen, the didactic approach is directive—it *tells* (or indirectly tells by means of prompts or closed-ended, right/wrong questions). It aims to present sequentially a definite body of information and identified skills. The *experiential* approach is open-ended—many possible learnings may emerge and be "discovered," all equally "correct." Didactic and experiential approaches are prevalent in group contexts, although either can be used in one-to-one situations as well. These approaches have been publicized within the past twenty years by the human potential movement (which popularized the experiential), by the behaviorist and competency-based theoretical approaches in psychology, education, and psychometrics (testing), and by the availability of recording technologies to observe microbehaviors.

In Kadushin's study of supervision in social work (1974), two basic approaches to one-to-one, discussion-based supervision were identified: (1) *existential supervisee-centered,* where the focus was on the supervisee's self-understanding, self-awareness, emotional growth, on the process of the work, and on the worker-client relationship; and (2) *didactic,* where the focus was on the task, on thinking concerned with the development of the supervisee's professional skills, and on the worker's activities. These two different supervisory categories parallel roughly our classification of counselor and coach teaching-style types. They are mainly verbal, instructional, one-to-one teaching styles that need to be distinguished from the didactic/experiential, *training* approaches that occasionally appeared in the social work literature but that arose in related professions and used interactional more than conversational instruction (e.g., Gifford, 1968; Middleman and Goldberg, 1972a, 1972b; Papell, 1972; Anderson, 1975).

While didactic and experiential training approaches typically are associated with certain psychological schools of thought—the didactic with behavioral and the experiential with humanistic or phenomenological—they need not be. For example, Carkhuff approaches *affects* didactically: empathy, genuineness, and positive regard are broken down into component behaviors and practiced as skills to be learned (1969). On the other hand, the approach of Kagan and his colleagues (Interpersonal Process Recall) deals with *affects* experientially (1969). The instructional methods, techniques, and technology now exist for affective content to be presented didactically *or* experientially, and for cognitive and skills content to be presented experientially *or* didactically. A comprehensive reference and collection of numerous approaches to the teaching and evaluation of interpersonal helping skills is provided by Marshall, Kurtz, and associates (1982).

Understanding the difference between these two approaches will enable you to assess the general frame of reference of other teaching/learning events that occur in your workplace and to know when you are in one or the other area in your own supervision. *Structured groups* have grown increasingly popular as teaching approaches applicable to staffs and to clients (Drum and Knott, 1977; Anderson, 1980; Middleman, 1981a); they may be classified as skills groups (didactic), theme groups (didactic/experiential), and transition groups (experiential). The many didactic and experiential intervention approaches and their change goals related to perceptual, cognitive, emotional, and behavioral learnings are described in greater detail by Middleman (1983).

Didactic and experiential training approaches have become relied upon increasingly as one-on-one, talk-based supervision has been augmented or replaced by group, interactional training in organizations, and as skills training has appeared in social work education at both B.S.W. and M.S.W. levels (Clark, Arkava, and

Associates, 1979). This classification also has been used to identify supervisory approaches (often what we would consider group-training [i.e., training supervisees by having them participate in a group] approaches) in the literature of psychology, counseling, and organizational development. For example, in Hart's supervision *skill development model,* the focus is on understanding the client and on the effective application of this understanding through the use of appropriate treatment strategies and therapeutic techniques (such as confrontation, reflection of feelings, and behavior rehearsal). In the *personal growth model,* the focus is on supervisees' interpersonal relationships with friends, relatives, acquaintances (not clients or other professionals). This model also emphasizes the supervisee's feelings and ideas about older persons, the opposite sex, minorities, and so forth (i.e., the development of insight and sensitivity to others).

Most instructional training approaches are combinations of didactic-experiential (e.g., Gazda, 1971; Brammer, 1979), although the skills components tend to be presented didactically. Approaching skills didactically involves identifying the relevant knowledge domain and breaking down its component elements into microbehaviors that are presented according to some planned sequence. Then these components are practiced until they are mastered in the teaching/learning situation. This teaching/learning includes "homework" assignments through which learners try out new behaviors outside the "classroom" (i.e., transfer the learning to the work environment). Through verbal instruction and observational learning (modeling, imitation, role play, audio or video examples of "correct" usage), the learners learn *what* to do; through repeated practice plus corrective or reinforcing feedback, they gain a *predisposition to act* in certain ways; and through the homework assignments, they learn *how to act* in real situations.

The skills-learning approach begins didactically, and a coaching stance is used (i.e., telling, identifying, directing, showing, and modeling). Then discussion and processing of the experience, as well as role playing the skills interactionally, make the learning situation more experiential. In addition, the outside assignments are didactic/experiential. Table 7-5 identifies seven sequenced learning levels in the didactic/experiential mode of presenting skills, and it lists some of the diverse instructional possibilities associated with each level. Additional discussion of this progression from verbal instruction through behavioral assignments is offered by Morton and Kurtz (1980).

Many formats exist for the skill teaching, especially the elementary interviewing skills and the basic facilitative interpersonal skills (Danish and Hauer, 1973; Egan, 1975, 1976; Ivey, 1971). Skills training has been introduced as laboratory training in some social work programs, but it mainly has been foundational training for human-service personnel, paraprofessionals, and counselors, and foundational training for some therapy instructional formats. A comprehensive review of the empirical foundations of these various approaches is provided by Lambert (1980).

Aside from the basic interactional or helping skills, many other content domains (e.g., assertiveness, parenting, stress management) have been approached through skills-based formats. In fact, if enough of the microelements of *any* content

**TABLE 7-5  Hierarchy of Processes for Learning Skills**

| SKILL LEARNING PROCESS | DESCRIPTION | MEANS FOR ENHANCING THE LEARNING | |
|---|---|---|---|
| (Informal preparation) | Emphasizing experimentation and exploration with materials and elements without definite instrumental ends | Play; work; trial and error learned by pursuit of activities of interest | |
| 1. Observation | Emphasizing seeing and hearing ideal versions of the acts to be performed | Observe practitioner demonstration; video tapes; listen to audio tapes | *S K I L L S* |
| 2. Conceptualization | Emphasizing inspection, dissection of components, identification and analysis | Charts; lectures; written information plus discussion | |
| 3. Imitation | Emphasizing duplicating and reproducing the components of the act sequentially | Role playing plus feedback; video taping self in action; interactional games | |
| 4. Precision | Emphasizing accuracy, exactness, fidelity, and control with reduction of errors | Paper and pencil activities; group discussions; role play plus feedback; use of mirror/tape recorder for self-observation | |
| 5. Coordination | Emphasizing production of an articulated, integrated series of acts with concern for accuracy, speed and pacing | Role playing plus feedback; interactional games; videotape self | |
| 6. Habituation (automization) | Emphasizing repetition to make the act routine, consistent, automatic, natural and spontaneous | Deliberate use in real situations with others | *L I F E L O N G   L E A R N I N G* |
| 7. Instruction | Emphasizing designing and presenting to other learners with clarity the means for exploring and experiencing the skill learning processes, levels 2 through 6 | Repeated experiences with developing, offering and analyzing the impact of teaching attempts plus written/oral feedback (tests and evaluative measures) from learners | |
| and/or | and/or | — | |
| Stylization | Emphasizing adding one's individuality and humanity, elegance, simplicity, flexibility, intuitions, artistry, and warmth to the enactment of the whole | Repeated performances plus feedback from other(s) and continuous self-reflection and analysis | |

domain can be identified and described, a skills/didactic orientation may be developed. Teaching social skills is "big business" today (see Timnick, 1982, for a review of this phenomenon). Such training is even introduced to five- and six-year-olds (Spivack and Shure, 1974).

In social work, the skills-based approaches conceptualize the content domain either from a frame of reference emphasizing the *tasks* to be accomplished or one emphasizing the *process* involved. A task framework emphasizes limited, observable outcomes and uses a directive approach to present analytic skills, instrumental skills, or both. A process framework emphasizes the facilitation of social relationships and enhancement of interpersonal skills. These task and process perspectives have been elaborated at the direct-service level as group-related skills (Shulman, 1969), as overall service-delivery skills (Middleman and Goldberg, 1974; Shulman, 1979), and as supervisory skills (Shulman, 1982). Certain planning skills in the task or process perspective have also been identified (Gilbert and Specht, 1977).

The proliferation of *experiential* training approaches (variously called growth, human potential, sensitivity, awareness, values clarification) is well known. One recent article described the bigness of this *business*, launched mostly by psychologists, as follows:

> Social researchers say that 80 percent of America's adult population is actively engaged in seeking self-fulfillment. Increasingly, that search includes forays into seminars and workshops costing anywhere from $5 to $5,000. The so-called human-potential movement has grown to become a staple of the culture, showing up in schools, churches, YMCAs, holistic health and fitness programs, "new age" magazines, positive-thinking tapes and the ubiquitous crash courses in personal growth. . . . "We get 150 notices a week for seminars," said Marilyn Ferguson, publisher of *Brain-Mind* and *Leading Edge* bulletins and author of *The Aquarian Conspiracy*, the definitive compilation of "new age" thinking. Her Los Angeles office has installed a computer system to keep track of 15,000 subscribers and new information. (Smith, 1982, p. 19)

Experiential approaches emphasize action and interaction as routes to "whole person" learning. Their appeal in the broader culture is related to a search for respite from the press of technological and environmental complexity. The search is for the nonroutine, the "new" experience, the creative outlet. There are hopes for self-improvement—physical, emotional, social, intellectual, and spiritual.

Today, the telecommunication world impacts upon most persons and exposes them vicariously to a broad awareness of diverse cultures, alternative life-styles, and self-improvement "courses." Direct involvement with Eastern values, with different modalities of expression in the realms of ideas and activities, are more available for immediate experience—through travel, through the "tastes" of ethnic cookbooks, festivals, handicrafts, and so forth. The experience of the new and different has become a valued commodity in and of itself.

Experiential training approaches are well known in both the corporate and the nonprofit workplace. They are typically group-training approaches where interaction is required. The learning experience encourages the trainees to compare their actions and feelings to those of the others, to see any likeness or difference, and thus either to reinforce or to disconfirm and change their ways. The unexpected areas may be in the realms of values, feelings, cognitions, or behavior. And despite the interactional format, they may be as directive as a well-planned lecture. They may subtly guide the participants to "see" through the experience a particular concept (e.g., decisions are impaired by ambiguous information) or alternatively, they may emphasize many possible acceptable ideas or behavior.

A unique characteristic of experiential approaches is the emphasis on learning through all the senses, not merely through hearing or reading. The value of *talking over* or *talking about* has been eroded. More typically, such wrap-ups, processing, or debriefing occur *after* some involvement with other persons, things, or tasks—that is, you act and then make sense out of or reflect on the event and thereby transfer the actions, feelings, and intuitive "knowings" into cognitive, intellectual understanding. Nonverbal communication is of coordinate importance with verbal communication. Doing is as important as talking. In fact, some now see it as *the* important communication message. Immersion in activities where the rules, order of performance, roles, and expected behavior are known to the participants may be seen as the basic experience, the natural home of speech. What vary and need to be negotiated are turns at talking.

The learning experiences are constructed by the trainer, at least in terms of their key elements (not outcomes), and they are launched according to some plan. These constructed experiences, which form the core of experiential approaches, are defined as:

> . . . a closed system deliberately constructed and set in motion by the trainer or facilitator. It has a boundary which separates it from the talk about the situation as well. Within this boundary a set of conditions is established which affects the roles and/or rules, and/or the processes of interaction. Finally, the trainer or facilitator introduces a task to be pursued under the structured conditions. This task constitutes the moving dynamics of the learning situation. Participants must function within those particular conditions and experience both the opportunities for and constraints on pursuit of the task and on human behavior in general that are generated by these conditions. (Middleman and Goldberg, 1972b, p. 205)

Experiential approaches may fit with many theoretical orientations, but they are essentially existential and phenomenological. They start with the experience (the phenomenon) as perceived, and they describe more than define the totality of the experience (intellectual, emotional, behavioral). In fact, the variability among perceptions, as well as the uniqueness of your own perception of a situation, are the beginning points of emphasis (Goldberg and Middleman, 1975; 1980). The range of influences on behavior (e.g., physiological, psychological, and social) are matters to explore. While some experiential approaches emphasize attitudes, feelings, and the enhancement of personal and interpersonal awareness, others may focus on problem solving, thinking, and reasoning. Through constructed experiences (exercises, simulations, and games), the kinds of reasoning needed for problem solving may be learned.

As described in Chapter 2, thinking is done with words, with numbers and other symbols, and with visual images (and occasionally through taste, smell, sound, touch, or muscular movement). And so, reasoning practice may utilize many of these modalities in experiential training. The teaching approach and requisite reasoning skills may be *deductive*—rearranging the information so that one can start with given information, draw conclusions, and extract implications from what is known already. Or the approach and the reasoning may be *inductive*—extending the information to go beyond the information given (e.g., from the instance, to rules, to generalizations or common patterns). Or the teaching and the thinking may involve *analogic* reasoning—comparing information, bringing to bear upon the familiar a new perspective from another realm, comparing this experience to previous instances. And finally, the emphasis may be *evaluative*—critiquing the information to judge and examine the soundness of an idea or production. As we will show later in this chapter (see Table 7-8), the teaching approach and constructed experiences would vary according to the instrumental goal.

We have used an experiential approach to augment the didactic in teaching supervision in the classroom (Middleman and Rhodes, 1980), as well as in presenting this content area (and others) in workshops and institutes. Our research on the analysis of learning administered to six supervision classes revealed that the interactional teaching/learning was the most valued teaching modality in the areas of role dilemmas, role dynamics, and power dynamics. High valuation was placed also on the areas of

> . . . impact from one's oral, nonverbal, and written presentational style, impact in and through relationships in momentary interactional behavior, decision making, problem solving, and gaining knowledge/skill in consultation.
> . . . What seems obvious here is that one can't teach flexibility, strategic interaction, and responsiveness didactically. These must be experienced in order "to know." (Middleman and Rhodes, 1980, pp. 57–59)

*Didactic and experiential teaching in supervision.* As we saw in Chapter 1, the social work supervisor's efforts to provide educative supervision in organizations has been diminished, while other teaching/learning situations, imported from sister disciplines, have augmented or replaced the traditional one-to-one supervisory approach pioneered in social work. Kaslow described traditional supervision and five other approaches as didactic, a designation that is appropriate to the extent that the learner is directly (or subtly) led to perform in a predetermined way (viewed as "right" by the teacher or supervisor). We also linked the didactic mode with *training* and placed the more open-ended, evocative and experiential, inductive, and discovery approaches in the *educational* realm. Whether in the classroom or in a supervisory conference, the distinction of importance is how much latitude there is for many possible answers versus one right answer or way of acting. The primary consideration is whether the emphasis is on raising more questions or providing more answers—discovery versus transmission. The underlying dilemma in teaching practice is obvious. In any given moment the practice demands action, and a choice must be made as to which way you will intervene. There will need to be some consistency in your approach, rather than an array of "surprises" in what happens with clients. Yet any situation may be *conceptualized* in various ways (according to any number of theoretical orientations). A discovery approach in supervision leaves more room for entertaining alternatives, though it still may suggest a "right" way in the supervisor's judgment. It is hard to learn how to offer clients problem-solving experiences with alternatives if you have not experienced such an approach yourself in your own learning. Moreover, in real life it is difficult to know "the" answer. This issue is explored more fully elsewhere with respect to the supervising group leaders (Middleman, 1980a). In social work's traditional approach to supervision, the experiential component occurred as part of the service offered to clients. The review with the supervisor afterward in the office was essentially *didactic* (even when the supervision was "existential supervisee-centered" or focused on "insight" or "feelings," since the purpose of the supervision had the practical end of producing a learner who could act in informed and reliable ways). Yet the *rate* of "discovery" was *emergent* from the actual practice and related to the learner's process. The overall dimensions of the learning process were known. Robinson (1936, 1949) offered a detailed conceptualization of the process from its beginning to turning point to ending. She also described the learners' initial feelings of insecurity as universal and professional, not individual and personal. In addition, teachers and supervisors could be guided by Reynolds's conceptualization (1942/1965) of the learning process and of the requisite teaching requirements appropriate at each stage, a conceptualization that was available in the literature. In fact, Reynolds's contribution of certain expected stages (which ranged from "acute consciousness of self," where energies are concentrated on your own activity, through "teaching what is mastered," where your energies are fully available to the other) remains a classic, valuable conceptual scheme.

We have described much of current supervision in social work (and in other professions) as training or consultation. Interestingly, a recent psychotherapy text describes *all* teaching/learning arrangements as "*supervision* models" (italics ours), including lecturer, teacher, case review, collegial-peer, monitor, and therapist (Hess, 1980). Included in this array are guest lecturer (a performance with an audience of any size), classroom teacher, organization-based review team, informal collegial-consultations, external administrative monitors (evaluators), and clinical therapy supervisors. In our view, such factors as voluntary attendance at sessions and the demand for compliance with the teaching would differentiate among these didactic approaches. There is freedom of choice for learners to attend or not in the peer consultative situation; subtle pressures operate with the guest lecturer. There is some choice in classes, some-to-no choice in the therapist situation, and no choice in case reviews and monitor situations.

Experimentation with didactic and experiential teaching approaches, in classes and in one-to-one situations, differs within the helping professions. Kaslow related the "awakening of the psychiatric-psychological-social work establishment" to the family and the "rapid mushrooming" in the 1970s of training and supervision systems *outside* the schools of medicine, theology, psychology, and social work. These family institutes, marriage councils, and postgraduate supervised training programs were initiated by "practitioner-educators" to meet "the clamor from clinicians for additional post-graduate training and from the lay population for therapists who can treat couples and families." The training systems used a broad array of teaching approaches in addition to the traditional model of supervision (Kaslow, 1977, pp. 209–223).

Although social workers only recently have begun to use diverse teaching methods and techniques in training and supervision, the profession's concern for teaching and learning is not recent. Reynolds believed anything could be taught in a variety of ways; yet the subject matter's place should always emerge from "the active responses of living persons" (1942/1965, p. 202). Her innovations in teaching techniques predated their use (and even their identification) in other disciplines. For example, she described how to teach through discussion by beginning with a little common story or constructed generalized case instance, "the miniature." She described how to lead in-service groups building upon job-related problems, how to rank-order ideas and select priorities (something now called "posting"). In addition, she did "laboratory teaching" long before any NTL (National Training Laboratory), and described "dramatization of interviews" before there was a concept called role play. Her "working notebook" is now known as a learning log or diary. Her "projects" and "experiments" on observation and interviewing, and her teaching of recording by means of "headlined paragraphs," illuminated the best of what is now known as discovery or experiential teaching/learning.

In traditional social work supervision, the approach to providing opportunities for learning was experiential in the best sense. It began with a real experience of offering help to clients or groups (i.e., doing the actual tasks and then discussing the experience and the learnings derived). This approach now is called "do-look-learn." But the tradition in social work supervision was discussional. The supervision was actually a second "experience" (variably directive, i.e., didactic). It was not "experiential" in the current usage of this word. A counseling text conveys the sense of the current "experiential" approach:

> The helper actually interviews a person seeking help: then the helper and helpee describe how they felt about the experience and what they did. The observers, if there are some, offer their emotional and cognitive reactions. Then, the principals and the observer group discuss what they *learned* from the experience—about helping skills, communication skills, or listening methods. . . . There is an ethical question about assigning a naive student helper to a helpee struggling with real problems. In formal training settings this issue is resolved somewhat by the usual presence of an experienced supervisor and fellow trainees who provide support as well as critical feedback on training performance.
> Various growth groups designed to provide helper trainees with self-awareness and skills practice fall in this experiential learning category. Here, the

trainees arrange themselves in a group and interact at increasingly more trusting and close interpersonal levels. Learning outcomes flow from the frequent efforts of the leader, or learning facilitator, to stop the action and to look at both the learning process . . . and what is happening to them as individuals. During the group process itself, however, members are constantly giving and receiving feedback to their helping skills. (Brammer, 1979, p. 163)

In social work's supervisory tradition, training occurred in the context of the help-offering, even by a novice, followed by a detailed written description of the process and discussion afterwards in a conference. The "ethical" problems involved in a novice-and-client helping situation were managed through the close attentiveness and investment of time and effort involved in the supervisor's back-up posture. The supervisor stood behind the substance of the efforts, yet gave room for the supervisee's learning through direct experience. In contrast to the counseling method just cited, there were no other observers (fellow trainees or group participants) to offer "emotional and cognitive reactions." The reactions to the substance of the work came only from the supervisor. Kadushin's 1973 survey of social work supervision points out a "classical dilemma":

> No use is made of modern technology to obtain data of on-the-job performance. Audio tapes, video tapes, and one-way mirrors are rarely used to observe the worker's competence: the principal basis for such assessment is the "supervisee's written case records," "the supervisee's verbal reports of case activity" and "the supervisee's correspondence and reports." (Kadushin, 1974, p. 295)

This situation, although described in terms of evaluation, also pertains to teaching—even if there have been shifts since 1973. According to Kadushin's description of major instructional methods:

> The supervisor can offer a small lecture, engage the supervisee in a Socratic dialogue or a give-and-take discussion, offer a demonstration, participate in a role play, listen to and analyze with the supervisee a tape-recorded playback, and offer material for reading." (1976, pp. 167–168)

The approach was retrospective discussion, which Kadushin described as a mix of direct, expository, telling, and indirect questioning and commenting—a dialectical-hypothetical approach resembling the guided discussion method. He saw the conference as a place for

> . . . systematic introspective-retrospective review of work that has been done, for thinking about the work as "recollected in tranquility." Experience is fragmented and seemingly chaotic. The supervisor helps the supervisee impose some order and meaning on experience . . . by asking questions, requesting clarification, freeing, supporting, stimulating, affirming, directing, challenging, and supplementing the worker's thinking . . . calls attention to errors in the worker's performance, missed opportunities, apparent misunderstandings, gaps and inconsistencies . . . introduces new ideas, shares relevant knowledge

and experience, explains and illustrates similarities and differences between this and other situations, enlarging the worker's perspective . . . poses relevant alternatives for considerations. (1976, p. 167)

The approach could be deductive—moving from the general to the specific, from presenting concepts, practice theories, rules, and techniques that could then be applied to the particular instance. It would be ordered through some planned sequence. Or it could be inductive—moving from a particular instance or critical incident experienced by the supervisee (whether or not the supervisee noticed its importance). The key points (committed or omitted) could be identified by the supervisor so as to stimulate the discovery of significance in the situation. Then, the insight could be applied to other comparable situations. These ways of teaching are *telling* or *asking*. The asking refers to a particular kind of telling (probe) that subtly leads to the learner's discovery of what the supervisor wishes the supervisee to see. In either case, as the following excerpts from Gitterman's records (1972) of supervisory conferences will illustrate, *the supervisor controls the teaching/learning situation.*

### General instance to specific—telling:

It sounded, I said, as though she felt that the other types of activity we had discussed . . . were not "social work." She responded, "yes, that's it, it's just not dignified." I explained why we provided these activities . . . (p. 29).

### Specific instance to the general—telling:

She commented how difficult it was for her and how a change to a "new approach" of work was frightening. I explained, . . . "by controlling the action of the group by preconceived plans and constantly directing its actions, [you] felt safe and secure; that the uncertainty which accompanies one in flowing with the unexpected of group process was frightening." She responded, "I guess so." (p. 30).

In the telling instances, the supervisor maintains control over the process, either by providing the correct responses, or by "Socratically" asking leading questions through which the worker "finds" a predefined solution. In either case, the supervisor is an expositor. As Gitterman points out, the supervisor is a dispenser of information who offers expertise in a didactic way, emphasizing general concepts that can then be applied to various comparable situations. In the next excerpt, the supervisor, still in control, does more questioning.

*Specific to general—asking and telling:* The worker wonders whether or not he should see the individual group members before their first meeting, since some of them seemed afraid of riding in elevators. The supervisor suspects that the worker out of his anxiety is more concerned about making sure they come to the meeting.

I wanted him to gain this insight into himself and thus asked, "Why did you decide to go by for them—What were you thinking and feeling?" He looked as if he had been "caught" and laughed nervously, and replied that he really hadn't thought about it, and just "decided on the spur of the moment to go up for them." I said, "But you had to think about it, what was underneath your decision?" He continued to look "caught" and seemed to resent my probing. I asked, "Am I making you angry by asking these questions?" He denied his underlying anger and insisted "I simply went up to pick them up and that's all." I asked him how he was feeling when he went by their apartments. He explained. . . . I asked him to look at his record in which he stated, "Today I went up to see whether or not any member would be coming . . ." He agreed that he really didn't know and this was part of the reason he went. I said, "Right, one of your underlying reasons was to influence the members to come to the meeting. Can you get an insight into yourself from this?" He sat in silence. (pp. 32-33).

We are fortunate indeed in having this glimpse of a supervisor's recordings of the teaching process, which, in itself, reveals a deep concern for dealing with supervisees, for time and energy investment in the actual process of the supervision. Most supervisors, even when the *how* of supervising is deemed important, do *not* devote this meticulous attention to the particular internal happenings of the conference; nor do they write them as a process to be examined. (The advent of audio and video recordings, of course, offer the interested supervisor opportunities for private, postsession reflection on processes and dynamics.)

The knowledge domain of communication and this domain's special class of teaching-type communications have benefited in recent times from theoretical and empirical research on their subtleties. More concepts and descriptive labels have been identified and classified, making it easier and possible to identify *how* the telling and dialectical-hypothetical questions and comments work so as to lead the supervisee toward an intended insight. These subtleties involved in the content domain of question posing are now described clearly in the interviewing and teaching literature—questioning is no longer an intuitive "art," to be cultivated through years of hard work.

There are the closed questions, answerable with yes or no, which add directionality to a process or bring it to a close. And there are the open-ended questions, which seek opinions, more elaborate responses, and leave the questionee free to explore many directions. Curwin and Furmann (1975, pp. 201-203) describe a range of five question types, from closed to open. Servey (1974) devotes a whole book to "the knack of asking questions." Using such insights for our analysis, we can determine *how* the supervisor led. Questions 1, 4, 6, and 7 in the last excerpt of dialogue (Why? Am I? I asked (told) him to, and Can you?) are closed questions. Interspersed are questions 2, 3, and 5 (What? What? How?), which are a bit more open.

In this review of didactic/experiential approaches in supervision and training, we see that the supervisor is directive, either overtly or subtly guiding the learning process. The justification for this is the need for supervisees, in real-live service situations that involve others, to learn so as to do particular things that supervisors can be held responsible for if something goes "wrong." Another cause for this directiveness is the fact that the supervisor is expected to know more than the supervisee about the workings of the organization.

When supervision involves others, teaching is more public, and potential influences upon the learning experience arise from additional sources besides the supervisor (i.e., from all who are part of the situation). In instances where teams or groups are the context of supervision, the centrality of the supervisor and the degree of directiveness may be decentralized or shared, but this is not necessarily the case. The specific content or belief system to be taught will also affect the directiveness of the supervisor. For example, it is impossible to imagine nondirective teaching of structural family therapy, since the method, itself, is directive. The supervision literature in this realm bears the stamp of directiveness: The supervisor's job is to protect the client from a beginning therapist; if client change is not taking place, the supervisor is a failure (Haley, 1976). Live supervision, in contrast to the usual situation, assumes that the supervisor does not have to wait until after the damage has been done to attempt to repair events (Montalvo, 1973). The student is a trainee who must carry out the supervisor's directives (Rickert and Turner, 1978).

Comparable thinking applies to co-therapy, where it is claimed that the number and extent of "therapeutic errors" can be reduced and that learners can build upon their own intervention skills better in the company of a more experienced practitioner who gives them a share of the supervisor's process (Kaslow, 1977). These issues of directiveness, which we shall return to in another section, must come to mind as you consider, "What kind of supervisor shall I be?" As a way of thinking about this question, we shall look at certain influences on how you will view yourself.

### The Supervisor's Self-View

As supervisor you will, through your teaching, be the arranger of the environment for learning. You will bring some specialized knowledge to the construction of means through which supervisees may develop their inherent interests and capacities. Devising your teaching plan is essentially an intellectual task. You will be influenced by your self-view, by the arrangements you make, and by traditions of the social work profession as well as other professions. As we have pointed out, your own professional socialization experiences, as well as "the ways" of other professions, affect present-day approaches to supervision.

Three main perspectives, associated views of the helping process, and the means for teaching them come to mind. We think these will play a part in just how you think about and view yourself:

*The assessor-instructor*—This perspective is linked to the behaviorist tradition. It is a controlling, directive one and employs procedures and interventions that feature exactness and prescriptiveness. The focus is on cognitive processes that may cause adaptive and maladaptive behavior, and on skills and behavioral learning (from an assumption that cognition controls emotions and actions). There is an emphasis on the reciprocal interaction of person and environment; on self-directed modes of learning; and on specialized, technical procedures, including performance-based objectives, preferably measurable.

*Facilitator*—This perspective emerged from the human-potential movement and the third-force (humanistic) psychologies. The teacher occupies a less central and controlling position in the helping process, sometimes disappearing into the group altogether, or assuming a nondirective stance and thereby forcing the learners to create their own structures. The emphasis is on the interaction—on feelings and emotionality, expressiveness, new ways of perceiving and reacting to others, and on the process and dynamics of giving and receiving help.

*Ecologist*—This perspective is linked closely with social work's traditions and value base in its concern for both persons and environments. An ecological perspective aims at more than the environment; it concerns the balance between individuals and environments. This perspective has been described in the social work literature by Germain, 1979; Germain and Gitterman, 1980. Using this perspective, the supervisor is concerned with selection and distribution of roles, power, resources, tasks, and problem-solving activities. Attention is devoted to the physical, cultural, social, psychological, and behavioral influences affecting the fit between person and environment, and the plans and energies that might make for a more harmonious situation. The directiveness of the supervisor with such a frame of reference would fall midway between the assessor-instructor perspective and the facilitator perspectives.

These three general stances or self-views are metaviews that, although derived from diverse realms, will inform your choice of supervisory design, techniques, and procedures. In any case, these will need to be adapted to social work purposes as you purposefully synthesize the components of your supervisory design. This is essential so that your supervision will be practical and fit the service delivery and learning needs of your supervisees. They play a part, along with other elements, in the orientation of the supervision that you will use.

## FOUR SUPERVISION ORIENTATIONS

Earlier, we identified four supervisory orientations—skills/information, self, transactional process, and pattern—and stated that any of these might be used with a given supervisee. Still, the skills/information orientation, with its linkage to task and context competencies, will be most appropriate at the outset. While these four orientations and related emphases will be considered independently (for analytic purposes), they are not discrete in terms of outcome. All share the common goals of effective service and supervisee learning; but the routes toward these goals differ in terms of the stress placed upon certain competencies and, therefore, upon the focus of the work. For your teaching purposes, it is useful to view them separately and make use of certain structures, procedures, and techniques to support concentration in any given area. With a supervisee who may be a novice to the delivery system, it is apparent that you might view these orientations sequentially. But no one (in light of life experience, prior training, and other learning experiences) is a *total* novice with respect to the elements emphasized in these orientations. So probably, you will move among them, clarifying the shifts with the individual supervisees.

Recall that we separated the task competencies of supervisors' and supervisees' professional assignments and claimed that you, as supervisor, assumedly possess the supervisee task competencies. You will begin by helping supervisees to learn the functional requirements of their work—that is, to grasp the task and context competencies. However, in focusing on task and context competencies with a skills/information orientation, you may need to move into the self-awareness area (self orientation) if you find that a lack of sensitivity and understanding of self and others gets in the way of the work. Then, depending upon the mutual assessment process which will reveal what they know, want to learn, need to learn, and what you know how to offer and can offer in view of time constraints and other demands, you may periodically renegotiate your focus with the supervisee. Table 7-6 summarizes various key dimensions in the orientations. We highlight certain distinctions in the following descriptions.

### The Skills/Information Orientation

The focus here is on developing conceptual knowledge and acquiring specific techniques and skills related to learning the elements of the presenting tasks (assuming various roles, delivering services to varieties of client populations in diverse configurations, connecting with and reaching the community, and developing resources) and to negotiating the complexities of the context of the offer of service. This is a generalist orientation concerned with individuals, groups, families, and communities; it calls for a mix of increased, purposeful interactional and intervention skills, as well as an understanding of clients and others. Here, a basic assumption is that knowledge of certain concepts and critical information, together with mastery of basic activities, roles, and skills, will lead to competent practice. In social work practice, it is through specialized activities that the core functions are actualized and performed according to the values and norms of the profession and the organization; these activities require an extensive unit of attention and a fund of knowledge and skills beyond merely the interviewing, interpersonal-focused offer of service. For instance, it is necessary to have the knowledge and skills needed for organization-aware work, unwilling clients, and noncollaborative colleagues.

In this orientation, the supervisor's main role is coach. You view yourself as assessor-instructor. Your major teaching approach is didactic. Your relationship with the supervisee is focused on instructing the novice about the intricacies of service delivery.

### The Self Orientation

Here, the focus is on self-awareness, insight, control of feelings and behavior, and subtle application of understandings and skills. It is directed toward the competencies of self—that is, the knowledge and skills connected with self-understanding.

**TABLE 7-6  Orientations to Supervision: A Summary**

| | SKILLS/INFORMATION | SELF | TRANSACTIONAL PROCESS | PATTERN |
|---|---|---|---|---|
| Goal | Task; context | Self | Relationship | Context |
| | | ←— Improved service delivery through enhanced worker learning —→ | | |
| Emphasized competencies | Knowledge, skills, roles | Purposeful self-awareness | Reciprocal impact of self/others | Strategic plans and actions; multi-impacts; power/influence |
| Focus | Certain specific behaviors and information comprise the basic professional task | Increased insight and affective sensitivity lead to control of self and compassionate helping | Attention to the mutual causal process, not only own action; leads to responsive service | Continuous change and conflicts of interest must be noticed and affected |
| Basic assumption | Coach | Counselor (clinician, therapist) | Counselor; then conferee | Conferee (sometimes coach, counselor) |
| Role | Transmission of content | Discovery (transmission of content) | Transmission, exchange, discovery of content | Transmission, exchange of content |
| Educational Goal | Assessor-instructor | Facilitator | Facilitator | Ecologist |
| Sees Self As | Skills: Present Information: Present/past (future) | Present/past | Present; cyclical | Future, present/past |
| Time-Focus emphasis | Didactic | ← – – – – Experiential – – – – → | Experiential | Didactic |
| Teaching Methods/Techniques | Teacher/novice | Helper/helpee | Helper/helpee; co-investigator, collaborator | Teacher/novice, co-investigators, planners |
| Supervisory relationship | Expert | Expert | Information; referent | Informational; referent |
| Basis of Power (aside from legitimate and assumed expertise) | | | | |

A basic assumption underlying this orientation is that supervisees need to know and claim their own attitudes, perspectives, ideas, values, feelings, and actions as differentiated from those of others. They need to gain purposeful, conscious control over self, so as to be available to clients and to offer consistent, responsive service. Through increased insight (knowledge of interpersonal behavior) and affective sensitivity (awareness and understanding of emotions that surround interpersonal exchanges), the supervisees may gain increased understanding of *what* they think and feel (more than *why* or *what caused* the thoughts and feelings). Such self-awareness and heightened consciousness will help supervisees remain close and empathic with clients, yet separate and not personally caught up with or overwhelmed by the emotionality of the others' problems or situations. Self-knowledge encompasses one's likeness to and difference from others. It is needed for becoming a compassionate helping person who can let the others have their problems, yet stay closely connected even when the problems resonate with comparable past or current situations of one's own.

At the organizational level, self-awareness and controlled behavior relate to how the supervisees function as a part of a larger, sometimes abrasive, collectivity. These learnings condition not only how supervisees deal with the hardships of clients, but also how they cope with their own conflict with authority, impulse control, attention and sensitivity to colleagues, personal appearance and behavior in the organization, accommodation to stress, routines, time, and so forth.

Your main role as supervisor in this orientation is counselor (clinician or therapist). That is, you model the helping stance in your relationship with the supervisees, through using your knowledge and skills and also through identifying and discussing relevant knowledge and skills as they occur in the supervisory relationship or in the supervisees' interactions with clients and colleagues. You see yourself as a facilitator, and your approach may mix didactic and experiential emphases.

### The Transactional Process Orientation

This orientation addresses the relationship competencies—that is, the supervisees' increased understanding and deliberate self-control as they focus on the process. The self/other interactions are seen as transactions—that is, as exchange units where each or all involved mutually affect one another. The use of this orientation assumes prior familiarity with the emphases of the skills/information and self orientations. A basic assumption is that events and interactions are mutual/causal, rather than cause-and-effect outcomes, and that process is cyclic, not linear. The focus is on deepened sophistication in self/other transactions; on more spontaneity and subtlety in using the behavioral and affective skills and understandings involved in relationships; and on appreciation of the reciprocal effects of self/other transactions. In other words, concentration is on *process* (how things happen) and *impact* (consequences of transactions).

As the supervisees gain comfort and confidence in their ability to offer service purposefully and consistently, they may be less concerned with their part of the helping situation (what to do or not to do) and more able to consider the others' effects on themselves. Complexity is seen as the human reality, the desire for certainty gradually suspended. Instead, multicausality, equifinality, ambiguity, approximation, and nondeterminism are concepts of interest. Differential approaches may be compared and contrasted as supervisees focus on cultivating an emergent, fluid practice, where spontaneity and versatility are valued and where mechanical or "packaged" interventive techniques are abandoned. Concern turns to developing their unique personal styles.

Awareness of and attention to impact also may lead to more systematic ways to assess impact, to the development of a practitioner-researcher orientation, and to involvement with methods of capturing the data of the helping situations. (Once involved in practice research, these requisite competencies may be applied also in the skills/information orientation, especially if the focus with clients is also on the learning of skills.)

As supervisor, you may begin in the counselor role; but eventually, you will probably shift to the conferee role, which is more consultative and collegial. As interest grows in the mutual, transactional approach to the work, the view of the supervisor/supervisee relationship also will assume a similar character. You will become co-investigators and collaborators in devising the work and assume a mutually sharing orientation. Your self-view will be as a facilitator of the learning process.

### The Pattern Orientation

The focus here is on strategic practice, on whole-system, global, future-oriented interventions with clients and others, and on the strategies and tactics that make the planning and interventions work. The pattern orientation connects with the context competencies as these impinge upon self and others at all levels of the organization: colleagues, supervisors, and other influentials, as well as those who seek service (clients). A basic assumption is that the organization is an arena characterized by continuous change and conflicting interests. Power and influence upon the inevitable shifts and changes, although differentially distributed in hierarchical organizations, may be purposefully applied at any level in the formal organizational structure. For effective service delivery to occur, the most important behaviors may be planfulness, awareness of the formal and informal patterns that are operative, and use of strategic behavior involving others with like interests.

The focus is upon understanding the "big" picture, the network of alliances and impediments, the natural, expected rhythms and unusual reverberations that surround the expected and unexpected events comprising organizational life. The organizational dynamics and impinging forces that affect the delivery system become foreground rather than background in this orientation, as supervisor and supervisee pursue their core functional imperatives, aided or constrained by the system in which they play a part. Key elements involved in planful, strategic behavior are the politics, maneuvers, coalitions, and other subtleties of the workplace.

In this orientation you share your knowledge and savvy with the supervisees.

Your main role is conferee: planning, directing, collaborating, consulting, and exchanging information with supervisees as the situation warrants. You see yourself as an ecologist, one who seeks a balance among the diverse contextual forces and persons. At times you may move into coach or counselor roles, depending upon the sophistication and experiences of the supervisees, who may need to learn strategies of manipulation, negotiation, or coalition formation more than they need communication and helping skills.

## THE PARTICULARS OF THE CONSTRUCTED TEACHING/ LEARNING COMPONENT OF SUPERVISION

By now it must be apparent to you that constructing teaching approaches with supervisees is a complex task of arrangement that depends upon an array of relevant variables, rather than a tidy one-way approach. This fact may strike you as a liturgy of overwhelming confusion or, alternatively, as a fascinating kaleidoscopic opportunity for challenging intellectual work. Recall that we promised you neither road map nor blueprint; only a more sensitized you in the driver's seat negotiating "the way" more knowledgeably in your travels with each new or seasoned supervisee. In some cases the supervisees will be assigned to you by the organization, and you will seek to "make it" with them, no matter their reluctance to the required engagement. In other cases, they may have selected you as the person they want to learn with, and this very voluntariness offers different presenting dynamics.

In Chapter 2, we pointed out that you and the supervisees will look at and think about the work as influenced by the individual cognitive styles you both have developed, by the values and conventions of the culture in which you live, and also by the norms and traditions of the social work profession. In addition, you must consider the influences of the teaching approaches of other professions, the influences of the community's expectations and determination of what social work should be like (Chapter 4), and the influences stemming from your organizational policies and procedures (Chapter 6). We also encouraged you to try to get a rough reading on where you are in terms of your own perspectives through various questionnaires, and through our discussion of the traditions and current features of supervision. A dominant theme throughout our discussions is the contrasting polarity between the one "right" way of thinking or doing (convergent) versus the many possible alternative ways of approaching ideas and actions (divergent). This applies in terms of your overall frame of reference about how the world works (Chapter 2), and it applies in terms of supervisory roles, functions, tasks, activities, and teaching approaches. Our persistent "answer" to this dilemma has favored consistently a stance of knowing much (i.e., understanding the wide variety of possibilities, adopting a stance that appreciates the values and contributions of various approaches to thinking and doing), and *not* settling for the one "right" dogma, school of thought, or way of teaching others.

This same perspective applies to the many little conceptualizations of method and technique that exist at the level of the technical aspects of service delivery and affects the ways to teach it. A major intellectual task is to think through the areas of performance and the possibilities for teaching them, so as to determine which components *are* open to opinions and variability and which are closed (i.e., are inherently right or wrong so far as competent performance goes). This judgment needs to be balanced by a second consideration, namely, whether or not the supervisee knows this already, knew it in the past but forgot it, or does not know it at all. For an elaborate description of how to determine where your supervisee may be on this continuum, consult Mager and Pipe (1970) or the summary of their work presented by Austin (1981, pp. 231-234).

**Who Needs to Know What?**

The conceptual scheme in Figure 7-4 can orient your determination of what to do when you know these differential learning needs. As we consider what and how you should teach, a major theme distinguishes the two main approaches. (1) You may construct your particulars out of a meticulous analysis that connects the goals of service and learning with what you can offer (the design for supervision); this is an emergent approach with its own logic—for example, a series of sequenced "important" learnings; or an incident-by-incident, inductive approach derived from the particular experiences encountered. (2) You may begin with what appeals to you, or what is written up as an exercise and can be "slotted into" your situation, or what is in vogue at the moment—a cookbook or mechanistic approach. In short, we have emphasized that anything may be taught in a variety of ways, but the way you go should not be merely the packaged-by-others, plastic approach. At the method and technique level, this difference between the tailor-made (adapted), constructed teaching/learning experiences versus the ready-made ones takes on great importance. There now exists the general advantage of access to many specific designs that are public knowledge and are described step by step in the training literature—an interior view of teaching methods that was obscured in the past. So, you are assisted by the conceptual efforts of others. But the potential disadvantage is that these designs may be used (put on persons) by the naive or that they may be adopted without examining their purpose, appropriateness, and potential consequences.

We have pointed to distinctions between didactic and experiential approaches and cautioned that either can be directive (closed) or evocative (subtly leading, hence partially closed), regardless of whether the appeal to the learner stresses hearing and reading or whether it stresses interaction and diverse sensory, perceptual modes. Perhaps the most fundamental question involves who determines the desired outcome: you? supervisee? you and supervisee? Or, in other words, where is the locus of control in terms of what should be learned, and how it should be learned? Or better, what parts must you control, and where are the areas that should be jointly determined?

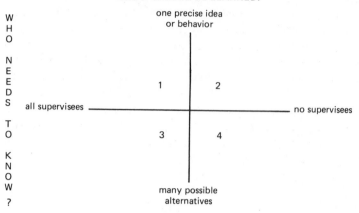

WHAT SHOULD BE LEARNED?

Quadrant 1:   a situation calling for clear, involving, dogmatic presentations,
e.g., lecture, memo, handouts, lecture + discussion to examine
confusions, skills training groups: dogmatic/convergent.

Quadrant 2:   a situation calling for differentiated, individualized formats.
The lecture, memo, handouts, lecture + discussion may be for only
those needing to know; or special roles created to acknowledge that
some do know, e.g., a buddy system where one helps another to
know, or skill practice with the knowers having more complex
responsibilities: dogmatic/differentiated.

Quadrant 3.   a situation calling for exchange of beliefs, biases, comparisons,
contrasts, suppositions, open examination of a range of ideas,
e.g., group discussion, consultative exchange, nominal group
technique, brainstorming, case conferences, problem-posing
opportunities: divergent-reflective.

Quadrant 4:   a situation calling for a mix of the elements suggested in Q2 and
Q3, i.e., differentiated, individualized formats which emphasize
speculation, exchange, and the development of many possible
approaches, ideas, "solutions." For those who may think they know,
the challenge is to re-think the old ideas, embellish, or innovate
different ways: divergent-reflective/differentiated.

**FIGURE 7-4.  What should be learned?**

Furthermore, you need to come face to face with the different types of
"knowing" that connect knowledge with skills, a matter we have approached
through using the organizing concept of knowledge/skills competencies. But actually, there are inherent distinctions here, as well as differential responsibility for
the teaching of these "knowings," which are shared by classroom teacher, supervisor, agency or outside training, and "street" teachings (entirely aside from any
intentional, purposeful, formalized teaching). There are the distinctions of knowing *about* something, knowing *what to do about* something, knowing *that* you
can do a thing that is needed *when* you need to, and knowing about what you
*have done* (i.e., the outcome or consequences of applying your knowledge in
action).

### The Systematic and Technical

The building blocks of teaching, at the technical level, are often described as methods, techniques, or strategies. This implies that there should be some order and systematic means of presentation to teach a given skill, concept, or task. For example, in teaching a skill, you might plan to move from cognitive understanding to action and then to reflection opportunities, in order to examine variable applications; or in planning a way to deal with perception or value differences, you might decide to begin with the action experience and then use reflective discussion to conceptualize the various feelings and conflicts that emerge. But having a system means having the progression you will follow in mind, while at the same time leaving room for dealing with the unanticipated reactions and experiences that will emerge from the learners. It is system plus unforeseen embellishments.

Since there are many ways available to you, the important thing is to have a repertoire of possibilities, and then to be consistent and orderly after you have determined your way. In any case, you need to know your objectives (shared and determined with the learner), how you intend to pursue these together, and how you will determine whether or not something, as intended, *was* learned or applied. This general orienting framework applies regardless of the particulars that need to be learned. In this sense, there is a method involved, a systematic approach, whether the outcome stresses a one-best or varied set of possibilities. Morton and Kurtz (1980) offer a detailed description and analysis of sequenced teaching strategies. The approach moves from teaching *what to do* (through verbal instructions followed by observations), to *putting the knowledge into operation* (through various practice strategies), to *transferring* the learning to the service tasks (through specified behavioral assignments and tasks).

As we have discussed, the utilization of technology and diverse instructional formats is an aspect of supervision in social work education and training that has lagged in comparison to usage in other professions. This type of instruction has lagged in classroom teaching as well as in supervisory approaches. (Most social agencies have *not* had money for expensive communications technology.) One extensive literature review of competency-based approaches in social work education found that there was least success with the instructional-design components, as contrasted with attention to the development of performance objectives or measures for evaluating the instruction (Gross, 1981). An impetus at the instructional-design level stems from a multidisciplinary route toward supervising and teaching family and group practice, from training packages developed in various institutes, and from the profitable consultative activities of "stars" and many derivative "asteroids" whose focus is organizational development or individual worker enhancement (through transactional analysis, gestalt, neurolinguistic programming, hypnosis, and so forth). These initiatives have shared a common goal of enhancing individuals' competence and, for the organizational development pioneers, of incorporating humanistic values into the workplace. Their thrust was toward organizational effectiveness, an ambiguous concept that often meant personal and interpersonal effectiveness to the trainers, and profit and increased productivity to the organization (Krell, 1981). This confusion is exemplified by the push toward quality-circles training in both profit and human services organizations (Middleman, 1984).

You will find these technical components identified in the literature as techniques, strategies, technologies, exercises, learning modules, structured experiences, and so forth. It may help to analyze them in terms of these elements:

*Needed configuration*—individual, dyad, small group, large group

*Inherent structures*—planned elements of the learning situation, such as chairs, tables, timing, equipment and materials, instructions, arrangement of the flow of doing and talking, one-way mirrors, video or audio devices

*Procedures*—forms of communication without content of their own that are used in various contexts for particular purposes, such as observers to watch the interaction, round-robin ways of trying a new behavior, feedback time, voting, fishbowl arrangement

*Main learning domain*—cognitive, affective, behavioral, perceptual

*Purpose*—acquisition of new knowledge, mastery of a skill, application of understanding to a new situation, reflection, discovery, integration of several ideas or behavioral elements, becoming more flexible, and so forth

These elements form the constructed teaching/learning experience you will devise. Table 7-7 lists examples of the great variety of techniques in the literature. The potential array is too vast to elaborate here. However, the elements (configuration, structures, procedures, learning domain, and purpose) should be explored as you consider any specific technique to determine its suitability for your teaching situations, and to show that *what* and *how* (or content and process) are really *content/process*.

As a route into the vast literature of these particulars, we can offer a few suggestions. Walter and Marks (1981) describe "classical" teaching methods (well known to you from your own learning experiences): lecture, case examination, reading, written tasks, and "supporting methods" such as process observation, alone time, fantasy, audiovisual methods, instrumentation, projects, and excursions. Certain additional methods are described as central to experiential learning: simulations, exercises, group interaction, role playing, and body movement. They offer, in addition, a comprehensive bibliography in the area of experiential teaching approaches. A second main source of diverse, detailed designs is the series of *Structured Experiences* handbooks published yearly since 1969 by Pfeiffer and Jones, together with their *Annual Handbooks* published since 1972. For interactional approaches specifically directed to organizations, examples are Vaughan and Deep (1975), Kolb, Rubin, and McIntyre (1974), Certo (1976), Morris and Sashkin (1976). The writings of Taylor and Walford (1972), and Ruben and Budd (1975) are among the many sources that deal with simulations and games; Shaw, Corsini, Blake, and Mouton (1980) offer a broad consideration of approaches to role play; and Akamatsu (1980) presents a comprehensive discussion of the empirical research

**TABLE 7-7  Some Examples of Teaching Techniques**

Process records, discussed after the fact
Critical incidents (written or described); work samples
Case notes; psychosocial summaries; case conferences
Role plays and simulated experiences; the empty chair
Direct observation by one or many, plus discussion
Sitting-in on individual or family interviews; co-leadership of groups
Construction (verbal, written) of alternative scenarios
Observations (global or discrete categories), plus feedback and exchange
Verbal, written self-reports; logs; journals
Skills practice in trios with differentiated roles: helper, helpee, observer
Perception and reflection practice: experiencing silence, experiencing not seeing, not hearing,
    not moving with both legs, etc.
Brainstorming; examining polarities; contrasting dichotomies with analogies, continuities with
    discontinuities
Models: live; videotapes; audiotapes
Constructed tasks: paper and pencil; interactional
Checklists; profiles; instruments that lead to a theory discussion or personalized insights
Nonverbal or action techniques: drawing, moving, pantomime, mapping, diagramming

on role play and simulations. Middleman offers a review and analysis of three types of structured group experiences (1981a), and a more general discussion of the place of content and activities throughout social group work's history and current group practices (1980b).

### Locus of Control

We introduced the notion *locus of control* in terms of who decides what should be learned and what different kinds of knowing should be clarified—that is, the *content.* Now we consider this concept from the perspective of the *process* involved. This issue concerns how much control over the teaching/learning process you will share with the supervisees. (This issue also would appear with respect to the evaluative and administrative functions as well.) Munson recognized this issue in calling attention to the "interactional ground rules" that need to be established at the outset of the supervisory situation, as well as to what the roles of supervisor and supervisee would be (as we have explored earlier). He posed certain questions to help clarify the arrangements:

> Who sets the agenda? Who establishes the frequency, time, and length of the sessions? Will emphasis be placed on case discussion, worker growth, or both? Will the supervisor present case material? Who will make what decisions? Who establishes the structure of presentations? Who establishes the content of presentations? (Munson, 1979, p. 338)

These subtleties influence profoundly the quality and orientation of the teaching/ learning situation, and ideally, they are open to negotiation if you are willing to involve the supervisees in having a hand in their own learning.

A second issue related to locus of control refers to the outcome, but it also influences the process. Here we remind you of the choice between supervisee-initiated versus supervisor-determined meetings, between voluntary versus involuntary relationships, and between following through and reporting back on determinations versus a take-it-or-not arrangement where supervisees are free to consult, yet free to follow their own decisions after reviewing the situations. (Recall the summary of teaching/learning events presented at the outset of this chapter in Table 7-1.)

We also dealt with the control issue when we explored didactic or directive teaching (whether through telling or asking selected questions). This is another instance of process (and content) control. But, beyond these considerations, the most profound determination of locus of control concerns how you learn about the supervisee's work. This factor, we think, influences the learning process more than whatever theoretical orientation to persons and practice you favor, and it results in radically different teaching approaches. *By this we mean how the supervisor knows about and deals with the work—*a combination of possibilities we now review.

Two basic perception and information-processing modes, direct observation and screened information, are possibilities. Each is related to a fundamentally different theory of teaching/learning. The question becomes: Will you want to watch what the supervisees do, then pick and choose what needs to be the focus of attention (correction or encouragement), sometimes intervening directly as "helper" or corrector in the practice situation? Or will you work with those aspects that the supervisees perceptually screen, that the supervisees determine that *they* wish to examine? This is a perception issue—the raw data of the actual encounter versus the screened data that supervisees want to (are able to) handle. And this is also an action issue—immediate versus delayed instruction.

These distinctions are explored in the research literature, not in the teaching literature. Bloom (1975) contrasts "subject-data" and "observer-data." Subject-data

**TABLE 7-8  Teaching Methods[a]**

| Thought Process | DEDUCTIVE | INDUCTIVE | S U P E R V I S O R  A C T I V I T I E S | |
|---|---|---|---|---|
| *Activities* | Presenting principles; rules | Summarizing principles | | Didactic (telling; guiding questions; showing) |
| | Asking for specific examples, applications of a general principle of production of behavior in accord with the rules | Seeking to discover the general principles to unit-specific instances or incidents | | |
| *Goal* | Mastery of skills; understanding of ideas | Discovery, dealing with problems | | Experiential, evocative (asking; interacting) |

[a]Gale Goldberg's help in preparing this table and Tables 7-9 and 7-10 is gratefully acknowledged.

are information obtained from the person directly through discussion (interviews). The major strength here is "getting the person's version of the situation, especially in subjective matters." This contrasts with observer-data, with information obtained from a person "interpreted by the observer or compared with norms from previous research, and it is the *observer's* responses [italics ours] or the normative scores which are the data under consideration" (p. 225). Elsewhere, Bloom raises this issue when considering evaluation of practice approaches: "To whom do the data belong? . . . When one person evaluates a second person, it is the first person's responses that become the data to be analyzed. The data are *about* the second person, but they are *from* the first person" (1976, p. 4).

Bloom also raises a second perceptual issue (which researchers think of as data collection) that is related to the subject/observer qualitative difference in the mode of obtaining information—that is, how intrusive is the information-getting mode on the information obtained? Here, Bloom contrasts "intrusive" methods, where the client may be aware of either the purpose or the process or both; and "nonreactive" methods, where intrusiveness is at a minimum and getting the information does not influence the situation (1975, p. 226).

Following a similar line of thinking with respect to teaching, Tables 7-9 and 7-10 show that you, as supervisor, can observe directly or more remotely (dimensions we term obtrusive and unobtrusive). Secondly, you may choose to deal with your observations either immediately (in the moment), or at some later time (after reflection both by you and the supervisee). We have listed some of the information-collecting and information-processing techniques that go with each situation.

So far as locus of control is concerned, you hold most control in Cell 1, and supervisees hold most control in Cell 4. That is, in Cell 1 you are part of the inter-

**TABLE 7-9   Type of Observation**

|  | OBTRUSIVE | UNOBTRUSIVE |
|---|---|---|
| *Immediate* | *1*<br>*Supervisor Sees All*<br><br>—Just watches<br>—Intervenes at times<br>—Co-therapist<br>—Not there, but injects messages (telephone, ear-bug) | *3*<br>*Supervisor and Others See All from Remote Position*<br><br>—Behind one-way mirror<br>—Watches video monitor |
| *Nonimmediate* | *2*<br>*Supervisee Records the Interaction*<br><br>—Videotape<br>—Audiotape<br>—Written notes | *4*<br>*Supervisee Submits Information*<br><br>—Written process notes<br>—Verbal accounts<br>—Critical incidents<br>—Log<br>—Diagrams, questionnaires |

**TABLE 7-10   Type of Teaching by Type of Observation**

| OBSERVATION TYPE | OBTRUSIVE | | UNOBTRUSIVE | |
|---|---|---|---|---|
| | 1 IMMEDIATE | 2 NONIMMEDIATE | 3 IMMEDIATE | 4 NONIMMEDIATE |
| TEACHING/ LEARNING TYPE | Demonstration and prompting by supervisor | Mutual examination after the fact by supervisor and supervisee | Feedback by supervisor; joint reflection after the fact; feedback of others | Reflection; review of key incidents as initiated by supervisee after the fact |
| | ←———— Re-created role plays, role reversals after the fact ————→ | | | |

action, even if simply sitting and watching. You see all that happens; and the client or family or group is aware of your presence. In Cell 4, the supervisees report to you what you should know about the encounter as determined by what seems important to them, what they know how to convey, how much they trust you with their difficulties, and how much they "forget." You, of course, are not bound to "know" only what the supervisees choose to report in Cell 4, since you may pick up on omissions, emphases, interpretation, and so forth. But here, you begin with what matters to the supervisee.

You can see distinctions within these categories—for example, whether or not you would "take over" the work at times, as in co-therapy, or whether or not you hear an entire audio tape or ask the supervisee to select the places of importance. You may use this framework to categorize numerous other activities beyond the individual conference, family, or group situation. Other ways to "observe" the work, for example, include accompanying your supervisee on a home visit or to a community meeting, watching your supervisees' interactions with other staff, and hearing from the agency grapevine. The category scheme is suggestive of the many possible variations through which you may determine your instructional approach. In Table 7-10, the immediacy/nonimmediacy dimension is nested within the obtrusive/unobtrusive dimension to show certain types of teaching that are congenial to each category and lead to four main approaches: (1) modeling/identification, (2) modeling and discussion, (3) feedback and joint reflection directly after, and (4) reflective discussion in a second, delayed teaching/learning experience.

Qualitative differences are associated with each teaching mode. For example, in Cell 1 the learning may be quickest and most economical; the supervisor's control is greatest; and client service is not hindered by worker learnings (unless the very fact of the added influence of two persons imparts a special problem). But the variability among "right" approaches may be diminished, and the possibility is greatest here that the supervisor's style and manner will be duplicated by the learners. Cells 2 and 3 allow for more degrees of choice by the supervisee, and possibly more reflectiveness. In Cell 3, benefits from the supervisor's awareness (through immediate debriefing) of all that happened are important, yet the heat of the moment of recapitulation (directly after the engagement) may fall on the "exhausted ears" of supervisees. Cell 4 is the slowest approach and the most time-consuming for the supervisor. But these situations have a great potentiality for the learners' development of their styles of conceptualizing and dealing with others. Depending on the quality of the relationship between supervisor and supervisee, there may be a powerful, positive impact, or possibly what has been called an occasion of "sanctioned trauma" (Murdaugh, 1974).

Systematic comparison among these four instructional approaches and the associated outcomes is an area that merits serious empirical study. Learning theories agree that learning (changed behavior) is a consequence of corrective feedback after the action, through which you alter aspects of thoughts and actions. Feedback may come from your own insights or may come from those of others; it may be positive (continue or accentuate what you are doing) or negative (correct or change actions in relation to intentions). The feedback of Cell 1 is external and normative as per the supervisor's judgment of "the right" thing to do. In Cell 4, the feedback is intrinsic and internal first—your own felt assessment of your work, and your subsequent determination of which parts of the situation you want to or need to review with the supervisor.

Certain perspectives and operating practices of the researcher can benefit the practice acts and the supervisor's teaching approaches. Yet there are differences in the norms and conventions of research and practice, as determined by their distinctive purposes. A good example of opposite imperatives that guide the two realms is the well-known Hawthorne effect (see Note 1), which every student of research methods learns to suspect (i.e., that the investigation itself, the noticing of the subjects may contaminate the effects of the investigated variables and make *the* difference). And yet, for teaching and training purposes, this Hawthorne effect is an advantage. When workers are given the opportunity to participate in special teaching/learning opportunities (whether or not the learners *learn* what the in-service event intended), the human relationship effects alone may affect morale, humanize the workplace, and combat burn-out. What is contamination in research is a precious by-product in training.

In general, many perspectives derived from the precautions of the researchers may have fruitful application to practice and its teaching. In fact, the matter of the obtrusiveness of the means of teaching, as well as the whole area of performance evaluation (learning) in social work education, is gaining increased notice. For example, Bloom analyzed 50 systems of evaluating student learning in social work programs (1976). The main evaluative mode was intrusive (60 percent)—that is, learners were aware of the process, content, or both; and it was external, normative (80 percent)—that is, "judgmental" in that the defined attributes and their units of measurement lay in the "sensitive" minds of the evaluators. Bloom contrasted this judgmental stage in evaluatory method with other possibilities, for example, assessments of observed behavioral performances, or of the specifics of problem-solving competence—the ultimate attributes of professionalism. While this analysis of evaluation approaches examined contrasts in methods of evaluation of learning, it would also be valuable if there were a leading-edge imperative that would review methods of teaching along similar dimensions.

*Locus of control as power.* Locus of control has been examined in terms of its influence on content/process, learning, and the supervisor's underlying intentions: correcting? undoing? modeling treatment? problem solving? facilitating? adjusting? The mutuality or unilateralness of determination, the freedom or compliance ambience, and the overall relationship arrangement of supervisor and supervisee lead us to a reconsideration of *power*.

Earlier we identified two main bases of supervisor power, derived from the classic studies of social power and influence by French and Raven (1959). We claimed that you held a positional power, *legitimate* power, because of your place in the organizational hierarchy, and that this power also includes the responsibility for evaluation and personnel actions (in relation to promotions, terminations, hiring, and so forth). Additionally, you have *expert* power (to the extent you *are* expert in various aspects of the work). At least, you are assumed to be expert until or unless the supervisee has reason to believe otherwise. The other bases of power that this research identified were reward, coercive, and referent (identification between supervisor and supervisee). This fuller range of influence possibilities suggests a wide spectrum of impacts on the teaching/learning process.

When expert and legitimate power are exercised in supervision, it follows that reward and coercive powers may be resorted to as means of emphasizing compliance with the directives stemming from the expert or legitimate realms. And when considered in relation to career socializing, referent power (or its absence) may play a key role in the learning, through identification of values, attitudes, and the integration of professional behavior.

Subsequent research, building upon the original formulations of French and Raven (Raven and Kruglanski, 1970), revised and further elaborated certain aspects of the original conceptual scheme, especially in extending the exercise of influence to instances where there are conflicts of interest between the parties involved. The five power bases just mentioned were revised as follows:

1.  Coercive and reward powers (the mediation of punishments *and* rewards) were collapsed into a single category, although the underlying monitoring and enforcement dynamics would differ.
2.  Referent power (including negative reference or the wish to be different from the power-wielder) was described as related to similarity or desired identification. "Liking" emerged more as "being like" rather than personally liking the other.
3.  A new category, informational power, was posed and differentiated in dynamics from expert power.

We think informational power holds enormous importance for social work supervision; and the differentiation between it and expert power bears careful attention.

Expert power (potential to influence another) depends upon the supervisor's superior knowledge and skill, and on the supervisees' trust that the supervisors, indeed, possess the requisite expertise. This expertise is seen as a personal attribute that is inherent in "the expert." A problem arises when the expert becomes involved "as expert" in content domains where the expertness does not apply (as, for example, when a physician's eminence in a medical specialty may lead to insistent and powerful opinions in the social realm, or when an actor's expertise in delivering messages impactfully leads others to trust the content of the appeals). With expert power, if there is a conflict in goals between the supervisor and the supervisee (e.g., if the supervisor's emphasis is on agency requirements and the supervisee's main goal is learning in a particular area), the power of the expert is not inherently influential. (In contrast, it would be influential in instances where conflicts existed in terms of what means should be used in reaching mutually acceptable goals.) Moreover, the supervisor's very expertise, as the means of influence, may also be a *separating* influence—that is, the supervisor's superior knowledge accentuates their difference—"The infallible expert is rejected as a basis for self-evaluation, [and this] may lead to a process of moving away in identification and interaction" (Raven and Kruglanski, p. 80).

Informational influence, on the other hand, is described as providing information not previously available and pointing out contingencies or possible consequences. It is separated from the giver of the information. Provided the information fits in with the supervisee's values and needs, change can then be internalized and not remain dependent upon constant reminders or surveillance. The information is power, depending upon its inherent value. That is, does it fit with the other's values and ideas? Is it useful and important? *The receiver of informational influence rapidly becomes independent of the influencer.* The use of informational power as a basis of influence applies to instances where you share your knowledge/ skills competencies through your way of teaching the supervisees. This stance also would include the acknowledgment of the possibly, as yet, unknown "answers," and offer opportunities for supervisees to learn how to face their work situations with increased autonomy. It also applies to the many other instances in agency life where supervisees learn from others—even from other supervisees.

### Learning Environments

Up to this point we have focused on you, the supervisor, teaching and devising the learning experiences. The main emphasis was on the substance of what needs to be learned and the diverse components, processes, and contingencies involved in your constructed approaches. A second way of arriving at what you will do is to look at the learning environment (with you and the supervisees as components within it) so as to examine how environments may demand, through their impinging tasks, particular knowledge and skills. This leading-edge transactional orientation, which directs attention to the environment's impact upon individuals, is currently encouraging research in diverse fields, including education, creativity, and child development (see, for example, Feldman, 1982). We shall use, as a primary example, the work of Kolb (1976); Kolb, Rubin, and McIntyre (1979).

Kolb developed a theory of "experiential learning" that began with the Lewinian formulation that behavior is a function of the person-environment interactions. At the person end of the transaction, he elaborated four "learning styles" by taking two dimensions of the learning process and juxtaposing them as Cartesian coordinates. These were (1) the *perceiving* or taking in of new situations in ways that range from concrete experience (sensing/feeling) to abstract conceptualization (thinking); and (2) the *processing* or dealing with the situations in ways that range from active experimentation (doing) to reflective observation (watching). Kolb proposed that all learning demands the perception and the processing processes and that the resultant learning styles are individually variable. The learners' dominant abilities may be the result of heredity and of particular past life experiences. They are also influenced by the demands of the current work environment. Learning, then, is transactional—partly related to what you have already learned and partly related to what is demanded by the environment. Your learning style may shift when the environment requires new responses (as, for example, when you move from the direct-service practitioner role to become a supervisor).

In Kolb's formulation, the four emphasized learning styles (or preferred ways of taking in and dealing with tasks) are termed *divergers,* who are sensors/feelers and watchers; *assimilators,* who mainly are thinkers and watchers; *convergers,* who are the thinkers and doers; and, finally, *accommodators,* who are sensors/feelers and doers. Finding these variations among persons led Kolb to look at the environment to see what, if any, variations in learning environments might have a relationship to persons' preferred way of learning.

Wolfe and Kolb (1979) described the research on various occupations and the learning requirements in different fields (as emphasized by schooling and subsequent working situations), and found that different occupations and disciplines valued distinctive learning styles. For example, the divergers perceive concretely and process reflectively. They start with what they see, then generalize—a demand affecting, for example, social scientists and organizational development consultants. The assimilators perceive experience abstractly and process it reflectively. They start with an idea and then reflect about it from different perspectives—an emphasis demanded in research and design. Still others, the convergers, perceive abstractly and process their experience actively. They start with an idea and try it out through experiments or tests to see if it works, which is a valued approach for engineers. The accommodators perceive experience concretely and process it actively. They start with what they see, hear, touch, and feel, and then move to try it out in action—orientations stressed in marketing and sales.

McCarthy (1980) studied Kolb's learning-style types, compared these with investigations by several others whose work followed similar lines, added the dimensions of right- and left-hemisphere brain-research findings, and developed a composite model that aimed to translate major learning-style characteristics and theories into directions for teaching. She relabeled Kolb's descriptive categories with more down-to-earth (and positive) descriptors and built instructional formats matched to the predispositions of the learners. Accenting each learner's strengths, Kolb's divergers became McCarthy's *innovative* (imaginative) learners; assimilators became the *analytic* (or theoretical) learners; convergers became the *commonsense* (practical) learners, and accommodators became the *dynamic* (intuitive) learners.

It is interesting to consider the varied tasks facing social work learners, since the profession's tasks are diverse and since various specialties within the profession make demands that relate to each of the four styles. For example, workers with families and groups, consultants, and administrators would need diverger strengths: seeing situations from many perspectives and organizing the relationships into a gestalt. Others, specializing in research, planning, policy, and model building, would need the assimilator's strengths: developing conceptual schemes, prioritizing, and selecting among the alternatives. Others, for example, discharge planners, supervisors, and those following a particular theoretical framework, would draw on converger strengths: problem solving and evaluating solutions and consequences through application of known methods. And finally, others whose work is outreach, community development, and training might draw specially on the accommodator's strengths: risking, acting, dealing with change. Such "typecasting" is hazardous at best. Social work practice spans all these styles. In applying Kolb's learning-style inventory to several classes of master's degree students, we have found that students fall into each of the four categories, although a preponderance have tested as accommodators.

Also of interest, in any case, is Kolb and Fry's discussion (1975) of business students' responses to the learning demands emphasized in various teaching approaches. *Divergers* preferred open-ended, self-directive activities and needed to know the time limits and constraints so as to learn more in given situations where the goal was to apply and test ideas. They liked the open-ended, unstructured homework papers and self-diagnostic activities, rather than peer interactions in class. They seemed to react most to the lecturer as a person, to conferences, talks by experts, and faculty feedback on papers. *Assimilators* did not like group discussion except in those activities requiring some conformity to directions, rules, assigned readings, and theory inputs. They (as well as the divergers) liked lectures, but they seemed to prefer the presence of the authority figure per se. They also valued assigned readings, exams, and tasks. *Convergers* liked the expert inputs and readings that linked class to the real world. They least liked open-ended peer discussions and group autonomy. *Accommodators* liked discussion classes, peer interaction, lack of structure, and lack of an authority figure.

These findings are cited to suggest the variability in how congenial and familiar the different instructional approaches are to the differential learning orientations among students—whether in the classroom or in agency work. While we do not assume that you have a measure of your supervisees' tested styles, these ideas might help you understand how your ways of presenting information may click with some and not with others. Let us turn from the individuals to the learning-environment side of the transaction.

Wolfe and Kolb's research (1979) on occupations, career demands, and the attraction of individuals to certain fields led to a conceptualization of working and learning environments as differentially complex (Kolb and Fry, 1975). That is, the environmental press could stress behavioral, affective, symbolic, or perceptual complexities, and it could exert differing role pressures in terms of the quality of the environment.

For example, environments that are *behaviorally complex* place emphasis on action, decision making, and generating useful results; and those who work in these situations face role pressures for quality decisions and solutions. *Affectively complex* environments require empathy and understanding, and they involve role pressures of having an appropriate value system so as to use these attributes. In *symbolically complex* environments, the demand is for the integration of complex issues through abstract reasoning, and for logic, comprehensiveness, and currency in the needed knowledge domain. Here, role pressures are related to the depth and quality of the thought processes. Finally, in *perceptually complex* environments, persons must be able to function in stable *or* turbulent situations with role pressures related to what they recognize, become aware of, attend to, and experience as the organization's shared reality.

In other words, behavioral complexity involves impulsive and active involvement; affective complexity involves childlike perspectives of wonder and freshness, and immersion in the immediate, concrete experience; symbolic complexity involves seeing situations from many viewpoints, thinking in terms of analysis and synthesis, and having freedom from the constraints of previous concepts; and perceptual complexity involves reflectiveness, manipulation of images or symbols, and speculations.

Then, according to Kolb and Fry's formulations, behaviorally complex learning environments focus on doing and completing tasks; affectively complex environments emphasize feelings, values, and opinions; symbolically complex ones emphasize problem solving, analysis, and best solutions; and perceptually complex environments emphasize understanding.

Fry (1978) described these learning environments further:

*Behaviorally complex*—These aim for learners to apply skills and knowledge to practical problems that they will probably experience professionally. The focus of information flow is on getting the task done, which is derived from previous work, plans, critiques, evaluations of progress, preparing for a presentation, and so forth. Output is evaluated against criteria of practicality and feasibility. The learners make their own decisions about the use of their time. Choice and actions at one point in time influence what occurs next. The teacher is a consultant or coach, available at the learners' request to summarize or impart knowledge of the field.

*Affectively complex*—These aim for learners to experience events or activities and become aware of their feelings as they do. The main sources of information dealt with are personal feelings, values, opinions, and ideas in the present situation. Feedback is personalized according to the learners' own needs and learning goals. Learners are encouraged to express their feelings, opinions, and values. Teachers portray themselves as models of the profession and colleagues, so that learning occurs through identification.

*Symbolically complex*—These focus on solving problems and obtaining solutions through the use of theory and analytical skills. The source of information is abstract ("there and then" rather than "here and now"). Content is derived from readings, lecture, compiled data, and the like. Performance is evaluated against the right or best answer as judged on the basis of a body of knowledge or the teacher's expert opinion. The learning activities and communications are governed by rules of inference, methods, concepts, often subject to the learners' memory recall. The teacher is the expert authority—interpreting the field of knowledge or judging what is correct, competent, acceptable performance, and enforcing rigor, methods, or rules as stipulated by the body of knowledge involved.

*Perceptually complex*—These aim for learners to understand, to know how and why things relate to one another. The main source of information comes from examining how things happen, and from focusing on the process as well as reviewing past events. The learners determine the criteria for evaluation and are left to devise their own criteria for performance. They are encouraged to observe, listen, write, think, and discuss in order to determine the meaning and relevance of the content for themselves. The teachers are nondirective, reflective, and nonevaluative. They teach by helping learners to discover their own perspectives, insights, and so forth.

Perhaps these descriptions can be used to help you review the demands of your organizational setting, or those you have known in the past. Also, they may help you conceptualize which aspects in the above descriptions are mainly stressed and which are most salient for the particular assignments you and your supervisees face, according to the demands of your work. The match of persons with learning environments and the tasks that impinge upon them is an area of study in its infancy, but as a facilitator of performance, it appears to hold more promise than IQ or achievement measures. Mitroff and Kilmann (1978) (see Note 2) have approached the area of knowledge development in the social sciences from a comparable perspective, which also yields four very different traditions and valued normative conditions affecting the methods of inquiry and orientations of individual investigators. Davis explored the fit between cognitive style orientations and work environments in service provision arenas (Davis, 1984). You are not likely to have a learning-style inventory of either your supervisees' or your own preferred learning styles. But perhaps the descriptions of these subtle differences (as well as reflection on your responses to the "Irregular Object" presented in Chapter 2) and your now sensitized review of the complexities stressed by your organization can offer clues to inform the ways you will individualize your teaching approaches.

## ISSUES AND CHOICE POINTS

The array of components we have examined is, in essence, kaleidoscopic—possibly dazzling or intimidating. But could it be otherwise? We shifted from types of teaching/learning events (supervision, training, consultation) to the work of social workers and the competencies needed by supervisors and by supervisees. We saw the differentiated functions that separate supervisors from supervisees in the task and context areas. Then, the career socializing and teaching functions became the focus as we looked at supervisee learning needs. All the while, aspects of the organization, of power differentials, and of self-questions shifted from periphery to center view. Next, various approaches to teaching and their interior elements came to the foreground, and the design became variegated again. Elements of power and control reappeared in new configurations. And finally, the view turned again to individual differences, this time in learning styles, and then back to variability of demand in learning environments—a four-figured vision that magnified emotional, behavioral, perceptual, and intellectual stresses.

Now we return to teaching as a many-faceted design. We aim to sharpen your perspective by looking at bits and pieces arranged within an arbitrary classification for focus. We shall highlight certain issues that require choice on your part, so as to place some order on the complexity and to help you elaborate a system for supervision that will match the complexity of the situation.                          •

### The Context

Returning to the context, the situation that connects you with supervisees, the choice becomes, *How invested in the teaching aspect of supervision will you be?* And the underlying issue here concerns the supportiveness of the organization. You have examined organizations you have known (Chapters 4 and 6), and now, with their learning possibilities in mind, you may re-view the scenes. You may consider their stresses and climates as learning environments. Every organization has an overall atmosphere that envelops you and supervisees (and all staff) with its powerful impact and its daily "lessons" in diverse realms—behavior, feelings, ideas, and points of view.

As you consider how committed and adventuresome you will become in the teaching aspect of your work, and how much of a priority it will be, you will imagine the rewards for such energy. Such efforts may be valued or not by "them" (your superiors, others in your hierarchical level). The teaching aspect may (or may not) have consequences for your advancement, monetary gain, or other forms of acknowledgment. Its value may (or may not) derive from the supervisees' heightened morale and professional development, from your awareness that services are improved, or it may come only from your own sense of self-reward for your involvement.

Ultimately, you are "them"; you and "the system" are one. You will need to consider many contingencies that affect the you/them unit, attending every practice act and affecting whether or not you will make waves or play it safe. As you reflect on the consequences of energies devoted to matters beyond the fulfillment of the routinized and developed ways of meeting the workaday tasks, you will evaluate your own credibility, vulnerability, confidence, and know-how and assess what knowing more would ask of you in job and time pressures.

As you consider such issues, you may review the whole gamut of teaching/learning events within the organization—the case conferences, unit meetings, special speakers, and training events (which may be the first to "disappear" when budgets are cut). Within this whole spectrum, you may find ways of connecting your teaching within or through these formats. You will consider how much of the teaching you share and how *central* you must be in the supervisees' learnings.

### The Supervisor/Supervisee Relationship

The working relationship between you and the supervisees determines what you do and how you do it, and the choice becomes, *How do you see yourself in relation to the supervisees' learning needs?* We have emphasized this theme from many perspectives. There are many aspects here: Do you have one main mindset, or are there diversified shifts over time—as a response to a supervisee's career development, or as a response to what needs to be learned, or as a response to where each supervisee may be coming from? But your self-view is a critical element at any given moment in time and space with each supervisee, even though it may be singular or variegated in and of itself. You will assume a working role in respect to what should be known (a functional relationship) that will demand a complementary role for the supervisees. Hart (1982) describes the pattern of relationships in "clinical supervision" as teacher/student, therapist/client, or colleague-collaborators. We have described role possibilities as coach, counselor, and conferee, and we have identified teaching perspectives that may inform your instructional stance: assessor-instructor, facilitator, or ecologist. Other elements coloring the working relationship are the power dynamics involved (expert, referent, informational), as well as the voluntariness or compliance aspects these introduce. Many, not one, types of teaching are involved. Each approach differs in terms of the amount of the teacher's prerogatives that are shared with the supervisees, and the balance that results may condition the working relationship in a basic way—to be one where supervisors act as either expert, as co-inquirer, or as administrator/planner of the learning environment.

### The Content

The issue here involves what needs to be learned. The question becomes, *What balance will you strike among the needs and expectations of clients, organization, and supervisees' learning?* Involved here are the distinctions among different types of knowing that are important for performance. These types range from *abstract* knowledge "about" to *applied* knowledge and actions. These include: the values and ethical imperatives that must condition social work practice and organizational interests, inclusive of their fit or misfit; a conceptualization of the work (competencies in the realms of task, context, relationship, and self); and orientations that may emphasize and focus upon the requisite learnings (skills/information, self, transaction, and pattern).

Moreover, once you and the supervisee have determined what needs to be learned and which specifics need emphasis, you face decisions. These decisions include the variety or limited amount of conceptualizations that exist for problem situations, client behavior, and action options; and how many or few options and orientations you will acknowledge. Such decisions will affect the approaches that you will teach or tolerate as valid. It is also important to determine the learning domains that need emphasis and the congenial ways of instruction that are available. For example, in the domains of thinking, feeling, valuing, and acting, possible approaches include telling, self-instruction, guided asking, and interactions. The "best" approach within the domains remains unclear, but some planned sequence needs to be followed, regardless. Should it be know, then judge? Or act, then feel? Or block the emotions, then think and decide? Lewin and Grabbe (1945) described the separateness of the cognitive and values domains. Zajonc's research (1980) similarly separates changes in feelings from those in the thinking realm. So, you are open to devise your most congenial way of sequencing the learning. There is little room for dogmatism at the present time.

### The Teaching/Learning Process

The process of teaching and learning (in fact inseparable from content in dynamics and issues) raises the basic issue, *How open will you be in how you teach?* Various instructional orientations have been described in terms of closed/open, didactic/evocative, experiential/interactional, and discussional (in its variations). These, with their emphases and priorities, affect the diversity and flexibility of the instruction. Other process considerations include orientations to the learning process itself: the universal stages involved in moving from the unknown to the known, plus individualistic variability as, for example, in preferred learning styles and the match or mismatch between supervisor's and supervisees' ways of perceiving and dealing with information. Moreover, the one-to-one stance (supervisor/supervisee) and stances in a more public realm (team or group contexts) are, first, part of the openness and variability of the learning process, and second, an element of power and locus of control. Matters of supervisee autonomy as a self-directed learner and matters of learning the problem-solving aspects related to practice are discussed with respect to the classroom (Bloom, 1976, p. 9) and in training groups (Harrison, 1977). Another learning-process issue, linked closely with context, concerns the openness of the organization to the supervisees' venture into untried realms, the value of becoming more adept at the known (specialization emphases) versus acquiring new knowledge and skills.

*Structures.* Among the many structural arrangements you will make (frequency of meetings, initiation of the meetings, composition and setting for them, length, development of agendas, and other supports for the teaching), a central underlying question is, *When do you give feedback and how do you learn about the substance of the work?* Here, the matter of obtrusive/unobtrusive means of learning about the supervisees' practice and the timing of your response become the major issues that will distinguish your supervisory style and impact on all the other elements: context, relationship, content, and process.

As we have discussed, the timing of feedback (in the moment, or immediately after the episode of service, or at a later, second teaching/learning conference remote in time and place from the practice) will need consideration, as will the presence or absence of other observers. This decision powerfully shapes your work as well as the decisions regarding dealing with common problems of supervisees in a group context and venturing into the individuals' learning issues publicly in the group, or only privately in the individual supervisory session.

*Evaluation.* As a final issue related to the complexity of teaching possibilities, the question is, *How will you evaluate your teaching efforts?* The underlying issue here is your ongoing professional development, your stance as a continuous co-learner. Depending upon the format (context) of your supervision, there is opportunity for the informal, process remarks of appreciation, dissatisfaction, anger, and so forth from the supervisees, especially if you allow room for these reactions as part of their evaluation. You also may gain some evidence of the impact of your teaching from observations of supervisees' changed behavior and knowledge acquisition. Remember, however, that these learnings may not be directly attributable to your teaching effectiveness; they may have been learned from many other sources. Mostly, assessment of supervisors' teaching remains *ad hoc* at best. This is an area where you may plan your own means of self-evaluation, for example, through tape recordings of your teaching process and reflective examination of your methods over time, through setting objectives you wish to pursue in your teaching methods and ways you may measure your progress.

## THE ACTION CYCLE

Now that you have reflected on these issues and come up with some preferences about how you will order your approach, and now that you have determined what choices you will make in your work, we briefly outline some general stages of the teaching process:

1. *Plan the climate of your teaching/learning situation.* This will be determined by the context, relationship, structure, and process aspects we have just reviewed.
2. *Assess the learning needs with the supervisee.* This will be informed by the presenting task requirements from an organizational perspective; from background material you may have received about the supervisees' prior life and formal learning and working experiences; and from in-person dialogue with the supervisees that includes their expectations, interests, felt competencies, and confidence. This may be augmented by your observations of how the supervisees begin and take hold of the initial assignments. You also may begin to sense, through discussion and observation, their general learning-style strengths.
3. *Develop a contract with the supervisees* that specifies the ground rules of your supervisory arrangement and the desired emphases of the teaching from your perspective and the supervisee's perspective. As a central part of this planning, you will carry out stages 4–10 of the action cycle.

4. *Formulate the main goals for service and for learning.* This will include discussing and reviewing the means you will use, as well as the time frame and methods for evaluation of progress toward and achievement of the goals.

5. *Select and order the goals, subgoals, and performance objectives.* This will enable you to arrive at priorities, sequence of attention, aspects of emphasis, and so forth.

6. *Determine the conditions for the learning.* This will relate to the specified goals (e.g., how you will teach these, who else will be involved in the learning events, what content, process, and structural elements will apply).

7. *Initiate your mutually planned supervisory design.*

8. *Give feedback and discuss achievement of learning objectives.* This will be done regularly, as part of the teaching (weekly, monthly, or as arranged).

9. *Keep your design up to date.* As certain learning objectives are achieved (or unanticipated problems arise), *substitute or add* by mutual negotiation different or new learning objectives, *assess* the progress at specified times, *identify* new emphases or different teaching/learning formats.

10. *Renew a supervisory design.* Your renewed design will be based on the new insights that have emerged.

## CONCLUSION

Among your major functions as supervisor, you will work differentially with each supervisee in the areas of career socializing and teaching. In your work, these are the functional imperatives that will vary most in terms of who you are supervising. They will form the heart of your efforts to aid directly in the supervisees' professional development and job satisfaction. The career socializing work will be carried out through role modeling, mainly, and also through periodic discussion and explanation of issues and events. Mostly, it will be achieved through *how* you perform your other functions (e.g., from your efforts in the realms of humanizing, managing tension, evaluating). That leaves *teaching* as your major deliberately constructed emphasis. This is the function we have emphasized in this chapter. It is the place where your energies, deployed within your heavy workload, may be differentially apportioned. Toward this end we have presented many variables that may contribute to your informed approach in an area of enormous complexity.

When you help another person learn the important particulars of the professional assignment, you are engaged in one area within the larger realm of adult education. Adult education, a territory that has been named *andragogy,* has grown enormously in the last several decades. It is an area characterized by both conceptual developments and fads. The flavor of these shifts is captured by Knowles, one of adult education's gurus, in reminiscences after forty-four years' involvement. He cites these "fads": From 1935 to 1950 it was group work, especially group discussion. After World War II mass media (radio) and audio-visual aids were "in." In the 1950s, it was human relations training, programmed instruction, and community development; in the 1960s personal growth, encounters, and organization development; business games and simulations; . . . in the 1970s computer assisted instruction, competency-based education, multimedia, modular learning, behavior modification, behavior modeling, self-directed learning, individualized instruction, learner controlled instruction, contract learning (Knowles, 1979).

Social workers work inductively, pragmatically, and empirically. They rely on a value base and belief system and on *ad hoc,* partial knowledge rather than generalizations or laws. This is part of the uniqueness and appeal of a practice with persons—one that demands intuition, creativity, judgment, inprovisation, and expressiveness more than rules, formulas, or cause-and-effect and logical relationships. Some of the time social workers will work methodically, systematically, and consistently, so as to apply what has been determined to be most beneficial in such instances (i.e., they must be *competent*). And yet they also need to work in situations with few or no known guidelines to rely upon (i.e., they must be *imaginative*). They are immersed with the actual, yet seek the possible. They deal concretely with specific events more than abstractions. Yet they must also seek to relate the specifics to more general instances, and they must draw back, reflect, and devise ways not merely to "live with" the given, but to change it. Their plans and interventions are affected by what has been learned empirically to be effective with others, to the extent that they are aware of and committed to contributing to systematic evaluation of their own impact and that of others. As Lewis pointed out, where any given supervisees may be, both in terms of judgments (from rule following to using various theoretical formulations) and in terms of actions, will differ according to their professional level of preparation (1982).

But two central learning objectives will pertain, no matter the job level or the supervisory teaching orientation you use:

1. Supervisees must master the particulars needed to handle themselves with respect to others, to the environment, and to the world of ideas and tasks—that is, they must learn "the rules of the game."
2. Once they have achieved some measure of comfort in the first area, they may move beyond this coping-learning to innovation and development of a unique style of working.

These basic sets of learnings are related to discipline and innovation and, therefore, to discovery and invention.

*Discovery* is a process of inquiry into *what is.* It comprises much of what formal academic work emphasizes, including the methods of science, the rules of the experiment and the canons of logic, and the conventions of analysis and systematic observation. Through these mainly verbal/linguistic and mathematical skills, you try to make sense out of the world and pursue an incremental, methodological means of discovering. Through this discovery orientation you learn the rudiments of a particular form and then become proficient in controlling the elements so as to produce the expected outcome by means of the selected use of your most reliable actions (i.e., various intervention methods and related techniques).

*Invention* is a process of creation of *what could be.* Involved here is disciplined use of the imagination, rather than leaving this to chance. Sometimes this process is called divergent thinking (entertaining many possible perspectives), or lateral or first-stage thinking (breaking away from known modes of processing information and introducing discontinuities), or intuitive thinking (moving from the inner world to the outer rather than vice-versa), or holistic, right-brain thinking. Invention and artistry involve a recombination of elements in a realm where right versus wrong is less important than novelty, new insights, and sometimes a reorganization of elements into a composition never before expressed: the creative (not merely the idiosyncratic).

A clue to understanding the distinctiveness of discoveries and inventions is suggested by Feldman's theory and research on individuals' achievements in both scientific and cultural realms. He explores the general to specific learnings as phases affecting a mastery range of learning accomplishments, and he also finds a place for the genetic, gifted, extraordinary accomplishment of young prodigies within the typology (1980). Feldman differentiates among the learned achievements that are associated with universal, cultural, and specific discipline-based expectancies and demands. These lead to certain universal achievements learned by all (e.g., talking), to culturally determined achievements (e.g., speaking English versus German), to specific achievements related to criteria levels of mastery determined by a particular discipline, and finally to idiosyncratic or unique or creative accomplishments attained by fewer individuals. These latter ones require special environmental inputs and highly specific tutoring. From his study of prodigious achievement, the following interplay of forces is proposed: the person's own unique qualities; the knowledge domain sufficiently evolved to serve as inspiration, resource, and challenge to the aspiring neophyte; a set of catalytic (educational) forces to help the learner move through the elements of the knowledge domain; and the opportunity in time and space that permits all the other forces to interact.

As supervisor, you will be dealing with the twin requirements of discipline and innovation, of discovery and invention, in your own work as well as encouraging these attributes in others. You will, at times, need to redirect priorities in supervisees, for some will wish to innovate without possessing the prerequisite discipline first, without knowing "the rules" before changing them. In other instances you may need to push others to dare to move beyond the obvious, to entertain the new possibilities. We shall consider this further in Chapter 8 as we look more carefully at what we call the *opportunity field*—the possibilities that await supervisors and supervisees who wish to improve upon the given and build new dimensions into their work.

## NOTES

1. The Hawthorne effect (a sacred cow of researchers) is still taught as an important concept to guard against, despite the fact that reanalysis of the data more recently disproves the findings of the original studies (which were that the main effects were due to the attention and special treatment of the experimental group) (Parsons, 1974).

2. Mitroff and Kilmann first examine the traditional method of scientific inquiry, that of the *analytic scientist*; and then they explore three other emerging styles of inquiry—the *conceptual theoretic,* the *conceptual humanistic,* and the *particular humanistic.* These emergent styles are posed as valuable approaches for the social sciences, neither less truthful nor less valid than the conventional ways of thinking about and practicing science. Each style of inquiry is governed by a different logic, ideology, and methodology. The styles are attuned to different phases of the inquiry process and may be integrated or applied sequentially in approaching the complexity characteristic of social problems and issues affecting the human condition. Interestingly, the analytic scientist and the conceptual theorist place greatest value on thinking while the conceptual humanist and the particular humanist value feeling first, thinking secondarily. (Mitroff and Kilmann, 1978)

## REFERENCES

AKAMATSU, T. JOHN, "The Use of Role-Play and Simulation Technique in the Training of Psychotherapy," in *Psychotherapy Supervision,* Allen K. Hess, ed. New York: John Wiley, 1980.

ALEXANDER, CHAUNCEY, "Implications of the NASW Standards for Social Service Manpower," *Journal of Education for Social Work,* 11, no. 1 (Winter 1975), 3–8.

ANDERSON, JOSEPH D., "Structured Experiences in Growth Groups in Social Work," *Social Casework,* 51, no. 5 (May 1980), 277–287.

_____, "Human Relations Training and Group Work," *Social Work,* 20, no. 3 (May 1975), 195–199.

AUSTIN, MICHAEL J., *Supervisory Management for the Human Services.* Englewood Cliffs, N.J.: Prentice-Hall, 1981.

AXELROD, JOSEPH, *The University Teacher as Artist.* San Francisco: Jossey-Bass, 1973.

BLOOM, MARTIN, "Analysis of the Research on Educating Social Work Students," *Journal of Education for Social Work,* 12, no. 3 (Fall 1976), 3–10.

_____, *The Paradox of Helping.* New York, John Wiley, 1975.

BRAMMER, LAWRENCE M., *The Helping Relationship: Process and Skills* (2nd ed.). Englewood Cliffs, N.J.: Prentice-Hall, 1979.

CARKHUFF, R.R., *Helping and Human Relations: A Primer for Lay and Professional Helpers* (Vols. 1 and 2). New York: Holt, Rinehart, & Winston, 1969.

CERTO, SAMUEL C., ed., *Sourcebook of Experiential Exercises: Interpersonal Skills.* Terre Haute, Ind.: Clearinghouse for Experiential Exercises, Bureau of Business Research, School of Business, Indiana State University, 1976.

CHERNISS, GARY, and EDWARD EGNATIOS, "Clinical Supervision in Community Mental Health," *Social Work,* 23, no. 3 (May 1978), 219–223.

CLARK, FRANK W., MORTON L. ARKAVA, and Associates, *The Pursuit of Competence in Social Work.* San Francisco: Jossey-Bass, 1979.

CURWIN, RICHARD L., and BARBARA S. FURMANN, *Discovering Your Teaching Self: Humanistic Approaches to Effective Teaching.* Englewood Cliffs, N.J.: Prentice-Hall, 1975.

DANISH, STEVEN, and ALLEN HAUER, *Helping Skills: A Basic Training Program.* New York: Behavioral Publications, 1973.

DAVIS, ANNE, "An Approach to Resolving Issues in the Workplace: A Study of Cognitive Styles," unpublished Ph.D. dissertation, University of Louisville, 1984.

DINERMAN, MIRIAM, "Options in Social Work Manpower and Education," *Social Work,* 20, no. 5 (September 1975), 348–352.

DRUM, DAVID, and EUGENE J. KNOTT, *Structured Groups for Facilitating Development.* New York: Human Sciences Press, 1977.

EGAN, GERARD, *Interpersonal Living: A Skills Contract Approach to Human Relations Training in Groups.* Belmont, Calif.: Wadsworth, 1976.

————, *The Skilled Helper.* Monterey, Calif.: Brooks/Cole, 1975.

FELDMAN, DAVID H., "Developmental Approaches to Giftedness and Creativity," *New Directions for Child Development,* 17, no. 3 (September 1982), 31–45.

————, *Beyond Universals in Intellectual Development: Six Interpretive Essays.* New York: Praeger, 1980.

FINE, SIDNEY A., and WRETHA W. WILEY, *An Introduction to Functional Job Analysis: A Scaling of Selected Tasks from the Social Welfare Field.* Kalamazoo, Mich.: W. E. Upjohn Institute for Employment Research, 1971.

FRENCH, JOHN R.P., and BERTRAM RAVEN, "The Bases of Social Power," in *Group Dynamics* (3rd ed.), Dorwin Cartwright, and Alvin Zander, eds. New York: Harper & Row, 1968, 259–269.

FRY, RONALD E., "Diagnosing Professional Learning Environments: An Observational Framework for Assessing Situational Complexity," unpublished Ph.D. dissertation, M.I.T., 1978.

GAGNÉ, ROBERT M., and LESLIE J. BRIGGS, *Principles of Instructional Design.* New York: Holt, Rinehart, & Winston, 1974.

GAZDA, GEORGE M., *Group Counseling: A Developmental Approach.* Boston: Allyn & Bacon, 1971.

GERMAIN, CAROL B., ed., *Social Work Practice: People and Environments.* New York: Columbia University Press, 1979.

GERMAIN, CAROL B., and ALEX GITTERMAN, *The Life Model of Social Work Practice.* New York: Columbia University Press, 1980.

GIFFORD, CUTHBERT, "Sensitivity Training and Social Work," *Social Work,* 13, no. 2 (April 1968), 78–86.

GILBERT, NEIL, and HARRY SPECHT, "Process Versus Task in Social Planning," *Social Work,* 22, no. 3 (May 1977), 178–183.

GITTERMAN, ALEX, "Comparison of Educational Models and Their Influences on Supervision," in *Issues in Human Services,* Florence W. Kaslow, and Associates. San Francisco: Jossey-Bass, 1972, 18–38.

GITTERMAN, ALEX, and IRVING MILLER, "Supervisors as Educators," in *Supervision, Consultation, and Staff Training in the Helping Professions,* Florence W. Kaslow, and Associates. San Francisco: Jossey-Bass, 1977, 100–114.

GOLDBERG, GALE, and RUTH R. MIDDLEMAN, "It Might Be a Boa Constrictor Digesting an Elephant: Vision Stretching in Social Work Education," *Contemporary Social Work Education,* 3, no. 3 (1980), 213–225.

————, "Visual Teaching," workshop and paper presented at the Annual Program Meeting, Council on Social Work Education, 1975.

GROSS, GERALD M., "Instructional Design: Bridge to Competence," *Journal of Education for Social Work,* 17, no. 3 (Fall 1981), 66–74.

HALEY, JAY, *Problem Solving Therapy.* San Francisco: Jossey-Bass, 1976.

HALL, EDWARD T., *The Silent Language.* New York: Doubleday, 1959.

HARRISON, ROGER, "Self-Directed Learning: A Radical Approach to Educational Design," *Simulation & Games,* 8, no. 1 (March 1977), 73–84.

HART, GORDON M., *The Process of Clinical Supervision.* Baltimore: University Park Press, 1982.

HESS, ALLEN, "Training Models and the Nature of Psychotherapy Supervision," in *Psychotherapy Supervision: Theory, Research, and Practice.* New York: John Wiley, 1980.

IVEY, ALLEN, *Microcounseling: Innovations in Interview Training.* Springfield, Ill.: Charles C. Thomas, 1971.

KADUSHIN, ALFRED, *Supervision in Social Work.* New York: Columbia University Press, 1976.

_____, "Supervisor-Supervisee: A Survey," *Social Work,* 19, no. 3 (May 1974), 288–297.

KAGAN, NORMAN, "Interpersonal Process Recall," *Journal of Nervous and Mental Disease,* 148, no. 4 (Fall 1969), 365–374.

KASLOW, FLORENCE W., "Training of Marital and Family Therapists," in *Supervision, Consultation, and Staff Training in the Helping Professions,* Florence W. Kaslow, and Associates. San Francisco: Jossey-Bass, 1977, 199–234.

KELMAN, HOWARD C., "Compliance, Identification, and Internalization: Three Processes of Attitude Change," *Journal of Conflict Resolution,* 2, no. 1 (March 1958), 51–60.

KNOWLES, MALCOLM, "How I Coped with Fads in Training," *Training and Development Journal,* 33, no. 9 (September 1979), 36–38.

KOLB, DAVID A., *Learning Style Inventory: Technical Manual.* Boston: McBer and Company, 1976.

KOLB, DAVID A., and RONALD FRY, "Towards an Applied Theory of Experiential Learning," in *Theories of Group Process,* Gary L. Cooper, ed. New York: John Wiley, 1975, 33–57.

KOLB, DAVID A., IRWIN M. RUBIN, and JAMES W. McINTYRE, *Organizational Psychology: An Experiential Approach* (3rd ed.). Englewood Cliffs, N.J.: Prentice-Hall, 1979.

KRELL, TERENCE C., "The Marketing of Organization Development: Past, Present, and Future," *Journal of Applied Behavioral Science,* 17, no. 3 (July-August-September 1981), 309–323.

LAMBERT, MICHAEL J., "Research and the Supervisory Process," in *Psychotherapy Supervision,* Allen Hess, ed. New York: Wiley, 1980.

LEWIN, KURT, and PAUL GRABBE, "Conduct, Knowledge and Acceptance of New Values," *The Journal of Social Issues,* 1, no. 3 (August 1945), 56–64.

LEWIS, HAROLD, *The Intellectual Base of Social Work Practice: Tools for Thought in a Helping Profession.* New York: Silberman Fund and Haworth Press, 1982.

_____, "The Structure of Professional Skill," in *Social Work in Practice,* Bernard Ross, and S.K. Khinduka, eds. Washington, D.C.: NASW, 1976, 3–13.

MAGER, ROBERT F., and PETER PIPE, *Analyzing Performance Problems.* Belmont, Calif.: Fearon Publishers, 1970.

MAIER, HENRY W., "Chance Favors the Prepared Mind," *Contemporary Social Work Education,* 4, no. 1 (May 1981), 14–21.

MARSHALL, ELDON K., P. DAVID KURTZ, and Associates, *Interpersonal Helping Skills: A Guide to Training Methods. Programs, and Resources.* San Francisco: Jossey-Bass, 1982.

McCARTHY, BERNICE, *The 4Mat System: Teaching to Learning Styles with Right/Left Mode Techniques.* Chicago: Excel, 1980.

McKEACHIE, WILBERT J., "Implications of Cognitive Psychology for College Teaching," *Learning, Cognition, and College Teaching: New Directions for Teaching and Learning,* no. 2 (1980), 85–94.

MEINERT, ROLAND G., "What Do Social Workers Do? A Survey," *Social Work,* 21, no. 2 (March 1976), 156–157.

MIDDLEMAN, RUTH R., "The Quality Circle: Fad, Fix, Fiction?" *Administration in Social Work*, 8, no. 1 (Spring 1984), 31-33.

————, "The Role of Perception and Cognition in Change," in *Handbook of Clinical Social Work*, Diana Waldfogel, and Aaron Rosenblatt, eds. San Francisco: Jossey-Bass, 1983.

————, "The Pursuit of Competence through Involvement in Structured Groups," in *Building Competence in Clients*, Anthony Maluccio, ed. New York: The Free Press, 1981. (a)

————, *A Study Guide for ACSW Certification*. Washington, D.C.: NASW, 1981. (b)

————, "Co-Leadership and Solo-Leadership in Education for Social Work with Groups," *Social Work With Groups*, 3, no. 4 (Winter 1980), 39-50. (a)

————, "The Use of Program: Review and Update," *Social Work With Groups*, 3, no. 3 (Fall 1980), 5-23. (b)

MIDDLEMAN, RUTH R., and GALE GOLDBERG, *Social Service Delivery: A Structural Approach to Social Work Practice*. New York: Columbia University Press, 1974.

————, "The Interactional Way of Presenting Generic Social Work Concepts," *Journal of Education for Social Work*, 8, no. 2 (Spring 1972), 48-57. (a)

————, "The Concept of Structure in Experiential Learning," in *1972 Annual Handbook for Group Facilitators*, William Pfeiffer, and John Jones, eds. Iowa City, Iowa: University Associates, 1972. (b)

MIDDLEMAN, RUTH R., and GARY B. RHODES, "Teaching the Practice of Supervision," *Journal of Education for Social Work*, 16, no. 3 (Fall 1980), 51-59.

MITROFF, IAN I., and RALPH H. KILMANN, *Methodological Approaches to Social Science*. San Francisco: Jossey-Bass, 1978.

MONTALVO, BRAULIO, "Aspects of Live Supervision," *Family Process*, 12, no. 4 (December 1973), 343-359.

MORRIS, WILLIAM C., and MARSHALL SASHKIN, *Organization Behavior in Action: Skill Building Experiences*. St. Paul, Minn.: West, 1976.

MORTON, THOMAS D., and P. DAVID KURTZ, "Educational Supervision: A Learning Theory Approach," *Social Casework*, 61, no. 4 (April 1980), 240-246.

MUNSON, CARLTON E., ed., *Social Work Supervision*. New York: The Free Press, 1979.

MURDAUGH, JESSICA, "Student Supervision Unbound," *Social Work*, 19, no. 2 (March 1974), 131-132.

NATIONAL ASSOCIATION OF SOCIAL WORKERS, *NASW Standards for the Classification of Social Work Practice, Policy Statement 4*, Task Force on Sector Force Classification. Silver Spring, Md.: NASW, 1981.

————, *Proceedings, National Conference on the Validation of Social Work Classifications*. Washington, D.C.: NASW, 1977.

PAPELL, CATHERINE P., "Sensitivity Training: Relevance for Social Work Education," *Journal of Education for Social Work*, 8, no. 1 (Winter 1972), 42-55.

PARSONS, H. McILVAINE, "What Happened at Hawthorne?" *Science*, 183, no. 4128 (March 8, 1974), 922-932.

PASCALE, RICHARD T., and ANTHONY G. ATHOS, *The Art of Japanese Management*. New York: Simon & Schuster, 1981.

PFEIFFER, J. WILLIAM, and JOHN E. JONES, eds., *Annual Handbook for Group Facilitators*. San Diego: University Associates, 1972 and yearly.

————, *A Handbook of Structured Experiences for Human Relations Training*. San Diego: University Associates, 1969 and yearly.

PRIMOFF, ERNEST E., *How to Prepare and Conduct Job Element Examinations.* Washington, D.C.: U.S. Civil Service Commission, Personnel Research and Development Center, Government Printing Office, 1975.

RAVEN, BERTRAM H., and ARIE W. KRUGLANSKI, "Conflict and Power," in *The Structure of Conflict,* Paul Swingle, ed. New York: Academic Press, 1970.

REYNOLDS, BERTHA C., *Learning and Teaching in the Practice of Social Work,* 1942; rpt. New York: Russell and Russell, 1965.

RICKERT, VERNON, and JOHN TURNER, "Through the Looking Glass: Supervision in Family Therapy," *Social Casework,* 59, no. 3 (March 1978), 131–137.

ROBINSON, VIRGINIA P., *The Dynamics of Supervision Under Functional Controls.* Philadelphia: University of Pennsylvania Press, 1949.

_____, *Supervision in Social Casework.* Chapel Hill, N.C.: University of North Carolina Press, 1936.

RUBEN, BRENT D., and RICHARD W. BUDD, *Human Communication Handbook: Simulations and Games.* Rochelle Park, N.J.: Hayden, 1975.

SCHWARTZ, WILLIAM, "The Classroom Teaching of Social Work with Groups," paper presented at the Annual Meeting of the Council on Social Work Education, 1964.

SERVEY, RICHARD E., *Teacher Talk: The Knack of Asking Questions.* Belmont, Calif.: Fearon, 1974.

SHAW, MALCOLM E., et al., *Role Playing: A Practical Manual for Group Facilitators.* San Diego: University Associates, 1980.

SHULMAN, LAWRENCE, *Skills of Supervision and Staff Management.* Itasca, Ill.: Peacock, 1982.

_____, *The Skills of Helping Individuals and Groups.* Itasca, Ill.: Peacock, 1979.

_____, *A Casebook for Social Work with Groups: The Mediating Model.* New York: Council on Social Work Education, 1969.

SMITH, LYNN, "Potential for Growth," *Courier-Journal Magazine* (August 22, 1982), 18–21.

SPIVACK, GEORGE, and MYRNA SHURE, *Social Adjustment of Young Children.* San Francisco: Jossey-Bass, 1974.

TAYLOR, JOHN, and REX WALFORD, *Learning and Simulation Game.* Beverly Hills, Calif.: Sage, 1972.

TIMNICK, LOIS, "Now You Can Be Likable, Confident, and Socially Successful for Only the Cost of Your Present Education," *Psychology Today* (August 1982), 43–49.

VAUGHAN, JAMES A., and SAMUEL D. DEEP, *Program of Exercises for Management and Organizational Behavior.* Beverly Hills, Calif.: Glencoe Press, 1975.

WALTER, GORDON A., and STEPHEN E. MARKS, *Experiential Learning and Change.* New York: John Wiley, 1981.

WOLFE, DONALD M., and DAVID A. KOLB, "Career Development, Personal Growth, and Experiential Learning," in *Organizational Psychology* (3rd ed.), David A. Kolb, Irwin M. Rubin, and James M. McIntyre, eds. Englewood Cliffs, N.J.: Prentice-Hall, 1979, 535–563.

ZAJONC, ROBERT B., "Feeling and Thinking," *American Psychologist,* 35, no. 2 (February 1980), 151–175.

# CHAPTER EIGHT
# ORGANIZATIONAL IMPERATIVES AND THE OPPORTUNITY FIELD

## INTRODUCTION

We have explored different possibilities and approaches to competent and imaginative supervision that are consistent with our preference for viewing the world as kaleidoscopic—as a scene of shifting patterns. These ideas have included using *super*vision, adopting a foursome mentality with the fourth dimension always seen as the constant, changeable context, a potentially expandable volume of imaginative possibilities. Mainly, we have urged you to assume a readiness to welcome the kaleidoscopic pattern of patterns that recur in slightly different configurations as you meet the challenges of the workplace—the work with your supervisees and others in the internal environment, and the felt forces from the external environment.

Such a view calls for a mindset beyond a mechanistic action-reaction or cause-and-effect, deterministic mentality. It goes beyond preoccupation with increasing disorder and diminishing options. This kind of viewpoint values fluctuations and instabilities as opportunities for seizing occasions to connect with the organization's thrust toward new levels of unimagined order out of chaos.

To think about and see the mission of supervision in kaleidoscopic terms involves accepting the inherent variability of supervisees, colleagues, and superiors. It involves seeing the uniqueness of individual clients and the differences between various populations and groups of clients. So, it involves an understanding of the diversity of social work practice contexts. As we suggested in Chapter 7, you and your supervisees can pursue competent performance, and then imaginative judgment making, in ways that are flexible yet supportive of common interests—the balancing of service and learning needs. You will be able to work toward these goals, always affected by your professional values and ethical injunctions, as you assume all of the nine functional imperatives (Chapter 5) that comprise your central supervisory task.

Now, we will explore the opportunities within your work situation for detouring around obstacles in your travel toward the possibilities for developing your supervisory relationships and staff responsibilities. Ultimately, such efforts will contribute to the organization's development as a system that meets its imperatives of stability (survival), effectiveness, and adaptability. These efforts will form the basis of your pursuit of internal integration (coordinated activities), quality service delivery, and linkages within the wider services systems of this service-dominated 20th-century world.

## THE OPPORTUNITY FIELD

The concept *opportunity field* owes much to Lewinian conceptualizations of life-space and field of forces, which characterize the person/environmental situation, and which affect persons' movement (learning, change) as a result of interaction with the immediate spatial context (*context* here means what people notice that is *actually* there and what they *imagine* is there) (Lewin, 1948; 1951). These forces may restrain or drive individuals and whole organizations toward either maintaining *status quo* (equilibrium) or introducing change (disequilibrium). We see the disequilibrium situations, so characteristic of current human service organizations, as the opportunity field—certain areas within your overall context. Here, there are the life-space forces (persons' needs, motivation, morale, goals, and ideals) and the boundary-zone forces (rewards and punishments, barriers and supports, and degrees of freedom for movement) that are interdependent, continuously fluctuating and competing for more room. If you think of these life-space and boundary-zone forces as an "opportunity field," a "window of opportunity"—rather than merely assume a reactive stance aimed to close a "window of vulnerability"—we think your basic strategy toward the complexities of the workplace will be a proactive one.

This special way of looking at problems as opportunities is analogous to "creating a new game" for supervision and service delivery. It involves a fundamental shift in your thinking about the forces in your surroundings; and it increases the possibilities that you will affect your context so that personal choice plays a greater role (Cohen, 1980). As described in Chapter 6, the human service organizations, even more than the for-profit organizations, possess greater areas of disequilibrium simply because the three competing domains (the policy, managerial, and service domains) operate with discordant values and norms that make coordinated action difficult at best. Still, these disjunctions also may be viewed as your "opportunity field." Their very discordance permits maneuvers and trade-offs to "play with" the barriers and loose linkages among these zones.

As noted by Minahan, during periods of reaction and contraction in responsive service provision, many social workers are active in promoting cooperation among organizations and groups. Yet conflict and dissension may increase within the social agencies themselves. This may happen, especially when "workers believe they have no control over their workplace and work life and no place to turn for information and support. Cynicism, distrust, and conflict result. Workers and their clients suffer" (Minahan, 1982, p. 207). Worries about job security, unemployed colleagues, and maintenance of quality service in the face of increasing workloads and diminishing resources are almost overwhelming, well-known consequences of boundary-zone encroachment on life-space circumstances. They constitute an opportunity field that must be spied with the magnifying glass. Nevertheless, we can identify the elements that comprise opportunity fields, so that they may be easier to identify and attend to.

The opportunity field is comprised of four dimensions: constraints, demands, supports, and context. The first three of these dimensions will enlarge or diminish relative to the fourth, context (which also shifts), and according to the tenor of the times. For example, the demands or constraints may seem mammoth (for example, when national security propaganda urges seeing the "window of vulnerability" instead of speaking to supports for human life-space needs and enlarging the "window of opportunity" for collaboration—rather than escalating defensive statements and suspicions). We prefer a reflexive stance where constraints, demands, and supports are seen as entities that may be turned to opportunities and as possibilities for inventing new "solutions" in order to test the possible degrees of freedom available for action.

Let us consider each of these dimensions with your workplace in mind. *Constraints* may include time pressures, resources, rules and regulations, cultural and organizational values, public opinion, and political vested interests. *Demands* include the needs of supervisors, of supervisees, clients, and the agency. Such needs are intimately related to the quantity and quality of services. *Supports* may come from agency colleagues, from organizational interdependence norms, from your own developed sense of competence, confidence, and other coping attributes, and from others outside the workplace, such as other colleagues and the profession, spouses, friends, and your diversionary interests, activities, and hobbies. Finally, the *context* is the workplace with its past, present, and future existences. These dimensions, in their interrelated magnitudes, will form the ground of the opportunity field.

Payne's study of the relationships among constraints, demands, and supports, and the behavior of individuals and groups suggests some clues of interest for us (1981). For example, persons in demanding, higher-level jobs experience stimulation and development rather than frustration and alienation because the relationship between their life-space and organizational boundary zone has generally strong

TABLE 8-1    The Opportunity Field

| DEMANDS | CONSTRAINTS | SUPPORTS | OUTCOMES |
|---------|-------------|----------|----------|
| High | Low | High | Stimulation |
| Low | High | Low | Alienation |
| Low | Low | High | Relaxation |
| High | High | Low | Exhaustion |

supports and moderate to low constraints. In contrast, assembly-line workers experience boredom and loss of interest, owing to a life-space boundary zone relationship characterized by low demands, low supports, and high constraints. Similarly, prison inmates and unemployed persons exhibit low degrees of psychological activity, apathy, and depression because their situations also are characterized by low demands, low supports, and high constraints. In situations where there are low demands, high supports, and low constraints, such as vacations and social gatherings with family or friends, the experience is one of relaxation and renewal. Finally, in situations of high demands, low supports, and high constraints, such as economic crises, divorce, and war, the affected individuals and groups are likely to experience exhaustion and/or collapse. The relationships among demands, constraints, supports, and outcomes are depicted in Table 8-1.

Following these observations derived from study of small groups, we hypothesize that the opportunity fields you would want to create are characterized by minimized constraints, moderate to high demands, and high supports. Further, we think that situations with high constraints or high demands need to be approached by deliberately using your position and connections within the organization to foster *higher* supports for those with whom you interact. These *higher* supports might apply to both superiors and subordinates, to colleagues, and to the creation of mechanisms for your own self-support. Moreover, while there may *appear* to be little room for making the high demands of the workplace more moderate, on closer reflection you may make some differences (in actuality or in your supervisees' *perceived* actuality) through such actions as job rotation, flexibility in daily hours, redistribution among caseloads, encouragement of interdependent planning and workload management within your unit, and so forth.

## THE OPPORTUNITY PERSPECTIVE

In large part, we are suggesting that the opportunity field will become more apparent when you adopt an opportunity perspective. Frequently, discussions of opportunity are couched in terms of costs. For example, if one program is supported, then there will be fewer resources for another one; or, certain actions are likely to preclude other ones (Gray and Gray, 1981). This political/economic view, one focused on limits, is derived from the world-as-lottery perspective, which assumes resources are scarce and inexorably diminishing. An alternative view of opportunity is one of benefits. This view includes the social purposes involved, not merely the political and economic considerations, and is attuned to matters of social efficiency and the social good. Such a view may hold several valued results: personal goal attainment by supervisors, supervisees, and clients; increased participation in decision-making processes; heightened identification with and commitments to the organization; satisfaction of individuals' intrinsic needs and organization's survival needs. The opportunity benefits rather than opportunity costs may lead to the pursuit of options that minimize constraints, maintain moderate to high demands, or increase supports.

Such a view does not lessen the responsibility for analyzing the forces involved in the opportunity field. It increases the possibilities of channeling energies and competencies in an effort to direct these forces toward individual, group, and agency benefits. While there may be some risks involved, and some need to make strategic choices as to which instances should be restructured from costs to benefits thinking, the challenge and potential developments of the organization and those who depend upon it may make considered action worth the risk.

To adopt an opportunity perspective, we shall propose two general strategies and then return, with certain other suggestions, to the dimensions of constraints, demands, and supports. As we have pointed out earlier, these will be mainly working-approximation possibilities. They will need to be tempered by your workplace, your credibility, competence, imagination, energy, security, and other personal and organizational attributes that would make opportunity-engaging attractive and worthwhile for you.

### The Proactive Stance

To establish among your supervisees a climate that will foster the pursuit of opportunities, you, as supervisor, must take preliminary initiatives. You can engage in proacting so as to develop group cohesion among your unit and help supervisees experience successes in risk taking (Johnson, 1981). Proacting involves your support of supervisees in bringing issues to the surface either directly or indirectly by asking questions during staff meetings and at other times that you structure for purposes of issue identification and strategic decision making. Also, proacting will require that you encourage supervisees in contributing to decisions for which you and the agency will be held accountable. Proacting is essential to creating the sense of we-ness (supports) in order to address constraints and demands not as problems but as opportunities.

### The "Reawakening" of the Structure

As a second general strategy, you may take the initiative to "reawaken" the structure by working with your supervisees to see what exists in the organization as possibilities, and by bringing them to life (Johnson, 1981). For example, you may identify mechanisms for input on current policy in the making, in addition to the more usual policy revision, and then work to elicit supervisees' contributions to these issues. In this way, supervisees will learn to experience the power of making unique, yet simultaneous contributions to the organization that are greater than the simple summing of their individual efforts. These processes may be seen as contributing to amplifying rather than damping out the possibilities and fluctuations. Thus, such moves and involvements may help transform the "givens" in the organization into higher levels of functioning. This growth will offer possibilities and probably more fluctuations, which may result in other opportunities for the reawakening process to happen again.

This is the mechanism of order out of chaos. Through these initiatives, you may enhance flexibility among your supervisees and help them gain competence in identifying available opportunity options. Further, you may build feelings of success and power in pursuing changes at these lower levels of the organization. You may find approaches to achieve what is needed, and to increase feelings of potency and interdependence. When problem situations are turned into possibility situations, cooperative behavior will be encouraged and competitive behavior will be discouraged. This will affect the very atmosphere of the workplace.

## THE FRAMEWORK OF CONSTRAINTS, DEMANDS, AND SUPPORTS

We now propose some further ideas within the constraints, demands, and supports framework. We first look at constraints.

### Constraints

We shall identify some ways in which you may work toward reducing constraints by treating them as opportunities.

*Develop a scarce resource.*   The human service organizations are increasingly beset with inadequate resources for meeting their service missions. These needs for resources offer opportunities for you and your supervisees to develop a resource that is important to the agency, yet not available widely, and that you can use as leverage in minimizing constraints. It has been noted that the world changes at one pace and organizations at another (Pruger, 1973). By developing a badly needed scarce resource, you and your supervisees can share in the benefits accruing to the organization. In part, this begins to make real the philosophy of involvement and participation in decision making, as well as increasing the potential for a long-term commitment to the organization. For example, in developing an important resource not available among higher-ranking members of your agency, you and your supervisees are likely to have power over them (Mechanic, 1962). Moreover, if you solidify your grasp on the competencies associated with this scarce resource, it is less likely that you or your supervisees will be easily replaceable (Mechanic, 1962). This in itself constitutes an important reduction in constraint. Scarce resources that you might develop may be in the areas of program development, program evaluation, grant writing, needs assessment, and strategic planning.

*Employ the principle of least contest.* In attempts to minimize the negative consequences of constraint, it will be important for you and your supervisees to exert the least pressure necessary to loosen constraining forces. It has been noted that force tends to generate counterforce. Low-pressure initiatives tend to evoke less resistance, so they are more likely to result in success (Middleman and Goldberg, 1974). One constraint that confronts many social service professionals is the tendency for agencies to proliferate forms and other types of mandatory paperwork. The more forms there are to be completed, the less time will be available for working with clients and the community in delivering effective services. This is an element of the quality/quantity dilemma, which we have emphasized throughout the book.

Since rules and procedures are never self-implementing (Pruger, 1973), you and your supervisees might opt to complete only those forms that seem to be related most directly to ensuring quality of service delivery (e.g., eligibility certification). Such limited compliance is likely to result in even greater emphasis on paperwork from the higher level. Another option might be to organize your clients to protest about limitations on staff time in working with them to meet their needs. Again, this approach is likely to trigger more pressure from higher-ups, as they interpret the client protest as an indication of worker deficiencies in service delivery.

From a least-contest perspective, you and your supervisees might employ a lower-level strategy designed to lessen the constraint of too many forms in the interest of higher quality and quantity of service delivery. You and your supervisees might work with other supervisors and supervisees in identifying alternatives for dealing with this constraint. You might develop a task group to develop new forms that are fewer in number and that capture all the information required by the agency and its funding sources. Then you would be in a position to propose your redesigned forms as a method for enhancing quality and quantity of service delivery, as well as worker and agency accountability. You and your supervisees are likely to be more successful with this approach, since decision makers attach more credibility to policy- or procedure-change initiatives that emphasize improved service than to initiatives that they perceive to be only in the self-interest of supervisors and supervisees (Patti, 1974).

*Capitalize on staffing differences.* We have described the current human service organization as comprised of a heterogeneous staff from diverse backgrounds and career socialization experiences. We have discussed the inevitability that staff members will have differing perspectives and interests that they deem valuable and supportive to working and surviving in their career choice. This diversity may be viewed as a constraint or as an opportunity to be exploited. As Shortell (1982) found in the health organizations, it may be easier for workers to empathize with their clients than to empathize with or understand one another's roles.

In Chapter 7 we described, as part of the competence you will wish to extend, various ways to acknowledge and deal with such differences through the particulars of your teaching design for supervision. Beyond this, you may capitalize on these differences through distinguishing among the service-delivery tasks and developing career assignments and occupational routes that help supervisees perform in areas suited to their interests and potentials. You may highlight and distinguish between the generic and specialized competencies, seek job-enrichment opportunities, and find ways to enhance collaborative, respectful, interdependent pursuit of agency goals. In many subtle ways, through how you devise, apportion, and structure the workload, you set the tone of mutual respectfulness and mutual striving toward valued activity.

*Use rules wisely.* Rules and regulations are a fact of organizational life. Often they are viewed as major constraints that must be tolerated, if not subverted. Mechanic suggested a more flexible orientation to the uniformity and coordination that rules and standards aim to achieve:

> It should be clear that full compliance to all the rules at all times will probably be dysfunctional for the organization. Complete and apathetic compliance may do everything but facilitate achievement of organizational goals. (Mechanic, 1962, p. 594)

As Filley (1978) pointed out, rules can be used (1) as obstacles to freedom when they are inflexible and not understood, (2) as barriers when they change at the whim of the supervisor or administrator, or (3) as useful tools for creating freedom and effective action. His parable of the traffic light and two towns highlights how rules may be simply traditional, arbitrary, or tools for coordinating action. In the first small town, the traffic light was donated by the town's founder and placed by the town's center near the only hotel. Over the years, the light broke down. No one knew how to repair it or wished to bother the benefactor. So, the traffic pattern had to shift away from the center, and the hotel gradually went out of business. Still, the light remained as a monument of earlier times and to tradition. In a second town, the mayor installed three traffic lights, but developed the rule that each morning he had to be telephoned so as to determine whether red would mean stop or go. In time, the necessary telephone lines grew extensive and his daily calls and decisions kept him so involved with the traffic light that he had time for nothing else. In fact, he was eventually hit by an outsider who did not know that green meant stop on that particular day. So they finally hired a city manager. He declared that red would mean stop and green go; and gradually the townspeople could predict one another's behavior and their own actions were coordinated. Although one person thought the system was too impersonal, most saw their time better used and found more freedom to pursue the nonroutine matters and creative effort from knowing what to expect (Filley, 1978, pp. 11–14).

In using rules wisely, you and your supervisees need to become knowledgeable so as to distinguish the merely traditional, nonfunctional rules from the arbitrary and the useful rules that simplify and coordinate while leaving more room for nonroutine activities. Moreover, you may look outside the organization to rules and regulations contained in the governmental and other policies that are pertinent to the service delivery of your agency. For example, if you work in an agency receiving Title XX funds and recognize that this policy contained provision for funding of primary preventive services if such services were in the state plan, you have the opportunity to begin to affect the agency constraints on these services. In this instance, you could use your knowledge of these rules to approach higher-ups in efforts to engage them in advocacy with state planners to include primary prevention in the future state plans. It is likely that in your agency and in the policies that determine its programs and funds, there abound such opportunities for using rules for their potential rather than for their constraining force.

### Demands

We turn now to demands and will examine how these, too, may be flexibly approached. While high demands often contribute to development and excitement about applying competencies to assigned work, uncontrolled demands can lead to fatigue, stress, and conflict. We have identified some possibilities for maintaining moderate to high demands without detracting from the quality of service delivery.

*Conserve energy.* In the context of increasing and often conflicting demands, there can be a tendency to squander personal and professional energies. This squandering of energy resources is most likely to occur when we are overly dependent on higher-ups for recognition and appreciation (Pruger, 1973). In order to conserve energy, you will need to encourage your supervisees to give recognition and feedback to each other rather than depend only on you or higher-ups. Additionally, conserving energy involves putting less desirable demands in perspective. Rather than using time to avoid keeping statistics in order, or meeting the reporting and collaborative requests from other agencies or for-profit organizations or other discipline-based interest groups, these requisite time-using activities, which support service delivery, can be viewed as opportunity possibilities. Other related groups can be a source of supports in addressing difficult or controversial service-delivery issues, can increase their familiarity and understanding of your programs and specialized expertise, and can provide supportive personal and professional relationships. Moreover, through networking and coalition building, you may be able to promote alternative service-delivery strategies, including the use of mutual-aid groups and helping networks of clients. In this way, the efforts committed to service provision may be decentralized and staff may be freed to become precious resources deployed to the most needed problems.

*Determine priorities among demands.* While there will always be a high demand for accountability, for responding promptly to forms and requests, for linkage to other agencies, and so forth, you can help your supervisees select the priorities among these demands, work at meeting these in an appropriate sequence, and plan for the time needed to meet the essentials. These demands are related to quality and quantity service delivery, to the very life of the organization and to its survival. In an atmosphere of mutual recognition and encouragement for timely action on the less intriguing demands, you and your supervisees will be able to redirect the energy conserved to the formulation of new initiatives and ideas. In turn, this will allow opportunity for engaging in the creative demands of practice which are essential to the vitality of yourselves and the agency (Pruger, 1973).

In order to maintain vitality in the context of high demands, you and your supervisees will want to increase your skills in assessing where to enter the opportunity field with the most impact. It is no less important to conserve energy in this area than in other areas of service delivery. You will want to work together in identifying and defining the specific components of constraints, demands, and supports that affect you and service delivery.

### Supports

Concentrating on supports for others can be a means of counterbalancing the effects of high constraints or of high demands. Because of the positive nature of these actions, they are well-known aspects of the social worker's traditions, value base, and competence (knowledge/skill) learnings. Offering some acknowledgment of the others' worth and sense of meaning in the organizational enterprise is an activity that is rated among the more pleasant aspects of the workplace. Supports are important to maintaining morale and commitment in the turbulent world of service delivery, especially in the complexities of organizational workings. All persons want to feel good about themselves, to feel valued by others, and to feel their efforts have some ultimate meaning. Supports are also important to feeling comfortable, relaxed, and self-renewed. For you and your supervisees, a number of options are available that can foster positive, personal self-value, as well as an organizational atmosphere that is, itself, supportive.

*Increase the attractiveness of the service staff.* Staff feel supported when they are liked and valued by their superiors. You can work at increasing the power and value of those in the lower organizational statuses by discovering ways to make them more attractive to the key decision makers at the top. As Mechanic found, "people who are viewed as attractive are more likely to obtain access to persons, and, once such access is gained, they may be more likely to succeed in promoting a cause" (Mechanic, 1962, p. 593). With such an approach, you open opportunities to simultaneously increase supports and minimize constraints.

There are many ways you can work at increasing the attractiveness of your supervisees (and at the same time increase the organization's attractiveness to them). These possibilities could include: making special assignments to task forces; providing public-speaking opportunities on behalf of the agency; noticing and supporting their selection of self-directed, continuing education efforts to develop or enhance their self, relationship, task, or context competencies.

Some options for increasing your own attractiveness include volunteering to work on a pet project of key influentials that you believe in, walking the extra mile to comply with deadlines during crisis periods, commending higher-ups on policy or program initiatives they have supported, and so forth. It is important for you to recognize that increasing attractiveness may take time and can only result if your actions with the higher-ups are genuine.

*Use trialogues more than dialogues.* Using trialogues suggests that you always seek information from more than one source, and that you welcome different points of view about all events in the work situation. Another implication of the trialogue emphasis is openness to many other ideas and interpretations (as opposed to decision-making based only on your own interaction with a given person or situation).

Given the complexity of organizations, it is important for you and your supervisees to learn to develop supports. The value of peer supports, along with the pursuit of practice issues openly among groups of staff, further extends the multivisioned trialogue—the threeness that pertains to all that is beyond the twosome. This is consistent with the ideas explored in Chapter 3.

As part of the extended trialogue, while any two persons are interacting, others beyond these actors are observing and reflecting on the transaction, and providing other viewpoints and possibly more dispassionate appraisals of the happening. Interactions that include threes (or more) not only decentralize and equalize power differentials, but they also introduce more possibilities for observation, reflection, diversity, and the unimagined. You may increase the dimensions of supports for yourself and others, and also deal more thoughtfully with the interactional effects of the accompanying constraints and demands.

*Encourage support groups.* Hanlan (1971) pointed out that the development of collegial support groups where staff interact as peers rather than superordinates and subordinates is one way to debureaucratize an agency. Such groups can encourage the use of professional judgment and can diminish more routinized orientations to rule following and requirement following. You can encourage the development of support groups for yourself and urge this for supervisees also. Some general guidelines for launching and structuring support groups have been formulated by Kirschenbaum and Glaser (1978). These mutual-aid enterprises, which may occur during lunch hours or at other times outside the workplace, have been found helpful for maintaining morale, stimulating ongoing professional development, and combating burnout. Such group experiences allow members to take some control over their own career development, to increase options for self-directed professional growth, and to receive social confirmation in the support-group context for ideas possibly dismissed by others on the job. You also may extend the support group concept into the broader community through developing coalitions and networks so that you can align with others whose interests and needs may be similar to yours.

*Foster a spirit of interdependence.* Perhaps the most vital route to strengthening the supportiveness of persons to persons and cultivating an atmosphere of supports in the organizational environment will grow from fostering a spirit of interdependence through your plans, actions, and involvements. Through such an orientation, you, your supervisees, and others may mutually search for and find your opportunity fields. Let us suggest ways to see and gain entry to such arenas that do exist within your context of service delivery.

## SEEING AND ENTERTAINING THE UNIMAGINABLE

Certain common consensual definitions of constraints, demands, and supports will be important to your success in shaping and redefining problems as opportunities. Some possible areas for enhanced proficiencies in entering the "unimagined" opportunity field can be suggested. First, to reinforce feelings of hopefulness and success, learn to choose issues with the probability of making the most difference with the least risk. Second, look for weak links in the chain of resistance and opposition to opportunities as you have defined them. Then focus your energies on these leverage points, in order to increase your probabilities of achieving positive changes. Third, select your opportunity emphasis with an eye to what is significant yet manageable. Finally, look around to discover who else sees or experiences problems or situations as you do (e.g., other supervisors and supervisees in your agency, supervisors and supervisees in other agencies, NASW, client-advocacy coalitions, clients of your agency, and so forth).

Our view of supervision is future-oriented and grounded in imperatives of professional competence and excellence in meeting quality and quantity expectations for service delivery. The future orientation is captured in our emphasis on making imaginative judgments. In the opportunity field, you will encounter circumstances for giving free reign to your imagination and that of your supervisees. You will want to encourage seeing the pattern of patterns, which may not yet be imagined or known by others. As an example, if you and your supervisees assess the prevailing ideologies of local, state, and federal policy makers, you can imagine future directions in policies and services and be prepared for them. Alternatively, you can concentrate on developing competence in lobbying and policy formulation in order to influence future demands more akin to social work values, client needs, and quality service delivery. We think that by now, you and your supervisees have imagined many possibilities and opportunities beyond those we have managed to address in this book. To make the high demands productive of development and excitement rather than fatigue and frustration, devote some of your energies to seeing and acting in anticipation of the unimaginable within the opportunity field of service delivery.

## CONCLUSION

In this chapter we have sought to expand on the kaleidoscopic array of possibilities for competent, imaginative supervision. We have linked prior considerations of the nine functions of supervision and the design for supervision to the dynamic forces conceptualized as the life-space and boundary zones. We have sought to help you envision the opportunity field as your opportunity to create a "new game" of relationships for you and your supervisees to play. This new game involves a redefinition of constraints, supports, and demands as legitimate opportunities for enhancing the simultaneous satisfaction of professional, client, and agency needs.

We imagine that some of you may be wondering about the legitimacy or illegitimacy of the various means we have identified for creating a new game in which constraints, supports, and demands are opportunities to seize upon rather than avoid (see Cloward and Ohlin, 1960, for discussion of legitimate and illegitimate means). From the purview of social work values, we can identify these means as legitimate yet risky, depending on the context, competence, and judgment used in carrying them out. At the same time, you are likely to encounter some who will say these means are illegitimate. We would expect these reactions from those who prefer hierarchical arrangements with primacy given to the use of power from the top down. We think that if you reexamine the options, you will now see them as legitimating opportunity power from the bottom up. It is this perspective on opportunities that, in part, underlies our view of the present and future possibilities for a social work *super*vision that works in behalf of supervisee, client, agency, and profession interests. By participating in the development and implementation of possibilities in the opportunity field, you can satisfy your professional needs and those of your supervisees. In turn, this increased need satisfaction changes the climate of the organization toward a philosophy and culture of involvement. Increased involvement is the key to establishing service-delivery organizations with a mutual and more equal commitment of staff to the agency and agency to staff.

## REFERENCES

CLOWARD, RICHARD A., and LLOYD E. OHLIN, *Delinquency and Opportunity.* New York: Crowell-Collier, 1960.

COHEN, BURTON J., "Coordination Strategies in Complex Service Delivery Systems," *Administration in Social Work,* 4, no. 3 (Fall 1980), 83–87.

FILLEY, ALAN C., *The Compleat Manager.* Champaign, Ill.: Research Press, 1978.

GRAY, CHARLES M., and VIRGINIA H. GRAY, "The Political Economy of Public Service Options," *American Behavioral Scientist,* 24, no. 4 (March/April 1981), 483–494.

HANLAN, ARCHIE, "Casework Beyond Bureaucracy," *Social Casework,* 52, no. 4 (April 1971), 195–199.

JOHNSON, ALISON H., "A Study of Power-Sharing as an Organizational Change Strategy," unpublished essay, Kent School of Social Work, University of Louisville, 1981.

KIRSCHENBAUM, HOWARD, and BARBARA GLASER, *Developing Support Groups: A Manual for Facilitators and Participants.* La Jolla, Calif.: University Associates, 1978.

LEWIN, KURT, *Field Theory in Social Science,* Dorwin Cartwright, ed. New York: Harper & Brothers, 1951.

———, *Resolving Social Conflicts,* Gertrud Weiss Lewin, ed. New York: Harper & Brothers, 1948.

MECHANIC, DAVID, "Sources of Power of Lower Participants in Complex Organizations," *Administrative Science Quarterly*, 7, no. 4 (December 1962), 349–364.

MIDDLEMAN, RUTH R., and GALE GOLDBERG, *Social Service Delivery: A Structural Approach to Social Work Practice*. New York: Columbia University Press, 1974.

MINAHAN, ANNE, "Conflict Within the Workplace," *Social Work*, 27, no. 3 (May 1982), 207–208.

PATTI, RINO J., "Organizational Resistance and Change: The View from Below," *Social Service Review*, 48, no. 3 (September 1974), 367–383.

PAYNE, ROY, "Stress in Task-Focused Groups," *Small Group Behavior*, 12, no. 3 (August 1981), 253–268.

PRUGER, ROBERT, "The Good Bureaucrat," *Social Work*, 18, no. 4 (July 1973), 26–32.

SHORTELL, STEPHEN M., "Theory Z: Implications and Relevance for Health Care Management," *Health Care Management Review*, 7, no. 4 (Fall 1982), 7–21.

# CHAPTER NINE
# CONCLUSION

As we conclude, we are reminded of another book concerned with the whole (Reynolds, 1942/1965). It aimed at a broad audience in the profession, that is, beyond social caseworkers—at workers, supervisors, executives—and it opened with a chapter entitled "Seeing It Whole." By *whole,* Reynolds justified her inclusion of social group work and community organization, fields she imagined might be a rapidly "growing edge" in social work. She claimed that social casework might make its best contribution to the wholeness of the profession "in what it can give to the other fields, and to administration, in understanding of human relationships" (p. 11). She made this choice "looking forward," believing that "it is important that the whole of social work move forward, emphasizing common elements rather than differences." Her whole also included attention to the confounding social conditions of the times, filled with the fierce heat of war and crisis, and some wonder about such a book that looked backward about learning to do and teach social work.

Although her hopes for the future did not come to pass, her writings continued to guide her times, and they live now. We think of her aim at a distillation, although we have no pretentions that our effort should be thought of in any sense as approaching her imprint. Our connections are merely with her wholeness theme, with doubts about whether writings aimed both backward and forward will have much merit, and with the sense of world crisis we all face in our times.

Using the leading-edge knowledge of her day, Reynolds claimed, "The whole is more than the sum of all its parts." We think she would be excited to know of the extension or revisions made of this gestalt principle today. The work of neuro-psychologist Karl H. Pribram on brain imaging patterns and storage, the theories of David Bohm in physics, and the technological uses of lasers in photography combine to lead to the hologram and holography, with its principle, "The whole is contained or enfolded in its parts."

Our whole is not of a profession unified in theories, tasks, settings, or common interests. Yet we think each social worker shares in a common wholeness, an entity derived from professional identity and values that are enfolded within the seemingly diverse activities that social work encompasses. The wholeness resides in commitments to values, often not shared by other professions and occupations, to competence and to being imaginative. It is these features that have led to the profession's survival, diversity, and growth, regardless of the odds against any particular individual's impact at a particular time.

We conclude with these themes—supervisory competence and imaginative approaches to the ordered and the chaotic in your workplace (and all workplaces). These themes matter for your own work and for your work with supervisees and others you are connected with, so that you might mutually value competence and innovation in daily task performance. We shall start with competence.

## COMPETENCE

We propose the following practice principles to guide your supervisory efforts. You will find a general principle and several subcomponents for each of the nine functions introduced in Chapter 5 as central imperatives forming the supervisory task. As you consider each of these, mentally add, "The supervisor should . . . ." or "The supervisor will strive to . . ." as a lead to each statement.

1. *Humanizing—Make the workplace responsive to the human component of the organization.*
   1.1 Seek and provide opportunities for others' satisfactions and recognition.
   1.2 Model collaborative and cooperative behavior.
   1.3 Maximize egalitarian rather than hierarchical person-to-person relationships wherever possible.
   1.4 Attempt to see and appreciate the others' perspectives.
   1.5 Differentiate private messages from public ones and deal with the private messages in private.
   1.6 Help the others save face in the face of embarrassment.
2. *Managing tension—Attend to the imperatives of the professional and the organizational cultures in ways that do not compromise the ethical or the practical in terms of the values and norms of client, worker, organization, and profession.*
   2.1 Encourage the expression of and the dissipation of tensions.
   2.2 Recognize the conflicting interests, values, attitudes, and ideologies among staff as natural.

  2.3 Approach differences and conflicts as inevitable, as inherent in the organizational situation, and as often desirable.

  2.4 Mediate among different orientations and interests.

  2.5 Urge the development of some system of yield-and-prevail decision-making pattern.

3. *Catalyzing—Make the workplace an interesting, rewarding, and involving context for the delivery of services.*

  3.1 Inject excitement and enthusiasm whenever possible.

  3.2 Value novel and unusual ideas.

  3.3 Appreciate and acknowledge risking, revising points of view, and entertaining alternative perspectives.

  3.4 Encourage experimentation and "think time" for yourself and supervisees (for example, an opportunity each week to reflect and replan the work, or to consider alternative approaches and issues).

4. *Teaching—Create a work climate where the opportunity for learning and ongoing professional development is valued, available, and attainable.*

  4.1 Promote the acquisition of new knowledge and skills and the specialization (refinement) of known competencies.

  4.2 Encourage mutual exchanges of information among members of the work unit.

  4.3 Involve the supervisees in the determination of their learning needs.

  4.4 Make expectations explicit at the outset of the relationship in a participatory manner.

  4.5 Devise ways to meet these learning needs through individualized and unit-wide instructional formats.

  4.6 Connect your efforts with those of others in the organization whenever and wherever possible.

5. *Career socializing—Act as a role model to supervisees, as a person who exemplifies the ideals, values, and standards of the social work profession and the service mandate and mission of the organization.*

  5.1 Make your actions and the ways of pursuing the task imperatives congruent with your verbal and written directions and appeals.

  5.2 Know that in instances where actions and words are not congruent, the influential action "message" will make the greater impact.

  5.3 Act in ways that reflect understanding of the multiple careers of supervisees—agency, personal, professional—and the differentials among professional identities that diverse professional socialization imposes.

  5.4 Temper your assumptions about the normative expectations for role performance by sensitivity to differences between yourself and supervisees as influenced by gender, ethnic, racial, and age-related perspectives.

6. *Evaluating—Design evaluation procedures so that the process captures the unique and changing achievements of each supervisee.*

  6.1 Distinguish with supervisees those areas of managerial accountability and quality control where compliance is mandatory from those areas of the work where degrees of freedom for individual judgment and discretionary performance are valued.

  6.2 Establish a process of mutual feedback between yourself and supervisees and among the supervisees in ways that preserve dignity and promote wisdom.

  6.3 Determine performance objectives and other criteria for achievement in a participative way that reflects individual differences in education, experience, and difficulty of workload.

  6.4 Develop evaluative procedures, processes, and criteria that value interdependent work, collaboration with others, understanding others' work, problems, needs, and the "big picture" of organizational life.

7. *Administering—Mediate between agency objectives and worker activity—the critical task that brings credibility to your efforts and leverage for your pursuit of the other functions.*

   7.1  Be accountable for the competent execution of organizational productivity and efficiency needs and for the quality of service delivery.

   7.2  Translate the broad statements of organizational purpose into the concrete, operationalized components of priorities, assignments, and activities.

   7.3  Involve those responsible for the implementation of decisions in making the decisions that determine these activities.

   7.4  Delegate authority and responsibility for service delivery activities to the extent of your jurisdiction limits.

8. *Advocating—Seek to eliminate inequities and injustices that may have detrimental effects on workers and on agency goals.*

   8.1  Act persuasively on behalf of worker issues that pertain to the quality and quantity of service delivery.

   8.2  Focus energy on issues of fairness and justice within the agency, as well as within external groups and organizations in the larger service-delivery system.

   8.3  Protect the supervisees from organizational assaults to professional or high-quality service delivery where possible, even when such a stance may result in unpopularity.

   8.4  Support the promotion of well-qualified persons who have experienced discrimination (in terms of gender, race, ethnicity, or age) to positions of importance in the structure of the agency.

9. *Changing—Expect continuous fluctuations in the agency and its environment.*

   9.1  Use your own and the workers' critical positions within the organization to influence these fluctuations in the direction of organizational development and enhancement.

   9.2  Initiate collective efforts to move the organization to higher levels of functioning within the constraints imposed by the priority of service delivery.

   9.3  Differentiate between short-term and long-term opportunities in terms of priorities, patterns, organizational arrangements, and intervention choices; and work strategically in both realms.

   9.4  Help those who experience pain, loss, or dislocation during changes to find a new sense of value, self-worth, and competence.

These principles are directly related to the competence theme, which we have emphasized as the first requirement of supervisory practice. They spring from a particular perspective—one that acknowledges diversity among the possible perspectives that persons may hold. They acknowledge an indebtedness to the conceptual efforts of many others in social work and other realms who have pondered similar issues and who have contributed to the incremental accretion of our point of view. We have explored the variability of perspectives and the subtleties of perception that form the core from which competent performance springs. It should be an expanding, changeable, and tentative activity used with all possible deliberateness and consciousness.

The shock waves generated in the realms of national and international politics and economics, in the core values and culture of all nations, in the physical, biological, and social sciences have led many to question old theories and assumptions, and to seek new ways to encompass yet move beyond former orientations and beliefs. There are conflicting reactions to the discovery of the limitations in old theories, to acceptance or rejection of new models and assumptions that are superseding or subsuming former ones, and to the need for finding a perspective that allows for working at the work of social work while also entertaining a sense of wholeness and integration despite inherent contradictions, complexities, and vast areas of partial knowledge.

Social work, as a value-based, service-oriented profession, has been influenced by philosophy, theology, the natural and social sciences, and the arts and other professions. Sometimes this has been to its advantage, and other times, to its disadvantage. One advantage, for example, is reflected in the profession's embrace of the extensive complexity necessary in attempting any understanding of the human condition and its potentialities. One disadvantage has been succumbing to the limitations of other sciences' and professions' theories and models as, for example, to linear causality, now known as insufficient for directing remediation or enhancement efforts in many situations. In addition, there has been the difficulty of adapting abstract perspectives that may yield broad understanding but little direction to the practice act.

We have identified a mounting shift in assumptions and speculation by many scholars and practitioners as they seek to re-order their thoughts and actions both in the world and in the subworlds of their occupations and preoccupations. We have considered changes in shared meanings and perspectives, and in the diversity of competing approaches or meanings that unsettle all realms (e.g., politics, science, education, and social work). And yet, we find instances of new shared perspectives. For example, there is a coming together between physics and psychology, two realms where respective past assumptions and traditions were decidedly foreign to each other. Each realm shows evidence of looking beyond a more narrow, Western scientific, empirical tradition as the only way to interpret reality. Also in each field, Eastern thinking is seen and appreciated with more openness. Certain common realizations and connections are surfacing. For example, consider the shared notion that objective observation is impossible.

The move among disciplines toward new groupings and alliances with common metalanguages and transdisciplinary activities, as illustrated by cybernetics and linguistics, constitutes a search for multiple levels of understanding. It is a search for pattern, now occurring in astrophysics, higher dimensional mathematics, data handling, and neurophysiology. Also, it is a move away from the mechanistic and behavioral 19th-century models toward some method of interrelating the contradictions within society and within ourselves, a point elaborated with pictures as well as words by Albarn and Smith (1977), much as we have tried to suggest herein.

As is the case with all practitioners, social workers are mainly busy at their mandate and use the best of what they have learned to guide actions, with little support and opportunity to reflect on essences and existences. They harbor vague discomforts with the limitations of what is known and what needs still to be known for competence in practice. Certain disputations and in-fighting may occur as practitioners seek new knowledge and ways to act, while clinging to what they already know and know how to do. With this in mind, we have tried to frame principles that reflect general directiveness and also that point towards openness and avoidance of the dogmatic and doctrinaire.

## IMAGINATIVE JUDGMENTS

Our second theme concerns the imaginative. We see this as the vital link between your given situation—the *is*—and the possibilities within your situation—the *what could be's*. This quality is also related to perspective, since the very way you view things will offer opportunities or restrictions according to the limits of your vision. There is a spate of information appearing these days on ways to manage our institutions. Such information usually boils down to investigations of how "they" manage to manage us, and what to do about such a thing. We have tried to emphasize that you *are* the organization, rather than considering the situation as a me/ them circumstance. To the extent that you see yourself as part of "them," you will have embarked on a route to affect, from your vantage point, a difference. To the extent that you begin to think in terms of "problem posing" and "issue finding," instead of problem solving (most problems are merely rearranged or re-ordered, not "solved" once and for all), you will find opportunities to imagine an array of ways around the problematics of organizational life and of engaging in your context: the changeable constant.

The imaginative or the creative grows from the competent. Competence comes first, then possibly imaginative judgments. The linkage is comparable to the craft and the art, or the methodical and the unorthodox or radical leap. It involves the mastery of the alphabet, so as to know how to speak and write, before being able to make up your own words. As with any artistic expression, rigor and discipline in the particulars precede innovation. It is akin to Toffler's advice, when asked for some words of counsel on writing a book of some complexity: "Pay close attention to craftsmanship and have a passionate theme" (Ingalls, 1979, p. xi).

We have distinguished the innovative from the merely idiosyncratic—the lucky impulse or breakthrough that occasionally, accidentally happens to shake up a regular course. While these naive accomplishments are not to be minimized as valuable, they are chancy rather than probable or reliable, as compared with the seasoned, disciplined mustering of the mastered elements.

We have suggested some deliberate ways to court the imaginative: through visualizing your situation (throughout the book) and through doing something about your situation (Chapter 8, The Opportunity Field). Certain other action particulars that are imaginative, for Western-style organizational behavior, are described as the "foreign" ways of Japanese managers, the "Zen and Art" (Pascale and Athos, 1981, pp. 85–115). They are imaginative in their cultural difference from our ordinary ways of thinking and doing. Some of these "different" ways are: valuing gradual change; letting time wither away organizational obstacles; winding around obstructions rather than encountering them head on; and gaining deeper perception through contemplation (see also Ouchi, 1981).

Other "foreign" mentalities, beginning to be noticed in the literature of complex organizations (hospitals, higher education, corporations), are those of women, many of whom seek more recognition and power in determining decisions. So far, they have been more acceptable as board members and at lower levels in organizations; they have had least access and acceptability at middle levels. It remains to be seen whether their "success" will require more conformance to male norms and the more customary ways of "doing the business," or whether their presence may add a new dimension to organization life (Shortell, 1982; Middleman, 1983, 1984).

Occasionally, however, the imaginative comes from the fresh perspective of a person, aside from the system of ideas that has guided the competent ones, the experts within a given field. Maltz (1960) considered such new knowledge to be the highly developed knowledge from within one field that implodes the prescribed boundaries of another with transforming consequences—the impact of "inperts" rather than "experts." Such was the case with the impact of engineering and cybernetics upon psychology and social work, and with Maltz's own thinking as a plastic surgeon, which brought innovation into psychology. As he claimed, "Pasteur was not an M.D. The Wright brothers were not aeronautical engineers but bicycle mechanics. Einstein . . . a mathematician [not] a physicist . . . Madame Curie was not an M.D. but a physicist, yet she made important contributions to medical science" (p. viii). We also think of Montessori, an M.D., and her impact upon childhood education, of the physicist Maxwell, whose discovery of electromagnetic waves and fields of forces was translated by Lewin into a field theory, which greatly affected social science and systems thinking, color photography, and, of course, moved physics away from Newtonian perspectives. And we think of Jane Addams, social worker, and her impact upon international pursuit of peace.

The imaginative most often, then, comes from disciplined openness and competence within the boundaries of the known within one's field of expertise; but also it may be imported from the application of knowledge and insights *outside* the "givens" we have been taught to accept as the conventions of our field. In any case, we see the imaginative as the expression of mastery more than happenstance. The chimpanzees may intrigue us with their paintings, but their products are not modern art.

## COMPETENCE AND IMAGINATION—ORDER AND CHAOS

Both competence and imagination are ways out of disorder or chaos. No one wants a world without order. We seek to create order in our world and try to impart some order even in the midst of chaos, confusion, complexity, and disarray. This longing for order has animated the most lofty philosophical speculations about the cosmos, as well as the humblest activities in the ordinary workaday world of supervisors and workers in the bustle, the hassle, the hustle of daily affairs.

We seek to create order in our world. We seek explanations and look for the elusive "facts." We try to construct some order through organizing information, persons, objects, and experiences into aggregates that may have some meaning in terms of what we already know and what we want to "see." And we reorganize or re-order, from time to time, as new information and intuitions demand some adjustments or restructuring of the known. The whole history of scientific investigation may be thought of as a massive, continuous incremental search for order. Likewise, the collective energies devoted to the arts may be seen as highlighting (through the particular expression or event) the aesthetic order—or as accentuating our awareness of its absence, through emphasis on deliberately depicted disorder. Whether or not any person's organization of entities is "true" is debatable. The "real" order of the world remains a metaphysical, a philosophical matter.

We might wonder about the world, about organizations, about the social work profession, and about supervision in terms of order and chaos. Are these in chaos? Are they in order? Are they to be thought of in either-or ways (as Aristotelian logic would require)? Or are they merely examples of a dialectical process—polarities on a continuum that we could label *harmony* or *coherence* or *integration,* or what have you, with order at one pole, chaos at the other—with some order within the chaos and some chaos within the order?

The order/chaos dialectic pertains to your thinking and feeling experiences, and so, it affects your visualization of situations and imagination of their elements. In addition, it affects your determination of available responses, or the actions you will take. But you are experienced through everyday affairs, with the demands posed by these perceptual, conceptual, and emotive requirements, and also experienced with the *doing* aspect. Let us illustrate this with two examples:

> EXAMPLE: Can you recall the excitement of a visit to a circus? You were bombarded with chaos—the three rings, three simultaneous spectacles. Each moved in diverse ways and yet demanded your attention. Each was furiously alive and in motion as spectacles of astonishing performances—animals and people—all marvelously competent and skillful, even imaginative as they reached for your laughter and appreciation. And, perhaps, there were also clowns wandering about at the periphery, distracting or enticing you with their antics.
>
> Although the apparent disorder may have unsettled you at first, you found coherence in the "big picture." You integrated the cacophony into a grand event that was whole. Perhaps the three-ring (frivolous?) circus is the analogue for what you must do every day in the workaday world. Perhaps its inherent craziness and the humor evoked offers a survival clue: *You forced your perception to take in the whole.*

> EXAMPLE: Or let us consider the *doing* part. You have just returned home from a one-week (two-week?) absence, and you are greeted with a chaos of mail, newspapers, magazines, and other items that clutter and discourage

your entry. You are experienced in dealing with this in quick order: the wastebasket for the junk mail, the bills and checks (?) carefully put aside, the occasional personal letter attended to happily or unhappily, and the magazines or other potentially useful announcements arranged somewhere for future consideration. Also, the mounting assortment of appeals for a variety of contributions (some with the wrong name) are sorted according to their importance and your quick estimate of your resources. You are probably amazed at the impact of the current political and economic circumstances on the good fortune of the postal system. But, no matter, you *did* it: chaos into order! And this skill also stands you well in your negotiation of your workaday world.

Returning now to supervision, we have tried to suggest some order in visualizing this many-faceted area. We have urged you to seek for patterns, recurring cycles, accents among seeming dissonance, dimensional, depth perspectives. We have urged you to expect confusion more than order. This is the stuff of the workplace—occasional order. Noise, according to information theory, is the *non*sense, the *non*-information. It is random, the accidental or incidental, rather than the meaningful signals. But noise is also the stuff of which music is made, when the sounds are organized with competence and imparted with artistry. Turning noise into music repeats the life course of all composers. Turning confusions into coherence repeats the life struggle of all supervisors.

## THE WORLD AS KALEIDOSCOPE

So we return to our world view captured as a tumbling kaleidoscope whose pieces and elements continuously move and shift so long as there is life force, turbulence, and restlessness. We believe we have used a congenial metaphor to picture your picture, to suggest the "big picture"—one that has inherent changeableness, beauty, and whimsy as its characteristics. Imagining that the permutations of kaleidoscopic patterns were infinite, we sought expert advice on this subject from Martin Gardner, known for his thirty-some books on popularized mathematics, science, and physics as well as his twenty-five-year "Mathematical Games" column in *Scientific American.* His response (1982) was confirming:

> I think it depends on how you look at the situation. [*Sic!*] If you make a kaleidoscope by putting two pocket mirrors on a large picture, at a 60-degree angle, and look into the V, you see a theoretically infinite regress. But if you place the V over a *small* picture, it forms a hexagonal pattern at the center of your vision. Most kaleidoscopes limit the portion of the plane that you view, so you see only this single pattern. The theoretically infinite plane is of course an endless repetition of the same fundamental region. As for the number of combinations possible with a finite set of colored pieces of glass, the number of patterns is theoretically infinite, since any individual piece can be in an infinity of positions and rotations. Thus the number of possible patterns is what in Cantorian set theory is called aleph one, the second order of infinity. It is sometimes called an "uncountable" infinity.

Plate 29, Floral design. Norma Y. Finkel and Leslie G. Finkel, *Kaleidoscopic Designs: And How to Create Them.* New York: Dover, 1980.

The kaleidoscope is "on the move" again these days, not only as our metaphor but in actuality. It is estimated that at least twenty-four craftspersons make their living constructing varieties of these wondrous instruments (McDermott, 1982); no longer are they merely for children. Kaleidoscopes of intricate wood and copper design, seascopes with shells that mystify, polarizing scopes, musical scopes, shifting colored emulsions, and tiny pendants may be found to delight adults. Replicas of antique scopes can be enjoyed. For cameras, there are even kaleidoscopic attachments that deliberately break up the ordinary picture of the world into patterns of the scene's inherent elements . . . the familiar into its particulars, rearranged into new configurations.

The kaleidoscope was a serious invention of the physicist Sir David Brewster in 1816 as he pursued his interest in the polarization of light. He had high hopes for its contribution to scientific thought as he pursued his interest in particle theory and vigorously opposed the emerging wave theory, which surfaced in his times. His

A kaleidoscopic photo. (*Photo courtesy of Edward L. Herser.*)

hopes for the kaleidoscope included its high contribution to all the ornamental arts—to the design of architectural ornaments, Gothic windows, carpets, jewelry, and so forth. It was an overnight success: 200,000 sold in Paris and London within three months of its first production. But despite its 150-year existence, it remains peripheral to "serious" thought. Antique examples have not survived as have comparable vintage telescopes and spyglasses, perhaps because of their mysterious workings, which led the owners to destroy them by taking them apart to determine how they worked. Or it may be that they have been trivialized as children's toys. And yet, children are the most open people and are the ones to be imitated by adults when viewing the world. Children see the world with fresh eyes, not jaded nor habituated to view the world as is. They are ready to entertain outrageous perceptions and possibilities as "natural."

We leave it to you to synthesize, make sense of, connect with, apply and extend the views encountered here—to experience what a kaleidoscopic orientation may do for your perspective, to live with its "uncountable infinity." If some clues, some excitement and clarity result from your and our efforts, so much the better. If some comfort and greater familiarity with chaotic-seeming circumstances, or even some optimism, become your orientation as you look ahead, we shall be overjoyed. If you learn to value your own inherent flexibility and to become suspicious of rigidities as you sense these affecting your perspectives and actions, we shall be encouraged.

These qualities of openness, flexibility, and adaptiveness seem imperative for all persons today, and certainly for social workers. Singhal (1982) argues for the appropriate yardstick when evaluating other cultures and cites a story of a prosperous ancient kingdom where a murderer was to be hanged, but the noose was too large for his neck. He cautions against using your own yardstick on others whose ways may not be measurable by your own standards. And Ragade (1981) calls attention to our "mindscapes" that tint our frame of reference:

> A physical object needs at least two views to completely define it. A view is more than a single dimension. We must add an experiential frame to an experimental frame when considering the views of a human observer. (p. 2).

We are reminded, further, of Bateson's emphasis on "double description." He urged an eye on the longer view, the larger gestalt, the wider perspective about perspectives, the two-eyed way of seeing things yielding an extra dimension—depth, and an act of comparison: "We can achieve insight by comparing more than single instances" (1979, p. 97). We need at least two versions of anything with their differences before we notice, or attend to, *any thing*. What we notice is the "information," the "unchanging is imperceptible unless we are willing to move relative to it." (p. 107). And we have urged you, in everything you view and try to understand, to employ a foursome mentality, comprised of the me/it/context/history.

These thoughts share a common theme: They deal with perception, and thus with perspective. They return us to our beginnings in Chapter 2, where we initiated this larger, more versatile view as an orientation to be grasped in considering supervision. The changes that are our constant context, the patterns that the kaleidoscope accentuates, remind us to keep seeking the shifting meanings, the patterns which recur, albeit in new configurations. The folklorist Sabine Baring-Gould (1892, pp. 299-301) found these verses in a Cambridge University undergraduates' magazine before the 20th century, and they talk of our kaleidoscope:

> I was just five years old, that December,
>     And a fine little promising boy.
> So my grandmother said, I remember,
>     And gave me a strange-looking toy;
>
> In its shape it was lengthy and rounded,
>     It was papered with yellow and blue,
> One end with a glass top was bounded,
>     At the other, a hole to look through.
>
> 'Dear Granny, what's this?' I came crying,
>     'A box for my pencils? but see,
> I can't open it hard though I'm trying,
>     O what is it? what can it be?'

'Why, my dear, if you only look through it,
    And stand with your face to the light;
Turn it gently (that's just how to do it!),
    And you'll see a remarkable sight.'

'O how beautiful!' cried I, delighted,
    As I saw each fantastic device,
The bright fragments now closely united,
    All falling apart in a trice.

Times have passed, and new years will now find me,
    Each birthday, no longer a boy,
Yet me thinks that their turns may remind me
    Of the turns of my grandmother's toy.

For in all this world, with its beauties,
    Its pictures so bright and so fair,
You may vary the pleasures and duties
    But still, the same pieces are there.

From the time that the earth was first founded,
    There has never been anything new—
The same thoughts, the same things, have redounded
    Till the colours have pall'd on the view.

But—though all that is old is returning,
    There is yet in this sameness a change;
And new truths are the wise ever learning,
    For the patterns must always be strange.

Shall we say that our days are all weary?
    All labour, and sorrow, and care,
That its pleasures and joys are but dreary,
    Mere phantoms that vanish in air?

Ah, no! there are some darker pieces,
    And others transparent and bright;
But this, surely, the beauty increases,—
    Only—*stand with your face to the light.*

And the treasures for which we are yearning,
    Those joys, now succeeded by pain—
Are *but* spangles, just hid in the turning;
    They will come to the surface again.


Brewster thought that when a figure in the kaleidoscope is once lost, centuries may elapse before the same combination returns. Perhaps this is so. But we can become familiar with similar patterns, and recognize their commonalities. This may happen if you distinguish kaleidoscopes from pencil boxes, fireplace matches, or other practical features of everyday life, and especially when you "stand with your face to the light."

## REFERENCES

ALBARN, KEITH, and SMITH, JENNY M., *Diagram: The Instrument of Thought.* London: Thames & Hudson, 1977.

BARING-GOULD, SABINE, *Curiosities of Olden Times.* Edinburgh: J. Grant, 1892.

BATESON, GREGORY, *Mind and Nature: A Necessary Unity.* New York: Dutton, 1979.

FINKEL, NORMA Y., and LESLIE G. FINKEL, *Kaleidoscopic Designs: How to Create Them.* New York: Dover, 1980.

GARDNER, MARTIN, Personal correspondence (February 22, 1982).

INGALLS, JOHN D., *Human Energy: The Critical Factor for Individuals and Organizations.* Austin, Texas: Learning Concepts, 1979.

McDERMOTT, JEANNE A., "The Kaleidoscope: Magic in a Tube Is Enjoying Revival," *Smithsonian,* 13, no. 3 (November 1982), 98–107.

MALTZ, MAXWELL, *Psycho-Cybernetics.* Englewood Cliffs, N.J.: Prentice-Hall, 1960.

MIDDLEMAN, RUTH R., "The Quality Circle: Fad, Fix, Fiction?" *Administration in Social Work,* 8, no. 1 (Spring 1984), 31–44.

―――――, "An Holistic View of Quality Circles," Program of the 27th Annual Conference; Society for General Systems Research, 2 (1983), 535–545.

OUCHI, WILLIAM G., *Theory Z.* Reading, Mass.: Addison-Wesley, 1981.

PASCALE, RICHARD T., and ANTHONY G. ATHOS, *The Art of Japanese Management.* New York: Simon & Schuster, 1981.

PRIBRAM, KARL H., "The Role of Analogy in Transcending Limits in the Brain Sciences," *Daedalus,* 109, no. 2 (Spring 1980), 19–38.

RAGADE, RAMMOHAN K., "Towards Applied General Systems," *General Systems* (1981), 1–5.

REYNOLDS, BERTHA C., *Learning and Teaching in the Practice of Social Work.* 1942; rpt. New York: Russell and Russell, 1965.

SHORTELL, STEPHEN M., "Theory Z: Implications and Relevance for Health Care Management," *Health Care Management Review* (Fall 1982), 7–21.

SINGHAL, KALYAN, "The Sociopolitical and Economic Context in Evaluating Productivity and Implementing Management Science Techniques," *Interfaces,* 12, no. 2 (April 1982), 77–82.

# APPENDIX A
# FOR FURTHER THOUGHT
# AND ACTION

## CHAPTER 1

1.  Explore the practices of other professions and occupations in terms of teaching the substance of the work, monitoring and accountability for performance, standards and hierarchical levels of identified mastery, ethical issues, licensure requirements, and the lack of these features. For starters, find out: What happens at beauty operators' conventions? What rules and requirements must plumbers meet? What are the developments and requirements in nursing? Select a profession and systematically investigate it. Compare and contrast it with social work.

2.  Explore your current agency or work situation to determine what orientations to supervision are used by various supervisors. Can you identify their frame of reference with any aspects of the historical emphases discussed in this chapter?

3.  Do a time-log review of your agency for one month and calculate the proportion of time devoted to supervision, training, and consultation as ways through which learning opportunities are approached.

4. Listed below are nineteen sayings that have been used popularly over the years to guide actions. On your own or with a small group, make connections between these aphorisms and ideas encountered in this chapter. Also, discover suggested connections you can make to issues within social work and related professions. Perhaps brainstorm other sayings of your own.

   a. Too many cooks spoil the broth.
   b. Two heads are better than one.
   c. Nothing ventured nothing gained.
   d. A watched pot never boils.
   e. When the cat's away the mice will play.
   f. I paddle my own canoe.
   g. When in Rome, do as the Romans.
   h. A rolling stone gathers no moss.
   i. Don't cry over spilt milk.
   j. Horses run fast when they feel the sting of the whip.
   k. One's reach should exceed one's grasp.
   l. In the land of the blind, the one-eyed man is king.
   m. A stitch in time saves nine.
   n. Better be safe than sorry.
   o. You can lead a horse to water, but you can't make it drink.
   p. 'Tis an ill wind that blows nobody any good.
   q. Rome was not built in a day.
   r. Every dog howls in its own backyard.
   s. As the twig is bent, so is the tree inclined.

5. In-class simulation

   SITUATION: You are a supervisor in a detention center employing a staff of 50: your 6 supervisees, who are social workers (B.S.W. and M.S.W.); 12 teachers; and 31 security personnel. You are aware of the tensions in relationships between the teachers and social workers and security officers. The security personnel view the professionals as too easy on juveniles, allowing them to get by with things. The social workers and teachers often deal with security personnel with disdain and see them as too strict, inflexible, and punitive.

   a. The class is divided proportionally, into three units representing social workers, teachers, and security personnel. Units are given 10 minutes to plan the components of their orientation in specific terms. Then these groups are brought together into an all-agency staff meeting (30 minutes). They are instructed to work on this situation collectively so that services may not suffer from the results of the apparent staff tensions.
   b. Option: In work groups of four to six members, the task is to reconsider this organizational problem in terms of six approaches to teaching described by Kaslow (see p. 32). Groups have 20 minutes to devise what they think would be the "best" approach among these options. They then present their plans to the class.

## CHAPTER 2

The tasks described below will extend your understanding of ideas presented in this chapter:

1. Select a situation to consider both globally and discretely (as was done in Chapter 2 with the Irregular-Object). Look at this situation and try to get to the overall pattern of relationships, then the specific details. Places to look include: your agency, a staff meeting, a classroom, your home, your neighborhood. Practice this once a day, and share your observations and experience in class.

2. Think about the concepts *stress* and *burnout*. Develop a brief written analysis of these concepts from each of the following perspectives:
   a. individual (your usual cognitive style)
   b. cultural prescriptions you can identify
   c. elements you believe are derived from norms and traditions of social work
   As a class project, select additional concepts to think about in these three ways, and practice with a new concept each week.

3. Select a paragraph at random from something you are reading, and try to capture its sense in a drawing or picture clipped from a magazine.

4. Bring a cartoon or picture without a caption into class and practice conveying its message to others in words. Or see what different meanings individuals will put on this picture.

5. Compare and contrast the experiences and outcomes of items 3 and 4 above. What is lost and gained by each way of communicating?

6. At your agency, take any memo and try to convey its message by a picture or diagram.

7. Think about others you encounter daily, and estimate their preferred styles of processing information: holistic? analytic? theoretical? process-oriented? contextual? right brain? left brain? Listening to their "code" words may help you make your judgments.

8. For in-class emphasis on the variability in how people "see" a situation, it will be useful to post and categorize the results of each of the profiles explored individually in this chapter. In this way you can begin to gain a picture of the totality of differences represented in this class. These compilations merit in-depth discussion, both in terms of the impact of these findings upon the learners, and in terms of the implications for work with clients as well as for supervising.

9. Observe a sporting event on TV carefully. What explanations might you offer in an analysis of what is going on using each of the three world views (world as machine, as lottery, as kaleidoscope)? Does any one of these views seem most adequate to account for the interactions? Discuss with others. Compare and contrast the differing analyses.

10. Apply kaleidoscope thinking and looking to your home or apartment, agency, or supervisor. What insights can be derived from this perspective? What new images, relationships, and patterns come to mind?

11. Think of the role of the supervisor as a conveyor of information from the administrator to the staff and from staff upward. Write an essay in which you describe and analyze this situation in terms of each of the three perspectives.

12. In-class role play: Divide into triads. Each group discusses this proposition: The paperwork of organizations continuously increases to the point where it interferes with providing services.

    During this discussion, have each person adopt, enact, and project a particular perspective on the situation, exemplifying one of the three world views: machine, lottery, kaleidoscope. After discussing this situation for 20 minutes, discuss the impact, the conclusions that each view encouraged, the utility of each perspective, and the constraints posed by each. Conclusions from each triad may then be shared with the entire class and may be discussed further.

# CHAPTER 3

1. Take some familiar dichotomies (either-or's) and transform them into trichotomies (e.g., black/white: black/gray/white). What difference does this make? What "problems" are created?

2. Apply trichotomy thinking to some social work dichotomies. Start with the following, and then add to this list as a class.

   Person—_____—situation
   Social policy—_____—direct service
   Internal—_____—external
   Thinking—_____—feeling

3. Practice analyzing various situations using a foursome perspective (you, looking at it, in context, and history) once a day for a week. Pick out events or situations at school or home to study, one each day, and analyze the elements. These trials may be discussed in class at week's end.

4. Transform the following words to lead from fixed to open possibilities (example—ability: potentiality).

   instinct: _____          deviant: _____
   trait: _____             alcoholic: _____
   old: _____               resistance: _____
   handicap: _____          barrier: _____

   Add to this list.

5. In-class simulation

   SITUATION: A family service agency recently added a new refugee services program, responsive to the influx of immigrants from Vietnam, Laos, and South America. Two factions emerged in the staff; individuals from each faction approached you, the supervisor, privately with complaints about "those others." The two factions stuck together at lunch and generally avoided those in the other "camp." The carping and complaining about others' behaviors increased weekly. In general, one faction seemed to think the new program would be a threat to older, established services. Individuals in this faction were uncomfortable dealing with persons who were hard to understand and who had practices considered objectionable. The other faction was excited about this new service as an opportunity for outreach to persons in need, largely ignored by the broader community. Moreover, they considered the other faction a bit elite and too "professional," —that is, they considered the first faction's preciousness about practice to be often time-consuming and open-ended, so that they spent too much time with too few clients.

Task—Divide the class into four groups. They are to do the following:
a. Analyze this situation in terms of the *dominance* factors described in this chapter (supervisor; worker; client; context), and determine which among the components they wish to view as being *the* dominant aspect that has unbalanced the agency situation (20 minutes).
b. Devise a strategy in relation to this analysis, responsive to bringing about a new realignment through either reducing or increasing its influence. Plan a scenario that will highlight their approach, and enact it with the class (20 minutes).
c. Have the groups reconvene. Have each group coach one of its members to act as supervisor, informed by that group's scenario. The class then experiences each of the four approaches. While one member of each planning group acts as supervisor, the others are to be observers of the ensuing process. Observers are to take notes on the dynamics set in motion by their plan.
d. After the four scenarios are experienced, the observers report their recorded observations. The whole group discusses the implications of all the experiences in terms of "best" approach, consequences of all approaches, relative ease of reducing or increasing the salience of components, and other related topics.

## CHAPTER 4

1. Using "A Snapshot of Your Community's Provisions" (pp. 328-331), explore matters concerned with responsive provision by collecting the data indicated in this instrument. For those in small communities, one person might pursue the project alone; for large cities, the project would be best pursued by apportioning the categories among members of a team. This project may be used as a basis for class discussion.

2. Select three individuals in responsible positions. These may be persons in your personal experience or national figures. Try to analyze their style in terms of managership versus leadership concepts.

3. Using the concepts derived from discussions of leadership and organizational life course, analyze the historic and current circumstances of women, blacks, or other special populations.

4. Collect newspaper pictures, headlines, or cartoons that deal with the non-dignity of persons. Make a poster of these that may be used in class for a clothesline exhibit or other event.

5. Using the social service organization Activity Cycle typology in Figure 4-4, plot your agency's current activities in terms of *can, may/must,* and *ought.*

6. In-class simulation

SITUATION: In the adult services unit of a comprehensive care center, the supervisor received increasing pressures from higher-ups that all workers provide 30 contact service hours per week and keep their records current and accurate. These pressures mounted as the budget was reduced. Expectations increased for greater quantity without any reduction in quality. The workers' complaints mounted: the impossibility of doing intakes, crisis work, keeping scheduled counseling appointments, and submitting up-to-date paperwork weekly. Enthusiasm and dedication of workers were eroding; paperwork was the first responsibility deferred in the effort to meet the pressing needs of clients. At the same time, messages from the top were beginning to "haunt" the supervisor with increased regularity, especially since it was just announced that an unexpected visit from the state auditors would occur in two weeks.

Task: Divide the class into three teams. The following options are possible.

a. Each team may analyze this situation and devise a scenario responsive to the problem within one of the three general concepts: competent supervisor; responsive provision; and dynamic organization. Analysis should include the subelements elaborated within each general area. Teams would be asked to propose interventions within the overarching analyzed concept (20 minutes).

   Reconvene all the groups, and have each one present its plan for action to the other two groups (10 minutes).

   Following this, have the whole class discuss the viability of each plan. It is then possible for the class to discuss the interrelationship among all three components and insights obtained about the interdependence of staff competence, service provision, and organization.

   This simulation is most suitable for classes of twenty or more.

b. For smaller classes, the situation could be approached through three units, whose members might make analyses and proposals similar to option a, above; however, concentrate on the interconnections among particular levels—such as leadership/resources/adaptability or wisdom/skills/effectiveness, or dignity/needs/stability.

7. What instances can you recall that illustrate indignity for workers, rather than dignity? How might these be changed by a supervisor interested in respecting others' dignity? Fill out the following indignity list with some ideas.

| OFFENSES TO DIGNITY | PROPOSED ALTERNATIVES |
|---|---|
| 1. | 1. |
| 2. | 2. |
| 3. | 3. |
| 4. | 4. |
| 5. | 5. |
| 6. | 6. |
| 7. | 7. |
| 8. | 8. |

## A Snapshot of Your Community's Provisions

Using census data, municipal yearbook, city, county, and state government public information files, *Statistical Abstracts of the United States,* and county and city data books, determine the following characteristics for your community (see Note 1).

### POPULATION CHARACTERISTICS OF YOUR COMMUNITY

|  | Male | Female | White | Nonwhite | Age Ranges |
|---|---|---|---|---|---|
| Marital status | | | | | |
| Employment status | | | | | |
| Educational status | | | | | |
| Family household status | | | | | |
| Income range | | | | | |

What is the median income of your community's families? _____

What percentage of the residents of your community live at or below the poverty level? _____

From the appropriate state or local office, collect information on the following:

|  | STATE BUDGET, LAST FISCAL YEAR | STATE BUDGET, CURRENT FISCAL YEAR | LOCAL BUDGET, LAST FISCAL YEAR | LOCAL BUDGET, CURRENT FISCAL YEAR | NUMBER OF CLIENTS SERVED |
|---|---|---|---|---|---|
| Aging | | | | | |
| Mental health | | | | | |
| Mental retardation | | | | | |
| Developmental disabilities | | | | | |
| Public welfare | | | | | |
| Corrections | | | | | |
| Vocational rehabilitation | | | | | |
| Health care | | | | | |
| Public schools | | | | | |

In the past fiscal year, how much revenue did your local community receive from each of the following major sources of income?

Property taxes _____  Fines _____  Shared taxes _____
Local income or occupational taxes _____  Fees and licenses _____
Sales taxes _____  Assessments _____ Other _____
Sale of property _____  Grants in aid _____

If you had to classify your community according to its major economic base, into which category would you place it?

Manufacturing _____          Research and development _____
Industrial _____             Educational _____
Farming _____               Amusement/resort _____
Mining _____                Government center _____
Wholesale _____             Transportation center _____
Retail _____                Other (specify) _____

Does your community have a public transportation system serving and connecting all geographic areas of the community? Yes _____ No _____ If no, which areas of the community are underserved? _____ Which population groups suffer the most because of gaps in public transportation? _____

Which of the following community organizations are involved in planning and coordinating social services provision in your community?

United Way or Community Fund _____      Council for Retarded Citizens _____
Red Cross _____                        Mental Health Association _____
Health and Welfare Council _____         Area planning and development
Health Systems Agency _____                agency _____
                                           Others (please list) _____

From the respective local professional associations (e.g., NASW, AMA, ABA), develop a list of the type and number of professionals in your community.

Physicians _____              Lawyers _____
Psychiatrists _____           Registered nurses _____
Dentists _____                Nurse practitioners _____
M.S.W. social workers _____    Teachers _____
B.S.W. social workers _____    Clergy _____

List each of the following types of cooperative groups that are active in your community.

Consumer coops (e.g., food)          Self-help coops

Health coops

Insurance coops

Farmers coops

Purchasing coops

Marketing coops

Energy coops

Other coops (please list)

Using information from the U.S. Department of Housing and Urban Development, the U.S. Census of Housing, and your local housing authority or planning and zoning office, answer the following questions:

How many dwelling units are there in your community? _____

How many of these are:

  Owner-occupied? _____

  Renter-occupied? _____

  Vacant? _____

  Condemned? _____

How easy or difficult is it to find suitable housing in your community for purchase or rent?

| | PURCHASE | | RENT | |
|---|---|---|---|---|
| | Easy | Difficult | Easy | Difficult |
| Low price range | | | | |
| Medium price range | | | | |
| Upper price range | | | | |

Which of the following services are provided by local churches in your community?

Settlement house/community center _____

Recreation programs _____

Summer camps _____

Counseling services _____

In-kind benefits _____

Residential (children, elderly, disabled, and so forth) _____

Which of the following resources are available in your community?

| | CENTRALIZED LOCATION | SCATTERED SITES IN COMMUNITY |
|---|---|---|
| Public hospitals | | |
| Private hospitals | | |
| Primary care centers | | |
| Health maintenance organizations | | |
| Family services | | |
| Planned parenthood | | |
| Community mental health centers | | |
| Spouse abuse centers | | |

|  | CENTRALIZED LOCATION | SCATTERED SITES IN COMMUNITY |
|---|---|---|
| Child abuse services | | |
| Rape relief services | | |
| Child guidance clinic | | |
| Vocational rehabilitation | | |
| Public assistance | | |
| Correctional facilities | | |
| Psychiatric hospitals | | |
| Visiting nurses | | |
| Probation/parole | | |
| Unemployment services | | |
| Services to the blind | | |
| Services to developmentally disabled | | |
| Services to migrant/seasonal families | | |
| Services to immigrants | | |
| Drug/alcohol services | | |
| Public library | | |
| Adult education programs | | |
| Public parks | | |
| Public zoo | | |
| Public recreation facilities (e.g., swimming pools, ball fields, tennis courts, bicycle trails) | | |

### Notes

1. "A Snapshot of Your Community's Provisions" was adapted from ideas in Roland L. Warren, *Studying Your Community*. New York: Free Press, 1965; Neil Gilbert and Harry Specht, *Coordinating Social Services*. New York: Praeger Publishers, 1977; and Keith A. Neuber, *Needs Assessment*. Beverly Hills, Calif.: Sage Publications, 1980.

## CHAPTER 5

1. Using your experience as supervisor or supervisee, develop a list of additional supervisory activities for each of the nine functions. Compare and contrast your list with the lists prepared by other learners.

2. For learners now working in an agency as supervisor, keep a one-week record of time spent on each of the nine functions and the activities you performed related to each function.

    For learners who are not supervisors, approach someone who is, and ask this individual to keep such a record for a week and then review it with the supervisor.

At the end of the week, compare and discuss your findings with those of other learners.

3.  In-class simulation: Divide into groups of three, with each person assuming responsibility for one cluster of functions (i.e., integrative, service delivery, linkage). On the basis of your perspective, analyze the following situation and work out an approach to the problems consistent with the functions in your cluster. Work on the situation as a group. At the conclusion of the time allotted, discuss how the various supervisory functions can connect and combine in enhancing the possibilities for working with supervisees and agency problems.

SITUATION: You are a foster care services supervisor in a large public agency serving a metropolitan area. There are several foster care teams within the agency, with six to ten social workers on each team. Each social worker is responsible, on the average, for 50 foster children and for related services to natural parents and foster parents. During the last six months it has become apparent to all involved in foster care services that there are serious issues that require action. The agency director, who is concerned about the situation, reports that there are no additional resources for hiring more social workers, and that the agency is legally mandated to care for all foster children in the community. Specific problems that have been noted include: (1) More than 50 percent of workers' time is devoted to crisis management (e.g., foster child being expelled from school, foster family refusing to keep a child, natural parents demanding return of a child, foster parents not receiving their monthly allotment). (2) Community hospitals, schools, and other social agencies are increasingly resistant to addressing the special needs of foster children. (3) The absenteeism rate among workers is increasing. Today you are meeting with the other foster care supervisors to discuss the situation and develop a plan for addressing the concerns of clients, workers, and the agency.

## CHAPTER 6

1.  Look at an organization you are presently a part of, and draw its bureaucratic form, using the 5-by-5 rule. Now redesign this organization into a different pattern, if you think it could work better that way. You may present your ideas and the justification for your changes as part of a class discussion.

2.  Did you complete the seven questions on pages 210–211? Now apply these to your school. Discuss your judgments with your classmates.

3.  Engage in some action research: Interview a supervisor or agency administrator about the experiences this person has had with social work supervision throughout his or her career. Your interest should be in exploring this person's experiences in the past with the discussion of educative supervision in this chapter. The conclusions of these interviews may form the basis of further in-class discussion of supervision's traditions in social work.

4.  Explore the job titles in your organization. If possible, list numbers of workers in each category. Calculate the percentages of staff devoted to the policy,

service, and managerial activities. In class discussion, share findings and discuss implications in terms of your organization's goals, major avowed purposes, and the allocation of staff, status, power, and so forth.

## CHAPTER 7

1. Study flyers and promotional materials about training events that you may receive in the mail, notice on bulletin boards in school, or find out about some other way. Practice making a connection between the various content areas and any of the nine functional areas of supervision. Are certain offerings impossible to place within this framework? Compare and contrast your list with the lists of others in class; discuss the items that do not fit.

2. Using the framework presented on supervisor and supervisee competencies, analyze your knowledge and skills in terms of current strengths (as supervisor or as supervisee). Project where you would like to focus most attention immediately.

3. Recall that persons in organizations may have several "careers" (e.g., organization person, ACSW social worker, parent) that may send different "messages" in relation to particular agency happenings. Construct a few vignettes that illustrate these dilemmas, and use these for in-class discussions.

4. One recent supervisory-skills inventory listed the following "most necessary skills areas" to successful supervision. Try to connect each area with the nine functional areas comprising the supervisory task competencies. (Our answers appear upside down.)

|   |   |
|---|---|
| 1. Setting goals | 7. Maintaining, controlling materials and equipment |
| 2. Planning and organizing | 8. Building teams |
| 3. Directing and delegating | 9. Assuring safety |
| 4. Solving problems | 10. Evaluating performance |
| 5. Enforcing work rules | 11. Training and coaching |
| 6. Relating to and supporting staff | 12. Reacting to stress |

*Answers:* 1. Administering, teaching, evaluating. 2. Administering, teaching, changing. 3. Administering. 4. All functions. 5. Administering. 6. All functions. 7. Administering. 8. Catalyzing. 9. Humanizing. 10. Evaluating. 11. Teaching. 12. Managing tension.

5. In-class simulation—an in-service event: Each student should select one chapter or article from the course bibliography and prepare a five-minute lecturette as part of a mini in-service event. In class ahead of time, develop criteria for content, delivery, clarity of communication, and other elements. Apply these criteria by a predetermined observational format, using instruments that can capture feedback for the presenters. Observation results can also form the basis for discussion of effective performance in conveying a specific bit of information to others.

6. How does field instruction differ from supervision? Develop your own means for investigating this.

7. Review the assumptions about consultation (see Chapter 1). From the following bibliography, select several references on consultation:

BERKOWITZ, MORTON K., *A Primer on School Mental Health Consultation.* Springfield, Ill.: Thomas, 1975.

GOODSTEIN, LEONARD D., *Consulting with Human Service Systems.* Reading, Mass.: Addison-Wesley, 1978.

HOLLISTER, WILLIAM G., and MILLER, FRANCIS T., "Problem-Solving Strategies in Consultation," *American Journal of Orthopsychiatry, 47,* no. 3 (July, 1977), 453–465.

KADUSHIN, ALFRED, *Consultation in Social Work.* New York: Columbia University Press, 1977.

LIPPITT, GORDON, and LIPPITT, RONALD, *The Consulting Process in Action.* La Jolla, Calif.: University Associates, 1978.

MEYERS, JOEL, PARSONS, RICHARD D., and MARTIN, ROY, *Mental Health Consultation in the Schools.* San Francisco, Calif.: Jossey-Bass, 1979.

RAPOPORT, LYDIA, "Consultation in Social Work," *Encyclopedia of Social Work* (Vol. 1, pp. 155–161). Washington, D.C.: NASW, 1972.

SCHEIN, EDGAR H., *Process Consultation: Its Role in Organization Development.* Reading, Mass.: Addison-Wesley, 1969.

Construct an approach to consultation in outline form, using material from your reading. Find someone to whom you can be consultant. Pursue your planned approach in relation to some problem or situation that your person may have. (Your consultee may be a friend or an employed worker of your acquaintance.) After you complete your experience, analyze it in terms of the following:

a. Situation: With whom did you consult, about what, when, where, how long?

b. The nature of your help: What was your approach? What of value did you offer? How?

c. Outcome: How was your offer to consult received? How do you know this?

d. Insights: What insights have you developed from this experience and its analysis?

## CHAPTER 8

1. In class, jointly select an issue of importance to social work supervision. Divide into pairs and have a dialogue about this issue for five minutes. Then, with a third member, engage in a trialogue on the same issue for five minutes. Afterward, compare and contrast the two experiences. What do you see as

advantages and disadvantages of each opportunity for communication, problem solving, and support?

2. Arrange three chairs so that they form the points of a triangle; label them *constraints, demands,* and *supports.* Have three people sit in the chairs. Take turns moving the position of the chairs, always making sure to retain the form of a triangle. Discuss your feelings and observations about opening and closing the space of the triangle in relation to the window of opportunity for creating a new game. What are the possibilities for applying this experience to your practice as a supervisor or supervisee? Discuss in class.

3. Outside of class time, reflect on experiences you have had with constraints, supports, and demands in family, at church, in school, at work. Make a list of these experiences and how you responded to them. Can you identify similarities and differences, depending on the context? Are these related to differences in the magnitude of each of the components? In class, share and compare lists, and work on translating these into additional opportunity strategies for supervisors and supervisees.

## CHAPTER 9

1. Although this book has concluded, there really is no conclusion to the matter of your ongoing professional development as a supervisor. Make a plan for pursuing your self-directed further instruction for the coming year, and be prepared to do something similar at least once a year.

2. Experiment with the kaleidoscope idea:
   a. Color the kaleidoscope pattern shown in Figure 9-1. Or make several photocopies of it and experiment with making different versions.
   b. Make your own kaleidoscopic pattern.
   c. Find a tube and construct your own kaleidoscope. You will need two mirrors almost as long as the tube, and you should angle them into a V. Then place some small objects of your choice at one end within a transparent circular container that fits the tube. Finally, make a peephole at the opposite end.

3. Practice using the kaleidoscope imagery as you view patterns in school, organization, and elsewhere. Can you identify the recurring patterns, the elements that surface from time to time? Can you spot cyclic thinking and returning "figures" in your own discussions with others?

4. Construct your own list of additional persons whose training and experience in one field or discipline was applied to a different area with transforming impact.

5. Recall the postvacation mail pile in the example on pages 315–316. Construct your other metaphors that illustrate the everyday tasks of making order from disorder.

6. Identify the chaos of your everyday experiences, and make plans to identify and to partialize out the little islands of order that exist within it.

# INTRODUCTION
# TO APPENDICES B-E

When you follow the directions for completing the questionnaires and profiles in Appendices B, C, D, and E, we encourage you to make copies of each one. Then complete each Appendix as indicated, and put them all away in a safe place. Upon completing the book, return to these Appendices, and without referring to your first set of responses, do them again. Then compare your two sets of responses for each Appendix. Note where you have stayed the same, where you have changed, and in what ways, and reflect on why the responses are similar or different.

Before you enter these Appendices, we want to issue a cautionary note. These paper-and-pencil tasks are approximations of reality. The interpretations can be viewed as ideal types in the sense of the best estimates we can offer, based on available knowledge and the value system underlying this book. Yet we encourage you to recognize the constant variability in behavior and contexts that characterize the world as we prefer to view it, in kaleidoscopic terms. As a result, the interpretations do not connote good or bad, right or wrong, desirable or undesirable, or one best approach or response. Your responses and the corresponding interpretations are clues to where you are right now, while at the same time we acknowledge that you and your context are changing even as you read this and respond to the tasks and interpretations in each Appendix. Our intent is to increase your awareness of who and where you are right now in relation to social work supervision, and to open your vision to the possibilities of who you are becoming as a social work professional and a supervisor, now or in the future.

# APPENDIX B
# SUPERVISOR
# PREFERENCE CHECKLIST

The following statements represent characteristics commonly found in the practice behavior of social work supervisors. These characteristics represent different supervisory approaches for which supervisees express varying preferences. On the scoring checklist that follows the list of statements, mark an X in the appropriate square for each statement, if it is broadly true that you would prefer this characteristic in your supervisor. If you think the statement does not reflect a characteristic you prefer, leave the space blank.

### I PERFORM BEST WHEN MY SUPERVISOR:

1. Closely monitors the way I organize and carry out my work.
2. Has developed practice mastery from blending personal sensitivity and skill with social theory and interventions.
3. Emphasizes the organization and group role components of our relationship.
4. Expects me to learn by watching how he or she does the work.
5. Judges my performance on the basis of my skill in dealing with feelings.
6. Bends the rules and procedures when necessary.
7. Makes most of the decisions.
8. Stimulates my personal/professional development by sharing his or her personal insights into feelings and behavior of workers and clients.
9. Emphasizes both internal and external system forces in problem solving.
10. Gives me feedback on my work that focuses on specific directives for change.

11. Relates the way I organize and carry out my work to my own personality development.

12. Has developed practice mastery from combining practical experience with knowledge of social theory and interventions.

13. Emphasizes the task components of our relationship.

14. Expects me to learn by exploring my feelings and behavior with her or him.

15. Judges my performance on the basis of a mutually determined set of goals and objectives.

16. Uses a strict approach to rules and procedures.

17. Helps me gain insight into myself in making decisions.

18. Stimulates my personal/professional development by challenging me to integrate ideas from various sources.

19. Emphasizes agency regulations in problem solving.

20. Gives me feedback on my work that focuses on my expression of feelings in doing the work.

21. Allows me to organize and carry out my work pretty much on my own.

22. Has developed practice mastery from many years of job experience in the school of hard knocks.

23. Emphasizes the emotional components of our relationship.

24. Expects me to learn by mutual examination of my knowledge and skills in the light of contemporary social theory and interventions.

25. Judges my performance on how he or she would do my job.

26. Is responsive to my feelings about the enforcement of rules and procedures.

27. Encourages me to make most of my own decisions.

28. Stimulates my personal/professional development by sharing her or his fund of practical knowledge from prior personal experience as a worker.

29. Emphasizes the emotional forces involved in problem solving.

30. Gives me feedback on my work that focuses both on constructive criticism and on praise for work well done.

## INTERPRETING YOUR PREFERENCE

Count up the Xs in each column and put the total at the bottom. While these scores are merely a snapshot of you at this moment and are not necessarily permanent, they should tell you something about your preferences in a supervisor. The statements reflect the following aspects of supervision: work and task structure; basis of practice mastery; interpersonal style; teaching/learning approach; evaluation; use of authority: decision making; personal/professional development; problem solving; and feedback.

> *Column 1*—You scored high on statements reflecting your preference for a supervisor who is highly structured and closely monitors your work and the work of other supervisees. You prefer a supervisor whose expertise and mastery of activities derives from extensive experience in the "school of hard knocks." You believe that you benefit the most from an upfront, directive supervisor who shows and tells, is fair yet follows the rules, and expects you and others to do the same.

**SUPERVISOR PREFERENCE
SCORING CHECKLIST**

| 1 | 2 | 3 |
|----|----|----|
| 4 | 5 | 6 |
| 7 | 8 | 9 |
| 10 | 11 | 12 |
| 13 | 14 | 15 |
| 16 | 17 | 18 |
| 19 | 20 | 21 |
| 22 | 23 | 24 |
| 25 | 26 | 27 |
| 28 | 29 | 30 |

*Column 2*—You scored high on statements reflecting your preference for a supervisor who is highly concerned with the feelings you have as you respond to the difficult tasks in practice. You prefer a supervisor whose practice expertise derives from using personal sensitivity and skill in applying theory and technique. You like the emphasis on relationship between the supervisor and the supervisee and notice its impact in work with clients. You believe that you gain the most from a supervisor who stresses emotional support, is comfortable in dealing with feelings, and helps you gain insight and make sense of what is going on in your work as well as your own developmental process.

*Column 3*—You scored high on statements reflecting your preference for a supervisor who approaches the organization, supervisees, and the work from a living systems perspective. You value expertise in managing the dynamic interactions of supervisee-client-organization based on the supervisor's synthesis of experience, social theory, and interventions into a workable approach. You appreciate a supervisor who is willing to take risks in bending the rules as needed. You believe you gain the most from a supervisor who focuses on tasks related to needs and links these to ideas that support various alternative approaches. You prefer a supervisor who shares responsibility with you for setting standards and criteria for accountability and then encourages autonomous practice within these limits.

Return now to Table 1-1 in Chapter 1. You will notice that coach relates to column 1, counselor to column 2, and conferee to column 3. These role orientations are a chronology. *Coach* was the role of Mary Richmond and Jane Addams, of the early district secretaries and settlement workers (and of many present-day trainers); *counselor* flourished from the 1920s to the mid-1960s; and *conferee* has been an active role orientation from the mid-1960s to the present time. All orientations may be observed currently, as influential for a given supervisor in the 1980s, yet one particular orientation will usually predominate in any one supervisor.

# APPENDIX C
# CURRENT PROFILE

Think about the work environments where you have felt most comfortable. Use this work context in working through each of the statements below. In the grid that follows the list of statements, please mark an X in the appropriate square if you think the statement is broadly true for your work behavior in the work context you are using as a referent. If you think it is not true, leave the square blank. Do not spend a lot of time on each statement; a few seconds is long enough.

1. I work well in situations that are ambiguous or unclear.
2. I need the feedback and opinions of others before I make up my mind.
3. I am particular about details.
4. I see myself as different from the others.
5. I enjoy working in groups, even when the process is time-consuming.
6. I am able to do my work, even when there is a lot of noise.
7. I can produce many ideas quickly.
8. I avoid working alone when I could work with someone.
9. I like to check with my supervisor before doing differently.
10. My ideas are often unusual ones.
11. I work well when guidelines are spelled out clearly.
12. I do my best work on my own.

13. At times I deliberately avoid being serious.
14. I am more confident when I know what my supervisor thinks.
15. Having to involve other people often frustrates me.
16. I avoid early commitment to an idea.
17. Staff meetings ought to include time for staff to socialize.
18. I grow irritated when I have to depend on someone else to complete part of a joint project.
19. I separate who says something from what is said.
20. I usually give in so as to avoid conflicts.
21. At work I think people would describe me as an independent thinker.
22. When I get involved, I follow a problem wherever it leads.
23. I like my workday to be predictable.
24. I value my self-evaluation as much as my supervisor's evaluation of me.
25. I like to toy with the elements of a situation.
26. I take others' actions as a guide for my own.
27. I like it when people do the unexpected.
28. I am rigorous with particulars before experimenting.
29. There is value to routine; it is important for competent work.
30. I rarely ask others' help.
31. I am impulsive and playful.
32. I rarely oppose decisions that most people seem to want.
33. I am not known for winning a popularity contest.
34. I dislike conforming, prefer differentness.
35. I am sensitive to group pressure and generally conform.
36. At times I seem awkward and miss interpersonal nuances.
37. I spend time on analysis and exploration without discouragement.
38. When I come into a room, I am aware of everyone present at a glance.
39. I grow impatient with group efforts.
40. I suspend judging an idea until I consider it fully.
41. Sometimes people would describe me as being too sensitive.
42. I tend to focus on what to do more than who is involved.
43. I take risks and find this pleasurable.
44. Direct confrontations are hard for me.
45. When stressed, I express anger directly.

## INTERPRETING YOUR SCORE

Count up the Xs in each column and put the total at the bottom. While these scores are merely suggestive and not necessarily fixed, they should tell you some of your preferences. Column 1 reflects aspects of creativity and imagination. Column 2 contains aspects of a field-dependent cognitive style (Witkin, 1977), and column 3, aspects of a field-independent style. Columns 2 and 3 should be viewed along with your score in column 1. (That is, the imaginative or creative can accompany either

**A CURRENT PROFILE
SCORING CHECKLIST**

| 1 | 2 | 3 |
|---|---|---|
| 4 | 5 | 6 |
| 7 | 8 | 9 |
| 10 | 11 | 12 |
| 13 | 14 | 15 |
| 16 | 17 | 18 |
| 19 | 20 | 21 |
| 22 | 23 | 24 |
| 25 | 26 | 27 |
| 28 | 29 | 30 |
| 31 | 32 | 33 |
| 34 | 35 | 36 |
| 37 | 38 | 39 |
| 40 | 41 | 42 |
| 43 | 44 | 45 |

of the other two styles. In fact, we suggest that your scores for field-dependent or field-independent style reflect aspects that contribute to your sense of competence.)

Here are some of the components contained in the creative/imaginative column: conceptual fluency; originality; unbiased evaluation; persistence; independence of judgment; sees self as different; visualizes; can live with ambiguity. The field-dependent column includes these aspects: prefers operating within a predetermined structure; receives and values the opinions of others, especially authority figures; relies heavily on external referents as guides for actions; relates socially to people and avoids isolation; experiences self and events globally. In the field-independent column, these elements were involved: prefers an environment that allows one to create structure and experiment with new roles; relies heavily on internal referents as guides for action; evaluates own work; pursues functioning independently and prefers not to be forced to participate in group efforts; experiences oneself and events analytically (See Note 1).

## NOTES

1. We acknowledge the work of Anne Davis (1984) in specifying categories in the areas of field-dependent and field-independent cognitive-style dimensions identified and studied empirically by Samuel Messick.

## REFERENCES

WITKIN, HERMAN A., "A Cognitive-Style Perspective on Evaluation and Guidance," *Proceedings of the 1973 Invitational Conference on Testing Problems.* Princeton, N.J.: Educational Testing Service, 1974.

# APPENDIX D
# HOW I LOOK
# AT SUPERVISION

*Directions*—Assume that you are a supervisor, and think about how you would want to supervise another person. For each of the following 13 phrases, rank the four statements given in the order that completes the phrase to your best satisfaction. Give your *most* favored statement a rank of 4; your next favored, 3; your next, 2; and your *least* favored statement, a rank of 1. Place your numerical ranking for each statement on the line in the appropriate column to the right of that statement (see Note 1).

|  | COLUMN 1 | COLUMN 2 |
|---|---|---|
| 1. In planning for supervision, I would most likely: |  |  |
| Require process records and select critical incidents for discussion with supervisees | _____ |  |
| Begin with a contract specifying what we wish to accomplish, when, and how |  | _____ |
| Pinpoint the results I expect from supervisees and construct a work plan that will almost run itself |  | _____ |
| Consider the areas of greatest concern to the supervisees and plan to deal with them regardless of what they may be | _____ |  |

2. Supervisees learn best:

   When they are free to explore with limited direction _____

   When they are interested in what they are doing _____

   When they have access to someone who knows what he or she is talking about _____

   When they have opportunities for practice, feedback, and repetition _____

3. The purpose of supervision should be:

   To help supervisees develop competency and mastery of specific skills _____

   To help supervisees get the information and resources required to do the job efficiently _____

   To help supervisees learn to become autonomous, self-directed practitioners _____

   To help supervisees develop insight into themselves and their work with clients _____

4. Most of what supervisees know:

   They have acquired through a systematic educational process _____

   They have learned by experience in trial-and-error fashion _____

   They have gained through a natural progression of self-discovery, rather than through some "teaching" process _____

   They have learned as a result of consciously pursuing their goals, solving problems as they go _____

5. Decisions on what should be covered in supervision:

   Are based on careful analysis of the situation beforehand _____

   Are made as the supervisory process progresses and the supervisees show their innate interests and abilities _____

   Are mutually derived by the supervisees and supervisor _____

   Are based on what supervisees now know and must know to do the work _____

6. Good supervisors believe:

   That they should gain proficiency in the methods and processes of supervision _____

   That they should assume supervisees are highly motivated and capable of directing their own learning, if they have the opportunity _____

   That they should master the field themselves and become effective "models" for supervisees _____

COLUMN 1    COLUMN 2

That they should consider the end behaviors they are looking for and the most efficient ways of developing those behaviors in supervisees    _____

7. As a supervisor, I am least successful in situations:

Where I have to criticize or go against what the supervisee wants    _____

Where there is no structure, and goals are unclear    _____

Where there is no right answer    _____

Where I have to deal with the abstract rather than the concrete and practical    _____

8. In supervision, I try to focus on:

The particular episodes of practice, and to develop capacities for dealing with them    _____

A work environment that facilitates self-discovery, expression, and interaction    _____

A stimulating environment that attracts and maintains the committment of supervisees while fostering their ongoing professional development    _____

Identifying a variety of resources that are useful to supervisees in meeting client needs    _____

9. Emotions in the supervisory process:

Are utilized by the skillful supervisor to help the supervisees develop skills in dealing with feelings    _____

Are a distraction to be avoided    _____

Will propel the supervisee in many directions which the supervisor may follow and support    _____

Provide opportunities for focusing on problems or questions    _____

10. To help supervisees improve their practice, my approach:

Would be relatively flexible but present real challenges    _____

Would be determined by the situation    _____

Would emphasize trial and feedback    _____

Would allow freedom for the individual supervisee    _____

11. When supervisees are uninterested in an in-service event, it is probably because:

They do not see the benefit to their job    _____

They are not ready for the topic    _____

The specialist has not adequately prepared the material    _____

The event has not been well planned    _____

12. Supervisees are all different:

Some will learn from me, but others may do better with another person    _____

|  | COLUMN 1 | COLUMN 2 |
|---|---|---|

The best approach is to teach the basics well and put them on their own after that _____ (Column 1)

With an effective presentation and discussion, most tasks can be mastered by the majority of supervisees _____ (Column 2)

An experienced supervisor, properly organized, can overcome most difficulties _____ (Column 2)

13. Supervisees seem to have the most regard for a supervisor who:

Helps them work through a problem, regardless of how painful _____ (Column 1)

Guides them through experiences with well-focused feedback _____ (Column 2)

Systematically leads them in step-by-step problem solving _____ (Column 2)

Inspires them and indirectly influences their lives _____ (Column 1)

Totals _____ (Column 1) _____ (Column 2)

## INTERPRETING YOUR SCORE

Total the numbers in columns 1 and 2 to determine your main preference and compare with the following descriptions:

*Column 1*—You scored high on statements indicating that you believe supervisees are internally directed and that they prefer independence, autonomy, and a chance to control their own destinies. As a supervisor you will tend to approach the teaching function by designing learning opportunities that encourage self-directed discovery, offer practical experiential activities, and in other ways support learning by doing. In the area of interpersonal relationships you emphasize the importance of self-awareness, spontaneity, and openness. When conflicts arise, your preference will be for a thoughtful, reasoning approach to problem solving, combined with direct feedback on the process. You believe that good relationships are the key to quality and quantity in service delivery. As a consequence, you will work to foster a supervisee-centered, task-oriented approach to relationships and the work. Your strengths as a supervisor include providing opportunities to learn, to take risks, make mistakes, and receive supportive corrective feedback. You tend to model a sensitive, empathic approach to people and to tasks, to help others to develop and utilize opportunities, and to give recognition for work that is well done.

    *Column 2*—You scored high on statements indicating that you believe supervisees are externally directed and that they respond to forces around them and prefer guidance from you or the environment. As a supervisor you will tend to approach the teaching function by carefully structuring and directing learning opportunities. Your emphasis will be on specific learning objectives for carefully delimited segments that, when learned, sequentially lead toward integration into the whole. Your method will be one of teaching via demonstration, followed by practice with prompting, feedback, and reinforcement. In interpersonal relationships your approach reflects a supervisor-centered, task orientation. You believe supervisees respond best to interpersonal conflict and problem solving when the situation is planned, organized, presented, and evaluated by the supervisor. Your strengths as a supervisor include thoroughness, clarity, and precision. You present information in a systematic fashion and stress planning and organization in doing the work. You tend to model behavior that indicates you are a strong leader who is committed to building trust and protecting the interests of your supervisees.

## NOTES

1. This questionnaire and its scoring and interpretation are adapted from Richard Brostrom, "Training Style Inventory," in John E. Jones and J. William Pfeiffer, eds., *The 1979 Annual Handbook for Group Facilitators.* La Jolla, Calif.: University Associates, 1979.

# APPENDIX E
# YOUR WORKING STYLE

*Directions*—The following items present situations that supervisors often encounter. Respond to each item according to the way you think you would most likely act. Put the appropriate letter to the left of each number, as follows: (A) always, (F) frequently, (O) occasionally, (S) seldom, or (N) never.

As a supervisor, I would:
1. Most likely help the workers by doing things for them
2. Encourage workers to go the extra mile
3. Allow them complete freedom in their work
4. Encourage the workers to follow certain routines
5. Permit others to use their own judgment in solving problems
6. Stress making the most of oneself all the time
7. Respond with help more readily when I know I am needed
8. Joke with workers to get them to work harder
9. Try to help the workers, even when they don't want it
10. Let workers do their work the way they think best
11. Be working hard to set a good example
12. Be able to tolerate postponement and uncertainty
13. Speak for others if they have not been effective themselves
14. Expect others to keep working even when discouraged

15. Allow the workers to try out their own solutions to problems, even when I know these will not work
16. Settle conflicts between people
17. Get swamped by details
18. Present an individual's position to others if that individual is unclear
19. Be reluctant to allow new workers much freedom of action
20. Decide what should be done and how it should be done
21. Push people toward high-level functioning
22. Let some people have authority which I could keep
23. Think things would usually turn out as I predict
24. Allow people a high degree of initiative
25. Stick to the things I know how to do even when others want other things from me
26. Make exceptions to the rules for some workers
27. Ask workers to work harder
28. Trust workers to exercise good judgment
29. Schedule the work to be done
30. Not explain my actions
31. Persuade others that my ideas are to their advantage
32. Allow others to set their own pace
33. Urge people to keep aiming higher
34. Do things without consulting the workers
35. Ask the workers to follow standard rules and regulations

**FIGURE E-1. Supervisory orientations.**

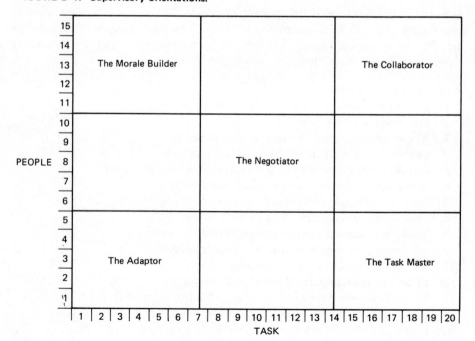

### DIRECTIONS FOR SCORING

1. Circle the following numbers: 1, 4, 7, 13, 16, 17, 18, 19, 20, 23, 29, 30, 31, 34, 35.
2. Put a 1 outside all those circled numbers where you put S or N.
3. Put a 1 next to all those *uncircled* numbers where you put A or F.
4. Circle the 1 next to numbers 3, 5, 8, 10, 12, 15, 17, 19, 22, 24, 26, 28, 30, 32, 34.
5. Add up the uncircled 1's. This total is your T (*task*) score.
6. Add up the circled 1's. This total is your P (*people*) score.
7. Plot your P score on the supervisory orientations matrix (Figure E-1), counting upwards 1 to 15; plot your T score according to the numbers 1-20. Connect these two values by drawing a line perpendicular to each number so that the two lines intersect at a point.

The following brief profiles describe your score.

## DISCUSSION OF SUPERVISORY ORIENTATIONS

We bring to situations our own patterned, learned way of responding to them. Two important attitudes are highlighted in this questionnaire: concerns about the task to be accomplished; and concerns about the people who are involved (see Note 1). Sometimes these two components seem to be in conflict. The supervisor needs to find a balance between both demands. According to how much the supervisor values each part of the work—responding to the human side of the organization, and getting the work done—one of five patterns can be described.

We have created our own labels for these patterns as an alternative to the preferred-achievement orientation reflected in other such questionnaires and scoring grids. We do not join others who suggest one best way or who use labels that connote good and bad, desirable and undesirable patterns. In this sense we are consistent with the concept of the world as kaleidoscope and with the notion that for the competent, imaginative supervisor, the choice of response to a given situation is a matter of, It all depends . . . on people, task, and context.

> *The task master*—You scored high on work and low on consideration for others. You may claim, "Nice guys finish last." The push is to get the work done well in the most direct and efficient manner, to sum up the situation quickly, decide what needs doing, and do it. The task master sees others as either effective or ineffective, right or wrong, with you or against you. You are highly persuasive, especially when in command, and you may evoke respect or fear. You value hard work, expect to be right, and are intolerant of roadblocks. You expedite and decide.
>
> *The morale builder*—You scored high in concern for others, low in concern for the work. Your motto may be, "The important thing is not winning, but how the game is played." You enjoy personal friendships, avoid being critical, use personal loyalties, expect consideration, think positive, believe in team spirit, and use yourself to relieve tensions. You show consideration by shifting

your opinion, and value peaceful, harmonious relations between people. You believe the work suffers if others are unhappy, angry, demoralized. You harmonize and accommodate.

*The negotiator*—This is a middle position, some concern for the task and for others—firm with tasks, fair with people. You think, "You win some, you lose some," and "Don't rock the boat." You see life as a compromise, like to be practical, value reasonable solutions, argue skillfully, and influence by using diplomacy. You push to get things done, but only to a point; you are considerate of others, but not all the way. You concentrate on the immediate and get it out of the way as quickly as you can. You are strategic in managing information to strike the bargain, to do the expedient thing. You bargain and settle.

*The collaborator*—You are very concerned about the task and the persons involved. Your motto is, "The most important part of an iceberg is that part below the surface." You expect conflict and believe it should be openly confronted. You believe people want to work hard, be involved, seek best solutions, are valuable resources, and can cooperate. You work for solutions that meet the situation and others' needs for respect and pride. You expect you might be wrong. You encourage emotional expression and full expression of opinions. You collaborate and go all out.

*The adapter*—You are not concerned much for either the task or others. Mainly your concern is for yourself. Your motto is, "I may not become the administrator, but I'll not get ulcers." You value objectivity, usually go along with the majority, listen a lot, believe in live and let live, delegate as much as you can, and want to survive. You take a back seat, avoid the action, avoid taking sides, and try to get along with minimum effort. You delegate and go along with.

In plotting your score on the supervisory orientation grid in Figure E-1, some of you may have found your score in a box without a label. The interpretation we have presented is our best estimate of the major orientations, and as such, it is not proven or absolute. Given the variability of configurations of context, task, and people, it is not unusual for some to end up in a blank box. To help those of you in this situation, we can offer the following ideas.

If your point in an empty box is closer to one labeled box than to any of the others, you are probably oriented in the same direction as the pattern described for that labeled box. If your score is basically in the middle of an empty box, you are likely to vary your approach to fit the particular configuration of people, task, and context. For example, if you fall in the middle of the blank box in the upper center, you probably recognize that depending on the particulars you sometimes follow the pattern of the morale builder, sometimes the negotiator, and other times the collaborator. You can make this same self-assessment for each of the other blank boxes in relation to the labeled boxes that surround it.

Finally, regardless of which box your score falls into, we suggest that you return to the questions and the scoring instructions to identify which questions and responses produced your location in the grid. For those of you who want to develop further ideas on how to modify your responses to fit a particular pattern, this reflective analysis may offer some clues.

## NOTES

1. Ideas in this questionnaire draw on the work of the following persons in the area of managerial style: Ralph M. Stogdill's Leader Behavior Description Questionnaire (Ohio State University), as adapted by Thomas Sergiovanni, Richard Metzcus, and Larry Burden, "Toward a Particularistic Approach to Leadership Style," *American Educational Research Journal,* 6, no. 1 (January, 1969), (62-79); and the 9.9 grid framework of Robert Blake and Jane S. Mouton, *Managerial Grid* (Houston: Gulf Publishing Co., 1964).

# APPENDIX F
# ORGANIZATIONAL
# LIFE-COURSE PROFILE

This profile asks you to make various lists. It is easier to do this on other sheets of paper that you have.

1. In what year did this agency first offer services in your community? _____
2. List the original services and benefits offered.
3. List the original client populations served by the agency.
4. List, by year, any changes in services and benefits offered.

| TYPE OF SERVICE | INCREASED | REMAINED THE SAME | REDUCED | TERMINATED |
|---|---|---|---|---|

5. List, by year, any changes in proportion of client populations served.

| | INCREASED | REMAINED THE SAME | REDUCED | NEVER SERVED |
|---|---|---|---|---|
| High income | | | | |
| Middle income | | | | |
| Low income | | | | |

6. List, by year, any changes in client needs identified by the agency.
7. How would you characterize public attitudes toward clients served by the agency?

Positive _____     Indifferent _____
Negative _____     Generally unaware _____

8. How would you characterize public attitudes toward the agency and its services?

Positive _____     Indifferent _____
Negative _____     Generally unaware _____

9. Identify, by year, shifts in public attitudes toward the agency.

Positive to negative _____
Negative to positive _____
Positive to indifferent _____
Negative to indifferent _____
Indifferent to negative _____
Indifferent to positive _____

10. List, by year, any shifts in criteria for agency accountability.
11. List, by year, any shifts in standards for performance evaluation of personnel.
12. List, by year, any changes in geographic location of the agency.
13. How many clients were served when the agency first opened? _____

5 years ago _____
3 years ago _____
1 year ago _____

14. List, by year, trends in staffing patterns.

More professionals than nonprofessionals _____
More nonprofessionals than professionals _____
More M.S.W.s than B.S.W.s _____
More B.S.W.s than M.S.W.s _____
Increased ratio of administrative staff to direct-service staff _____
Increased ratio of direct-service staff to administrative staff _____

15. List, by year, any crises the agency has experienced, how it responded, and the consequences.
16. Chart the funding sources and pattern for the last five years.

|  | FEDERAL | STATE | LOCAL | CLIENT FEE |
|---|---|---|---|---|
| Increased |  |  |  |  |
| Decreased |  |  |  |  |
| Remained the same |  |  |  |  |

17. Has the agency used any of the following procedures during the last five years?

**PROCEDURE**                                                                      **YEARS**

Freeze on hiring
No cost-of-living raise
Reduced direct services
Reduced clerical staff
Reduced direct-service professional staff
Reduced non-direct-service professional staff
Used part-time staff from outside the agency
Increased use of volunteers
Reduced working hours

## ASSESSING YOUR AGENCY'S LIFE-COURSE PROFILE

Most of us enter organizations after they have existed for some time and have already faced one or more of the life-course issues. Given the historic precariousness of social services, it is important for you to be aware of the life course of your agency. The current picture may be a reflection of whether the agency was created during a period of expanding, contracting, or regrouping within the mandate for responsive provision. To develop a sense of your agency's pattern in the life course, look at the year in which it was founded. Was your agency created during a decade of expansion, contraction, or regrouping? Next, look at the years in which major changes occurred, and consider what else was happening during the decade in which these changes occurred.

To assess your agency's current life-course stage, consider how long it has been in existence. If your agency is new (i.e., founded within the last three years), it is likely to be dealing with the problems of the creation stage while moving into the growth stage. If there have been numerous recent changes in services, clientele, resources, or goals and objectives, your agency is probably in the growth stage. An agency that has experienced few changes in the last three to five years is probably in the maturity stage of its life course. Finally, if your agency has been through numerous negative shifts in the areas of public attitudes, decreases in clients, funding sources, and personnel, it is likely to be facing the life-course issues of decline and demise.

When you have developed a picture of your agency and its stage in the life course, reflect on the problem cycles of *can, may/must,* and *ought.* What challenges are confronting you as a supervisor or supervisee? Can you translate these challenges into action possibilities for yourself and others? To assist you in this analysis, we suggest you synthesize your findings and interpretations into the analysis foursome: *you* (supervisor or supervisee); *it* (*can, may/must, ought*); *context* (pattern of wider forces, e.g., public attitudes, funding sources); and *history* (past, present, and future actions and reactions of your agency across the life course). When you have completed your assessment of your agency's life course pattern and present stage, share and discuss it with others who have completed the same assessment of their respective agencies.

# INDEX